THE TIGER
AND THE
CHILDREN

Fidel Castro and the Judgment of History

Roberto Luque Escalona

Translated by
Manuel A. Tellechea

**FREEDOM
HOUSE**

TRANSACTION PUBLISHERS
NEW BRUNSWICK (U.S.A.) AND LONDON (U.K.)

Library of Congress Catalog Number: 91-46477
ISBN: 1-56000-027-9 (cloth); 1-56000-593-9 (paper)
Printed in the United States of America

Library of Congress Cataloging-in-Publication Data

Luque Escalona, Roberto, 1936–
    [Fidel, el juicio de la historia. English]
    The tiger and the children: Fidel Castro and the judgment of history / Roberto Luque Escalona; translated by Manuel A. Tellechea.
    p.   cm.
    Translation of: Fidel, el juicio de la historia.
    ISBN 1-56000-027-9. - ISBN 1-56000-593-9 (pbk.)
    1. Cuba–History–1895– 2. Castro, Fidel, 1927–   . I. Title.
F1786.L9613   1992
972.9106–dc20
                                        91–46477
                                        CIP

To "Jersey Joe" Walcott, who showed me,

the night of September 23, 1952,

how to fight the clean fight.

Contents

Acknowledgements

Freedom House would like to thank those whose efforts made this work possible: Manuel A. Tellechea, the translator; Irving Louis Horowitz and Scott Bramson of Transaction Publishers; and Christopher Kean, who met with the author in Havana and brought out of Cuba a new epilogue. Thanks also to those who read and provided comments on the manuscript: Barbara Futterman, Lisa Garcia, Oliver Schultz, Antonio Fins, Scott Sleek, Eric Singer, Victoria Thomas, and Charles J. Brown.

This project is part of the Freedom House Cuba Roundtable. It would not have been possible without the solidarity and support of Manuel J. Cutillas, Francisco Blanco, Richard O'Connell, Modesto A. Maidique, Guillermo Marmol, Carlos M. de la Cruz, Alfonso Fanjul, Goar Mestre, Carlos Ripoll, Felix Granados, Alberto Tellechea, and Armando C.Chapellí, Jr.

Transaction would like to thank Esther Luckett and Sandy Klein-Suriano, who served as manuscript editors; and Joe Bertucci and Valerie Stefani, who coordinated production.

Prologue

I don't think that I am wrong to affirm that the publication of this book constitutes an unprecedented event, as much for the circumstances that surround its appearance as for the personality of the author.

In 1970, the author of this book, my father, wrote a novel with political content entitled, *The Funeral Rites of Hector*, which he submitted to the annual contest sponsored by "Casa de las Americas," but because the ideas that it contained departed from the *fidelista* line, he was fired from his job at the Cuban news agency, Prensa Latina.

Eighteen years later, in 1989, he again took up his pen; this time he wrote a short account of his efforts to emigrate entitled, "It Just Wasn't My Day," and, later, during a grueling three month period, he wrote the present work.

One afternoon in March of that year I was surprised to receive by certified mail a package from Cuba. On opening it I found two issues of *Economy and Development*, a journal where my father worked as a proofreader. Several pages had been cut out and in their place were the first pages of this book. And so, little by little, the rest came.

During all that time I couldn't stop thinking what would happen to my father if this book were published, as was his wish. The consequences would perhaps be grave, but if it could call attention to the critical situation in my country and avoid worse misfortunes, then surely its publication would have been worth whatever risks or consequences might attend it.

The Tiger and the Children

In mid June, I received a long distance call from my mother and learned that my father had declared himself on a hunger strike. The news was bad enough, but even more painful and troubling to me when I considered what I knew to be my father's character, and what I believed to be the regime's attitude toward political reform. It will never allow it. It would be its undoing.

Fidel Castro is besieged by internal and external pressures and the worsening economic crisis in the country caused by changes now taking place in the Soviet Union and other countries that have begun to liberate themselves from Marxism-Leninism. Fidel knows he is cornered and his distress is evident; he made it quite plain in his July 26th speech, which could not but have distressed those of us who really believe him capable of making good his promise to sink the island rather than permit a form of government that doesn't include him.

As my father states at the beginning of this book, he is not a persecuted political figure or a world famous dissident; or at least he wasn't before he wrote it. Nor does he write from prison as others have done. He belongs to the immense anonymous majority that suffers in silence the consequences of a dictatorship -- the most defenseless and least remembered part of the Cuban people. He has defied Fidel from his position as a free man-- free at least in spirit-- and, conscious of the consequences, he has raised his voice above the silence imposed on the Cuban people to speak for them.

Like my father, I hope this book will facilitate a reassessment of the historical causes that led to the rise and endurance of a phenomenon that has influenced, almost always for the worse, the lives of all Cubans: Fidel Castro. The law did not absolve him in 1953, and neither shall history absolve him on the day he is finally judged. Let us hope that day will come soon.

Verónica Luque

September 1990

Introduction

I can't stand it anymore, old man. You will not listen to reason, protest or plea. You mock everything. You tolerate nothing but blind obedience to your blind orders.

--Melville

Of all the human rights violations that the Cuban people have suffered over the last thirty years, the most severe arise from the *fidelista* regime's restrictions on emigration. Such restrictions, which masquerade as laws, vest in the State the prerogative to permit or deny any citizen the right to leave his country and settle in another. What is worse -- if anything can conceivably be worse--these "laws" also enable the State to prevent any citizen from returning to his country, if he so wishes.

Because of the suffering that these restrictions have caused by dividing families and therefore an entire nation; because of the millions of people who have been affected adversely by them; because of the horror of countless deaths they have caused--it is far worse to be eaten by sharks, to drown, to lose your life from thirst, or to be burned to death by the sun, than it is to be shot by firing squad. because of the non-belligerent character of victims who only wished to express the natural desire of every man and woman to flee from where he is not esteemed or respected; because of all the weddings, baptisms, Christmas dinners, births and funerals that have taken place in the absence of loved ones; because of all the broken

1

marriages and frustrated loves; because of the humiliations to which hundreds of thousands of people have been subjected in exchange for permission to do with their lives as they thought best; because of this massive and daily suffering, without even the rewards of heroism, I think that migratory restrictions are the worst crime committed against our people.

Yet, little is said about it. The victims of these restrictions have almost always been common or ordinary people, who are not prisoners, or exactly persecuted. They are unimportant people, oppressed by despotism, but unimportant.

Here and there, however, in this confraternity of millions, you will find an occasional well-known personality, such as the greatest Cuban novelist, José Lezama Lima.

Separated from his exiled sister and nephew, and condemned to watch his elderly mother suffer the pain of that separation, José Lezama Lima penned these words: "How have we come to be in this blind alley, without a glimmer of hope, surrounded by death?"

I want to attempt an answer to that question. I want to find out where and when we lost what we lost and why. For this, as for all other enterprises, the best place to start is precisely at the beginning.

I. The Colony

It all started in 1492. We shall soon mark the 500th anniversary of that pivotal year, when the acts and decisions of one woman would alter radically the destinies of a people, and affect not only all future generations of Spaniards but also those like me who carry the blood of Spain though we have never set foot in that country. In 1492, Isabella the Catholic, Queen of Castile, destroyed the kingdom of Granada, the last Arab redoubt on the Iberian peninsula; initiated the search of the Indies, which led to the discovery of the New World; and expelled the Jews.

The capture of Granada was the culmination of *la reconquista*, the seven-centuries struggle to oust the Moors and unite Christian Spain that produced a nation of proud men who, immersed or threatened by war generation after generation, fought for a cause that belonged to all alike: great and small, rich and poor. Spain was a nation of soldiers, not slaves. Such a nation ought by circumstances to have been the cradle of modern liberties.

One hundred years before the Magna Carta, Rodrigo Díaz de Vivar, "El Cid," the model hero of the Reconquest, addressed the future king of Aragón thusly: "We, who as men are worth as much as you, and who as a people are worth more than you, make you our king on the condition that you will respect our rights, and if you will not, then neither shall you be king." Such were the harsh words that the heir to the throne of Aragón was made to hear before being invested as king. And, moreover, El Cid made Alfonso VI swear that he had no part in the murder of his own brother, Prince Sancho, before pledging his allegiance to him. "You press me much, Rodrigo, but I swear," replied Alfonso. Later, Alfonso would exile El Cid, but his oath remains an example of power awarded consensually and conditionally.

The great literature of Spain's Golden Age is rich with examples of this same attitude toward honor, individuality and the right to dissent. The Count de Benavente obeys Carlos V's order to board his French general, the Comte du Bourbon. But when the unwanted guest, despised because he lacks honor, departs, Benavente burns to the ground his palace in Toledo to protest having been required to do something against his conscience.

But it was not only the nobles and *hidalgos* (lower nobility) who so jealously guarded their honor; the peasants, whether from the city or the country, maintained the same code. Calderón de la Barca immortalized in one of his plays the humble Pedro Crespo, but he didn't invent him. He drew him from life -- the everyday reality of XVIth century Spain. Crespo does not hesitate in avenging himself on the well-born captain who has besmirched his honor, and before the king, asserts his right to do so: "To the king, I owe my estate and my life, but my honor is the patrimony of my soul, and my soul belongs only to God."

Honor is simply the right of every man to be respected. Whether a man is free or not can be judged by his behavior before the powerful, his so-called "betters." Freedom itself is judged by how well it functions before the limitations placed on it by power. In the end, England became what Spain should have been: the cradle of modern liberties. Still, it would be difficult to imagine situations similar to those already described occurring under the reign of the Tudors. [Thomas More, who like El Cid stood up to his king, though not in so brazen a manner, was beheaded by Henry VIII, who, unlike Alfonso VI, did not suffer the rebuke of his subjects patiently or punish it with exile.]

4

In our own country, right now, can anyone imagine members of the Central Committee of the Cuban Communist Party imposing conditions on Fidel Castro? Who can conceive of a Pedro Crespo (so many Cubans bear that name!) asserting before Fidel his right to be respected, as did the future mayor of Zalamea before Felipe II? No. Imagination has its limits. And progress is a very relative concept. Especially the progress of the soul.

In 1492, Spain was united but the people of Spain were torn asunder. The great queen, misled by religious fanatics, decreed the expulsion of the Jews from the kingdom of Castile. Her husband, Fernando II, also a great king, followed suit in Aragón, misled by his own avarice. The expulsion of the Jews was a great blow to modernity and to Spanish liberties. The Jews dedicated themselves to commerce and the sciences because all other fields of human endeavor were closed to them. They were at the heart of an emerging bourgeoisie -- the class that most needs democracy, and that, consequently, would have done the most to install it. By destroying the nascent bourgeoisie, the Catholic kings attacked indirectly but profoundly the liberties of the Spanish people. It is from such a people that we inherited the fundamental elements with which our own nation was formed.

Liberty, which had begun its slow agony in Spain, would in 1492 find a better habitat. On October 12, Christopher Columbus arrived in a New World that someday would become a haven for so many persecuted men searching for a little dignity and well-being. Not all of the New World, however; just the North, colonized by Anglo-Saxons, would enjoy such fortune permanently. For it was England that, in the end, would displace Spain as the home of free men. Her thirteen North American colonies eventually would occupy the leadership of the Free World. Close, very close, to the thirteen colonies that later would become the United States is our own island, where for a time the old Spanish liberties seemed to be reborn, but only to expire again as a promise unfulfilled. Our island, transformed today into one of the last redoubts of totalitarianism.

But let us return to Spain, whose history was also ours for more than 400 years. After the death of the Catholic kings and several fleeting reigns and regencies, there ascended to the throne the young Carlos, grandson of Fernando and Isabella, but the product of a different environment: the solidly feudal world of the German principalities where there was no place for the likes of El Cid or Pedro Crespo. It was the Hapsburgs of Austria that inherited the Spanish throne and buried Spanish liberties.

Carlos V's Germanic style of government drove to desperation and revolt the inhabitants of the towns, cities and freeholds of Castile. Having defeated the rebels at Villamar and executed their chief, Juan de Padilla (a recurrent surname in the history of our own frustrated rebellions), Carlos next turned his attention to Valencia where a similar movement had broken out, crushing it as well. The remaining Spanish bourgeoisie, weakened already by the blow against the Jews, was brought down by royal fiat, and Spain sunk into totalitarianism, religious fanaticism and economic incompetence. All these words are familiar in Cuba today except religion.

Felipe II, son of Carlos V, completed his father's work by executing Chief Constable Juan de Lanuza because he gave asylum (as was his right) to Felipe's persecuted ex-minister, Antonio Pérez. Carlos V and Felipe II: one cannot write the history of the XVIth century without mentioning their names. They both were great but nefarious kings.

The monarch under whose rule I find myself (monarchy is defined as the rule of one alone; there is no king who is more "one" than Fidel nor one more "alone"), has a weakness for glory -- though he may deny it. But the years, the occasional failures and his growing isolation, have embittered his naturally good disposition. Taking all this into consideration, and in view of Fidel's limitless power over our lives and estates (mine included), it seems to me prudent to flatter his vanity with some historical parallels.

Fidel, like Carlos V, the king-emperor, trampled our liberties, emptied our pockets and embarked us on absurd enterprises. As for Felipe II, upon his ascension to the throne, there were already seven million sheep in Spain--those magnificent merino sheep that later would be the wealth of Australia. Upon his death, forty years later, there were only two million. The data that I have on livestock in Cuba are not, paradoxically, as accurate, but I can say that the number of cattle has diminished by no less than one million head in the thirty years of *fidelismo*.

It would appear that there are certain styles of government that are not very conducive to the reproduction and survival of certain species of animals. But what does this matter beside the glories that they achieve--Lepanto, San Quintin, Cuito Cuanavale? What importance could the disappearance of a few foul-smelling beasts have when compared to such meteors of glory? Only the mean-spirited would count bovines in the midst of such splendor.

After this adulatory parenthesis, let us return once more to Spain. (Would that I could return to that country which I have never visited, but how could I get a visa? Nobody listened, few listen now, and few will ever listen). In the XVIIIth century Spain was already a second-class power. The Hapsburgs never again produced anything even similar to the first Carlos or second Felipe, who were morally but at least not physically or mentally defective. Eventually, the Hapsburgs inbred themselves into sterility and extinction. In 1700, a French prince, a grandchild of Louis XIV, became *our* king (I say "*our* king" because in 1700, the Luques, the Escalonas and the other clans from which I am descended remained in Spain, as were the Castros who were Fidel's ancestors; in fact, it would take the Castros longer than it did us to get to Cuba). The new foreign dynasty, the Bourbons, proved as detestable and, of course, as despotic as its predecessor: in almost three centuries, it has produced only two good kings. By then, Spanish liberties were ancient history.

Meanwhile, what was happening on the island of Cuba, even without the Luques, Escalonas, Castros or Ruzes? Very little. Almost nothing. The country was populated very slowly; other lands in the Americas were far more promising for settlers. Cattle, free of authoritarian influences, did propagate, and were one source of wealth, but not a very great one. Cuban tobacco was gaining its

7

worldwide reputation, which it still retains to an extent, despite the ravages of Marxism-Leninism. In 1717, the tobacco growers staged the first rebellion of importance in Cuban history to protest the state monopoly to which they were forced to sell their product. This was the first state monopoly that exploited the labor of the island's inhabitants. It would not be the last.

Was there something else? Yes, the precious woods of a marvelous forest, long since disappeared, and, above all, the provision of the flotillas that would meet in Havana to make the voyage to Spain. That was Havana: a way station. The rest of the country consisted of pastures, forests, small valleys, tobacco, sugar mills with their primitive works, and towns that lived at the mercy of sea pirates. The inhabitants of these towns were always ready to fight or run from those evildoers, or, just as likely, join them in the business of hostage-taking and contrabanding. Drake, Jacques de Sores, Morgan, and the terrible Olones are names that fill the early history of Cuba--if such can be called history.

In 1759, Carlos III, one of the two good Bourbon kings, ascended the throne (the other is the current king, the astonishing Juan Carlos). But even good kings commit errors. Such a blunder was Carlos III's family compact with his kinsman, the king of France, which involved Spain in a war with England. In 1762, the English laid siege to Havana.

It was not a bad resistance. There have been better, but this was not at all bad. From it emerged the first popular hero of the Creoles, the councilor of Guanabacoa, José Antonio Gómez, or "Pepe Antonio," who, at the head of the militia of that village, proved himself a skilled fighter. But the resistance to the English didn't last for long. Pepe Antonio was dismissed by the inept Spanish governor and died a short time later, apparently from the rage occasioned by his unjust removal.

In the end the English captured Havana, remaining there for eleven months until the city was returned to Spain in exchange for the then-underpopulated swamplands of Florida. These were eleven important, fundamental months in Cuban history: we learned then, for the first time, the wonders of free commerce. There are things, persons and situations without which it is very difficult to live once one has known and enjoyed them. For the Creoles, free commerce was one of those things. When Spain again took control of Havana to the great rejoicing of its inhabitants -- for we were Spaniards then -- Carlos III seemed to understand the new situation, and maintained, to a certain extent, commercial liberties. We then ceased to vegetate and began to live as a nation. And for the first time, we started to have a history of our own.

Francisco de Arango y Parreño

Some years later, in the 1780s, a commission of landed Creoles visited the neighboring French colony of St. Dominique (today known as Haiti) to investigate how French planters managed to extract such riches from so small an area of land. One who formed part of that group, Francisco de Arango y Parreño, then 24, was destined to exert a fundamental and long-lasting influence on the life of our country.

The commissioners, particularly the young Arango, grasped thoroughly the secret of French methods: the generalized and intensified use of slave labor. They returned to Cuba and inaugurated the enterprise that they hoped would convert the island into the world's largest sugar exporter. They succeeded; after two centuries -- and despite centralized planning -- Cuba is still the world's principal exporter of sugar. They achieved their success, in part, at the expense of St. Dominique, whose social and economic institutions were swept away shortly thereafter by revolution. The slaves of St. Dominique rose up, killing the whites who did not escape and destroying the wealth created by their hands for the benefit of the French. St. Domingue disappeared and Haiti emerged. From its very beginnings to the present day, it remains underdeveloped and a slaughterhouse of men.

A few thousand Frenchmen survived the massacre and settled in Cuba where they contributed to the expansion of a new landed

9

class that would make the island one of the most prosperous countries in Latin America and certainly the most progressive. But that transformation was already underway when the French arrived, and I believe that their fundamental contribution was not technical or economic, but social. They contributed their knowledge of what a race war might do to a nation: the French émigrés were themselves a living reminder of the consequences of such a struggle. In any case, the French were an infusion of new blood that in time would produce personalities of all sorts: generals in our wars of independence, mayors of Havana, literary figures, painters, the founder of our most famous distillery [Bacardí], the Olympic world champion fencer at the turn of the century and the best swordsman in France [Ramón Font], and Karl Marx's son-in-law [Paul Lafargue]. Incidentally, the founder of scientific Socialism complained bitterly of the excessive boldness that the French Creole's hands showed during the courtship of his daughter Laura. [Marx also referred to Lafargue, who was of mixed blood, as the "African gorilla."]

The worthy French emigrants from Saint Domingue were most influential, however, in establishing a solid class of Creole landowners in Cuba -- a class that was entrepreneurial, progressive, receptive to new technology and absolutely modern (despite the manpower it utilized). The new Cuban gentry was led by a man of genius, Francisco de Arango y Parreño, who had already begun to be called "Pancho the Great." The planter class created the wealth of the nation, and removed Cuba, once and for all, from the obscure vegetative existence that it had led since the days of Diego Velázquez de Cuéllar, the island's first colonial governor. But it accomplished several even more important things: it isolated Cuba from the horrible carnage that would beset the rest of Latin America as a result of the Hispanic wars of independence, and saved us also from the aftermath of those wars -- the rule of barbaric *caudillos*.

At the beginning of the XIXth century the Bourbon dynasty reached the nadir of its degradation. King Carlos IV, quite apart from his incompetence as a ruler, was one of the most contemptible cuckolds in the history of mankind. As for his queen, María Luisa. . .

well, I dislike to speak ill of women. Prince Fernando, the heir apparent, was called in his youth "The Well-Desired One," and in his old age (he lived many, too many years) was given the epithet of "mule-brained and tiger-hearted." The royal family also included at this time one Señor Manuel Godoy, the queen's lover and the king's well-beloved. This complicated family situation excited the interest of the French emperor, awakening in him once more his voracious appetite for land and his incurable nepotism. Without thinking it through, Napoleon deposed the Spanish Bourbons and gave their throne to his brother Joséph. Joséph Napoleon was alone worth more than the three nobodies that filled the various places of Queen María Luisa's world, but the Spanish people did not see it quite that way, calling him "the usurper" (which he undoubtedly was) and *Pepe Botella* (Joey Bottles); and they rose against him.

Napoleon committed an enormous error in judging the Spanish people by their deplorable royal family. Nothing corrupts a people quite so much as a prolonged tyranny. Although they were not a nation of Pedro Crespos anymore, the Spaniards still had the daring to confront the all-conquering French and their all-but-invincible Emperor. So began Spain's war of independence, which not only was just, but logical and natural. You cannot simply impose a foreign monarch on a people who had been as great as the Spanish, who had retained the recollection of their past greatness.

This just, logical and natural war provoked other wars across the seas. Spain's colonies in the Americas also rebelled, but their wars were not in any way provoked by the imposition of Joséph Napoleon, an event far-removed from their everyday reality. Their wars were precipitated by concurrent factors: the removal of the recognized king and, therefore his power over them, and the disgust of local Creole oligarchies with the Crown's unwillingness to share its power with them. The Hispanic wars of independence were not the product of a natural process. The vice-royalties had not evolved internally or acquired the conditions for independence. It was an external factor that had occurred on the other side of the Atlantic,

11

thousands of miles away, that set in motion the independence movement in the Americas.

Almost all of Spain's American possessions were involved, sooner or later, in that 14-year struggle: some through their own initiative, others dragged in against their will by circumstances beyond their control. But Cuba was not, and neither was Puerto Rico.

In Cuba, the governor-general, the Marquis de Someruelos, and the sugar barons, led by Arango, formed a solid coalition that maintained the peace of the island. Other countries, such as Venezuela, whose social system and ethnic composition resembled our own, plunged into class wars of hair-raising ferocity. Simon Bolivar, the rich and aristocratic landholder from the Aragua Valley, and José Tomas Boves, an obscure merchant from Asturias who ruled the plains of Patagonia, rivalled each other in cruelty. Slitting the throats of enemies and neutrals became a natural fact of everyday life in South America, and was even sanctioned in a decree by Bolivar.

Fame and glory are not very serious mistresses, to put it as gently as possible. Who today is unacquainted with Bolivar the Liberator? Yet Francisco de Arango y Parreño is an unknown even in his own country. Arango created prosperity while Bolivar left in his wake only death and destruction. Karl Marx branded Bolivar as "A cowardly, vile and miserable swine." Marx had an animus against men who risked their lives, whatever their motives. Marx said nary a word about Arango, because he also never learned of his existence. However, it was a Marxist historian, Manuel Moreno Fraginals, who first showed me that the oligarch Arango was a genius.

You have to be a genius to become wealthy from the exploitation of slaves and at the same time realize what a nefarious institution slavery was not only for the country as a whole, but also for the sugar oligarchy itself. The only thing that blinds men more than money is love. The sugar oligarchies did not follow their leader in his rejection of slavery, because geniuses are few; but they did emulate his "fidelity" to the Spanish crown, which was really dictated by their own·interests.

Another factor helped us escape a premature and turbulent independence. Carlos IV and Fernando VII, those execrable kings of Spain, sent to Cuba a series of governors (Las Casas, Someruelos, Cienfuegos and Vives) possessed of enough common sense to gauge the strength of the sugar oligarchy and share power with them. Lastly, we must again mention the French emigrants, survivors and witnesses of a race war, whose presence in Cuba was a constant reminder of what could happen in our country.

Bolivar the Liberator. That's what his countrymen and his contemporaries always called him, and what he is still called today. Nonetheless, we might ask ourselves, who did he liberate? To whom did he bequeath this liberty? His native country, Venezuela, lived 130 years under a series of cruel and rapacious tyrannies, and its first tyrants were Bolivar's own comrades-in-arms. It was not until 1958 that democracy finally came to the land of the Liberator. Colombia, which is named for the discoverer of the New World, has lived since independence submerged in barbaric violence that never ends. Ecuador's history is one of continuous barracks coups, dictatorships and rebellions, although its last three presidential elections were settled in a peaceful manner, for the first, second and third times in its history. Peru has put aside for the moment its legacy of military dictatorships, but is now facing an insurgency of fanatic assassins who worship a bloody Chinese idol, the Maoist *Sendero Luminoso*. And Bolivia, the nation that bears the Liberator's own name, holds the world record for military coups d'état (more coups than it has lived years as a nation; historians argue the exact number.) Bolivia now enjoys a democratic system, although in the countries "liberated" by Bolivar, one can never be too sure.

Bolivar. Many times I have pitied the sad and solitary death of this singular man. But I ask myself: Did he ever pity the sad and solitary death of anyone? I doubt it. And since I have spoken so much of the Liberator, I want to take this opportunity to point out certain similarities between the Venezuelan hero and Fidel Castro. It never does any harm to adulate those who can crush us.

13

Both Bolivar and Fidel, or, better yet, Fidel and Bolivar, dreamt of a great pan-American nation, with themselves, naturally, at its head. They both detested Yankee imperialism although they each maintained cordial relations with other imperialisms; in Bolivar's case, the England of Canning; and in Castro's, Brezhnev's Soviet Union. And they both also detested Spain. But what most unites them, in my opinion, are two vaguely similar events. One occurred many years ago in Angostura, the other but a short while ago in Havana.

In 1817, after sustaining a series of defeats, Bolivar took refuge in Guiana, which had been won for the separatist cause by General Manuel Piar. In Angostura, a Congress convened that confirmed Bolivar's leadership. From there, the Liberator crossed the flooded plains and frozen Andes to defeat the Spanish at Boyaca. It is important to point out that Bolivar, unlike Fidel, personally directed his campaigns. Admittedly, there did not then exist the means of communications that later would enable Fidel to direct a battle in Angola from thousands of miles away. But let us return to Angostura (now Bolivar City) where a few months after his arrival, the Liberator signed the order to execute Manuel Piar, probably without his hand shaking, (just as Fidel's hand did not shake when he ordered the execution of General Arnaldo Ochoa, who had fought for Fidel and his cause in at least four countries, including Venezuela). How sad it must be to die by order of one whom you have served loyally for more than thirty years! When I die, I will have other sorrows but not that one.

But let us leave in peace those great men of old whose designs we cannot fathom, and return to our own affairs. We Cubans managed to elude these South American freedom fighters with their inveterate practice of killing all who crossed their path. We also avoided what followed. The Hispanic wars of independence had a terrible result: they produced the tyrannies of barbaric *caudillos*. Some, like Páez in Venezuela and Castilla in Peru, had been active participants in the independence struggle. Others, like Rosas in Argentina and Santa Anna in Mexico, had remained on the sidelines

14

or even fought on the side of the enemy. Their personal revolutionary histories really don't matter, however. What does is the phenomenon of a vigorous military man using the troops he commands as the fundamental argument for imposing his rule. That is the nefarious legacy of these wars of independence.

When a nation endures a succession of intense wars, it is inevitable that some generals should be transformed into political figures: five military men--Washington, Jackson, Taylor, Grant, and Eisenhower--were presidents of the United States in two hundred years. Dayan, Alon, Rabin, Weissman and Sharon are or have been important figures in Israeli politics, but in forty-one years, there has never been a coup d'état in Israel, the most threatened country in the world. There has never been a single case of an Israeli general who, entrusted with troops to save his homeland from the snares of its enemies, used them, in passing, to install himself in power. None of the U.S. generals already mentioned was in active military service when he assumed the presidency. By contrast, the characteristic means of transmitting power in Latin America since the first days of independence, has been through military insurrections or barracks coups, which is what "politics" means in that region even today. It is a custom, by the way, that is frantically emulated in the other regions that comprise what they call the "Third World."

The prudent sugar oligarchs, led by Arango, saved us from these barbaric *caudillos* and their barbaric tyrannies. In Cuba, there were in the early 19th century honest dreamers like the poet José María Heredia and the magnificent priest Félix Varela, who attempted to convince their countrymen of the benefits of a struggle for independence, but failed because of the indifference and rejection of those who exercised economic control over the island. Varela, after many years of preaching independence in his newspaper, *El Habanero*, came to the conclusion that Cuban landholders were more interested in increasing the production of their sugar mills and coffee plantations than in achieving independence for their country. Nevertheless, the planters were right and the priest was wrong. I do not doubt for a moment that Arango and his followers were thinking first

15

of their pocketbooks when they decided not to support independence, but their human motives were less important than the results of their actions.

And these were the results: In the period that ran from the beginning of the South American wars of independence in 1810 to the beginning of our own war of independence in 1868, the worst of the Spanish governors sent to Cuba, from the fat Marquis de Someruelos to the dulcet General Dulce, deserved to be, if not canonized, then at least beatified, when compared to the tyrants who wielded power in Latin America during those years. And, mind you, among these colonial governors were some, like Tacón and O'Donnell, of a decidedly despotic character. But the spiritual and political climate of the island, as well as the knowledge that they served at the pleasure of the king, prevented them from becoming tyrants. Put simply, we Cubans did not live in barbarism.

The most despotic of these governors, General Miguel Tacón, served from 1834 to 1838. He had a hellishly bad temper, aggravated by the resentment that he felt toward all Creoles because of the defeats that he sustained at the hands of Bolivar while governor of Popayán in Nueva Granada (Colombia). Now, it is well to ask, how many men did Tacón send to their deaths because of their political ideas in the four years he ruled Cuba? And how did his government end?

Throughout his tenure, Tacón had constant clashes with the Creole landowners. The most severe point of contention between Tacón and the sugar oligarchy was the exile of the reform-minded writer José Antonio Saco. But Tacón did not execute Saco. In fact, Saco died an old man in Madrid, and while in exile there, was elected a deputy to the Spanish Cortes (parliament) from Cuba. Then there also was Tacón's opposition to the construction of the Havana Bejucal railroad, the sixth to be laid in the world, because he did not think it seemly that a mere colony should be more advanced than the motherland. But the railroad was built by private investors, despite his opposition. Because of the railroad and other conflicts with the head of the Exchequer, Claudio Martínez de Pinillos, successor to

Arango as leader of the Creole oligarchy, the arbitrary Tacon was sacked by Fernando VII.

And now that I've mentioned Martínez de Pinillos, the first Count de Villanueva, I want to pay one last tribute to his predecessor as Creole leader, Francisco de Arango y Parreño. Like Pinillos, Arango was elevated to the nobility by Fernando VII, but unlike other sugar-aristos, he refused to present a certificate of purity of blood, an indispensable condition for the creation of Spanish noblemen, declaring that "everybody in Cuba knows who I am." When awarded the title even without the certificate, he refused to use it, so that I can't even remember what he was marquis of. I like people who are what they are and don't pretend to be anything else. Arango was bourgeois, a modern man who lived in the present and looked to the future. He was not a nobleman and never pretended that he was. He was only a great man who enriched himself and his country. Arango created wealth and took his share. Others -- the devil take them! -- know only how to generate poverty and are so "generous" they won't even take their share.

I have spoken of barbaric *caudillos* that never had the opportunity to impose their bloody presence on our country. To list them all, even summarily, would be a tedious and disagreeable task. However, there are two that I must mention: the "Illustrious Restorer" Juan Manuel de Rosas and "El Supremo" Gaspar Rodríguez Francia. Both were, in their own terrible way, precursors of totalitarianism in Latin America. Their style of government reminds us of other tyrants who, unfortunately, are not so distant in time.

Rosas imposed on Argentina a despotism based on something like an ideology, as vast and primitive as his own person. But it was an ideology nonetheless, one as mendacious and oppressive as those modern ideological systems that assign to the State the right and duty of oppressing and repressing men and foment the most abject cults of personality. That was the ideology of Rosas' "Holy Federation."

I have never bothered to investigate what this "Federation" could have meant or comprised in a country governed in the most centralized manner available in pre-Marxist times, nor what deeds made it "Holy." I know, however, that the citizens of Argentina who did not embrace the "Holy Federation" were called "swine, savages and filthy unitarians (i.e. centralists)." This reminds me of more recent epithets ("worms," "scum" and "anti-patriots" in Cuba; and "beasts" in Nicaragua). I have also learned that the unlucky wretches condemned to live in those days and in that country were required to wear on their clothes a red ribbon as a mark of adherence to the official ideology.

God only knows how the Illustrious Restorer came to choose red as the symbol of his oppressive system of government.

Francia, Paraguay's El Supremo, was also a precursor of the one-party state. He reached that category by turning his country into a prison, forbidding anyone to leave or enter it. An old Spanish proverb instructs, "Make a silver bridge for the fleeing enemy." El Supremo did not believe in proverbs, or, rather, he only believed in those that he himself proclaimed, such as "the best enemy is a dead enemy." Well, if not exactly in the grave, then at least locked away in prison or within the reach of his death squads. Of course, Francia did not violate Article XLII of the United Nations Charter, which endorses the right of every citizen to leave his country freely and return there whenever he wants. He did not violate this article because it was drafted more than a century after the wretch's death. But the U.N. Charter is in force today. Nevertheless, there are still nation-prisons similar to Gaspar Rodríguez Francia's Paraguay.

While Paraguay and Argentina and virtually all the rest of Latin America were sinking under tyranny in the XIXth century, the colonials in Cuba lived without the necessity of making constant public demonstrations of political adherence, without fear of death, incarceration or humiliation, misfortunes that frequently befell the citizens of independent republics -- sometimes as a result of mere carelessness or happenstance. In any case, if things went badly for us in Cuba, we always had the possibility of going to where we thought things might go better. Back then, Cubans seemed to have had good fortune.

But fortune is fickle. Still, we should not hurry along this story. Much more transpired before we arrived at our totally wretched fate. We then were slowly setting forth toward the formation of our national identity. Slavery, the socio-economic system on which our prosperity depended, was leading us, bit by bit, to our own struggle for independence. It was bit by bit, I repeat, and without external factors, pushing us -- just as Napoleon's invasion of Spain years earlier had driven the other Latin American countries -- to seek independence.

II. The Wars of Independence

Slavery could only serve as a means of accumulating initial capital, but never as a permanent system. Arango understood this in the early 1800s and pressed for gradual abolition, but this time no one listened to him. The sugar oligarchs, filled with entrepreneurial spirit, were always in search of new methods and technologies that would enable them to produce more and at lower costs, but the manpower that they utilized, the slaves, was a barrier to all attempts at modernization. The possibilities of the system had been exhausted, and the nation was already on the road to ruin. It was then with slavery as it is now with centralized planning of the economy.

The island's wealth began to change hands, and ended up, eventually, in the possession of reactionary Spanish merchants. Their greed, shortsightedness and lack of roots in the country to which they owed their prosperity would cause the Creoles to declare Cuba's independence forty-four years after Bolivar's victory at Ayacucho. Cuba was too great a country to be just a place where money was made only later to be spent in Spain. The Crown treated Cuba more and more like a simple colony in the spirit of 19th century imperialism, without taking into account that Cubans were not a conquered people. Most importantly, however, the Spanish failed to see that Cuba was too great a colony for so miserable a colonial power as Spain. Embroiled in the Carlist wars, the posthumous legacy of the calamitous Fernando VII, and governed by more or less obtuse

generals (Espartero, Narvaez and our own former governor, O'Donnell), Spain had no one capable of grasping this not-so-simple truth.

Meanwhile, the proximity of the United States to Cuba began
to figure ever more prominently in our historical development. It
became increasingly clear that this enormous and growing country
was the natural market for our exports and the most convenient
purveyor of what we imported. There were other attributes of the
United States that fired-up enthusiasm of a very different kind in
Cuba, attributes that contradicted each other: the solidity of American
democratic institutions and the survival of slavery in a part of its
territory.

There was yet another factor for Cubans to consider. England
had based its initial capitalist development on the slave trade, but
since had abolished slavery and become its most bitter enemy (for
humanitarian reasons, needless to say). It was pressuring a weak
Spain to do the same. The British bourgeoisie had realized Arango's
dream: it had used slavery *only* as a means of accumulating initial
capital.

Those who favored annexation to the United States did not
want for heroes, martyrs or outstanding leaders: the printer Eduardo
Facciolo, the first worker to die for a political cause in our country;
Joaquín de Agüero, whose execution caused the beauties of Camagüey to cut their tresses in mourning, and filled with tears the eyes
of a 10-year old boy named Ignacio Agramonte; Isidoro Armenteros
from the town of Sancti Spiritus; Ramón Pintó, a Catalan whose
death was decreed by his great friend, Governor Gutiérrez de la
Concha; Domingo Goicuría, shot by firing squad as an advocate of
independence in the Ten Years' War, but who once had been an
annexationist and a participant in William Walker's imperial
adventures in Central America (Goicuría, after Walker's execution,
raised such a fuss of his own, that Costa Rican authorities preferred
to let him depart in peace rather than continue to fight his private
army); Gaspar Betancourt Cisneros, "El Lugareño," the theoretician
of the annexationist movement who died a natural death surrounded
by the unanimous respect of his *lugareños* (countrymen); Miguel

21

Teurbe-Tolón, designer of our national emblem (which Henry Miller called "the strange Cuban flag"); the Venezuelan-born Narciso López, a general in the Carlist wars who raised our flag for the first time in the city of Cárdenas and who, undaunted in defeat, declared before dying, "My death shall not alter the destinies of Cuba." And he was right.

It was the Americans themselves who killed the Cuban annexationist movement, not the Spaniards. In 1865, the War Between the States concluded with the defeat of the South. The pro-slavery current of Cuban annexationism, like the idyllic life of the Southern slaveholders, was swept away by the outcome of that struggle -- one of the things that was gone with the wind. Not long afterwards, in 1869, Cuba's first constitutional convention, meeting in Guáimaro, addressed a petition to the U.S. Congress expressing the desire of Cubans to join the Union once they had achieved their independence from Spain. The Congress did not even deign to answer their petition, and the proud patriots who led the insurrection, silently and without reproach buried annexationism. But it was no coincidence that the Convention of Guáimaro chose the annexationist Teurbe-Tolón's flag as our national ensign rather than the flag that Carlos Manuel de Céspedes raised at Bayamo at the start of Cuba's war of independence. It was a tribute from the young general and parliamentarian Ignacio Agramonte to his boyhood hero, the martyred annexationist Joaquín de Agüero.

From José Antonio Saco to José Martí, some of the most prestigious figures in Cuban history have attacked annexationism. One of the fundamental and, indeed, overwhelming arguments against annexation is that a small nation cannot be grafted to the body of a larger one without inexorably being absorbed and dominated by it. Had their island been annexed to the United States, Cubans would have become second-class citizens in their own country, suffering the same fate as the Mexicans in California and Texas. It is a strong argument that seems irrefutable, and I myself regarded it as such until only recently.

Nevertheless, I now doubt it -- not Saco's conclusion that annexation was not the best thing for our country, but the argument on which he based his conclusion. First, I doubt it because of the advice of Karl Marx (one of the few cases where that very ill-advised man gave good advice): "Question everything." Second, I am unsure because of the brilliant accomplishments of the one million Cubans who have emigrated to the United States since the advent of *fidelismo*. The economic and social success of my exiled countrymen and their successful defense of their identity in the midst of American society causes me to ask myself whether we Cubans could not have accomplished in our own country, under the auspices of the Americans, what we have achieved in Florida and New Jersey? I ask myself, but do not dare to answer. It's not worth it. Annexationism has been water under the bridge for a long time now, and no mill will ever be moved by such currents again. But I now question Saco's argument and I will question it again if I see fit. I will question it and whatever else I please whenever I please, for questioning is the prerogative of free men and I am free, at least on paper.

While the annexationists preached their theories, fought and died for their cause, the reformers, led first by José Antonio Saco and later by the Count de Pozos Dulces, attempted what their party name implied: to reform the inoperative system that governed the country. They failed. They could not but fail because then as now, power was in the hands of men who clung to their privileges, prerogatives and personal interests, men for whom any kind of reform meant that they would cease to be what they were. Better to die, or better still to kill everybody else, than to surrender their status or the principles that sustained it. And so the war began.

It is called The Ten Years' War or the Great War. We were already a nation; were we lacking any element to make us so, the war itself would supply it. The Ten Years' War (1868-78) that began our struggle for independence and the War of 1895 that culminated in our independence were our finest moments as a people and the glories of our history. It is difficult to conceive of an armed movement that demonstrated greater respect for civil authority and freely elected

23

republican institutions, demonstrating an almost total absence of military *caudillismo*, authoritarianism, or ferocity.

As in all wars, military leaders played a fundamental role. But they were subordinate to civil authorities and institutions. The President of the Republic-in-Arms, his cabinet and the House of Representatives never had a fixed seat of government, not even in a small town: the war was carried out (on the Cuban side at least) with groups that almost never exceeded five hundred men, rarely enough to take a village and never enough to hold it. But this portable government, this civil authority that legislated in the woods, was obeyed. The military leaders recognized the supreme authority of civilians who did not fight.

Ignacio Agramonte was the greatest proponent of civilian government. The young general imposed it with his oratory at the Guáimaro convention, upheld it with his actions in war, and above all, adhered to the principle for which he had fought -- even when in conflict with President Céspedes, whose authority he recognized even when Céspedes was too authoritarian. Agramonte, soldier and parliamentarian, was killed at 32 in a meaningless skirmish. Had he lived, he would have been 59 when the Cuban Republic was established at the beginning of this century. It is better not to think what the death of his magnificent man cost us, or what he could have given to his country had he lived the full cycle of his life. Nothing so aggrieves as that which could have been but was not.

I have mentioned in passing the authoritarian character of Carlos Manuel de Céspedes, the initiator of The Ten Years' War and the first president of the Republic-in-Arms, who is known today as "the father of his country." In 1874, Céspedes was relieved of the presidency by the Congress and retired to the Sierra Maestra. What was Céspedes doing there? He was waiting to receive permission from Congress to go abroad. Naturally, the Congress had no means to prevent his leaving. Yet Céspedes obeyed because the Congress that had deposed him was the embodiment of constitutional legality, democracy and liberty for which he had sacrificed fortune, tranquillity, the life of his son and the love of a young wife who had bright-

24

ened his old age. Céspedes waited but permission never came. What did come was a Spanish detachment that ended his life. He died fighting as had Agramonte.

Just for the memory of men as these it is worthwhile to be a Cuban. There are so many others less known who performed similar deeds, and not only men, but women as well. If we had only their memory left -- and barely their memory survives -- for that alone it would be worth any sacrifice to attempt to recover our country.

But were there no *caudillos* among them? No individuals who considered themselves above the law? There were those who aspired to be *caudillos* -- but only aspired. Only one of these is worth the trouble of mentioning: Vicente García, a most able guerrilla fighter whose men adored him with that dangerous and corrupt love that makes some people who are not entirely bad but not exactly good second whatever action or decision is taken by their well-beloved leader, whom they regard as a father, a spiritual guide and a platonic spouse. I do not know which are more detestable: these spurious supermen or their worshipful admirers.

Vicente García led two rebellions against the legal government that was conducting the insurrection, very costly rebellions that were an important factor in the process that brought The Ten Years' War to an end. He was unable to induce other important generals to join his conspiracies. A frustrated *caudillo*, his actions served only to illustrate what could never be permitted to happen again.

I remember now another military leader: Antonio José de Sucre, the most brilliant general of South America's wars of independence. I admire Sucre even more for his kindness and generosity than for his martial deeds because he was kind and generous amidst ferocity, savagery and intrigues and also because he valued the love of his wife and daughter above power or honors. Sucre was something like a warrior saint. But saints also err; only God is infallible. One day in his short life -- for Sucre died very young, as might be expected of a man of his virtue (he was betrayed by a friend and assassinated when he was to be re-united at last with his beloved wife and daughter) -- Sucre said of Bolivar, "This man is the fatherland incarnate; against him, nothing."

No, my good officer and gentleman. The fatherland is not embodied by any one man: we are all the fatherland or there is no fatherland. We Cubans had a fatherland during The Ten Years' War because none of the exceptional figures that participated in that struggle pretended to be the "fatherland incarnate."

The Ten Years' War was called the Great War by those who took part in it. (Since it was the first war that Cubans fought, it is not surprising that they should call it so. But for Spain, which has fought a million wars, to call a mere colonial insurrection "the Great War" gives some idea of the epic dimensions of that struggle.) Great it was, and not only because of its duration -- the Angolan war has lasted longer. From that contest emerged, already formed, our national identity. There was no ferocious decree that condemned to death not only enemies but neutrals. We fought, on our side, like gentlemen, and the Spanish also, at times, fought like gentlemen.

During that decade, Spain sent no less than 150,000 soldiers to the island, more men than it had sent to Mexico and the whole of South America during their wars of independence. Even if you were to add to that total the soldiers and mercenaries used by George III to fight the Thirteen Colonies, you would still fall short of the 150,000 that Spain pitted against the Cuban rebels.

There are innumerable reasons to be proud of that heroic struggle. But ten years is a long time, a very long time, to spend in war. There was no hope of victory on the horizon. There was no scarcity of men but no horses on which to mount them. Regional disputes between rival military leaders also had done their destructive work.

The Spanish military governor, Arsenio Martínez Campos, more of a politician than a general, very ably took advantage of the situation and offered peace terms.

To offer an honorable peace without humiliations to an enemy that is tired of fighting but very difficult to annihilate seems, on first consideration, a simple exercise of logic. Nevertheless, it

26

required great common sense and also an absolute lack of interest in shedding the blood of others. These are characteristics rarely found among professional soldiers.

The accord that ended The Ten Years' War, the so-called Peace of Zanjón, has been severely criticized, especially by those who did not participate in the war (and could not have participated because they had not yet been born). I can see nothing in that accord that is reproachable; the absence of a vindictive spirit in Martínez Campos' actions, seems obvious to me. Yes, of course, the war was lost: for those who initiate an armed struggle anything that is not victory is a defeat. But there are many kinds of war, and many kinds of defeats.

Let us analyze another war and another peace. A century after Zanjón, Cubans now are the ones who cross an ocean to fight in a foreign land with which they have no ties whatsoever (except, perhaps, the vague ties of ancestry that some -- and only some -- of the expeditionary force have to that country). During thirteen years of war, Cuba has sent to Angola twice as many soldiers as Spain sent to Cuba. After thirteen years, apartheid continues in South Africa, even though Fidel Castro said that he would not remove his troops from Angola until it had disappeared. UNITA, the rebel organization against which our soldiers fought, controls no less than a third of Angolan territory. The MPLA government for which Cubans fought and died is now negotiating with UNITA. Nonetheless, Castro signed a peace treaty, although no one can accuse him of doing so enthusiastically.

What I write are my own opinions, not a work of historical documentation. Those who would like to know exactly what were the terms of the peace treaty signed at Zanjón will have no difficulty locating the document. Perhaps they will find something denigrating in it that may disprove my argument. I just want to point out that among its dispositions was one that freed all slaves who had risen in arms against Spain: these, the most humble of the insurrectionists, were rewarded with manumission, while the other slaves, who had abstained from the fighting, continued in slavery. But not for long.

To concede freedom to rebel slaves was an invitation to the other slaves to rebel. Four years after Zanjón, slavery was abolished in Cuba.

To dissent is as much a right of free men as is to question. The young General Antonio Maceo dissented, calling on his countrymen to continue the struggle in the much praised Protest of Baraguá, commended today as much as the Zanjón Pact is criticized.

"I am as white as I am black," so Maceo defined himself. Such a definition of someone of mixed race seems to me unobjectionable. But some do not share it. Raúl Castro, for example, described the Cuban cosmonaut Arnaldo Tamayo, with his fine lips, his almost straight hair, his tanned complexion and his nose -- which is at least as long as mine -- as a "young negro." It would appear that certain sons of Spaniards wish to erase all traces of Spain in Cuba, the better to advance their Third World politics. I stick to Maceo's definition: he was as white as he was black. The Protest of Baraguá is reliable proof of Maceo's Spanish spirit, a feat worthy of Don Quixote and, like all fights against windmills, short-lived and without success.

The last rebel action of Cuba's Great War was the so-called Little War; it was led by General Calixto García. The Little War wasn't really a war, not even a small one; it was barely a series of uprisings that were quickly dissipated by the general exhaustion.

In 1880, a period of peace began that would last fifteen years. They were interesting years. Young men from Havana followed and cheered General Maceo as he passed in front of the Louvre Café and Restaurant. A young lawyer and poet, José Martí, delivered a speech at a banquet attended by the governor general where he appealed for a new war to drive Spain from Cuba. "Never did I think that anyone would pronounce such words in my presence," declared the stupefied governor general. But he listened. The reformers, who were now calling themselves autonomists, won election to the Spanish parliament; the Cuban people were beginning to learn how to vote against their rulers. The journalist, Juan Gualberto Gómez, a son of slaves, published an article whose title could not have been more eloquent: "Why We Are Separatists." He was condemned to three years imprisonment by a Havana court, but his defense attorney -- for such did then exist in Cuba -- appealed his case to the Supreme Court in Madrid and his sentence was vacated.

All this may not seem to be much to some, but it is a great deal to me. How great it would be if those Cubans who so desire could acclaim not the person of General Ochoa, who is no more, but his memory! How wonderful to be able to elect to the National Assembly if not an enemy of the regime like Martí, then at least a reformer like Rafael Montoro! Or if someone in Cuba could publish an article entitled, "Why We Are Supporters of Perestroika," without being hauled before a court that has never pronounced a verdict of not guilty!

Martí was deported to Spain because of his speech. What, I ask myself, would happen to me if I published these opinions? Would they deport me? I doubt it. Deportation is no longer a punishment for Cubans but a dream; a dream that many times cannot be realized. No, I would not be deported. I would be sent to prison for spreading enemy propaganda, even though I am speaking about my own country in my own country. Or perhaps I would be set upon by an indignant mob of my fellow citizens who could not contain their anger at the shameless lies of this worm, this traitor, this scum, this miserable pseudo-intellectual in the pay of Yankee imperialism (and perhaps also suborned by those whose name it is better not to mention, those who are burying Socialism and destroying the work of Lenin).

In sum, one hundred years ago, in the 1880s, under Spanish rule, Cubans were able to elect representatives to press for reforms in the prevailing system, applaud on a public boulevard those who had risen in arms against the government, and publish opinions critical of the Spanish regime without going to jail or being mistreated by savage mobs. I, who lack such rights, regard them as very significant.

We have already mentioned in passing José Martí, but we must now pause before this extraordinary man, and examine not only his life, but, which is perhaps even more important, the spiritual

29

climate that made Martí's rise to the leadership of the independence movement possible.

A most essential harvest of The Ten Years' War was the crop of military leaders who were formed by it and survived it. Maximo Gómez, Antonio Maceo and Calixto García were all logical candidates to lead the movement because of their participation in the war. Martí, on the other hand, did not take part in it. He was only 15 at the start of the war. By its middle, Martí was already old enough to serve. He was the same age, in fact, as his son was when he joined the rebel ranks in the next war. At its conclusion, Martí was 25. Martí had, then, more than enough time to enlist but he did not. There were reasons why he did not -- or could not -- but those do not concern us here. What matters is that a man who did not participate in the first war was later recognized by its veteran generals as the leader of the second war.

José Martí's merits are immense and have been amply exposed for almost a century since his death in battle in 1895. How many Cubans, attempting to channel their heroic impulses, have done naught but imitate or tried to imitate this man!

Nevertheless, I don't wish to discuss his influence. Rather, I want to ask how it came to be that Martí was obeyed by so numerous and distinguished a group of generals, all of whom had the opportunity and the credentials to aspire to the post of *caudillo*, but who were also imbued, in a greater or lesser degree, with respect for civil authority and majority rule. Martí was chosen as head of the new insurrectional movement by Cubans in exile, then as now the only segment of the nation that could freely express its opinion. The military leaders of 1868 submitted to the will of that unarmed majority and accepted their choice. Martí, a man who had never fought in battle, convinced those who had fought so long to fight again and led the way to war.

Of course, there were dissensions, beginning with the frustrated Gómez-Maceo uprising of the mid 1880s and culminating ten years later at the start of the war in the verbal match between Maceo and Martí at the Mejorana ranch.

During the failed Gómez-Maceo conspiracy, Martí was little more than a peon, or at best an assistant; but even from his subordinate position, Martí objected whenever he thought it necessary. Of his differences with Máximo Gómez we retain a phrase that it is better not to remember very often because it is useless to cry: "General, you cannot govern a nation like a barracks." One hundred years later, we see a nation divided by hatred and distance whose entire territory has been converted into a military barracks in preparation for a war that has not come in thirty years against an enemy who has been made into one by the personal will of one man representing scarcely twenty percent of Cubans. And that twenty percent happens to be armed with the only arms in Cuba. A century after Martí's affirmation, we are a nation dominated by armed men who have no respect for any kind of law, not even the law that they themselves enact.

Martí did not live to know Cubans of that stamp. Days after the controversy at Mejorana, Martí, obeyed and respected, died in maiden combat on a steed that was a present from Antonio Maceo's brother, General José Maceo. Shortly before his death, Martí had been acclaimed by the troops as president, although he had not yet been elected as such and never would be. And Martí, the apotheosis of civilian power among Creoles, was made a general by the generals.

Antonio Maceo was also destined to die in battle a year after Martí. I cannot help asking myself: How many of the great figures of the wars of independence in this hemisphere died in battle? Not a one. Neither in North America nor South America; not a single distinguished general died in the American Revolution, nor in the wars of independence in South America or Mexico. We Cubans lost Céspedes and Agramonte in The Ten Years' War, and Martí and Maceo in the War of 1895. Only Máximo Gómez, with his incurable complex of not being a native-born Cuban, and Calixto García, who died of pneumonia shortly after the conclusion of the war, lived to see the culmination of our struggle for independence. Our tradition of heroic deaths has cost our country dearly.

31

The deaths of these leaders greatly affected the future of our country -- none more than that of Martí, who seemed destined to be a great statesman. He was a man of love, not hate, of laws, not violence, and of persuasion, not imposition. The war followed its course without him, and without them; but the Republic was born an orphan.

Cánovas del Castillo, one of those intransigent politicians who considered all reform to be treason, vowed that the Spanish would fight in Cuba "till the last man and the last *peseta*." Of course, he would not be that last man, nor would that last *peseta* come from his pocket. When the dizzying insurrection seemed to him to be impossible to contain by civilized means, Cánovas, an inveterate enemy of all compromise, sent to Cuba General Valeriano Weyler.

In the War of 1868, there had been one particularly bloody Spanish general, the Count de Balmaseda. But Weyler was another thing altogether. Weyler was a monster. He drove the peasants from the country into camps outside the cities, so that they would not be able to assist the rebels. He invented the concentration camp (he called it the "reconcentration" camp) and was the first to use barbed wire to corral men, women and children. Weyler starved myriads of country folk and made his own name synonymous with "monster" in Cuba and throughout the world. It might be well to ask ourselves what is a monster? I would define a monster as someone who is without limits. Blas Villate, the sanguinary Count de Balmaseda, was not a monster, just a bad man.

For all his monstrosity, Valeriano "Butcher" Weyler was still only a subordinate, the instrument of the policy of pacification at all costs devised by Cánovas del Castillo. When his cruelty was exposed as ineffective and even counterproductive from the point of view of propaganda, Weyler was simply relieved of his command. Weyler's unlimited cruelty was a brief interlude in our history, and when it reappeared in our own times in the person of the son of one of Weyler's soldiers, it took us entirely by surprise.

But nothing could stop the rebels. Even Cánovas, one of those architects of disaster who mistake stubbornness for firmness, at last had to agree to reforms. Now, however, it was the Cubans who did not accept these reforms. There was no reason to accept them.

Now, the United States enters. All American presidents from Ulysses S. Grant to Grover Cleveland had been hostile to Cuban independence. I can't help wondering if Grant's animosity toward Cuba may not have been the reason that a street in Havana is named "General Lee." That might also explain why our black national poet, Nicolás Guillén, never protested that designation. In any case, the United States is not the exclusive domain of whomever happens to be president.

Although the U.S. government was opposed to Cuban independence, it could do nothing to prevent Martí and others from advocating it on American soil, nor stop them from collecting funds for the rebel cause. Nor, for that matter, could it prevent something that was, on principle, illegal: the shipment of arms to Cuba. Regardless of what its presidents thought or did, the United States was then what it had always been for Cubans and what it would be again someday: our base of operations in our struggle for liberty. Of course, a little goodwill or at least common sense on the part of the American presidents would not have been at all bad. There was no goodwill. But after years of indifference, Cuba finally came up on the presidential agenda. The fruit had ripened, but it was not the Americans who had brought it to season, though it was they who would reap the harvest.

The story is well-known: the providential explosion of the armor-plated *Maine*; the Congressional Joint Resolution; the "Message to García;" the landing at Daiquirí (which was, more correctly, a stroll, because the Cuban rebels had already taken the coast); the unnecessary assault on the fort defended by the brave Spanish general Vara del Rey (which was opposed by Calixto García and cost the lives of hundreds of American soldiers); the battle of San Juan Hill; Teddy Roosevelt and his "Rough Riders;" the suicidal heroism of Admiral Cervera; the surrender of Santiago de Cuba; and The Treaty of Paris.

33

All of this has been the subject of many historians, although there are some things that I should like to add. I'd like to talk about the Congressional Joint Resolution that declared that "Cuba is and by right ought to be free and independent." How can one reconcile those words with the imposition of the Platt Amendment, which made Cuba, in effect, an American protectorate? I want also to talk about the "Message to García," an example of President McKinley's perfidy, because he addressed his request for support to the regional commander, Calixto García, not to the commander-in-chief of the rebel army, Maximo Gómez, or to the government of the Republic-in-Arms. McKinley treated García as if he were an independent and autocratic *caudillo*. But Calixto García was not Vicente García. He didn't move a single soldier until consulting with his superiors who, of course, instructed him to lend all assistance he could to the Americans.

When Spain surrendered the city, García's troops were prevented from entering Santiago, though they had secured the coast where the Americans had landed and been instrumental in the defeat of the Spanish forces. In truth, General Shafter was alone responsible for this ridiculous and spiteful act. Calixto García had shown himself Shafter's superior, and the obese American general opted for the vengeance of the mean-hearted. But it's another thing altogether with the rest of the indignities inflicted by the Americans on their Cuban allies: McKinley's "Message to García," the Paris Treaty, which was signed without the participation of the real victors, and the Platt Amendment. There is only one word for it: betrayal. Or, to put it in American jargon, a "double-cross." The U.S. presidents served poorly the cause of liberty in Cuba. The chain of perfidies forged by William McKinley has been exploited to the utmost by enemies of our country's freedom since 1898.

We Cubans did not rise to the occasion, either. Nothing better illustrates this than the treatment that the Cuban Congress accorded Maximo Gómez, which seems all the more remarkable if you consider that this body did not want for honest and talented men. They did not, however, prove as honest or as talented as the situation required.

How could they think of treating our greatest general as if he were an undisciplined sergeant? Did they not take into consideration, when they removed him, the total commitment of that cantankerous and acid-throated Dominican to the cause of Cuban independence and the services he had rendered to it? He was cantankerous and acid-throated, but he also was very honest and very much a good man.

"Fight foreign meddling with domestic virtue," advised someone, though I don't remember who [Manuel Márquez Sterling]. But we were short on virtue when we most needed it, for we lacked virtuous men. We were without Agramonte, Maceo and Martí, the oldest of whom, Agramonte, had he lived, would have been barely sixty years old at that time. The Argentines have a saying that God is an Argentine; the Brazilians say He is a Brazilian. I don't know what He is, but I can assure you, He is not a Cuban.

I want to return to Martí. The official perfidy of the United States, as I have said, has been shrewdly used to their advantage by the enemies of Cuban freedom, as have certain opinions of Martí about the country where he lived for so many years.

At only 15 years of age, the future apostle of Cuban independence was sentenced to hard labor for having written a letter in which he addressed a friend as a traitor and apostate because he had joined the Volunteer Corps, the attack dogs of Spanish intransigence. He spent some months in the San Lázaro stone quarry; not many months, because back then it was considered unbecoming to keep an adolescent in prison for political reasons. Martí was subsequently deported to Spain, returning briefly to Cuba only in 1879 when he left the Spanish governor dumfounded with his harsh words and again in 1895 to die in his first combat. Martí spent almost all of his life in exile, and the greater part of those years in the United States. He tried living in his beloved Mexico. He tried Guatemala, leaving with the bittersweet memory of María García Granados, his one true love. He tried Venezuela, the homeland of the Liberator. He tried living in all these countries but could not. This man could not live without liberty. He found it in only one country-- the United States.

35

Why, then, such harshness in judging a country where he lived for the first time unvexed by tyranny, and where he found that without which he could not live? First of all, because he was allowed to. In that country, so harshly judged by Martí and others, any man, native or foreigner, can criticize whatever strikes him as worthy of criticism. This is not the case everywhere; it is not the case, for example, here in Cuba.

As I see it, there is yet another fundamental cause of Martí's harshness: Martí was obsessed with pan-American unity and embittered by the greatest obstacle that then as now confronts it. I refer, of course, to the inability of Martí's "long-suffering (Latin) American nations" to maintain even a minimum of liberty and respect for the law. "Our long-suffering nations" is right. To live in them is to suffer and always has been.

The civic inferiority of Hispanic Americans in relation to North Americans crushed and tormented Martí, who, ever the poet, tried to erase it with words that today are used by a tyranny worse than any that he knew. But words cannot erase reality, not even words from a poet's pen. And what was then, what is now, and what has always been that reality?

Sometime in the 1820s, Father Félix Varela, a deputy from Havana to the Spanish parliament, voted in favor of the removal of Fernando VII. Victorious, the felon-king demanded the heads of all guilty of such contempt for "divine right." To save his life, Varela fled to the United States. For more than a century and a half, hundreds of thousands of Cubans persecuted for their political ideas have followed the path of the cassocked deputy to the United States and have found liberty, peace and prosperity.

José Martí was one of many. There he lived and wrote without fear of being imprisoned or murdered. There he predicated and prepared what he called, quite correctly, "the just war." From the United States -- not from the nations that comprised what Martí called "Our America" -- were launched expeditions with men and arms to aid the cause of Cuban independence. That's one side of the

American coin; on the other side appear Grant, Cleveland and McKinley.

I said, in referring to Sucre, that saints can err. Apostles also err. That's how I see things and that's how I write them.

Biding their time, McKinley, Elihu Root and Teddy Roosevelt played their cards well and defended skillfully the interests of the burgeoning American imperialism that they represented. It was we Cubans who failed. We lacked everything we needed. The birth of our republic was a national disaster.

The Pact of Zanjón was a victory when compared to the way that the War of 1895 ended. That pact at least we ourselves negotiated with the Spaniards. In the Treaty of Paris, however, Cuba appears only as a territory under arbitration, and the fierce struggle that the Cubans waged for their independence is ignored entirely.

In war, as in business or love, when we give all and risk all, it is natural to expect that we will be rewarded accordingly. In our case, this was not to be. That's why our independence and the birth of our republic is marked by the most complete frustration.

We suffered thirteen years of war (1868-78; 1895-98), and for what? To become something like a protectorate? One cannot fight so long and obtain so little. That is how our vital nation began its independence: in a state of total prostration and spiritual lethargy, comparable only to what it suffers today.

III. The New Republic

After four years of U.S. military occupation, the Republic of Cuba came into being on May 20, 1902. Tomás Estrada Palma was our first president, a wealthy landowner who lost all in The Ten Years' War, and who during that struggle had served for a time as president of the Republic-in-Arms. Captured by the Spanish and released by the Zanjón Pact, Estrada Palma emigrated to the United States where he resided for more than twenty years and founded his own school in Central Valley, New York. A close collaborator of José Martí (who had complete trust in his integrity), Estrada Palma was at war's end the Delegate (or Leader) of the Cuban Revolutionary Party in the United States. It is well to point out that Martí founded that party merely as an instrument of the independence struggle. Estrada Palma, following Martí's wishes and true to his non-partisan legacy, dissolved the party at the conclusion of the war. I make this clarification because Fidel Castro, having designated the Apostle of Cuban Independence as the intellectual architect of the assault on the Moncada barracks, has attempted to portray Martí as an exponent of the one-party state, which is as alien to our political traditions as it is vital to *El Comandante*'s authoritarian mindset.

Estrada Palma, known to Cubans as "Don Tomás," was an austere and honest man who cared nothing for riches and loved his country. But love, though it is the best thing in life, does not always bring good results. Don Tomás possessed undoubtedly all the

38

qualities I have enumerated, but he was also stubborn and not especially bright, a very ordinary man for very difficult days. Moreover, he admired the United States to excess. The admiration of the weak for the strong is always fraught with dangers.

And so, when his stubbornness would not allow him to leave office after his term expired in 1906, he committed two deadly sins: he made a mockery of his countrymen's right to elect their own leaders, and when this provoked an uprising among his political rivals that he could not control, he demanded and obtained the intervention of the United States. To be sure that I am well understood, I mean that he did the same thing the Czech Communists did in 1968 when they invited the Soviets to crush democracy in their country.

The responsibility for this second intervention lies entirely with him. Roosevelt did not want to send the Marines. But Estrada Palma renounced office and made all others in line of succession to the presidency resign, as well as all congressmen of his party, leaving the legislature without a quorum. The Cuban state was left acephalous and the Platt Amendment took care of the rest.

In the waning days of the Republic, an "Avenue of the Presidents" that would be lined with statues of all our chief executives was being constructed in Havana. Only two statues in this perhaps too ambitious plan had been erected when Fidel Castro seized power: Tomás Estrada Palma's and José Miguel Gómez's.

During the *fidelista* era, both statues were removed. But Communists can never do anything right. They carried away the body but couldn't wrench Estrada Palma's bronze shoes from the pedestal of his statue. It strikes me as symbolic that the nation honors its first president with a statue of his shoes. Because of his exemplary role in Cuba's wars of independence and his scrupulous honesty in the handling of public funds (and despite his colossal error), the shoes of this *mambi* (freedom fighter) deserve to be on a higher plane than those of the men who ordered the demolition of his statue. They remain on their pedestal still, ten feet off the ground, the bronze shoes of Estrada Palma.

There are many theories to account for this phenomenon. One I have already mentioned: there are people (and systems) that can do nothing right, not even demolish monuments. Others believe that the shoes are indestructible relics from a time when shoes were made properly in our country -- that is to say, before our economy was devastated by scientific Socialism. To the foreign observer, it might appear that the Cuban people -- who under Fidel's rationing system are allotted one pair of Russian shoes every two years -- have erected a statue to the Teutonic god Florsheim.

The U.S. intervention secured by Estrada Palma lasted three years (1906-09). We will let history have the last word on his shoes as well as the man who occupied them.

When Woodrow Wilson occupied Veracruz, he declared arrogantly that he "wanted to teach the Mexicans how to choose good men." Well, the Mexicans at least were luckier than us. Teddy Roosevelt apparently wanted to teach us the opposite because he sent to Cuba as governor general one Charles Magoon, a shameless political boss venal to his very bones. I don't want to say any more about him. I have enough with our own homegrown lazy grafters.

One such individual was General José Miguel Gómez, who was elected president in 1909. He was the first in a series of four presidents who were elected in a more or less orderly manner. This might seem insignificant to those unacquainted with the history of Latin America, but eighty years after the election of Gómez, there are still countries in Latin America that have never peacefully elected four consecutive presidents. No nation in Africa has managed it, and in Asia only India and the Philippines can claim that distinction.

General José Miguel Gómez, known to Cubans as just "José Miguel," was also popularly referred to as the "shark," because of his insatiable appetite for money. He founded a tradition of immorality in the management of state funds (or rather the "taxpayers' money," as the Americans very rightly call it and as we should also). Gómez also put down, with astonishing ferocity given his reputation as a good-natured person, an armed protest by black veterans of the War of Independence, led by Evaristo Estenoz and Pedro Ivonet, two poor devils who couldn't decide between a peaceful protest and a revolution, but who only wanted a little justice and equality for their people. That slaughter, a national disgrace, left for a long time blacks and mulattos in Cuba without the desire to participate in national politics, as would be reflected twenty years later in their total abstention from the struggle to overthrow Machado's dictatorship.

José Miguel Gómez was a bad man, but there was one misdeed that he never committed. He never sought to make himself a dictator. Neither did his successor, Mario García Menocal, despite his authoritarian character.

Menocal, another second-tier general -- the first tier was dead -- had studied engineering at Cornell University and was heavily involved with U.S. interests in Cuba. Before becoming president, Menocal had promoted and run the great U.S.-owned "Chaparra" sugar refinery in Oriente, which, together with his rough manners, earned him the nickname of "overseer of Chaparra."

When Menocal replaced Gómez as president, General Eugenio Molinet replaced Menocal as administrator of Chaparra. General Molinet ordered the assassination of my grandfather, Millo Escalona, one of the principal cane growers for Chaparra, because of a land dispute and a blow that my grandfather struck him which laid Molinet flat on a billiards table. Molinet, damn him, sent three hit men with orders to shoot his old comrade-in-arms in the back. The hit men mortally wounded my grandfather, but not before he had dispatched two to their graves and one to the hospital. Cuban independence was undoubtedly a good cause but not all men who fought for that cause were good men. It is always so in such struggles.

Mario García Menocal did nothing about the assassination, though my grandfather had served on his general staff during the war. However, he can't be accused of ever having devoted himself to the murder of political opponents. Menocal was a general without a penchant for blood. He declared war on Kaiser Wilhelm II as the Americans had asked, but refused to send any Cubans to fight in a foreign war.

41

In 1917, Menocal got himself re-elected in a fraudulent manner. His Liberal opponents, of course, were indignant. They made a grotesque attempt at a revolt, which has come down to us by the curious name of *La Chambelona* (the lollipop), the title of a popular conga of the day that was used as a campaign song by the Liberals. This vulgar brawl was systematic of a vulgar time.

In Menocal's second term the market price of sugar rose dramatically owing to the World War and Cuba experienced its greatest economic boom in history -- the "Dance of the Millions," it was called. The Dance of the Millions was followed by the worst depression in Cuban history, which almost wiped the weak Cuban bourgeoisie from the map. It wouldn't have been such a great loss; these "sugarcrats" weren't fit to hold a candle to those of Arango's day.

In 1921, the harsh "overseer of Chaparra" handed the presidency over to a strange man named Alfredo Zayas, the first non-general to be elected in twenty years. Although not a general, Zayas was a patriot who had endured three years at hard labor in Spain's infamous African penal colony of Ceuta for agitating on behalf of Cuban independence.

En route to Ceuta on a Spanish prison ship in 1895, Zayas was afflicted by a terrible case of rheumatic toothache. All the torment of the world seemed to be reflected in his face as he stood on the deck contemplating the sea. A fellow passenger and companion in adversity asked him kindly, "Doctor, does it hurt much?" Zayas braced himself and answered: "Nothing hurts me too much." At that moment, Zayas seemed a strong-willed man, as strong-willed as his brother Juan Bruno Zayas, an able and combative general who was killed in the war. Perhaps Afredo Zayas was strong-willed too. In that case, something must have cracked inside him during his years of incarceration.

Prison is intended to break men, especially political prisoners. Ceuta was so notorious for its destructive capacity that even today there are Cubans and Spaniards who use "Ceuta" as a curse word. However terrible the conditions, Zayas spent only three years in prison. Today, his sentence would have been thirty years. Zayas entered politics on his release, but was a very different man from what he had been when he had entered prison. So different in fact that I have had to recount the story of his toothache to be able to say anything good about him.

Nevertheless, this swindler at least had a decent respect for public opinion. Before leaving office, Zayas erected a statue of himself across from the presidential palace. Students would gather to throw stones at his statue. The police wanted to disperse the students, but Zayas stopped them. "Let them throw their stones," he said. "Someday they will place flowers." Prison may have crushed Zayas' will and honesty, but not his eternal optimism.

It disgusts me to speak of that time and of corrupt men who once were patriots or pretended to be. But before finishing up with those times and those men, I want to mention one last character who in my opinion, exemplifies as no other the state of degradation in which our country found itself as a consequence of the usurpation of its independence. Alberto Yarini was a pimp, or as those who dedicate themselves to this despicable activity also are called -- a "white slaver." This is an incongruous phrase, for he trafficked not only in white, but also in black, mulatto and Chinese women.

Alberto Yarini reigned supreme over Havana's demimonde of prostitution in those sad days. He was not, it is true, a common pimp. As a rule, pimps come from the bottom rungs of society, the economically disadvantaged, or what Marx calls the *lumpen* proletariat. Yarini was the exception. He came from a family of university professors, but while his brothers dedicated themselves to academic pursuits, he preferred to exploit the stupidity and weakness of others. That is the essence of a pimp's life, and whoever profits from degrading and terrifying his fellow human beings -- whatever his profession -- is a pimp.

Gómez, Menocal and Zayas were not tyrants. Alberto Yarini, whose prostitutes had to ask permission to take their eyes from their plates when they were granted the honor of dining with him, was a tyrant -- a petty despot and dime store tyrant.

Come to think of it, the only difference between this kind of tyrant and the ones who rule nations is purely quantitative.

This repugnant little man was admired, envied, praised and imitated in the very country, and the very city, which a few years earlier had acclaimed as heroes Maximo Gómez and Calixto García; and he held court in the very street of the Cafe and Restaurant "Louvre," where three decades before the youth of Havana had cheered Antonio Maceo.

When Yarini was gunned down by rival French colleagues in what the *fidelistas* would call an act of pimpish imperialism, he was given a funeral that evolved into a mass manifestation of national mourning. Many important political figures either attended or sent wreaths.

To such depths did we Cubans sink. We saw that our struggle did not get us what we expected, what we deserved, or what we had won. But we would not remain in total ignominy for much longer. The man who would force us out of that spiritual morass, by falling there himself, was elected president in 1925.

IV. Machado's Dictatorship

I have thus far spoken only about bad men -- the corrupt generals and doctors who were our first presidents, men who nonetheless had at one time fought and suffered for their country. Faced with the sorry panorama of those bygone days and the no less bleak picture that has been my lot in life to witness, I know the truth of Samuel Johnson's observation that "patriotism is the last refuge of the scoundrel." But that remark does not contain the whole truth. Did *all* men of good will who fought for our independence die in the struggle? Clearly in war as in all dangerous situations, the good and the generous perish first because they don't really take care not to die. But the good do not always die young. Were there no true patriots left in that detestable time? Were there no good men among Cuban politicians of that era, or among the survivors of that struggle? Of course there were. There always are.

I must ask myself, then, why Salvador Cisneros Betancourt, the bellicose Marquis de Santa Lucia, one of the initiators of our independence struggle, was not among our first presidents, when his merits and renown were greater than José Miguel Gómez's, Menocal's or Zayas's? And why didn't the good essayist and brilliant orator, Manuel Sanguily, also a surviving veteran of 1868, reach that position? Surely Sanguily was sufficiently good looking to win the ladies' approval but old enough not to inspire jealousy in the men. And what of the philosopher Enrique José Varona, who would live into the 1930s and who would become the example and inspiration of the magnificent generation of 1930?

Weighing these three men in the balance -- their successes and failures, virtues and defects -- one cannot but conclude that all three were worthy to lead the nascent republic. But Ortega y Gasset was right when he said: "I am me and my circumstances." The circumstances of the first three decades of the republic did not allow a place for men of real worth, but only for the likes of José Miguel Gómez, Menocal, Zayas and Molinet. Such circumstances made it possible for a pimp to become the paradigm of an age.

Well, enough already of those days. In 1925, Alfredo Zayas was succeeded by General Gerardo Machado, the last general of Cuba's War of Independence to occupy the presidency. As minister of the Interior in President Gómez's cabinet, Machado had put down a strike with such ferocious enthusiasm that even Gómez was impressed: "Woe to Cuba, Gerardito, if someday you get to be president!" And they say that no one is a prophet in his own land.

Still, Machado rode to the presidency on a greater wave of popularity than any of his four predecessors. There presents itself an obligatory question: What did the Cuban people see in that ignorant and course yokel, who was known as a thug and had the face of an ill-humored frog? One of history's enigmas.

What is also true about Machado is that despite all his shortcomings, he was during his first years in office the ablest administrator that Cuba ever had as a president -- or so I have heard it said by so many different people over the last forty years that I now believe it myself. Of course, the competition was poor.

Machado's greatest achievements were the construction of the Cuban Capitol and the Central Highway, which spans the length of the island. Sixty years after its construction, the Capitol is still one of the most imposing buildings in Havana. Gabriel García Márquez, the celebrated author and *fidelista* courtesan, has described it as a neo-classic monstrosity and a stone for stone replica of the Capitol in Washington, D.C. The courtesan is always at odds with reality, because he must say only what his lord and master wishes to hear.

Fidel, quite understandably, has never liked our Capitol -- a permanent reminder of democratic aspirations. Nor, for that matter, does he care for the Central Highway, which also was constructed in the late 1920s with great efficiency and at an amazing rate. The Central Highway still serves the bulk of the nation's automotive traffic.

But let us say no more about Fidel's bizarre phobias and García Márquez's courtly manners and return to the Capitol. On the doors that lead to the enormous Hall of Lost Steps, there are bas-reliefs depicting the most important events in our history -- and one not so important event. In this last relief, the central figure has been obliterated with hammer blows. It is the likeness of the man who built the building. Such was the whirlwind of hatred and violence that Geraldo Machado left in his wake.

The relative success of his first years notwithstanding, Machado soon, too soon, would begin to exhibit facets of his personality that would make good José Miguel Gómez's prophecy. He began to show his true self exactly two months into his presidency.

Armando André was a journalist and cartoonist who in his salad days during the War of 1895 had pioneered in Cuba what some call terrorism and others urban guerrilla warfare (depending on whether they sympathize or not with the objectives of the perpetrators). In his boldest act, André tried to blow up the Palace of the Governors General, with what I regard as the laudable objective of sending Valeriano Weyler to hell. He failed in his attempt. I cannot say that I am sorry because I have plenty of reasons to love that beautiful old building, even though Weyler richly deserved to be turned into mincemeat.

Three decades later, André would again be involved with explosive material: in this case, however, it was not gunpowder or dynamite but the pathological vanity of Geraldo Machado who (although already well past his prime) still regarded himself as a ladies' man. André published a cartoon showing Machado sprawled out on the floor, dressed like Don Juan. Leaning over him appeared to be a dissatisfied Dona Inés reciting to him these implacable verses: "Your powers are now long gone/ You are not up to such tasks/ You will

not do for Don Juan/ You are through with women and fantasies."
Armando André was assassinated in front of the door to his house.

This was not the only time someone was assassinated during
the first years of Machado's rule. In 1925, the union leader Enrique
Varona was murdered. Shortly thereafter so was another organizer,
Alfredo López. The most spectacular was the assassination of Noske
Yalob, a left-wing Jewish immigrant: bits of him were found in the
belly of a shark that was caught off Havana Bay.

These and other deaths, very few in number, did not raise a
stink, since none of the victims was a national figure. One needs to
be famous to have any claim to the tears of strangers. It was a very
different matter with the incarceration of Julio Antonio Mella, leader
of the reformers and founder of the Student Federation of Havana
University and the Communist Party of Cuba. Detained arbitrarily,
Mella declared a hunger strike. A delegation of Cuban worthies met
with Machado, asking him to set the student leader free. Among
those present was Rubén Martínez Villena, the poet and lawyer who
leaned toward Marxism. The meeting ended in a colossal brawl with
the president and the poet seized by twin tantrums. In an outburst of
lyric fury, Martínez Villena called Machado a "donkey with claws,"
an epithet that Machado would shortly do much to justify. Nonetheless, on this occasion, Machado relented. In those days it was
considered in very bad taste to allow someone on a hunger strike to
kill himself. Mella went into exile in Mexico, and was killed there
three years later.

If, God forbid, I were arrested someday for no apparent
reason as was Mella, and declared myself on a hunger strike as he
did, would I be released in 18 days and sent into exile? I would be
very grateful even if I were given only three more years to live
before they sent some hired assassin to finish me off.

And since we are talking about assassinations, it is well to
point out that José Miguel Gómez, Menocal and Zayas were never
accused of murdering their political opponents. Despite their shortcomings, these three -- like Estrada Palma -- always functioned
within the civilized bounds of a democracy. However precarious, it

was still a democracy. None of Machado's predecessors ever aspired to be a dictator. Machado tried and succeeded, although his dictatorship was short-lived.

It could not have lasted for long because our country was already being transformed. The nation was at last finding the strength to extricate itself from that spiritual and moral morass. New men were emerging who were neither second-class survivors of the shipwreck of our independence nor exploiters who profited from that catastrophe: Julio Antonio Mella and Rubén Martínez Villena, two resolute young men of spotless character, followers of a now outworn but then still vital creed, were living symbols of a nation that was being reborn. Later others would emerge like them. Pimps remained in Cuba, but now they were kept in their place.

Machado, with his pigheaded authoritarianism, would have had no difficulty imposing himself as a tyrant ten or fifteen years earlier. He came too late. The nation no longer required such services. But Machado did not see it that way. He had Congress extend his term of office from four to six years, later attempting something that is far more difficult for dictators to do, something that very few in fact have done: he tried to die in power.

Machado's relatively successful administration and his good relations with the Americans were the foundation for his aspiration. Naturally, he did not lack for camel boys in his caravan; he had a surfeit. Under his system of "cooperativism," he welcomed and rewarded hacks from all parties, virtually co-opting all of his old political opponents. These hangers-on gave themselves over completely to an orgy of adulation, creating a personality cult that only the *fidelistas* were able to surpass many years later. Machado was called the "Egregious One," a title that takes the cake. One can only imagine how such flattery affected a man so vain that he had a fellow human being killed just for having questioned his sexual prowess.

Machado had adulation to spare but he didn't have much luck. It makes me very happy to say so because there are already too many lucky bastards in this world. Not only had the nation overcome its apathy, but if that were not enough to undermine the general, Wall

49

Street -- which had financed his impressive public works program -- crashed in 1929, producing a depression that nearly wiped out capitalism and Western-style democracy. Four years later, it would do away with the government of our first dictator.

The economic disaster, however, was not the only factor that contributed to Machado's overthrow. Equally important was the tireless activity of a generation of thinking and fighting men such as our country had not known since the partial triumph of the independence struggle. Although Julio Antonio Mella was already dead by 1930, his generation is called the "Generation of 1930," perhaps because the student demonstration that initiated the open struggle against the Machado tyranny took place on September 30, 1930. Rafael Trejo, a law student, was mortally wounded in that demonstration. Also wounded, though not fatally, was Pablo de la Torriente Brau, a courageous and talented young man who held the promise of becoming one of our most brilliant journalists and politicians.

Many future celebrities took part in the September 30th demonstration. I want to mention two who were totally different from one another, both physically and in terms of character, who for the first and only time in their respective lives participated in violence: the corpulent José Lezama Lima, the greatest Cuban writer of the twentieth century and an honest man who refused to prostitute himself for *fidelismo* (which cost him dearly); and the gaunt Raúl Roa, a charming and fickle Communist buffoon in his youth, an anti-Communist in his maturity, and again a Communist in his dotage. Roa is the Cuban intellectual who most resembles Karl Marx both for his predilection for verbal assault and his aversion to physical violence.

In effect, a war broke out on September 30, 1930. Machado would amply demonstrate his ferocious character. Over the next three years the country would know a level of repression it had never before experienced during the republican era and few times in colonial days. Corpses started to be found on streets and the jails began to fill.

In Machado's prisons we find a flaw in his despotic character, a lapse in his tyrannic vocation. If we compare the recollections of political prisoners then and now, we are struck by the mildness with which Machado treated those of his enemies who for one reason or another were not assassinated but ended up in jail.

Small details illustrate great differences. Pablo de la Torriente was allowed to protest his imprisonment by growing his hair down to his shoulders and a beard that reached his chest. When the heat in his cell became oppressive, he could shed his prison clothes. It never occurred to anyone to force him to submit to a regulation haircut. When Pablo took off his prison uniform, it was because he chose to go *au naturel*, not because his jailers required him to wear the uniform of a common criminal or no uniform at all, as is the case with the naked *plantados* (or "unbending ones") in Fidel's prisons. No one in Machado's day thought to equate a political prisoner with a common criminal. Pablo pranced about naked because he wanted to, not because he was compelled.

Apparently, Machado subscribed to the now obsolete notion that prisoners, by virtue of being prisoners, no longer posed a threat to society and should be left in peace. Of course, Machado's political prisoners were considered enemies of law and order and established institutions, whereas Fidel's are no less than "enemies of the fatherland." The fatherland must be defended and avenged by every available means, including beatings.

The despotic general suffered from an extravagant fondness for amnesties. He decreed three amnesties in the final three years of his bloody rule, precisely when the opposition to him was at its most violent.

Machado had other political practices that have become obsolete in our own day. We have spoken already of his extreme susceptibility, aggravated no doubt by power and adulation. Recall the tragic case of Armando André, who drew the cartoon of Machado as a dissipated Don Juan. Still, Machado was sufficiently sure of himself to allow the publication and mass distribution of anti-Machado pamphlets, declaring categorically that "I will not be overthrown by little pieces of paper." (Frankly, I worry a lot about the catastrophes that might befall me as a consequence of these "little

51

pieces of paper" that I am writing, and I cannot dismiss from my spirit a strange longing for days I did not know, already history when I was born in 1936.)

But it was not only "little pieces of paper" with which Machado had to contend. Suddenly, there appeared men and organizations with the energy, courage and "combative imagination" (a phrase coined by Pablo de la Torriente Brau) for the fight that lay ahead. It was a violent and devastating repudiation of corruption in our country and of those who profited by it.

Antonio Guiteras was one of these new men. A pharmacist by profession and dishevelled in appearance, he was as anti-American as Mella or Martínez Villena. Yet Guiteras, whose full name was Guiteras y Holmes, was born and bred in Philadelphia, the son of a Yankee mother. He was not, however, even remotely a Communist. Rather he was one of the fruits of that ill-wind that the United States unleashed in Cuba as a result of its disastrous intervention in our War of Independence. It has always been disastrous for us. But in the long run, it also would prove disastrous for them.

The most prominent organization in the anti-Machado struggle was the cryptically named "ABC," a terrorist/urban guerrilla organization (I still insist that everyone has the right to choose whatever label he prefers). Somewhat influenced by Italian fascism, ABC was a secret organization that did not make public the names of its leaders. It was a strange combination of many different elements. Its symbols were the Star of David and green, the color of Islam. But it could all be explained: the six points of the Hebrew star signified the six basic points of the ABC program, and green also is the color of hope. ABC proclaimed itself "the hope of Cuba." When the ABC directorate, or central cell, shed its anonymity after the fall of Machado, we learned that it was composed of a group of brilliant intellectuals: Joaquin Martínez Sáenz (the chief, or "A-1"), Carlos Saladrigas, Jorge Manach, and Francisco Ichaso. As for being "the hope of Cuba," however, there is no doubt they exaggerated.

Many of the most bellicose young men joined the University Students Directorate, including Pío Alvarez, Ernesto Alpizar, Juan

Mariano González Rubiera. All three would die in the struggle. Two members, Carlos Prío and Eduardo Chibás, survived to play very different roles in the future of our country.

The struggle to overthrow Machado raged for three bloody years. To cite but one example of Torriente Brau's "combative imagination": men from the Directorate led by Pío Alvarez and Alfredo Nogueiras undertook to excavate a long tunnel from a safe house near Havana's Colon cemetery to the Vázquez Bello mausoleum, which they wired with explosives. When the tunnel was completed, they assassinated Clemente Vázquez Bello, the president of the Machado-controlled Senate. Then they sat and waited in the certainty that Machado and his entire cabinet would attend the burial, and they would have the chance to blow them all to hell. But destiny intervened in the person of victim's widow. She decided to bury Vázquez Bello in his native city (I don't remember whether Matanzas or Santa Clara, and they can hang me for all I care). In any case, many years would pass before the July 26th Movement and later the Uruguayan Tupamaro guerrillas attempted anything as daring.

On March 4,1933, Franklin Roosevelt became President of the United States in the midst of the Great Depression. He was a cousin of Theodore Roosevelt, but unlike the Rough Rider, Franklin Roosevelt was what they call a "liberal." The truth is that American liberals drive me mad. I think that one can justly say of many, if not most American liberals what Melville writes in *Moby Dick*: "You have as few principles as the Gods and are an apprentice everything and a master nothing." Of course, the phrase can be applied also to many who are not liberals or Americans, but it will always fit those who are both. American liberals, among other things, make a constant display of their magnanimity and concern for the liberty of others, as well as their rejection of any imperialist attitudes. This is always a false pretense and often entails catastrophic consequences. I will speak in due course of an American liberal president who wreaked havoc on our country in the Sixties, but now I am in the Thirties and must speak of Roosevelt.

"He is a son of a bitch but he is our son of a bitch," said Roosevelt of Anastasio Somoza. Apparently, Machado was not Roosevelt's "son of a bitch." In the Spring of 1933, shortly after assuming the presidency, Roosevelt sent Benjamin Sumner Welles, one of the State Department's star diplomats, to Cuba with the dual mission of getting the Cuban dictator and making sure that the revolutionary groups didn't get in.

Sumner Welles set out to work. His "mediation," as it was called, was welcomed enthusiastically by conservative sectors of Cuban society. To everybody's surprise, ABC, "the hope of Cuba," also became Sumner Welles' hope. Machado, for his part, discovered the tender mercies of anti-imperialism, although too late to do him any good.

The U.S. diplomat did not only confine his efforts to political sectors. The military also occupied his active attention. The Cuban military had never participated in a coup d'état in thirty years of republican government. Instead, it had dedicated itself to improving its battle readiness, though no one dreamed then of internationalist adventures for Cuba. This training had produced a solid group of capable professional officers who had no interest in politics. It included such men as José Martí's son and Lezama Lima's father.

Machado had succeeded in implicating a segment of the officer corps in his repression, thus beginning the long degenerative process which many years and events later, would culminate in the 1950s in an armed forces capable of toppling a constitutional government and at the same time utterly incapable of fighting with even a modicum of skill. By demoralizing the army, Machado laid the groundwork for that process. But the chief architect of that catastrophe was then only a sergeant stenographer in the army high command.

Sumner Welles worked with persistence, quickness and efficiency, confronting the growing anger of an increasingly "anti-imperialistic" Machado, who was then almost as "antiimperialistic" as that other scoundrel, Manuel Antonio Noriega. In the summer of 1933 events suddenly came to a head. A transportation strike had extended to other sectors of the economy and spontaneously become a general strike. Machado, may not have been cultured, but he was astute. He found the weakest point in the enemy front -- the Communists. The party committed its first great capitulation by agreeing to wage concessions from a government that was on the brink of collapse. It was as if the republic-in-arms had accepted the autonomy offered by Cánovas after Weyler had starved so many Cuban peasants. Moreover the Communists surrendered what was not theirs to surrender, for they did not control the strike and it proceeded without them.

In fairness, we should not be too hard on the Communists of that time. Their moribund leader, Rubén Martínez Villena, had only four months to live. One cannot successfully wage so violent a political struggle when one is in the final stages of tuberculosis. Martínez Villena's shattered body could no longer sustain the ideals of his ardent soul. Only a few years later, other Communists in perfect health would commit far worse deeds.

Corralled on all sides, the tyrant did justice to Martínez Villena's epithet: "the donkey with claws." Machado circulated rumors that he was resigning. The people took to the streets to celebrate. They encountered Machado's police, firing right and left. These were to be the last of Machado's victims. The army high command informed him that it no longer could support him, and the dictator, who loved his life better than power, decided to flee. Mussolini also loved life better than power; not so Hitler. That's why Hitler was worse than Mussolini, and Machado not the worst of our dictators.

Reading the accounts of his flight it is easy to see why Gerardo Machado, the very antithesis of patriotism, was able to rise to the rank of general in our War of Independence. There is no better situation to take the measure of a man than in defeat and flight. In defeat and in flight, Machado proved to be a brave man. He headed for the airport at Rancho Boyeros, but on arriving discovered that the plane that was to take him and his cronies to exile had malfunctioned. Machado decided then to take his siesta. He drove to his nearby hacienda and tormented his frightened companions with his hoarse snoring until word reached him that the plane was ready. The plane took off for Nassau in the Bahamas, but not before it had withstood several rounds of gunfire courtesy of the boys from the Directorate, who arrived just a few minutes too late.

V. From Batista to Prío

Machado left in his wake the worst outbreak of hate and barbarism ever recorded in the history of Cuba to that time. Machado's henchmen were beaten to death and their corpses dragged through the streets. The mansions of the tyranny's great beneficiaries were sacked. At the estate of the ex-minister of public works, Carlos Miguel de Céspedes, the pursuers themselves became the pursued when one of those sunshine patriots happened to uncage a black panther that the minister kept as a pet -- one of those whims of wealthy men.

Sumner Welles had provided against every eventuality, or at least that's what he thought. He quickly set up a government that was acceptable both to anxious conservatives who had nothing now to conserve but their wealth and to the ABC. Welles' choice for the presidency was Carlos Manuel de Céspedes y Quesada, a career diplomat whose only merit was his illustrious ancestry. He was the son and namesake of the father of our country. I do not know whether he was also related to the minister who loved panthers.

But then, to Sumner Welles' despair, things got complicated. The army -- or, rather, its top brass -- had been left in a precarious situation due to its collaboration with the tyrant. This in turn provoked a general breakdown of discipline among the ranks, the greatest and most catastrophic manifestation of which was a movement headed by four sergeants; one of these, the most harmful sergeant in our history.

On September 4, 1933, the sergeants, supported by the corporals and privates at the Columbia military barracks, mutinied against their superiors. But it was not a coup d'état. The sergeants' demands were limited to a series of pay increases and improvements in living conditions. Some of these strike us as ridiculous, such as the demand that they have the right to wear more buttons on their uniforms; but ridiculous or not, these demands constituted a breach in discipline and a challenge to the principle of hierarchical command, without which no army can function.

With the police disbanded and the army in mutiny, the Céspedes government was left without the means to make itself obeyed. The Directorate and other revolutionary groups were quick to exploit the situation. In what would prove a fateful decision, they gave their support to the sergeants' movement, lending its leaders the prestige and renown that none of them possessed. The Céspedes government collapsed, and all the best laid plans of American mediation went to the devil.

Sumner Welles himself must have asked the devil to take him too when he saw how things turned out in this damned country, where sergeants and students, joined later by a terrorist pharmacist from Philadelphia, could smash in a few hours the most carefully wrought diplomatic labor.

But Welles and his government were not the only losers. On September 4, 1933, the Cuban army ceased to exist, and would not emerge again until the *fidelista* era. The sergeants were turned into colonels, and then generals; eventually, a new officer corps would emerge. There was something in Cuba like an army but not really an army, if by the army we mean an armed organism with a real disposition for combat. In the 1950s, a man who then demonstrated great sagacity would set out to conquer power based on his understanding of that fact. On September 4, 1933, he was not yet a man and I can't imagine that he was very sagacious. Fidel Castro had just turned seven.

The sergeants and their student allies replaced Céspedes with what can only be described as a "political extravagance." What else can we call a collective presidency on the Swiss model, comprised of five members? Three of the five were of no significance. We must, however, speak of the other two.

Sergio Carbó, a brilliant journalist and friend of Batista, had been instrumental in winning civilian support for the sergeants' movement. Carbó was famous for having led an armed expedition to overthrow Machado. It had landed at Gibara in 1932 and been quickly smashed by army. He was the only nationally prominent figure in the so-called Pentarchy. Perhaps because of this, Carbó did not feel that he had to consult his four pentarchic colleagues before committing the blunder of promoting Sergeant Batista to the rank of colonel and naming him head of the army.

Carbó was one of Cuba's most distinguished journalists for as long as journalism existed in our country. But his political career was short-lived, and given his performance during his brief stint in power, it was a good thing, too. If to govern means to set in motion disasters in the long, medium and short term, there can be no doubt that Carbó used to the fullest his five days at the head of the nation. Sergio Carbó wrote well, sometimes very well, but that was all.

The other noteworthy pentarchist was much less known than Carbó at the time, but was destined to enjoy a longer career in Cuban politics. Ramón Grau San Martín was a distinguished physician and university professor, who was very respected by the students. He entered public life precisely on that September 4, 1933 of unblessed memory. In time, he would show himself to be just another swindler, but no one could ever accuse him of being stupid. Never would it have occurred to Grau to name a sergeant as head of the army, much less an undisciplined and seditious sergeant, when he could still have his pick of officers without a *machadista* taint and with enough guts to put any subordinate in his place. The sergeants' movement made possible the Pentarchy's rise to power, but what did those sergeants really count for and what could they have accomplished without the support of the University Students Directorate, Guiteras' Revolutionary Union and the other anti-Machado organizations? No, Grau would never have named as head of the army the sallow and shrewd Sergeant Batista.

The Pentarchy, that strange Swiss import, lasted less than a week. On September 10, Grau, supported by the Students Directorate, assumed the presidency. The key man in the new government, however, would be Antonio Guiteras, the minister of the interior.

The Grau-Guiteras government was brief, fruitful and violent. It was besieged by the bourgeoisie and the Communists, by the United States and the ABC, by the old officialdom of the army that was deposed on September 4 and the new spurious officialdom that emerged that day, and by the continuing economic crisis. Many of the old officers, incited by a desperate Sumner Welles, dug in at the once fabulous National Hotel, daring the sergeants to attack them. The sergeants obliged with all the hardware at their disposal, including tanks and land and naval artillery. Before bowing to an overwhelming numerical and material superiority, the well-trained officers made a show of their expertise with little feats that nearly drove the ex-sergeant and neo-colonel Batista mad, such as picking off the tank drivers with their view finders. Various officers were murdered after their surrender. These were Batista's first victims.

ABC attempted its own thing in November, when it assaulted and took various military installations. Even Camp Columbia was bombed (but with little success) by the airman and old sports star, "Pepe" Barrientos. Finally, the ABC rebels converged on Fort Atarés, where they were decimated by able artillery commanded by Captain Gregorio Querejeta, one of the few black officers in the old army, who had gone over to the sergeants' side. The casualties exceeded one hundred, including those killed in battle and afterwards. In time, however, ABC and the sergeants would come to an understanding.

While bombs exploded and bullets flew, Guiteras was dragging Grau along radical paths foreign to his idiosyncrasy. In all fairness, though, we should point out that the physiognomy professor was not lacking in backbone. When the odd couple decided that Grau, on taking his oath of office, should refuse to swear allegiance to the Constitution of 1901, they made it clear that the Cuban government did not recognize the Platt Amendment, the infamous appendix to the Cuban constitution that legalized American intervention. In response, Roosevelt the good neighbor positioned U.S. warships within view of Havana. Guiteras ordered all the armed forces of the nation to fire at any foreign soldier who should attempt to set foot in Cuba without authorization. There was no landing. Years later, when Fidel was old enough to analyze these historical events, he must have taken very much to heart the Americans' lack of will to attack. As for the Platt Amendment, it was legally abrogated at the Montevideo Pan American conference of 1934. By then the Grau-Guiteras government had already fallen, but the Cuban delegation that attended the conference was appointed by them and represented their point of view.

Guiteras did more than just give exhibitions of his integrity. He dictated and Grau signed social legislation establishing the 8-hour day and a minimum wage. He nationalized the American-owned electric company after its arrogant management refused to observe new government regulations lowering rates. And he made plans for the distribution of uncultivated lands. Although this proposal might have materialized into a serious agrarian reform that would have expanded land holdings rather than create a state monopoly over them, nothing came of it. Nothing came of another Guiteras proposal that would have spared us endless disasters: in a meeting of government officials, a hoarse Guiteras accused Batista of treason for scheming with the failed Sumner Welles, and set forth the necessity of ousting him or better yet putting him in front of a firing squad. Unfortunately for Guiteras (who was killed by Batista's henchmen two years later) and for all of us, several of those present decided it was best to temporize and the traitor got away with just a scare. May God forgive them if he thinks He should. I wouldn't in His place.

The Roosevelt administration had already found its man in Havana, its "son of a bitch." In January 1934, the Grau-Guiteras government collapsed, leaving a trail of unfulfilled hopes. Upon Guiteras' death, Grau became the sole heir and depository of these hopes, and Batista the "power behind the throne" in a series of short-lived governments. The briefest of all these provisional governments was Carlos Hevia's. It lasted all of forty-eight hours. Hevia deserved a better fate. Next to occupy the presidency was Carlos Mendieta, a lieutenant colonel in Cuba's War of Independence. He had been in semi-retirement from politics for, among other reasons, his addiction to dueling. Batista formed a governmental partnership with Mendieta that resembled that of Grau and Guiteras, only far more homogeneous from a moral point of view. There took place under this administration the bloody suppression of the sugar workers strike of March 1935, and the assassination in May of Antonio Guiteras, as he attempted to leave the island clandestinely for foreign parts.

Guiteras. I cannot but invoke again the premature deaths of Agramonte, Martí and Maceo. How greatly those deaths affected the destinies of our country. Before attempting to flee the country, Guiteras had founded an organization that he called "Young Cuba," and collected $300,000 (or $3 million by today's reckoning) from a kidnapped sugar magnate for securing his release. Money, talent and determination: he had all that was necessary to wage a successful struggle. But Guiteras died, leaving only the money (which ended-up I know not where). I am acquainted, however, with Guiteras' political trustee, Ramon Grau San Martín. In 1952, when we so wanted for energetic leadership, Antonio Guiteras would have been 46 years old.

During Mendieta's presidency, which lasted slightly less than two years, obituaries became news of major significance in Cuba: the death of the striking sugar workers; the deaths of Guiteras and Carlos Aponte, who were gunned down on the coast of Matanzas Bay; the death of Roberto Méndez Peñate, a friend and unconditional supporter of Mendieta who committed suicide rather than endure the spectacle of his chief transformed into a puppet of an insolent sergeant; the death of Lieutenant Colonel Mario Alfonso Hernández, who though then a private was one of the organizers of the September 4 sergeants' revolt, a strange sort with too much personality to have ever been just a common soldier, who has always been suspected of representing something or someone, though we don't know what or who (in any case, he was assassinated at Batista's orders).

At the end of 1935 Mendieta resigned and the colonel-in-chief appointed in his place a gentleman as grey and opaque as a pearl, but without the pearl's special value. José Antonio Barnet's sole function was to preside over the presidential election of 1936, which was won by Miguel Mariano Gómez, the son of Cuba's second president.

In Cuban history, Miguel Mariano Gómez is known simply as "Miguel Mariano" to distinguish him from his father. Not that there would be much occasion for confusion since the son, unlike the father, didn't remain in the presidency for long. Barely a month in office, Miguel Mariano attempted to ascertain who really ruled Cuba, he or Batista. The president vetoed a law supported by Batista that established rural schools taught by sergeants. The Cuban Congress quickly put to rest all of Gómez's doubts. It overturned the veto and for good measure, impeached him.

However, 1936 is remembered not for the election and impeachment of Gómez, but for the start of the Spanish Civil War. Hundreds of Cuban leftists fought on the Republican side. All the nations of the Americas contributed men to that struggle, but none as many as Cuba. It was quite a demonstration of the adventurous spirit of Cubans and of their inclination to put their noses in other people's affairs. In future years, Fidel would exploit to the utmost these national characteristics in his internationalist adventures.

Of the hundreds of Cuban combatants in the Spanish Civil War, some did not live to tell of their adventure. The most notable casualty was Pablo de la Torriente Brau, a man of great talent and energy, brimming over with love for his fellow man. It was in Spain that Pablo happily gave his life for his ideals. Rolando Masferrer, who like Torriente was blessed with extraordinary qualities that, in him, were eclipsed by an evil nature, left not his life but only a piece of his heel in Spain and returned to Cuba to kill Cubans. We have always been unlucky as regards the destination of bullets.

63

But let us return to Colonel Batista and his presidents. The deposed Gómez was replaced by his vice-president, Federico Laredo Bru, the last veteran of Cuba's War of Independence to occupy the presidency and yet another "pearl" that I don't care to examine. His government (let's call it that) is notable for something that did not concern Bru at all: the beginning of the long idyll of Batista and the Communists. We must try to understand who Batista was and who the Communists were in order to discover the basis of their mutual attraction.

The illegitimate son of a very poor mulatto family, Fulgencio Batista had received a limited education. An uncertified railroad conductor and a soldier, Batista was a man who craved for acceptance. Although he managed to raise himself to the economic level of the wealthiest of the island's bourgeoisie by sacking the public treasury in an unbridled manner, they were long in accepting him as their social equal -- if ever they accepted him at all.

To be accepted by the rich was not Batista's only ambition. He also wanted to be loved by his own, those who inhabited the world that he had left: the poor, the humble, the workers. And who better to secure him their acceptance than the Communists? The Communists have never given any power to the workers although that has always been their promise, and an oft-repeated promise never wants for believers. Batista decided to try his luck with them.

The Communists had far less complicated reasons for lending their support to Batista: pure and simple opportunism and a total lack of ethics. "The Colonel has no one to love him. Let us offer him the love of the proletarian masses." And what did they get in exchange? For starters, their organizations were legalized in 1938. Later, they would get their own newspaper, *Noticias de Hoy*, and their own radio station, *La 1010*. Eventually, they would gain control of several labor unions and ultimately, of the Cuban Federation of Workers itself. (In Batista's day it was headed by Lazaro Pena -- a man whom many years later Fidel Castro would call the "Captain of the Cuban working class." Between 1938 and 1944 this captain was the faithful servant of a certain colonel.)

Batista accepted the support of the Communists magnanimously. The Communists extolled him, adulated him, addressed him always as "colonel," and later "major general," sweet words to the ears of a sergeant. Finally, Batista and the Communists formed the Democratic Socialist Coalition.

This coalition did not only include the Communists, however. An important part of the "popular front" was the old ABC, which Ruben Martínez Villena had accused of being fascist.

In 1940, Fulgencio Batista decided to put an end to his brilliant military career in order to dedicate himself entirely to politics. A constitutional convention was convened that year to draft a new fundamental law for the Republic. The Constitution of 1940 was undoubtedly a good constitution. That's important, but not very. Since 1917, Mexico has had a constitution that teems with democratic precepts, but it has not prevented a clique of politicians from monopolizing power in that country for more than seventy years, frequently through violent means. Great Britain, on the other hand, has no written constitution. It is not so much the law itself as the respect a people have for it that is the real foundation of a democracy.

I badly want to tell an anecdote about this Constitutional convention, and as I am a free writer, who follows only his own impulses, I shall do it.

Seated among the delegates were to the left, Blas Roca, secretary general of the Popular Socialist Party (i.e. the Communists) and a leading voice in the chorus that sang the praises of Colonel (or was he already a major general?) Batista; and to the right, the Italian-born Orestes Ferrara, a veteran of our War of Independence, a former Machado minister, and as dishonest a politician as he was honest as an historian (a paradox in human nature that may be explained, in part, by the fact that he practiced politics in the 20th century but wrote about the Fifteenth and Sixteenth centuries). Ferrara was also a man of biting wit. During one of the debates at the Convention, questions were raised concerning the lack of freedom in the Soviet Union. Blas Roca, as faithful a servant of Stalin as he was of Batista,

65

affirmed emphatically that in the Soviet Union everyone could freely express his opinion. As fast with his tongue as my grandfather was with his revolver, Ferrara interrupted: "One time only, Señor Roca. Only one time."

I ask myself, were Blas Roca alive today, would he defend the growing climate of liberty in the Soviet Union? No, I don't think he would. Carlos Rafael Rodríguez, Blas Roca's sole surviving comrade, has not and I suspect never will support it.

After the Constitution was ratified, there came the general elections, which were marked by instances of electoral fraud on such a scale as had never before been seen in colonial or republican history. Batista formally assumed the presidency after six years of managing puppets. The losing candidate, Grau San Martín, was confirmed as the heir of the promise and the hope of those one hundred days when he had headed but not guided the government.

The four years Batista was president transpired in a climate of relative calm. At the start of his term, the chief of the army, Colonel José Eleuterio Pedraza, one of those bedeviled sergeants of September 4, tried to stage a coup d'état and failed. With Pedraza out of the way, Batista's government lost its ferocity. Meanwhile, World War II had stimulated economic growth, which is to say, sugar sales went up.

With the country at peace (for dead men tend to be very quiet), and trusting in the popular support that the Communists promised and in which he had come to believe himself, the old railroad worker turned millionaire and sergeant turned major general, conceived the passing fancy he could win genuinely democratic elections. Here is a perfect example of the difference between an astute and reasonably intelligent man and a real political talent: never would it have occurred to Fidel to commit a similar blunder.

Batista could not run for re-election in 1944 because the Constitution did not allow consecutive presidential terms, but this was no problem for one who was used to governing by proxy. And so, Batista designated a candidate to run in his place, Carlos Saladrigas, the old "A-2" (or number two man) of the ABC, whose colleagues Batista had massacred in November 1933.

I firmly believe it was the Communists -- or, specifically, the two Communists in his cabinet, Juan Marinello and Carlos Rafael Rodríguez -- who convinced Batista to embark on this crazy democratic adventure.

On the occasion of the president's birthday, the Communist party organ, *Noticias de Hoy*, published on January 16, 1941 a congratulatory message that read in part as follows: "A president with profound ties to the people who is deeply rooted in democratic principles, Major General Batista guides our country along the path of national dignity and progress. . . ."

Apparently, a majority of voters did not agree with those sentiments. On June 1, 1944, Grau buried Batista and Saladrigas -- along with their allies, the Communists of the Popular Socialist party and the fascists of ABC -- in an electoral landslide.

Ramon Grau San Martín

On that June 1, 1944, around ten o'clock in the morning, my father made one last desperate attempt to convince my mother to vote for Grau. He had spent several weeks at the task, but my mother, who naturally was not going to vote for Saladrigas, a *batistiano* backed by the Communists, also refused to support Grau, arguing that she would never vote for a confirmed bachelor. On the morning of the election she repeated the same argument. Father, exasperated by her irrational woman's intuition, lost all patience and blurted out: "You are an idiot!" Mother, undaunted, simply stared at him in silence until my old man, who wasn't so old then, set out for the polling station with only one vote for his leader. The next day, when he learned the news of Grau's victory, I saw tears in the eyes of my father.

That argument, the only serious one that I can recall my parents ever having, is for me symbolic proof of the state of mind of the best among the Cuban citizenry of that day -- the sector to which my father undoubtedly belonged. It is an example of the fervor and hope that the Grau candidacy awakened among a majority of Cubans. That fervor and hope reached such heights as to cause a mild-mannered and respectful family man to so lose control of himself as to insult his wife in the presence of his small son because she refused to vote.

Unfortunately for all concerned, my mother was right, her point of view rational (although that may not be completely evident to some). A bachelor, which is to say a mature man who has not founded a family, is necessarily an egoist, a man without love for others, and without love one cannot be a true patriot. Grau was not a patriot. He was, in fact, the anti-patriot par excellence, a man who scorned the country where he was born.

When Grau revealed himself as an absolutely corrupt president, our country sustained the second of its great national traumas, exceeded only by the trauma provoked in 1898 by our nullified independence and the one that has affected us since 1959. A rich man who had made a fortune as a doctor but who seemed not to place too much importance on money, Grau had spent ten years preaching against corruption in government. Apparently, his real complaint was not that previous administrations were corrupt but that they couldn't do corruption right. Grau taught his cronies to rob more and better. There had been administrative corruption in Cuba since the days of Charles Magoon (1906). It was not something new, but from Grau it was unexpected.

Those two makers of national disasters who rose to prominence on September 4, 1933, Grau and Batista, had something else in common -- they were both scoundrels. Nevertheless, there was something that was essentially contrary in their personalities: while Batista desperately craved acceptance, Grau exuded contempt for everything and everyone. He respected nothing. His four years in government were marked by grotesque episodes. There are some that I must tell.

In the Capitol's "Hall of Lost Steps," as the rotunda is called, a 20-karat diamond encased under thick glass that was the official "point zero" from which all distances were measured on the island had been placed at the feet of a gigantic allegorical statue of the Republic. It had been used by Machado to lay out and demarcate the Central Highway, thereby joining symbolically the two great projects of his administration. There the "diamond of the Republic" remained for 15 years. One day, it mysteriously disappeared from the Capitol, causing a national uproar. But not for long: President Grau found it in his desk.

The Bell of Demajagua, which Carlos Manuel de Céspedes rang to signal the start of Cuba's struggle for independence on October 10, 1868, also mysteriously disappeared. Like the Capitol diamond, it also re-emerged a few days later. A young university student, Fidel Castro, very smugly had himself photographed with the recovered relic.

These two incidents, though they are not attributable to Grau personally, illustrate the moral climate that he engendered. Other scandals, however, were entirely of his own making and he must bear full responsibility for them. The most notorious of these involved his relations with Paulina Alsina, his brother's widow. Grau lived in the same house with his sister-in-law for many years before assuming the presidency, which may be of interest only to the evil-minded.

But then in 1944 he installed the woman in the presidential palace and named her first lady of the Republic. By protocol this position should have been discharged by the wife of his vice-president, Raúl Cérdenas, because Grau was a bachelor. This relationship coupled with Dona Paulina's notorious involvement in public affairs provoked a wave of commentaries and jokes of every kind, which the president listened to with great eagerness.

Another grotesque anecdote is told by Renée Méndez Capote, who was the victim of the story. She who would later become a successful writer was then a voluptuous woman in her forties whose well-rounded curves drove Latin men wild. Grau showed himself susceptible to her charms and asked her to become his lover, but she turned him down. So things stood when, one day, they chanced to meet at an official function in the presidential palace. I can't recall

69

the occasion; someone was to give a speech, I think. Anyway, Grau, who showed no resentment over the rejection, graciously gave up his place in the front row to Renee and sat in back of her. Then, during the speech, while the other few and bored listeners were lost on the moon, Grau, unnoticed by anyone, was busy fondling the ample buttocks of Doña Renée, who had to tolerate stoically and defenseless this public invasion of her privacy.

This little tale may seem amusing to some, and that's how it struck me on first reading the victim's well-written account of it. In my judgement, what makes it important is that it reveals in all its magnitude a fundamental character flaw: Grau's absolute lack of decorum.

I want to tell one last story from those times, one that also is revealing, but tragic: the encounter between armed gangs that took place in the Orfila section of Havana.

Before, we must speak a bit of the gangsters themselves. But they really weren't gangsters, because they didn't rob banks, traffic in contraband, control prostitution or illegal gambling, extort merchants or trade unions, or engage in turf battles. But like gangsters they settled their disputes with guns and were always well-armed. They also employed aliases in imitation of the criminal underworld: "El Colorado" (the ruddy one), "El Extraño" (the bizarre one), "El Italianito" (the little Italian); but they were just as likely to use their university titles: Dr. Rolando Masferrer, Dr. Eufemio Fernández and Dr. González Cartas. Almost all were white; among the most notorious I can recall only one mulatto, Policarpio Soler. Money was not a universal objective for them. The gangster whom I consider the most representative figure of that time was a decorated veteran of World War II, who lived in poverty and had a one-syllable surname sonorous as a gunshot: Tro.

What were, then, these men? They were, above all, the hangover of the revolution that overthrew Machado, violent individuals who had lost their natural leaders and lacked the qualities to fill the void left by their deaths. The term "revolutionary" was never missing from the names of their organizations: the Guiteras Revolutionary

Front, the Revolutionary Insurrectional Union, to name but two. They fought for notoriety, and they hoped to obtain a leading role in the political life of the nation, doing the only thing they knew how to do well: shooting.

Batista detested these thugs -- except, of course, those who were in his service. Grau, on the other hand, tolerated them, granted them sinecures in government with a fixed salary but no fixed obligations, leaving them free to pursue their real vocation. Those with the greatest celebrity among the gangsters he made officers in the National Police or appointed them *comandantes* in the army, a rank that laid between captain and lieutenant colonel in the hierarchical arrangement then in use. (Curiously, *comandante* was the rank that Fidel Castro chose for himself at the beginning of his struggle in the Sierra Maestra and that all guerrilla leaders in Latin America who have since attempted to follow in his footsteps have also adopted.)

On a date I don't care to recall, the house of *Comandante* Morín Dopico, with *Comandante* Tro present, was besieged by an armed group under *Comandante* Salabarría. Since gunfights were a part of the *modus vivendi* of these people, there would have been nothing extraordinary about this one had the combat not raged for several hours, erupted in broad daylight, and taken place less than five miles from Camp Columbia. When a truce was reached to permit Morín Dopico, his wife and small daughter to leave their house -- the objective of the attackers being Tro --something went wrong, and Aurora Soler de Morín, a beautiful woman in the final months of pregnancy, was felled by a sudden burst of fire. Tro, who went to her rescue, was also killed. Grau decided at last to send some army tanks to stop the fighting. Earlier he had said, "Let them kill one another."

One more story of gangsters and other people addicted to violence. I promise that this will indeed be the last. At about that time, a few of these hardened individuals, some of them bitter enemies, decided to liberate the Dominican Republic from the tyranny of Rafael Trujillo, once more putting into practice that old Cuban custom I spoke about of meddling in the affairs of others. They made preparations for the expedition without worrying too much about secrecy. They gathered at Cayo Confites, a remote islet situated at the Northern end of Isla Grande. Grau pretended not to notice for as long as he could, but when the ships set out for their destination, he ordered the Cuban navy to intercept the ships and arrest the would-be liberators.

Among the filibusters were such notorious figures as Doctors Masferrer and Eufemio Fernández, as well as some not so famous then, including the future Dr. Fidel Castro. When the prisoners were being conveyed across the Bay of Nipe en route to the port of Antilla, Fidel decided that he didn't want to go to jail even for a little while and threw himself into the sea. Nipe Bay is famous for its immensity and the abundance of sharks in its waters. Nonetheless, Fidel swam several miles without any shark showing any interest in him. He finally reached the coast and disappeared into the thousands of acres that bounded his father's plantation, where he was born. Sharks are capricious and stupid beasts that can't be relied on. I have always detested them.

I am going to finish with Grau. I have dedicated too much space to his government -- or rather to the spiritual and moral climate that it created. The personality of this intelligent, cultured, perspicacious and even brave man has always held a strange fascination for me. He could have been a great man, a great president; he could have been what my father and so many thousands of good men wanted him to be. He had all the requisite qualities. But he lacked something fundamental: the minimum of love and respect for his fellow men required for them to remember him fondly. The then- young swimmer to whom I have alluded also lacks the same thing.

But can anything good be said about Ramón Grau San Martín? Yes, something very important. Grau, whose personal conduct might lead one to suppose he respected nothing and nobody, not even himself, did show respect for democracy, liberty and human rights. Grau's scornful mien had limits, although one had to go a long way to reach his good side. I, who consider him a fraud, cannot help longing for that atmosphere of absolute political freedom that existed under his government. I miss him most of all when I am visited by fear, that omnipresent monster in our country; when I think of what awaits me should I be able to get these pages published -- the accusations of writing enemy propaganda, spreading false reports, and disrespect for authority. And I think of the mobs, those mobs I saw attack the Mariel refugees in 1980. I think of those mobs of madmen spitting, hitting and insulting me and I long for Grau. He was a bad man, but there are worse.

Grau, I want to repeat, was the second great trauma of our republican history. But the effect that this trauma produced on the Cuban people cannot be compared to the negative impact of the first two decades of the Republic (1902-25), about which it is so upsetting for me to speak. When the long fought-for and dreamt-about Republic turned instead into a protectorate, the nation's spirit collapsed and did not recover for twenty years. But when the man who had embodied the hope and fervor of his people showed himself to be a scoundrel, the reaction was quick in coming. A new leader, with the best of the country gathered around him, emerged from Grau's own party and hope was reborn. We were then a much more solid and mature people. We still suffered from social ills but we had not grown accustomed to them.

Carlos Prío and Eduardo Chibás

After Grau, Carlos Prío and Eduardo Chibás dominated Cuban politics from 1948 to 1952 (even though Chibás did not live for all four years). As young men, both belonged to the Directorate of University Students and subsequently became active in the *Auténtico* party that achieved the great electoral victory of 1944. Prío, however. was part of the corrupt political machine of the physician-president, while Chibás rebelled against it. In 1948, the *Auténticos* nominated Prío to succeed Grau. Chibás defected from their ranks and organized his own party, the *Ortodoxos*. In the 1948 election, Prío defeated both Chibás and the other candidate, Ricardo Nuñez Portuondo, a doctor

73

as eminent as Grau who had a vaguely *machadista* past. It is interesting to note that Chibás' campaign centered around a promise to manage state funds honestly. He did not have to promise democracy and liberty, because these were no longer aspirations but facts to which we already had grown accustomed.

Prío's government was in every way a continuation of Grau's: the same immorality and unrestricted liberty. The combination of these two contrary factors was the worst legacy of both presidents. Years later, it would be used as an excuse to crush democracy.

Identical conduct, but different men. Whereas Grau was scornful and lacked the capacity to love, Prío was weak. Our last democratic president was not a bad man, but a weak man. Moreover, whereas Grau had been the central figure in the country during his years as president, Prío had to share the limelight with Eduardo Chibás, whose party had in less than two years become the strongest political machine in Cuban history.

Eduardo Chibás had the same political origins as Prío, but his social origins were very different. While Prío came from the petite bourgeoisie that lives on the edge of proletarianization, Chibás was born a millionaire. And unlike Prío, he had abandoned his university studies to dedicate himself to politics with all the frenzy of his peculiar character.

Chibás was a brave man. In August 1933, pistol in hand, he confronted a mob that had hung the corpse of Ainciart, Machado's police chief, from a lamppost. He took the body away for burial, leaving the two-legged beasts without their toy.

Chibás was an excitable man. He once was watching a bullfight in a certain Latin American country when his hosts suggested that perhaps the reason that the sport had disappeared in Cuba was that his countrymen lacked the courage to face the bulls. Chibás jumped into the bullring. Another outburst: on a campaign stopover in Camagüey in 1948, Chibás was met by an enthusiastic crowd at the railroad depot. They so excited him that he made a flying leap from the platform of a railway car into the arms of his followers. Roberto Agramonte, the vice-presidential candidate, attempted to do the same, but crazy stunts can only be carried off by crazy men. The level-headed sociology professor nearly broke everything but his soul.

Chibás concentrated his proselytizing campaigns on the theme of administrative corruption, a weak point for Grau and Prío as well as all Cuban presidents since Estrada Palma. Indeed it is a weak point of the Cuban Republic itself and of our democracy. To fight corruption Chibás coined the slogan, "[Don't Lose Your Sense of] Shame Before Money," which was no less effective for being simple. On that front Chibás himself was not vulnerable. He had always had money, but he had never earned it. He had never had anything to do with money but spend it. Money didn't interest him, only power did. With the exception of Fidel Castro, I don't believe there ever was another Cuban politician more obsessed with power than Chibás.

Sunday after Sunday, at eight o'clock in the evening, Chibás spoke to the nation by radio; his oratory wasn't high-flown, but direct and very powerful. The subject of his weekly diatribe was always corruption, the chronic ill affecting the health of the nation. Skilled at directing the noise to where it found the greatest resonance, the leader would also attack the telephone and electric companies, neither better nor worse than other American-owned firms but much more irritating because they were public utilities.

Chibás' other media vehicle was the news magazine, *Bohemia*. Its editor and publisher, Miguel Angel Quevedo, was a mediocre journalist but a shrewd businessman who had made *Bohemia* the largest circulation weekly in the Spanish-speaking world. The heart of the magazine was the "In Cuba" section, whose editor, Enrique de la Osa, seemed to be everywhere.

The Cuban people responded to Chibás' message and his party grew and grew. Composed at first of dissidents from the *Auténtico* party of Grau and Prío, the *Ortodoxo* party fortified its ranks with the most prestigious university professors and distinguished journalists of the day. The *Ortodoxos* were a diverse party that accommodated both labor leaders and great landowners because when Chibás proclaimed "shame against money," he referred to the monies that had been

75

robbed from the public treasury only. It is well to note that the *Ortodoxo* party, or "the party of the Cuban people" as it was also called, was openly anti-Communist. Chibás refused to forget the collaboration between Cuban Marxists and the corrupt and criminal Batista administration. Among the *Ortodoxos* was a young lawyer, Fidel Castro, who had not had much success in politics and was not even very well known in his own party. This was before Fidel exhibited his now famous "charisma."

This is unusual because charisma -- the power certain personalities exercise over the collective imagination of the masses -- is said by the Greeks and some moderns to be an innate gift. Nicanor McFarland, when he was Fidel's age, had already shed his strange name and become nationally, even internationally known as Julio Antonio Mella. Guiteras was only 26 when he passed like a brilliant star over the Ministry of Interior. José Pardo Llada, a radio commentator with a bewitchingly convincing voice, received 80,000 votes in the congressional elections of 1950, more than twice the required number to win a seat in the House. Pardo Llada was barely four years older than Fidel.

Well, enough of these Greek meditations; let us return to serious things. By 1950, the development of democracy in Cuba was a serious process, even though there were still clankings in the system. In the elections of that year, Chibás himself ran for a Senate seat against Virgilio Pérez, a friend of President Prío and godparent to one of his children. Chibás defeated the government candidate overwhelmingly. In another important race, Antonio Prío, the president's brother and a shameless thief, lost the election for mayor of Havana. Pardo Llada, a Chibás' follower who, as I said, won a congressional election with 40,000 votes to spare, owed his popularity to the virulence of his attacks on the government, which rivalled those of Chibás.

The elections of 1950, the last free elections to be held in our country, were the high-water mark of Cuban democracy. The man who presided over them as president was Carlos Prío. The elections were not his only achievement, though it is no small thing to be able to choose among various options when deciding who shall exercise the powers of the state.

Besides respecting the public will, Prío created two extremely promising institutions: the National Bank of Cuba and the Office of Accounting. The former, a central bank in charge of issuing currency, was given control over the Cuban financial system, which until then had been rather chaotic. The latter was destined to become a vital instrument in the eradication both of the theft of public funds and of dirty business ventures that had been run under the protection of state authority.

Carlos Prío could have left a positive legacy, but he was, I repeat, a weak man. Weak men, when they occupy positions of power, often prove to be catastrophic. An example of Prío's weakness was his behavior toward Batista. Following his electoral defeat in 1944, Batista had voluntarily exiled himself to the United States. He had wanted to return to Cuba during the Grau administration but Grau had made it clear that while he had no objection to Batista's return, it would have to be as a private citizen. Batista would not be allowed to engage in his kind of "politics." The millionaire ex-sergeant, a man who never was guilty of rashness, decided to wait for better days.

Those came when Prío assumed the presidency in 1948. The new president, too preoccupied with not appearing resentful or vindictive, approved the return of Batista. He even assigned him a military escort that among other things, served as a point of contact between Batista and the putschists who would overthrow Prío on March 10, 1952. But what really set in motion this calamity was a series of events for which Prío had no responsibility whatever, and of which Prío's rival, Eduardo Chibás, was both culprit and victim.

Eduardo Chibás was not in the least interested in seizing other people's money. This is a common attitude among honest men, but it does not in itself constitute honesty. Chibás was not himself completely honest, as he demonstrated in his political battle with Aureliano Sánchez Arango, the minister of Education who was shaping up as a possible presidential candidate. With a good record

77

as an anti-Machado fighter and an acceptable record as a cabinet minister, Sánchez Arango might have become a dangerous rival. Chibás decided to neutralize him.

He accused Sánchez Arango of what he justly accused most of Prío's ministers: stealing funds from the budget of his ministry. Sánchez Arango challenged him to produce proof and Chibás promised to do so. But he couldn't. The evidence did not exist.

The complete certainty with which the leader of the *Ortodoxos* promised to substantiate his allegations and the details that he offered regarding businesses set up by Sánchez Arango in Guatemala with embezzled funds lead me to suspect that Chibás was the victim of a trap. Someone may have tricked him into making these accusations by offering to furnish the proof of the supposed theft. But had Chibás been a completely honest man, he never would have accused a political rival of wrongdoing without evidence .

Chibás found himself in a precarious situation in respect to public opinion. One indication was the astute Miguel Angel Quevedo's refusal to publish Chibás' column in an issue of *Bohemia* that carried numerous promotional advertisements from the Ministry of Education. Quevedo was Chibás' friend, but he was his own friend first.

Eddy Chibás, it is well to remember, was a brave man obsessed with power. To reach the presidency was the prime objective of his life. Now all was lost or in danger of being lost, beginning with his honor. Moreover, the leader of the opposition wasn't what you would call a model of mental stability, either. On seeing his dream turning to ashes, Chibás took a decision that was in keeping with his character. He read on his radio program a dramatic harangue against the dangers threatening the nation, among which he included, prophetically, communism. At the conclusion of his speech, he shot himself in the stomach.

There was a bit of everything in the *Ortodoxo* party. Chibás, unlike Fidel, liked to surround himself with talented men. For example, among the party faithful were Cuba's most eminent surgeon, Antonio Rodríguez Díaz, and two excellent clinicians, Drs.

Iglesias Betancourt and Bisbé. Taken immediately to Dr. Rodríguez Díaz's private hospital for surgery, Chibás was expertly operated on and given the best post-operative care available. All seemed to indicate the leader would recover.

Moved by his dramatic act, the people gathered in front of the hospital to await the latest news on Chibás' condition. They were disposed to forgive and not criticize him. Everyone knew that Chibás was an indispensable man, though no one knew then or could know, just how indispensable.

Meanwhile, the wave of fervor for Chibás left his political opponents in the cold. No one dared to label that drama a political maneuver; no one except Prío's prime minister, Manuel Antonio de Varona, who was covered with insults for it and presented with four horseshoes.

The people, the majority of whom were *Ortodoxos*, waited to forget, forgive and applaud. But none of this was necessary: an unforeseen complication took the life of Eduardo Chibás on August 16, 1951.

"Blondie!," Chibás called me, tousling my hair -- which was then like a cornstalk -- when he passed through my town on a campaign trip. It was 1944; Chibás was campaigning for Grau, whom he then supported and did so much to elect. Seven years later as I wept over his death, I remembered his happy smile, his starched *guayabera* [shirt], and his blue eyes that seemed so remote behind his thick glasses. Millions of Cubans wept that day and more than one hundred thousand attended his burial. In truth, we had reasons enough to cry, reasons that we could not even begin to imagine. Eduardo Chibás, despite all his defects, would have saved us from a great many things. Without his death, Batista's coup six months later and the tyranny that followed would not have been possible. Without that tyranny nothing that has transpired in the last thirty years would have taken place.

When the leader of the *Ortodoxos* died, little more than nine months remained until the next scheduled presidential election. While the *Ortodoxo* party had a little of everything, it lost what mattered most: an unquestioned chief whose personality was the glue that held it together. Still, the strength of the *Ortodoxo* party was such that even its enormous loss did not seem as if it would affect its rise to power.

The *Ortodoxos* nominated Roberto Agramonte as their presidential candidate. For vice president they chose Millo Ochoa. Gentle in appearance and solemn, but without the warmth, energy or attraction that the suicidal leader had had among the masses, Agramonte was nonetheless Chibás' natural heir, a man with a clean political slate and impressive academic credentials. This was enough: the political astuteness and experience -- if they were necessary -- would be supplied by Millo Ochoa. (Years later, by the way, a lack of political astuteness and experience would send another Ochoa from Holguín to his grave).

The *Auténtico* party nominated Carlos Hevia for president. He had occupied that office for one day in 1934. Aureliano Sánchez Arango had come off badly from the conflict that culminated in Chibás death. It doesn't make any sense, but that's just the way it happened. Irrational attitudes, whether individual or collective, can be criticized, but it's senseless not to take then into account.

Hevia was a spotless man. In Prío's administration, he had presided over the National Development Commission, an organism dedicated to the construction of public works, Hevia rejected the many possibilities for shady dealings that such a position afforded. The government gave him all the assistance it could, but still his chances were slim. Hevia could not capitalize on Agramonte's lackluster personality (the sole weakness of the *Ortodoxo* candidate), because Hevia was just as dull.

While a victory by Carlos Hevia was improbable, for Fulgencio Batista, the third candidate, it was impossible. He had not the least chance of winning. This did not seem to bother him too much. The ominous ex-sergeant was engaged in certain activities more in keeping with his character than electoral concerns: conspiracy and treason.

Chibás' death had opened the way for Batista. There was no other leader with the daring and popularity to get the people into the streets in defense of democracy. There were men with daring but without popularity (Sánchez Arango); and men with popularity but without daring (Pardo Llada). Fidel Castro was as brave and ambitious as Chibás, but in 1952, he was almost as unknown as I.

Evidence of this lack of leadership was demonstrated during the electoral campaign of 1952 -- the same campaign in which Fidel ran for Congress. During a demonstration, a youth was killed as a result of a brutal beating administered by two police officers. The two officers, *Comandante* Casals and Lieutenant Salas Cañizares, were relieved of their functions and indicted, but this did not quiet public indignation. Prío -- the weak, cordial and dishonest Prío -- was assailed by the *Ortodoxo* opposition, but not by Batista. The brutal Lieutenant Salas Cañizares was already a key player in a conspiracy to seize power.

During the murdered boy's funeral, Fidel proposed diverting the enraged crowd to the presidential palace and topple the government by force. Pardo Llada, Fidel's contemporary but unlike him already a national figure, opposed his suggestion and the funeral cortege continued on its way. Fidel's charisma had not yet appeared, but his ambition was already present. Only a few months away from the elections that were expected to bring his party to power, Fidel wanted to seize power by force. If Fidel had then enjoyed the renown and authority of Pardo Llada, Batista -- a prudent man if ever there was one -- would have had no choice but to wait once again for better times.

During his presidential term, Batista was less of an assassin and more of a crook than he had been during his tenure as colonel-in-chief of the army. Grau, a completely democratic president, was better than Batista. Prío, a better man than Grau, was a still better president. It all leads one to suppose that either Agramonte or Hevia would have done better than Prío.

81

The years between the Constitution of 1940 and the coup d'état of March 10, 1952 remind me of a scene from a Brazilian film, Glauber Rocha's *God and the Devil in the Land of the Sun*. Manuel the cowboy arduously climbs the steep ascent to Calvary carrying on his shoulders an enormous stone. At his side is Brother Sebastian, who excoriates him with a whip from time to time. Manuel travels a hard road with a heavy load and heavier company. But he forges onward and upward. That was Cuba on March 9, 1952. The next day Fulgencio Batista would begin the final act in the role that destiny assigned him in the destruction of our institutions and our liberties.

The destruction began long before March 10, 1952, with Machado. His tyranny, while short-lived, implicated the army in his tyranny, opening the way for the destruction of the armed forces through the introduction of politics into its ranks. The army thus ceased to be an independent organism capable of fighting.

One of the paradoxes of political life is that in no country at any time has the army been a bulwark of liberty and democracy. It cannot and never could be such a bulwark because the army is an institution that operates on blind obedience and without discussion. The proper function of the military in a democratic system is to abstain from politics; in short, to be inactive. In no case, and under no circumstances should the army participate in the nation's political life. That had been the posture of the Cuban army since the foundation of the Republic. This posture was inherited from the Republic-in-Arms, which had never been controlled by military men: the military fought and the civilians directed the independence movement (the officers who did participate in government had no troops at their command).

This tradition, the only one of its kind in Latin America, was lost, or began to be lost, on September 4, 1933. Over the next decade, the army was transformed into the principal wellspring of power on the island. Perhaps even worse, it became an armed band dedicated to plundering the country and incapable of defending it except under conditions of absolute superiority. Later, the governments of Grau and Prío had no time for nor showed any interest in reconstructing what had been destroyed. While new officers who had no connection to the Septembrist sergeants' revolt emerged, they were too few in number. The army remained in essence and ability what it had become between 1933 and 1944.

VI. Again Batista

Thus on March 10, 1952, the first military coup d'état in our country's history occurred. It was the first and the last: one was all that it would take to destroy Cuban democracy. "Batista is a reserve of Cuban democracy," declared Blas Roca on July 1, 1944, exactly one month after the Communists and the *batistianos* had been devastated electorally by Grau. The ex-sergeant had returned to active service.

Completely demoralized, Carlos Prío put up no resistance. Two hundred miles from Havana, Colonel Martín Helena, commander of the Matanzas regiment, denounced the coup and offered the president his support. In Santiago de Cuba, Colonel Alvarez Margolles, chief of the Moncada, the second-largest barracks in the country, also sided with Prío. Numerous students and alumni (including Fidel Castro and Rolando Masferrer) converged on University Hill, ready to fight. But Prío didn't want to fight. He didn't want help. The only thing he wanted was to flee, which he did, with his two young daughters and his beautiful wife. Smiling lamentably, Prío boarded a commercial flight bound for Miami.

I will never tire of saying it: if Chibás had been alive, there would not have been a coup. But even without him, it is well to ask ourselves what would have happened if Prío had decided to resist. In Batista we find a strange symbiosis of audacity and cowardice, with cowardice as the dominant factor in dangerous situations. As for his military followers, they were merely rats -- armed rats, but rats to the end, as they would demonstrate a few years later. Prío didn't take this into account. He didn't want blood shed -- especially his own. And thus Batista was again president.

Although a democracy that falls as a consequence of the death of an irrational and demagogic leader and the demoralization of one president could not have been very stable in the first place, it is well to point out that what is unstable can be fortified, a task infinitely simpler than resurrecting something that is dead.

Well then, we again had the sallow and shrewd sergeant of September 4 installed in the presidential palace, who had since his last occupancy acquired an extremely corpulent and prolific new wife and a numerous progeny that he had to provide for. I am in total and indignant disagreement with old Communists who swear that Fulgencio Batista was a generous man of noble sentiments. On the contrary, I believe that he was never anything more than a despicable scoundrel. Of course, if we compare Batista (or Machado, for that matter) to other contemporary Latin American dictators, he comes out smelling like a rose. But the merit isn't his. It is due simply to the fact that Cuba had no tradition of barbarism.

For Batista, an absolutely amoral man, the assassination of enemies posed no problem for his conscience. But neither did he regard it as a necessity. Batista wasn't Stalin, a psychopathic criminal. Batista's motivation for killing (or rather ordering or allowing others to kill in his name) was solely the necessity of defending his own interests when he feared they might be imperilled. He didn't shed blood for the sake of shedding blood. Batista had no impulsive blood lust, as almost all tyrants do.

It is clear that Batista in his first presidential term was much more benign than during his colonelcy. By the same token, the level of repression in the country during the first sixteen months of his second dictatorship was relatively low. Batista felt confident because his power wasn't threatened. In 1940, Batista's principal enemies were dead or had renounced insurrection. Throughout 1952 and until mid-1953, there appeared to be no serious threat to his rule on the horizon.

Repression, consequently, was kept at minimum. In those first sixteen months I can recall only two deaths: a worker killed during a strike at the Manatí sugar refinery, and a student shot during a demonstration (who, curiously, was the namesake of Rubén Batista, the dictator's eldest son). There were also some isolated cases of police brutality, but not very many if you consider that the police were under the command of that feral beast Rafael Salas Cañizares, the lieutenant whose brutality had so complicated Prío's life.

There just wasn't any reason for savagery. The *Ortodoxo* party, which until just recently had been a very powerful political machine, began to disintegrate as a result of internal squabbles of little consequence. It is not even worth the trouble to discuss the fate of the *Auténtico* party of Grau and Prío. As for the Communists, Batista ignored his erstwhile allies. They had already given him all they could, including bad advice.

Still, all was not peaceful. Fidel Castro presented before the courts a suit challenging the constitutionality of the de facto government. It was dismissed, of course, although nothing particularly disagreeable happened to the young lawyer. There are tyrants and then there are tyrants.

I will go so far as to affirm, though I do so at my own risk, that during the first sixteen months of Batista's dictatorship, there existed in Cuba freedom of press, freedom of assembly, and freedom of association. I can vouch that such rights would today be received by Cubans as marvelous and unexpected blessings.

But such a state of affairs could not last for long. Democracy had already reached such a state of development in our country -- despite the evils that it had to confront -- that a military dictatorship was regarded by the people as an anachronism, something from another time and place. To uproot the democratic system in Cuba required someone of greater dimensions than that greedy tin pot dictator Batista.

The first to conspire against Batista was Rafael García Bárcenas, a university professor. It was a serious (albeit somewhat romantic and idealistic) conspiracy. The professor intended to burst into Camp Columbia, armed not only with conventional weapons but also with his convincing oratory, which he would use to persuade the soldiers to do their civic duty. This episode puts me in mind of some verses from Guillén (I don't mean the good Guillén, who was a Spaniard, but Nicolás Guillén, Cuba's Communist "national poet): "I don't know why you think I hate you, soldier/When we are the same thing: you and I." I don't want to contradict the poet. It is possible that he and the soldiers were the same thing. But I am sure that García Bárcenas had very little in common with that throng of uncouth loafers.

In short, the conspiracy was uncovered. The professor was sentenced to several years in prison but had served only a brief time when he was amnestied.

Amnesty. There's a word that has disappeared from the Cuban political lexicon. Batista decreed several amnesties in his time, as had been the practice of all Cuban presidents throughout the history of our republic.

The second conspiracy was of a very different order. It differed from the first as Fidel Castro differed from García Bárcenas. Fidel Castro doesn't have a whit of the romantic in him, and although numerous cretins have described him as an "idealist," I maintain that there is no foundation for such an accusation.

I have already spoken about Fidel. I will speak a bit more. I am well aware that this entails risks, but at this moment I am inclined to be fearless. Fidel Castro was born in 1926 at an hacienda in Birán, northern Oriente province, near Nipe Bay where sometimes lethargic and irresponsible sharks prowl. His father, a Galician, was sent to Cuba as a soldier and fought on the Spanish side in Cuba's War of Independence. At war's end, Angel Castro made a decision that would have fatal consequences for millions of Cubans: he decided to remain on the island. By the time Fidel was born, Angel Castro had already become a wealthy landowner; how he did it, I have no idea.

87

Fidel began his secondary studies at a Jesuit preparatory school in Santiago de Cuba and completed them at Havana's very prestigious Belén School, another institution run by the Order. At about this time, Fidel's sister, Juanita Castro, was studying at a convent school run by the Ursulines. Fidel visited Juanita from time to time; on one of these occasions, he confided to a classmate of his sister that someday he would rule Cuba. The young girl from Bayamo was more interested in Fidel's physical stature and self-confident demeanor than in his incredibly precocious ambitions, but his affirmation would remain in her memory.

At the university, Fidel dedicated himself entirely to his chosen vocation, and took the first step toward his final objective and reason for existence -- power -- by becoming president of the Havana University Law Students Association. But after that initial success his career seemed to stall. He never was able to climb the next step of the ladder to become president of the University Students Federation, the famous USF founded by Mella. "And what of his charisma?" some will ask. Let them ask all they want, but don't ask me. I've already made it quite clear what I think of such Greek sorceries. As for other kinds of witchcraft, I refuse even to discuss them.

One day in 1948, on the eve of the Pan-American conference that was to be held in Colombia, Jorge Eliécer Gaytán, a very popular Liberal leader in that country, was assassinated in Bogota. Although political assassination is a more or less routine occurrence in Colombia, this particular one provoked one of the worst outbreaks of violence that anyone can recall in Latin America. Fidel was there. What was his role in that colossal brawl?

I should also like to know Fidel's version of his involvement in the gangster-led Cayo Confites expedition to "liberate" the Dominican Republic. What, if any, were his other contacts with the underworld? I am interested, too, in his colorless militancy within the ranks of the anti-Communist *Ortodoxo* party, as well as in his disagreement with Pardo Llada over the purpose of funerals. Many interesting things might be found in Fidel's memoirs. But while I await his decision to write them, I shall continue to write my own because

88

there are not enough good memoirs in this world. Men with good memories usually don't write memoirs.

The Assault on Moncada

For nine years (1944 to 1953), Fidel engaged in fevered but not very successful political activity. On July 26, 1953, he overcame at last his relative anonymity, mounting that higher plane that had eluded him so far, and became famous. Fidel achieved in one day what he could not do in nine years.

The assault on the Moncada barracks is a fundamental event in our history for it marks the political ascent of the most important figure in Cuban twentieth century political life. As a military operation, however, Moncada was not just a disaster but a completely botched job, a series of irresponsible improvisations in planning as well as execution.

The assailants had no contact whatever with other conspiratorial groups that already existed in Santiago de Cuba. Of the men who carried the guns with the greatest firepower, none was familiar with the city. Still, all the best-equipped rebels were assigned to the same car, which got lost on the way and ended up who knows where. Among their planned objectives was the Saturnino Lora Army Hospital, which housed convalescing soldiers and their dependents. Nothing was to be gained by endangering their lives. The already meager rebel forces were far too dispersed. Finally, the planners assumed that were they successful in laying siege to the barracks, the people of Santiago would lend them their resolute support.

Let's pause and consider this last point. The conspirators chose July 26 to begin their operation at the tail end of the tumultuous Santiago carnival so that while they were making preparations for the assault in the preceding days, they could pass unnoticed in a city that had given itself over heart and soul to the festivities. That much at least makes sense. What seems improbable to me is that men who had only hours before been wildly dancing the conga in the streets, emptying bottles of beer and kegs of rum, should suddenly awaken from the profound slumber that envelops exhausted debauchees, shake off their hangovers, and run to take arms at the behest of an unknown individual. Fidel, like all of his ilk, trusted in his luck.

Fortune would smile on Fidel many times in years to come, but not on this occasion. The assault failed and Batista ordered the first massacre of his second dictatorship. Fidel fell prisoner. It was then that his luck kicked in. I refer, of course, only to *his* luck: many of the other captured rebels were murdered, including José Luis Tassende, who was photographed alive and in captivity before being officially listed as a casualty of the assault.

And yet Fidel was saved. He was assisted by a combination of unexpected factors: the intervention of the archbishop of Santiago de Cuba, Enrique Pérez Serantes (a charming little old man who struck me as very intelligent when he visited my parents' house, but who, in July 1953, would have done better to copy Charlotte Corday and declare: "I have allowed one man to die in order to save 100,000"), and the attitude of two lieutenants. Two lieutenants saved -- or, rather, spared -- Fidel's life: the lieutenant who arrested him and the lieutenant who had custody of him during his trial. Both refused orders to assassinate Fidel. By the way, the second of these lieutenants, Yanes Pelletier, became Fidel's military mentor after he seized power. Later, he fell in disgrace, spending several years in prison. Now he is a political pariah. Pelletier belongs to one of those groups dedicated to the humanitarian but ingenuous task of demanding respect for human rights from a totalitarian state.

It wasn't only luck that was on Fidel's side. He was also assisted by our traditions, which still retained some of their influence. Fidel was given a public trial that was witnessed by journalists who were not salaried employees of the state. He was defended by the lawyer of his choice, someone genuinely interested in securing his acquittal -- namely, himself. If someday, God forbid, I am accused of writing enemy propaganda, spreading false reports, disrespect for authority or some similar gibberish, I would like (if the Revolution is generous enough to allow it) to be tried under exactly the same conditions Fidel had for the assault on Moncada, in which several dozen soldiers were killed. Of course, I would have to send to Miami or New Jersey for a defense lawyer. Here we have none.

Dr. Fidel Castro's defense is known to posterity by its Parthian shot: "History will absolve me." There are many interesting things in that speech. For example, there is Fidel's description of the Rule of Law that had been abolished by the coup of March 10, 1952. He said he wanted to restore it: "Everybody could assemble, associate and speak with complete liberty. If the government did not satisfy the people, the people could change it." To praise our maximum leader is an extremely convenient activity, but the opportunities for doing so are few -- at least for me. So when any opportunity presents itself, I must make haste to take advantage of it. And so I say, though it may annoy some: "Bravo, Fidel! Now you're talking!"

Fidel was sentenced to fifteen years imprisonment, and served twenty-two months. The amnesty, another tradition then in force but now only folklore, came to his assistance. Some years later, during the *fidelista* era, *Comandante* Huber Matos was sentenced to twenty years imprisonment in a case that did not involve the death of anyone. He served every year. Jorge Valls was also given a twenty year sentence. It almost isn't necessary to say so, but just in case, let me point out that Valls wasn't charged with any blood crimes, either. Valls is in fact a kind of Gandhi. Yet he also served his entire sentence.

How many men have served sentences of twenty years or more under Fidel Castro's government? If anyone knows the exact number he should publish it; perhaps it has been published and I am unaware of it. I am ignorant of so many things, but I won't go so far as to affirm like Socrates that "I know only that I know nothing." I do have some information. I know that Armando Valladares served 22 years in prison, Vladimir Ramírez 24, and Roberto Martín Pérez 27. Mario Chanes has just completed his 28th year in confinement.

In 1953, Mario Chanes participated in the assault on the Moncada barracks. He was sentenced to prison along with Fidel and like Fidel, amnestied by Batista. But Chanes hasn't had the same luck with his old chief and comrade-in-arms, Fidel Castro. Another veteran of Moncada, Gustavo Arcos, was crippled for life as a consequence of a wound he received there. He has been better served by Fidel: he has "only" had to serve nine years spread over two incarcerations. As I write these lines, he is not in prison. But I can't guarantee anything in respect to the immediate future.

"Free Nelson Mandela," was the hue and cry of thousands upon thousands of people who call themselves "progressives." But no one was shouting or singing for the freedom of Mario Chanes, who beat the leader of the ANC by two years for the world record of longest-held political prisoner. Having analyzed how very different is the attention accorded to each of these men and their respective misfortunes, I have taken an irrevocable decision: I am going to make myself famous.

Being more sagacious than me, Fidel arrived at that same conclusion at a very early age and achieved his prime objective a few days shy of his 27th birthday. The Moncada assault served first and foremost to make him famous. He risked his life and won fame. In future days he would risk his life again, but never unnecessarily.

Jail did not affect Fidel. There was no way it could have affected him, not just because of the brief duration of his stay, but also because of the humane treatment he received while in confinement. Batista accorded Castro the same treatment that Machado had accorded his political prisoners. In so doing, he was only following the tradition of our country. Once a prisoner had appeared before the courts, his life, person and dignity were respected. Prisoners were not beaten or humiliated; they were not kept incommunicado for months or prevented from seeing their families; they did not have their mail intercepted, nor were they kept in solitary confinement inside steel boxes -- none of that. Fidel was able to maintain an intense correspondence with his great friend Luis Conte Agüero, a radio commentator; his letters are very interesting because they record in minute detail the excellent treatment he received in prison. He also wrote to the author and historian Jorge Mañach, whom he seemed to respect and admire. Fidel received regular visits from family members, including his infant son. He was even interviewed in prison by a reporter from *Bohemia*, who did not obtain prior authorization for the interview from prison officials but who had no cause to regret his temerity.

His stay in prison, however, was not without its bitter cup: Fidel's wife deserted him, which is an occupational hazard of revolutionaries. Not all women (nor all men) can rise to the occasion in such circumstances. Martí was also deserted by his wife, Carmen Zayas Bazán, and he must have suffered much more than Fidel. Martí was a man of love, Fidel is not.

In any case, whatever griefs he suffered were worth suffering, for when he left prison Fidel was already a national figure. He immediately resumed his revolutionary activity. He founded the July 26th Movement, an organization that could have been the instrument of the restoration of democracy in our country, but was not. Some of its other founders have been forgotten or devoured by the Revolution. But others are still with Fidel: Raúl Castro, Pedro Miret, Armando Hart and Jesús Montané.

Special mention must be made of Haydée Santamaría, a brave and idealistic woman who fought at Moncada next to her brother Abel and her fiance, Boris Luís Santa Coloma, both murdered in the wave of repression that followed the failed operation.

Despite Haydée and her tragic and impassioned presence on the list of founders, I must add another name lest the list appear somewhat insipid: Gustavo Arcos.

Fidel did not tarry long on the streets of Havana. Anticipating a possible attack of lucidity on Batista's part (who had followed the democratic tradition of amnestying political enemies, but who was not even remotely a democrat), Fidel set out for exile. He established himself in Mexico, where he began preparations for the expedition that would bring the armed struggle to the Sierra Maestra.

"In 1956, we will be free or martyrs," announced Fidel. This business about a revolution on a fixed schedule seems a bit absurd to me but since things have gone better for Fidel than for me, it is best that I curb my critical spirit. Believe me, it isn't easy for me to do.

VII. The Sierra and the Plains

By 1956, there appeared on the national scene two figures who embraced Fidel's immediate goals but might have threatened his long-range plans. One was yet unknown to the general public, working in the shadows in Santiago de Cuba. Energetic, capable and brave as few men, Frank País would become famous on November 30, 1956.

País at least was active in the July 26th movement. The other, a product of the militant student tradition of Havana University, preferred to go at it alone. He was a tall, stocky, (or better yet corpulent) young man with rosy cheeks, the unaffected charm that Cubans find irresistible, and the blind courage of a fighting cock: José Antonio Echeverría.

Both Frank and José Antonio were students; Frank studied pedagogy and José Antonio architecture; and, besides bravery and patriotism, they had something else in common: their deep religious convictions. Frank was the pastor of a Baptist church and José Antonio was a fervent Catholic. Strange martyrs for a Marxist-Leninist revolution.

While Fidel was preparing for war, the Society of Friends of the Republic offered to mediate peace talks between the government and the opposition. This attempt at national reconciliation was led by Cosme de la Torriente, an old Conservative politician and one of the last surviving officers of our War of Independence, and José Miró

94

Cardona, president of the Cuban Bar Association. But such negotiations were doomed to fail from the start: Batista had been cured for good of all populist illusions by the elections of 1944.

The *Ortodoxo* party was split into many factions, and what had once been a formidable political machine, was slowly but surely coming apart. One of these factions decided to set up its tent elsewhere: Jorge Mañach and José Pardo Llada founded the Nationalist Revolutionary Movement. They then joined not the Revolution, but the controversial peace negotiations. The *Auténtico* party, which ruled Cuba for eight years prior to Batista's coup, practically had ceased to exist, though its leaders continued to speak as if it still existed.

In the plaza adjoining the Muelle de Luz, there was a mass gathering of the opposition. It was attended by representatives from the entire political spectrum, ranging from Grau to the University Students Federation. Only the unpopular Popular Socialist Party was excluded, because it had labelled the Moncada assault a "putsch" and "petite bourgeoisie adventurism." Fidel's supporters in the crowd sang in unison, "Revolution! Viva Fidel!" Tempers flared to the boiling point. Suddenly, someone was thrown headfirst from the grandstand and all hell broke loose. Everywhere in the crowd rival groups were beating up on one another, folding chairs were flying through the air like birds of ill omen, and the great meeting of the opposition broke apart.

We are in 1956, the year that Fidel had selected to begin the insurrection. Yet it wasn't only Fidel and his followers, or the boys from the University, who were plotting Batista's downfall. A clique of officers headed by ex-Colonel Ramón Barquín was preparing a coup d'état. Nothing came of their plans: someone turned informant. The conspirators were apprehended, spending the remainder of the Batista dictatorship in the stockade. That would be, however, less than three years.

The aborted conspiracy cost the army its most competent high ranking officer: José Ramón Fernández (dubbed "El Gallego" because he spoke like a Galician), the able artilleryman who years later would

95

play a pivotal role in what Fidel has called "the first defeat of imperialism in the Americas [i.e. the Bay of Pigs]."

Shortly before Fidel's 1956 deadline had expired, students under the leadership of José Antonio Echeverría founded a new insurrectional organization: the Revolutionary Directorate, which was almost from the first marked by a tragic destiny. José Antonio travelled to Mexico to sign an alliance with Fidel and Frank País.

Little time remained to make good Fidel's promise. In November 1956, the storied yacht *Granma*, with 82 men aboard, set out from Tuxpan, Mexico, bound for the southern coast of Oriente province, which is but a few miles from the Sierra Maestra. The yacht was expected to arrive on November 30. On that day, as planned, Frank País, who was always precise and reliable, led his men to action on the streets of Santiago de Cuba, in a diversionary operation that paralyzed government troops. The July 26th Movement accomplished its mission with only three casualties; and then went into hiding in the belief that the men of the *Granma* expedition were also safely ensconced in the Sierra Maestra.

But the *Granma* had not arrived; it would not arrive for two more days, and when it finally touched land, it was not on the coast of the Sierra Maestra, but on a mangrove swamp not far from Manzanillo on the Gulf of Guacanayabo. After a mile-long trek through the marshlands, the exhausted expeditionaries saw a vast plain before them, and in the distance, very far away, the outline of the foothills of the Sierra Maestra. That's about as close as most of them would get to their destination. The army caught them by surprise, cornered them, and many lost their lives. Others were taken prisoner and spent the last 25 months of the Batista regime in prison. Among the captured rebels was Mario Chanes, that much-persecuted man who has never had the good fortune of becoming famous.

Fidel was presumed dead, but, of course, he wasn't. A few days later, somewhere in the hills, a small band of survivors would re-group round their leader; they were twelve.

Much has been said about them, for they have not lacked historians; some enjoy international fame, and almost all have occupied

96

or still occupy high government office -- those, of course, who are still alive and have been able to retain Fidel's favor. There is no reason, then, to enumerate them.

I do want, however, to mention another small group of revolutionaries, not twelve, but fourteen men. When the July 26th Movement was disbanded in the wake of the news of the disastrous landing of the *Granma* and the supposed death of the movement's leader, there were only 14 urban fighters left alive in Havana. Since no one has ever mentioned their names, I shall.

Of the top men in the Movement, there were only two survivors in the capital: Gerardo Abreu ("Fortín") and Carlos Franqui. The others who were ready to resume the struggle, were Julio Alon, Julio Bauta, Federico Bell-Yoch, Sergio González ("El Curita"), Enrique Hart, Alonso Hidalgo, Ricardo Martínez, Francisco Miralles, José Pellón, José Prieto, Héctor Ravelo and Aldo Vera. When Faustino Pérez, one of Fidel's Twelve, was sent to Havana in late December 1956 to revive the July 26th Movement, he found that it was still alive.

Dr. Faustino Pérez, a physician and veteran of García Bárcenas' conspiracy, proved an underground leader difficult to surpass or even equal. Under his direction, the Movement carried out a long series of successful actions, overcoming the tyranny's repressive net.

Shortly after Faustino's arrival, Haydée Santamaría, who had been in Santiago during the tragic events of November 30, and René Rodriguéz, another of "The Twelve" but a very different sort of man than Faustino, were sent by Fidel to Havana on a mission which I am unable to clarify.

I know nothing about the objectives of the mission, but I do know the results: René Rodríguez, whom Haydée called "a little gangster," devoted himself to creating a group independent of the leadership of Faustino Pérez, with the connivance of the attorney Humberto Sorí Marín. Expelled from the July 26th Movement, Rodriguéz and Sorí Marín marched off to the Sierra Maestra, where, despite the expulsion dictated against them, they were received well enough for both to attain the rank of *comandante*.

Sometime later, in 1961, Sorí Marín was executed by firing squad. René Rodríguez had much better luck. He still occupies high office and has even achieved a kind of international celebrity: in 1982 he was indicted by a Miami grand jury for drug trafficking.

But let's return to the Fifties. The Revolutionary Directorate committed itself in the Mexico pact to supporting the *Granma* expedition with diversionary tactics similar to those carried out on November 30 by the July 26th Movement, but didn't do it. The Directorate decided instead to liquidate the tyranny with one blow, a great blow meant to decapitate it. While it prepared for that mission, the Directorate kept up a seeming passivity. The calm was broken by the assassination of the head of Military Intelligence, Colonel Blanco Rico, which was carried out with great skill. Next the Directorate would attempt to get the Colonel's boss.

Meanwhile, in the Sierra Maestra, the fledgling *fidelista* guerrillas, supplemented now by some peasant recruits but still small, gave some signs of life by attacking a small army barracks.

Nevertheless, the government continued to insist that Fidel had been killed in the *Granma* landing, as if it believed that its unshakable faith in a lie could somehow modify reality.

One of the first feats of Faustino Pérez and his men was to demolish this stupid legend. They arranged to bring Herbert Matthews of *The New York Times* from Havana to the Sierra Maestra. Matthews interviewed and photographed the "dead man," and so Fidel became an international celebrity overnight, and, in time, the most famous of Cubans.

But wars are not won with propaganda alone; men and arms are also necessary. Frank País came to the rescue of the decimated expeditionary group in the Sierra Maestra. He reinforced it with a detachment of well-armed and -equipped fighters that tripled the guerrilla force in one day. The July 26th Movement created the rebel army; in time, the army would devour it.

By the way, the reinforcements sent by the Movement were transported on trucks provided by "an *arrocero* from Manzanillo," as Ernesto Guevara was later to describe Huber Matos. When Dr. Guevara wrote those words he had already been in our country long enough to know what we Cubans mean by *arrocero*: a landowner who cultivates rice on vast tracts of land using the latest agricultural technology and with a great concentration of capital, as economists say. In short an *arrocero* is, as Guevara well knew, an agrarian capitalist. Except that Huber was, as Guevara also knew, a school-teacher with an enterprising spirit who had rented some trucks to transport the rice that others grew.

"I am extremely rigid in my actions," Dr. Guevara wrote on another occasion. I also can be quite rigid at times. Under certain circumstances, however, I wish I could be less rigid because I realize that being rigid doesn't do me any good. But respect for the truth won't let me. My veracity compels me to accuse Dr. Guevara of lying. He may be one of the major deities in the revolutionary pantheon, but he lied through his teeth when he portrayed Matos as bourgeois.

My love of the truth also obliges me to say, as I have already, that the Directorate did not live up to the commitment it made in Mexico. But in this case it was not due to bad faith; it had, quite simply, decided to stake all on one card. On March 13, 1956, the Directorate stormed the presidential palace with all the force at its disposal.

In an interview with a CBS reporter, Fidel labelled the attempted assassination of Batista "useless bloodshed," adding that "the dictator's life is of no importance." With a heavy heart, I must disagree. Batista's dictatorship, like Fidel's, centered around one man. There was no substitute for that man among his followers. With the death of the dictator, his regime would have been condemned to disappear immediately or in short order. To eliminate Batista was tantamount to destroying the dictatorship, which was all for the good. What Fidel found objectionable was that the Directorate should bring

99

about the fall of the dictator; such a contingency would have affected seriously his future plans.

As for the bloodshed, it was "useless" only because it did not directly benefit him. Moncada also ended in failure, but the blood expended there was not "useless" because it served to make him a national figure and put him on the road to power.

What is certain and undeniable, however, is that to assassinate Batista made much more sense than attacking an army barracks. The assault on the presidential palace itself was better planned and executed than Moncada. However, certain imponderables predominated that day, and to the great misfortune of many and the great luck of few, the Directorate suffered a terrible defeat that included the death of its leader.

While the assault was underway, José Antonio Echeverría burst into a radio station and read a somewhat impassioned and puerile communiqué announcing the death of the tyrant. It was a mistake. In politics, one shouldn't announce possibilities as facts, however feasible these may seem. The brave José Antonio didn't have the time to learn that axiom: he died a few minutes later in an encounter with the police on the street.

Hardly a few weeks had passed when we again had proof of the tragic fate that dogged the Directorate: four participants in the events of March 13 -- Fructuoso Rodríguez (José Antonio's successor and as intrepid as the fallen leader), José Westbrook (one of the most promising young men of his generation), Juan Pedro Carbó Servía (a medical student whose name now adorns a wing of the Havana Psychiatric Hospital -- an institution that will surely be investigated by the Secretary General of the United Nations whenever he decides to comply with his duty), and José Machado -- were ambushed and murdered in an apartment on Humboldt Street where they had taken refuge. It was not known then, but they had been betrayed to the authorities by a Communist informant about whom I shall have more to say in due course.

Meanwhile, in far off Santiago de Cuba, death continued to reap its harvest. Frank País was murdered; gunned down in the street, like José Antonio.

I have already compared these two young men who could have contributed so much to the restoration of democracy in our country. Today, far removed in time (and despite the sympathy that the recollection of a youth so filled with kindness and joy inspires in me), I believe that José Antonio never got to be more than he was: a youth. Not so Frank; this serious-minded native of Santiago was already a mature man, although no older than the brave student from Cardenas. "They don't know what a man they have killed," wrote Fidel on learning of Frank's death. On that day, he was truthful. José Antonio was the promise. Frank was the realization of that promise.

Two leaders died that would forever remain in our memory, but the struggle continued. In Matanzas, an armed group attempted to seize the Goicuría barracks. They got as far as the gates: the army was waiting for them, and the slaughter that ensued was the work of the curiously named Colonel Pilar García. Another group (which like the last was financed by ex-president Prío) disembarked on the Northern coast of Oriente, where they were ambushed and wiped out (only two escaped) by Colonel Fermín Cowley, commander of the Holguín regiment and a criminal psychopath who celebrated Christmas 1956 by distributing 25 corpses throughout the streets of the city.

In September, navy contingents supported by the July 26th Movement mutinied in Cienfuegos and took the city. They couldn't defend it against the army's Third Tactical Squadron and another massacre ensued. Batista had returned to his old ways: not since the days of his colonelcy had he shed so much blood. Attempts at mediation continued, but there seemed to be no peaceful way out of this situation. Batista would not compromise. He felt strong. He was sure that he could finish off all the revolutionaries.

Of course, the government also sustained losses -- important losses. On a day that would prove fatal for him and others, the ferocious General Salas Cañizares burst into the Haitian embassy in Havana with the objective of murdering a group of asylum seekers.

101

One of these men was armed and wounded Salas Cañizares in the lower abdomen before the general's henchmen killed him and all the other rebels under Haiti's protection. Salas Cañizares died amidst atrocious and prolonged suffering. It served that criminal right.

Cowley was luckier; they blew his head off with a sawed-off shotgun in an operation executed with much ability and luck. Later, the new chief of Military Intelligence, Irenaldo García Báez, son of Pilar García (the colonel with the woman's name), practically exterminated the forces of the July 26th Movement in Holguín. Among the dead was Manuel Angulo, my old high school gym teacher. I had always considered him an idiot because he let his students get away with so much, but he faced torture and death with admirable firmness. I pay tribute to his memory and offer these words as belated amends.

Batista cried publicly at Cowley's funeral. It was out of pure sentiment because in truth, he had henchmen to spare. Good henchmen who were merciless, amoral and sometimes even brave: Ventura, Carratalá, Martín Pérez and José Salas Cañizares, the spitting image of his late brother. And let's not forget Rolando Masferrer, another townsman of mine, who fought on the side of the Republic in the Spanish Civil War but later turned gangster in the Forties. Masferrer was ready to fight the putschists on March 10, 1952, but the next day embraced Batista's cause with all the enthusiasm of a new convert. The tyrant allowed Masferrer to dedicate himself to what had always been his vocation: killing. Masferrer was not a soldier or a policeman. He was a senator and editor of his own newspaper, but the vocation of which I spoke held a very strong sway over him.

No doubt about it, the henchmen were plentiful. They had all kinds of advantages to fight the July 26th Movement and what was left of the Directorate. What Batista didn't have, however, were officers, soldiers capable of leading men into combat. He had only one: Colonel Sánchez Mosquera, who attacked Fidel's guerrillas with the obstinate ferocity of a pit bull. But a *fidelista* bullet penetrated his cranium and damaged vital brain matter. The pit bull lived but lost his ferocity and obstinacy. Batista, who had a surplus of murderers, from then on had not a single warrior in his army.

The lengthy task of destroying the effectiveness of the army, initiated by Machado and continued in all aspects by Batista, was by now complete. The army no longer existed. Batista, despite his long military career, was unaware of it; after all, he was only a sergeant stenographer. Fidel did understand the situation. He always understood it. Before him opened the road to power. He still had a long way to go, but the road was free of obstacles.

Meanwhile, under the fierce and relentless pursuit of the not inefficient Batista police, the July 26th Movement continued to hit and hit hard in Havana. Havana was the principal theater of urban combat, not Santiago de Cuba, as official history claims. The men of the July 26th Movement, under the direction of Faustino Pérez, carried out a series of well-conceived and -executed operations, some even spectacular. On the way, they became the main source of financing for the rebel army.

It's not for me to write the history of their daring deeds. That responsibility and honor rests with those who lived for years under constant pressure from repressive forces and at the mercy of chance, and who confronted day after day the possibility and the reality of torture and death. I will cite only three of their successes: the so-called "Night of a Hundred Bombs," which drove the tyranny mad; the abduction of the Argentine Juan Manuel Fangio, the world champion professional race car driver -- a masterful tactical operation that in addition to generating loads of publicity, served to demoralize the enemy; and the blackout of sections of Havana, an operation that involved the excavation of a tunnel from a rented safe house on Suárez Street to the main electrical cables servicing the city just across that street.

Of all the men who have fought dictatorships in the cities of Latin America, I believe that only the Uruguayan Raúl Séndic equalled Faustino Pérez as a clandestine leader. And since I have already alluded to chance -- that terrible and unforeseeable enemy of clandestine fighters -- I want to point out that both Faustino and

103

Séndic were captured by chance. A police officer who knew Faustino happened to run into him on a street; and a detachment of police carrying out a routine house to house search knocked on the door of a residence where the leader of the *Tupamaros* happened to be visiting. I also want to point out how Faustino was freed from prison after undergoing the usual beatings. Judge Enrique Hart, father of two brothers of that name who were active in the Movement, got in touch with the examining magistrate in charge of the case and arranged bail for the revolutionary. The bond was posted immediately, Faustino was released and vanished. Human solidarity with a man in danger, risking livelihood and social position to aid a deserving man, is one of the traditions that has been erased by *fidelismo*. Such traditions saved the lives of many men and women who fought so that Fidel could reach power.

The urban fighters, the "plainsmen" as they were beginning to be called, withstood the hardest and most dangerous part of the fight against the tyranny, confronting the most efficient forces that the tyranny had at its disposal and living in a climate of permanent tension that the guerrillas in the mountains in no way knew. Although subject to material hardships, Fidel's men were spared the constant worry that is an inevitable part of the life of one who may lose his life at any moment, sometimes just by chance.

The harshness of war, or of any confrontation that involves the use of violence is in direct proportion to the degree of danger that the enemy poses, whether he is capable of doing us little or great harm. From this axiom of war, it naturally follows that it is impossible to compare the struggle waged by the rebel army and that waged by the clandestine resistance. To put up with hardships requires only a strong will, but to withstand torture requires strength of character.

How many men died in the mountains as compared to the cities? How many died in Havana alone? I have no answers to those questions. Those who do have the figures, answer if you are able. I can, however, point out some interesting facts. Of "The Twelve" who made it to the Sierra Maestra, only one died in combat: Ciro Redondo, who by the way was active in the Catholic Workers Youth. None was captured. None suffered torture, except Faustino Pérez, and this happened in Havana when he was fighting with the underground. By contrast, of the fourteen members of the July 26th Movement in Havana, four died: Gerardo Abreu ("Fortán), Sergio González ("El Curita"), Enrique Hart, and José Prieto. Another eight were detained and tortured. Aldo Vera miraculously escaped torture, but was imprisoned. Only one escaped unharmed. One in fourteen.

The publicity surrounding the insurrection centered on the guerrillas. Besides Fidel, other names were becoming famous: Raúl Castro, Cienfuegos, Guevara and Juan Almeida. The men of the urban resistance were photographed only when their corpses turned up or they were put on trial.

This was unavoidable: those who fought in the shadows had to shun the limelight. But what was historically unjust (and in the long run politically tragic), was that the struggle waged by the Sierra Maestra guerrillas was promoted as the sole image of the Revolution. That's where the theory of the *guerrilla foco* originated, meaning, of course, the *guerrilla foco* as the heart, brains and very center of the revolutionary struggle. Ernesto Guevara was the principal exponent of this theory.

The growing confrontation between "The Mountains" and "The Plains" is reflected, on a small scale, in an epistolary skirmish between Guevara and René Ramos Latour, who had succeeded Frank País as head of the July 26th Movement in Santiago de Cuba. Ramos Latour sent a shipment of arms to the Sierra Maestra that Guevara pronounced defective. In a letter to the urban leader, Guevara, an Argentine physician but now a *comandante*, complained of the poor quality of the arms with that asperity that Guevara considered one of the most beautiful adornments of his character. In a devastating reply, Ramos Latour told Guevara that in order to send him that defective shipment he first had to disarm men who were in constant danger of death.

These differences, which would become more pronounced with time, were not founded on mere jealousy. They were, to use the political jargon that has been imposed on Cuba in the last three

105

decades, "a manifestation of the ideological struggle." The rebel army was under the complete control of Fidel, who by then had discovered (although he was careful not to say so) that the dictatorship of the proletariat afforded the greatest felicity to those who rule. Guevara shared Fidel's point of view, as did (naturally) Raúl Castro, Ramiro Valdés and Juan Almeida (all of whom, as far as I can tell, have never had an idea of their own in their lives).

In the urban resistance movement, on the contrary, those who favored the restoration of democracy were in the majority. Facing an army that was every day more inept, corrupt and demoralized, the guerrillas began to spread out over the mountainous zones of Oriente. To the northeast of Santiago de Cuba, a second guerrilla front was established under the command of Raúl Castro. A third front commanded by Almeida cropped up in the very Sierra Maestra, just west of the capital of Oriente.

But it wasn't just the rebel army that was creating new guerrilla fronts. At the center of the island, a group of men rose under the command of Eloy Gutiérrez Menoyo, becoming the autonomous Second Escambray National Front. The decimated Directorate, now led by Faure Chaumont, took refuge in the Escambray mountains and was able at least to survive.

In April 1958, the ideological struggle between "The Mountains" and "The Plains" finally came to a head. After a long string of successes, Faustino Pérez and his men met at last with disaster: the general strike that the July 26th Movement had convened in Havana for April 9 was a complete failure.

"April is the cruelest month." I remember that April 1958 because it did indeed prove cruel for our country. Fidel, Guevara and the rebel army used to great advantage the Movement's reverse of fortune. Faustino Pérez couldn't rise to the occasion; his strength lay as a clandestine fighter, not as a politician. He also lacked ambition and independent judgement, qualities that every leader should have. As a result, the Movement of "The Plains" came completely under the control of the men of "The Mountains."

Emblematic of that control was the appointment of Enzo Infante to replace Faustino Pérez. I have a friend who is also friends with Infante and holds him in the highest esteem. I have myself met the gentleman on several occasions and he seemed a decent sort to me. But the fact remains that Enzo Infante was an absolute nobody then, surely no substitute for Faustino Pérez. Why wasn't someone chosen who was at least known in revolutionary circles? Why not, for example, the energetic and capable Manolo Ray, who led the Movement of Civic Resistance (a collateral arm of the July 26th Movement)? Or the respected Haydée Santamaría? Nothing stimulates men's courage more than the presence among them of a courageous woman. Her appointment would have constituted a promising token of that much vaunted but as yet unrealized "equal opportunity" that the Revolution would later promise women. Or if not Ray or Haydée, then why not at least name one of the survivors of the original fourteen, none of whom lacked courage?

Sometime in 1975, a conference was held in the economics department of Havana University to commemorate the fiftieth anniversary of the founding of the Cuban Communist Party. One of the superabundant cretins in attendance asked a panel member, Professor Sergio Aguirre, why Martí had named Tomás Estrada Palma as his replacement in the United States rather than Carlos Baliño, a Key West tobacco cutter who much later would become one of the founders of the party. Aguirre was an old member of the Popular Socialist Party but nonetheless an honest man. After explaining the role that each played in the independence struggle and their respective merits -- Estrada Palma's vast and Baliño's very modest contribution -- he concluded that the appointment of Estrada Palma was both natural and logical in view of his record. "Whereas if Martí had named Baliño, all would have asked themselves, 'why Baliño?', or what's worse, 'who's Baliño?'"

And so I ask myself, why Infante? Or worse, who was Infante? He was named Faustino Pérez's replacement precisely because he was an irrelevant figure, the ideal candidate if you wanted to minimize the July 26th Movement's role in the revolutionary process.

And minimized it was. In the days to come the Revolution would mean only the rebel army. And Fidel was the rebel army.

But that was not the only cruelty that April 1958 showered upon us. In Mexico, certain events transpired that have not been given much importance. Since they happened to be important in my life -- and this is my book -- I shall treat them, for I consider those events if not significant then surely symptomatic. When the yacht *Granma* departed from Tuxpan in November 1956, various members of that expedition were obliged to remain in Mexico for various reasons (imprisonment, illness). Among those left behind were Pedro Miret and Gustavo Arcos, two leaders and founders of the July 26th Movement who were entrusted with the mission of organizing and training a new group of recruits and sending them to Cuba in a reinforcement expedition.

Miret and Arcos set out to work. By April 1958 almost everything was ready. A few recently arrived recruits were still scheduled to receive basic training, but the arms and the ship had already been acquired. These were kept somewhere on the Yucatán peninsula under the custody of a small group of men.

In April, while Arcos was in Caracas, Miret learned that various members of the Movement were planning to fly a small plane from Costa Rica to the Sierra Maestra. Such an action could not be taken without Miret's approval, for he was chief of foreign operations for the Movement, with Arcos as second in command.

Miret decided to go to Costa Rica to impose his authority. Up to that point everything was done correctly. But then Miret assumed direct control of the Costa Rican group -- which included, by the way, Huber Matos -- and flew with them to Cuba, landing at Cienaguilla, a small plain on the foothills of the Sierra Maestra. The plane landed but could not take off again. While this did not affect those who intended to stay, Miret was supposed to return to Mexico.

With Miret in Cuba and Arcos in Caracas, the expeditionary group in Mexico was temporarily without a leader. Jesús Suárez Gayol, Heliodoro Martínez Junco, an American named Jay Silvester who was our military instructor, and the other custodians of the arms and the ship, decided, without consulting God or the devil, to set out for Cuba on their own, leaving behind the rest of their companions.

That is exactly what they did, sailing as far as the coast of Pinar del Río, which is at the opposite end of the island from the Sierra Maestra. Upon landing, they were detected by the army and lost everything except their lives, with which they were able to escape. The long and patient work of more than a year came to naught.

This seemed to me then, seems to me still and will always seem to me even if hailstones should rain on me for saying so, a signal instance of irresponsibility on Miret's part, and of irresponsibility, insubordination and lack of esprit de corps on the part of Suárez Gayol, Martínez Junco and the other adventuresome voyagers. Nonetheless they were not penalized. Fidel, who is always so unforgiving of errors (I mean, of course, errors committed by others), took no disciplinary measures against the architects of this disaster. Miret was named a *comandante* before finally returning to Mexico. Suárez Gayol remained in Cuba, fighting bravely in Las Villas and achieving the rank of captain. Martínez del Junco returned to Mexico a few days after the failed expedition. Some day he would become Minister of Public Health.

Of course, not everything was going wrong for the rebels. With his characteristic sagacity, which was then functioning at full capacity, Fidel understood just how near he was to the end of the struggle. So perhaps Fidel was inclined to forgive the perpetrators of the Mexican fiasco. One who was not forgiven, however, was Gustavo Arcos, who in no way was implicated in that disaster. *El Comandante* has shown an inexplicable hatred toward him. Perhaps I should say it was a hatred that has yet to be explained.

Another who did not rub Fidel the right way was Huber Matos. However, Matos must have been a very good guerrilla. How else do you explain the fact that he became not only one in a heap of *comandantes*, but the chief of a column? There were barely a dozen chiefs of column in the rebel army, including Guevara, Cienfuegos,

109

Almeida and Raúl Castro. In time, Matos would pay dearly for being "the stranger in their midst."

In Mexico, at the other end of that stage on which this April drama was played, were a group of disillusioned men who had been abandoned by their leaders; some of these individuals would later gain notoriety. José Abrahantes, for example, who, like me, saw the end of the struggle without shooting one bullet or placing one bomb, was named a captain on arriving in Cuba in January 1959. He then embarked on a brilliant career in repression, which ended just recently in complete ignominy.

We arrive now at the final stage of the Batista dictatorship, which signals the end of the presence in the public life of our country of that wretch without whose actions our present misfortunes would not have been possible. It was he who led the way to that "blind alley without a glimmer of hope," of which Lezama spoke.

The guerrillas came down from the Sierra Maestra and began to move west; at the end of the road in that direction, lay Havana and power. Some but not all of the rebel army came down from the hills; in fact, very few abandoned their mountain stronghold. Fidel was not among them. Two columns commanded by Ernesto Guevara and Camilo Cienfuegos crossed on foot the plains of Cauto and the flatlands of Camagüey, a total of more than 300 miles, until arriving at Las Villas.

This march has been compared to the Westward Invasion led by Generals Gómez and Maceo during our War of Independence, an absurd and disrespectful analogy that is in keeping with the Communist practice of using our national heroes for propaganda purposes. Gómez and Maceo were facing more than 100,000 enemy troops and had to fight every inch of the way. Yet our *mambises* broke through the box formations of the Spanish -- a feat rarely accomplished in any war.

The enemy that Guevara and Cienfuegos confronted was very different. Batista's army was no army. Perhaps Dr. Guevara recalled his uninterrupted hike through the plains of Cuba as he saw his guerrilla forces in Bolivia battered, encircled and finally annihilated by a battalion of army rangers. There was nothing special about those little Bolivian soldiers; they had been well-trained and -armed, and when their officers led them into battle, they fought. But Batista didn't have at his disposal a single battalion like that.

The trek of the two guerrilla columns was undoubtedly a great feat, but it wasn't a military feat, because that would have required an enemy willing to fight. The 300-mile hike instead was an impressive demonstration of physical resistance and forbearance in the face of material hardships.

Guevara arrived in the Escambray mountains and was received with cordiality by the Directorate and with cold hostility by Gutiérrez Menoyo's men. This was the beginning of the bleak future that awaited Gutiérrez Menoyo. Cienfuegos, for his part, proceeded to northern Las Villas, where a small guerrilla band hastily organized by the Communists operated. At the last moment, the Communists had decided to abandon their opposition to the armed struggle. "It's never too late to enjoy good fortune," says a somewhat incongruous Spanish proverb, which was fulfilled on that occasion. The veteran Stalinists were the last to climb on the bandwagon, but they're still aboard today.

Camilo Cienfuegos should have kept going west, where a guerrilla front organized by *Comandante* Escalona was waiting for him. Escalona commanded a "stationary front," to borrow a meteorological term. No fighting ever happened on that front. Its mission was to prepare a base of operations for when *Comandante* Cienfuegos arrived. But Cienfuegos never came: it wasn't necessary.

In the western mountains, Batista's army continued to demonstrate its absolute incapacity to fight. It was undermined by cowardice and corruption. The rapacious and shameless General Tabernilla, head of the Joint Chiefs of Staff, and his equally rapacious and shameless subordinates, turned the war into a business venture by selling materiel.

One example: Colonel Sosa Blanco, a fearless man when it came to murdering defenseless peasants and burning their thatched huts, but incapable of facing armed and dangerous people. One day

111

the Colonel and his troops arrived at the outbuildings of a sugar refinery, situated some twenty miles from Holguin. The soldiers hurriedly dismounted their trucks, falling over themselves in a mad scramble to get to a nearby park where there was a grove of coconut trees. The desperate soldiers climbed those trees like monkeys and knocked down every coconut, which they opened with their bayonets and devoured as if someone were going to take them away. Meanwhile, the townspeople and other witnesses looked on in astonishment. The frenzied enthusiasm that Colonel Sosa Blanco's troops demonstrated for coconuts had a very simple explanation: they were starving. Their scoundrelly colonel had sold their rations.

Batista's army continued to prepare and launch attacks on rebel positions, but they always had the same result: defeat and desertion. Although these were small fights, sometimes only skirmishes, Radio Rebelde, the guerrilla's clandestine station, referred to every encounter as a "battle." One of these so-called battles (not that it matters, but I don't remember what it was named) was described as "one of the greatest defeats ever sustained by a modern army."

How was it possible that such a propaganda fraud could have gone undetected? We didn't suspect. No one suspected -- even though the magnitude of those lies was self-evident -- because we were all overpowered by hope, which makes men blind. When Pandora opened her blessed box and let loose all those evils, the last to escape was hope. I sometimes think it would have been better if hope had stayed in the box.

The end came. Villages were captured, then towns. Finally, troops led by *Comandante* Guevara with the assistance of Directorate forces under the command of Rolando Cubelas attacked the city of Santa Clara. Batista sent an armor-plated train to reinforce the city. However, the train and its contents served only to rearm the rebels, who had captured it but rather had bought it from the colonel Batista had entrusted with this last-ditch mission. Santa Clara fell to the rebels in late December 1958.

On the morning of January 1, 1959, having fulfilled his historic mission, Batista fled the country. We thought then that all vistas were opening to us. And so it was, but only for the chosen few who have lived like princes since that day.

The fugitive tyrant headed for Santo Domingo. The Americans didn't want him in their country, even though they granted asylum to some of his worst henchmen. Batista made a bad choice: Rafael Léonidas Trujillo, the fiery Dominican despot, had many scores to settle with Batista and availed himself of this opportunity to get even. Trujillo moved him violently from one place to another; terrorized him (which wasn't hard to do); corralled him (which is the best word to use in his case); forced him to clean the toilet of his cell, and, lastly, stripped him of several million of his heart's dollars.

I know that this is of absolutely no historical importance, but I am a vengeful man and I take great satisfaction in narrating the misfortunes of scoundrels. Alas, Batista's travails were not many. Another dictator, Oliveira Salazar of Portugal, granted Batista asylum on the condition that he remain on the Isle of Madeira. There (and later in Estoril and Costa del Sol), Batista spent his final years, enjoying the golden exile of thieving rulers.

But I waited. I expected he would be punished as he deserved, either by Fidel or Providence. Years later, the Sandinistas signed a family pact with the Montoneros that entrusted the Argentine terrorists with the assassination of the deposed dictator Somoza, then living in Uruguay. Fidel attempted no such undertaking against Batista, even though he has managed (or rather others working under his orders have managed) to pull off much more difficult and risky things.

Providence failed me too. I had expected something like the cancer that killed Machado, but it was not to be. Many years after the fall of the tyrant, I was waiting at a stop on Santa María del Mar beach for a bus to take me back to Havana. Meanwhile, I was keeping one eye on a certain diminutive young man whose wild perambulations threatened the public safety. At a certain moment when he tried to cross the street, I took the necessary measures against the

113

subject in question. It was then that I heard, from passers-by on the street, that Fulgencio Batista had died of a stroke, sweetly and quietly, in his luxurious residence in Spain.

"Daddy, I'm a big boy," said my five-year old son Ernesto, enraged at what he considered excessive control over his person. I lowered my gaze and looked sadly at that tiny and mischievous being who meant the world to me. I recalled at that instant that Batista, while in the last years of his millionaire exile, had lost one of his numerous male offspring to leukemia, and I conceived the hope that the wretch loved his children as I love mine. A malignant idea, perhaps, but comforting.

The designs of Providence are inscrutable, as my mother used to say. But not so men's designs. As I scrutinize Fidel's designs, I can't help thinking that the indifference he demonstrated to Batista's fate, the *dolce vita* that he allowed the tyrant to enjoy in his exile, was in large measure due to a conscious or unconscious sense of gratitude.

Fidel has been able to do everything that he has done thanks to the Revolution. This is not my idea; it belongs, as far as I know, to Carlos Alberto Montaner. Without Batista there would have been no Revolution; without the aborting of Cuban democracy on March 10, 1952, there would have been no Fidel Castro. And even with Batista's disruption of the democratic process in Cuba, if only he had not destroyed the professional army and replaced it with a parody of an army after his own image and likeness, cowardly and corrupt like him. Then Fidel's fate would have been very different, as would have that of our country and all its people.

Fidel would then have had to face troops led by career officers of the caliber of a General Martí Zayas Bazán; Colonel Lezama ("according to his instructors at West Point, my father was capable of commanding an 100,000-man army," José Lezama Lima said proudly one day); men like Colonel Martín Helena, Colonel Barquín, or even the same Captain José "Gallego" Fernández who is today Fidel's unconditional follower. Had Fidel had such men as adversaries, he and his guerrillas would have met with the same fate

114

as the Salvadoran rebels, or, worse yet, Ernesto Guevara in Bolivia. I don't think that Gary Prado, the Bolivian captain who commanded the troops that annihilated Guevara's guerrillas, was a military genius; he was only a competent and gutsy officer.

VIII. The Revolution

As it turned out, the calamitous Fulgencio Batista fulfilled his historic mission with excruciating exactness. On January 1, 1959, he was done. Paradoxically, the day that today so many millions of Cubans would like to forget was the happiest in our history. The week that followed, which culminated in Fidel's triumphal entry into Havana, was our happiest week. Apotheosis is a strong word, but what other could I use to describe such an explosion of joy, fervor, enthusiasm and hope? If you know what it is to love, and only if you do, you might be able to imagine a nation where everyone (with a few exceptions that counted for nothing) was in love. Several millions were in love with Fidel himself, and the rest, less inclined perhaps to forming strong personal attachments in the realm of politics, were in love with the Revolution.

"The dream of reason produces monsters," Goya inscribed at the bottom of one of his paintings. In January 1959, reason slept the dream of the just in Cuba, while joy, fervor, enthusiasm and hope filled streets, filled homes, filled everything.

Some, not very many, would soon come to their senses. It would be years, however, before a majority of Cubans would awaken. In many cases, even after regaining consciousness, they continued to nap. Others have refused to awaken and have kept themselves in an artificial trance by resorting to all sorts of soporifics.

116

The monsters began to appear. The first of these nightmares come-to-life may be described, allegorically, as "justice mocked" and "human life cheapened." Batista's henchmen and informants were promptly placed in front of firing squads. There was not a single man among them who did not deserve to be executed. They were, one and all, the dregs of Cuban society. So it's not a question of whether they deserved their fate or not. It is criminal to condition a people to regard violent death as an everyday occurrence. Cubans had no experience of the firing squads, though, granted, one does not have to be blindfolded and stood against a wall to be the victim of a firing squad. Still, these officially sanctioned executions were new to Cuba. They are no longer a novelty. Since 1959, thousands of our countrymen have been sentenced to death and executed by order of the State.

I have no access to Spain's Archives of the Indies, which I very much regret. Is there anyone not so encumbered who, if it's not too much of a bother, could find out how many Cubans were executed by the Spanish government in thirty years of wars and conspiracies in Cuba between 1868 and 1898?

From Karl Marx I learned that quantitative changes in time become qualitative. After certain strictly numerical limits are exceeded, retributive justice becomes barbarism. I don't pretend to make myself out to be a particularly lucid or sensible man. Back then, I did not disapprove of the slaughter of the henchmen. But thirty years have passed. A few weeks ago I was surprised and moved by the execution of General Arnaldo Ochoa. I have no ties to Ochoa except that he was both a countryman and a townsman; we were both born in Holguín, but that, according to the Mexican actor Arturo de Cordova, "is of no importance at all." Fidel, on the other hand, had very important ties to this general, who dedicated more than thirty years of life to his service, and served him well.

Thirty years before Ochoa faced a firing squad, another general did not. It is important to understand why one general was spared and the other was not. In the waning days of the Batista dictatorship, General Eulogio Cantillo, a veteran of the barracks coup that had brought Batista to power in 1952, entered into secret

117

negotiations with the revolutionaries, promising to depose Batista and deliver him up to justice. Cantillo did not comply with the terms of this agreement, and, what is worse, tried to play smart with Fidel and grab power himself -- a very difficult and dangerous thing to do. He failed, as was only natural, but despite all his offenses, received a benign sentence of only ten years. Of course, the difference between these two generals, Cantillo and Ochoa, is obvious: Cantillo was inoffensive, a make-believe general; Ochoa was the real thing.

I have spoken of the mockery of justice. A spectacular example of this was the trial of Rafael Sosa Blanco, the colonel who brought death to so many peasants and drove his own starving troops coconuts by stealing their rations. Sosa Blanco's trial was held in the Sports Colosseum, an indoor stadium with a seating capacity of 13,000 that on the day of the trial was filled to the rafters. And so the trial of a war criminal was transformed into a gigantic farce by a furious and uncontrollable multitude.

"Am I in the Roman circus?" asked Sosa Blanco, who showed more courage before his judges than he had when facing rebel troops. He was right: it was as if that ancient spectacle had suddenly materialized in Cuba.

We never know when death might surprise us, so we might as well laugh in the face of death. To entertain myself, I sometimes imagine ludicrous situations. Right now, I imagine Comandante Sorí Marín, the presiding judge at Sosa Blanco's trial, banging on the bandstand with his gavel, and energetically and imperiously commanding: "Order in the court!"

Another mockery of justice was the trial of a group of Air Force pilots, who had been ordered by Batista to bomb the Sierra Maestra, but evaded that order by dropping dummies. They were tried and absolved by a revolutionary tribunal. As that well-known attorney and doctor of laws, Fidel Castro Ruz, was well aware, men found innocent cannot be tried a second time for the same offense. Still, *El Comandante* ordered a second trial on the same charge. This time, of course, the pilots were found guilty.

118

The law -- the basic principles of law -- what did they matter then? Who could bother with such things amid so much happiness and hope? Sage words did the Spanish master inscribe on his painting. While reason slept in our country, monsters did indeed appear, one after the other, destroying everything in their wake.

After the Rule of Law had been abolished, next to fall was that other fundamental liberty, freedom of the press. The government decreed that all articles critical of it should carry disclaimers stating that other employees of the newspaper did not agree with those opinions or rebuttals where any employee could assail the truthfulness of the facts contained in the article as well as the journalistic ethics of the reporter or editorial writer. That is how it all started. Today, if Cubans want a little information about what's happening in the world -- particularly the kind of information that lacks "truthfulness" and "journalistic ethics" -- the only thing for us to do is to listen to the "happy and friendly sounds" of the Voice of America's Radio Martí. On second thought, I can discard the quotation marks, because they really do live up to their own claims: Radio Martí is really happy and friendly.

The old laws were the first to go, but soon even the new laws -- that is, the first laws dictated by the Revolution -- also fell into oblivion. One example is the Agrarian Reform Law that everyone agreed was absolutely necessary. As originally conceived, the Law provided for the expropriation of all farms of one thousand acres or more and all cattle ranches that exceeded 1500 acres (thirty and fifty *caballerias* respectively, in Cuba's arcane system of measurements). The letter of the law never was applied. Confiscation merely became another means of persecution. I am personally acquainted with and can attest to such a case. Rafael Cruz Rubio, a friend of my family and a distant relative, had his farm near Holguín confiscated even though *La Nena* (we Cubans name, or used to name, our farms) was scarcely 300 acres. With such thunderclaps no landowner slept soundly in Cuba. It was not long before some farmers began to conspire, and that suited Fidel's purposes just fine. He ended up by confiscating all farms over 150 acres.

119

The Tiger and the Children

Late in 1959, I met up with Rafael Alberti, not the Andalucian poet of that name but my friend "Felo," the grandson of the owner of *La Nena* who complained bitterly about the injustice done his grandfather. I refused to acknowledge that he was right. "Everything was well, all would be justified or put right," I assured him. I myself was then submersed in that deep sleep of reason.

Cuba today is a country dominated by boredom and desperation. Only government officials, in their fairy-tale world of material comforts and foreign trips, can be happy. Those who have no ambitions in life, who live just because their mothers put them into this world and their time has not yet come to leave it, may be as happy here as anywhere else. But the rest of us who are not government officials or idiots know no happiness in our own country, only boredom and desperation.

Life was very different during those joyous first days of the Revolution; then it was impossible to be bored. Something was always happening and whatever happened was OK with us. We all applauded when President Manuel Urrutia was forced out by Fidel, who had appointed him. Urrutia had gained a certain notoriety when, as a judge on the appellate court of Santiago de Cuba, he had cast the only vote to acquit the captured *Granma* expeditionaries. Urrutia was not content solely with the title of president. He didn't exactly expect to govern but he at least wanted to participate in government. *El Comandante*, who was then prime minister, lost all patience with this ingrate. Fidel appeared on television to announce his own resignation. The people took to the streets to demand Urrutia's resignation instead, even as Fidel spoke and spoke and spoke (he preserves still that awesome staying power that makes me fear we may have Fidel for many years to come). This wave of popular repudiation caused Judge Urrutia to seek refuge in a foreign embassy.

To replace Urrutia, Fidel appointed Osvaldo Dorticós as president. Dorticós was a competent provincial lawyer with an oddly-shaped head but without any other attributes to attract public attention. Nonetheless, he turned out to be a practical man who knew his place and made the best of it. Slowly the president climbed the ladder of power until he occupied a relevant position, much higher than revolutionaries who had both celebrity and a past, qualifications that he lacked.

Dorticós holds several interesting records in our history. He both occupied the presidency for the longest period (twenty years) and governed for the shortest time (not a single minute). He shares that last record with presidents Barnet and Laredo Bru (both Batista puppets). Having lost much of his standing (and his title) and seemingly ill, Dorticós ended up committing suicide. Fidel has never forgiven him for it, but of what damn use is forgiveness to a dead man?

What happened to Urrutia was a tragicomedy, but what befell Huber Matos was a drama. One day in October 1959, the unruly *Comandante* Matos resigned as military governor of Camagüey; he was joined in that resignation by his entire general staff. As for motives, Matos said in a letter to Fidel that he believed the country was heading toward communism, and that he, Matos, was not in agreement with that course. Matos sat and waited for his replacement. But Camilo Cienfuegos had not come to relieve him, but to arrest him and all his subordinates. Matos was declared a traitor, tried and condemned to twenty years imprisonment, every day of which he served.

What was his treason? He repeated imperialist lies about Cuba's march toward Communism. "I am not a Communist. My political ideology is very clear," Fidel declared to *Bohemia* in January 1959. His political doctrine, he said time and again, was something called "humanism." He was still repeating it in October, when Matos was arrested, although he would not take much longer to baptize our Revolution as socialist. Somewhat later he would pronounce himself a Marxist-Leninist and announce the unshakable determination of the Cuban people to construct Communism in their country. No one seemed to remember that *Comandante* Matos had been arrested and was still in prison because he said Cuba was heading in precisely the direction where it in fact was heading. Reason continued its placid slumber. Well, let's be honest: many Cubans had already awakened

121

to the truth, but many more had not (including your obedient servant).

A few days after Matos' arrest, *Comandante* Camilo Cienfuegos disappeared while flying to Havana in a small plane. This gave rise to the legend that Fidel ordered his death. As far as I am concerned, I have had enough with the myths and legends of *fidelismo*, which I am forced to listen to daily. As was the case with Ochoa thirty years later, the popularity of Huber Matos among his troops and the influence that he exercised over his officers proved menacing to Fidel and led to Matos' ouster. Camilo Cienfuegos commanded the same loyalty from his soldiers and staff, and was, moreover, extraordinarily popular with the people. The popularity of others doesn't worry Fidel so much as whether such individuals are capable of having ideas of their own or adopting dissident positions that might challenge his leadership. In his short public life, Camilo Cienfuegos never demonstrated such propensities.

The iniquity of Matos' sentence had no important effects on the national consciousness. Today, in hindsight, it seems to me palpable proof that Fidel was something completely different, absolutely aberrant and without precedent in our republican history. Neither Huber Matos nor anybody else guessed -- or could have guessed -- that a man who was sentenced to fifteen years imprisonment for the bloody attack on the Moncada barracks and pardoned by the tyrant Batista (his enemy) just twenty-two months into his sentence, would be capable of condemning Matos, a not so cordial comrade-in-arms but a comrade-in-arms nonetheless, to twenty years imprisonment, leaving him to serve the full term without pardoning him.

All who have stood up to Fidel using the same methods and strategies that proved effective in combatting Machado and Batista, have paid with their lives or with long years of incarceration for their inability to predict him. Only a soothsayer would have been able to divine then that this man who had burst on our national life was unlike any other politician we had known or suffered; someone who knew no limits, implacable and immovable.

Stalin was. . . . Well, we all know what Stalin was. We have been able in recent years to read all about his crimes in *Moscow News* and *Sputnik*. But the cold-hearted Georgian had many predecessors, historical progenitors, men very like him in character who ruled the Russians by similar means.

Ivan *Grozni*, the celebrated Ivan the Terrible -- what was he if not a sixteenth century version of Stalin? Stalin was terrible to the Russians, the Byelorussians, the Ukrainians, and the other peoples that now make-up the Soviet Union, but these peoples had known rulers as ruthless. Stalin might have been the worst of all, more terrible than Ivan the Terrible, but he was by no means something new, unexpected or different.

And so, I ask myself: "Where the hell did Fidel come from?" We Cubans were taken by surprise, caught unaware. Inert: that was the word I was looking for. Fidel and his revolution -- because it is *his* revolution and nobody else's -- burst on the life of our country like a tiger on a kindergarten. The women in charge of looking after these children of one or two, could shout in horror or attempt to run. But children who have never seen a tiger do not know what a tiger is. And tigers, it cannot be denied, are very attractive animals.

From a very young age, Fidel dreamed of ruling his country. He didn't realize, however, that a country, unlike a revolution, has many owners, millions of owners, or at least it should. I have no objection to his dream, but every person should have a right to the same dream. It is not his aspiration to govern that I find infamous, but the nature of the government that he envisioned in his dream and brought forth into reality. What Fidel wanted, and what he has in fact achieved, is absolute power, without limits or responsibilities, the kind of power that only Marxism offers.

According to Marx and his disciples and followers, the principal means of production should belong to the State. "Principal" is a rather vague word; consequently, Marxists in power include among the principal means of production anything that suits their governmental interests. Marxist Socialism, as it exists to this day, is more than just a means of organizing an economy. It is a system for the domination of some men by other men. A centralized economy under state control leads inevitably to despotism. If, as Marx maintained, the economy is all-important and decisive in the final synthesis, then, it follows, that absolute control over the economy must lead to absolute control over every other aspect of life in the country.

Fidel demonstrated extraordinary sagacity in recognizing that the Cuban army, or, rather, Batista's army, was both in the short and long term, useless for war. He understood also that Marxism was made to measure for him, that it alone could contain his ambition for absolute power. And, lastly, Fidel understood that the United States, a giant full of contradictions, would not attempt anything really serious against him until it had exhausted its ample arsenal of intimidations. That would afford him the margin of time he required to consolidate his power. Conversely, American presidents have never seemed able to understand that it is impossible to intimidate a man who is at least brave in his own defense and who, obsessed with a desire to rule, would do anything when his power is at stake.

Marxism was Fidel's weapon, and the United States confined itself for a while to threats. Having set out from that original premise, Fidel plunged into a frenzy of confiscation. In less than two years, he placed the economy of the nation in his hands. Standing in the wings was the Soviet Union: what is not to the Americans' advantage will, in all likelihood, benefit the Soviets. Fidel played his cards and he played them well.

Luck was also on his side; he has always been lucky, at least until just recently. In fairness, however, Fidel has always known how to make the best of the cards dealt him. First, fortune favored him with the death of dangerous or potentially dangerous rivals: Frank País and José Antonio Echeverria, above all, but, also the hard and taciturn Fructuoso Rodriguéz; Rene Ramos Latour, a brave man with opinions of his own; and José Westbrook, a great talent in the making, as everybody that knew him says. At nineteen, Westbrook could already see through the secret designs of complex personalities.

El Comandante met him in Mexico and did not appear in the least taken with this adolescent with an Anglo-Saxon surname.

In November 1960, it was not the Grim Reaper that came to Fidel's aid, but the American voters, who elected John F. Kennedy to the presidency of the United States over Richard Nixon, a man infinitely his superior in all respects except physical appearance.

I have mentioned already my aversion to American liberals. The man who contributed the most to fomenting this animus in me was John F. Kennedy, and the basis of his contribution consists of the Bay of Pigs, the Kennedy-Khrushchev pact and the Vietnam war.

The Eisenhower administration at first expressed concern, then irritation about Fidel. Later, it threatened to apply and did in fact apply economic pressures. Finally, however, it learned that its concerns, irritations, threats and pressures didn't affect in the least Fidel's spirit. There was a precedent: Guiteras. The isolated and harassed Guiteras government had not allowed itself to be intimidated, either. But I doubt anybody in Washington remembered Guiteras, though he was a man well worth remembering. Fidel, for his part, did not feel either isolated or harassed, because the Soviet Union was at his side. At the helm of that nation was Nikita Khrushchev, a man who seemed crazy about Fidel, and who possibly was -- crazy, that is.

Eisenhower ordered plans to be drawn up for an invasion of Cuba. The plan called for arming the then-tiny Cuban opposition, flinging the exiles on a beachhead in Cuba, and installing a docile government there that would immediately solicit American assistance. The operation was to be carried out by Nixon, because the General was then in the waning days of his second term. But Nixon wouldn't become president, at least not then. Kennedy, the elegant Kennedy, defeated him by a hairbreadth.

The men and women who voted for Kennedy couldn't have imagined that they were also voting for Fidel. The new president didn't approve in the least of plans for an invasion. He regarded it as a clear and flagrant act of imperialism, and he, Kennedy, was no imperialist.

This is not to say that the plan should be scrapped. It was not even remotely, a model of military and political logic. The men who were to replace the then universally beloved Fidel lacked popular roots. The most well-known participant, Aureliano Sánchez Arango, proved too quarrelsome for the demanding organizers of the plan and was cast aside. The military command of the Brigade was entrusted at first to Colonel Martín Helena, the same who had opposed Batista's coup of 1952. But when the well-known colonel resigned, for whatever reasons, he was replaced by two lieutenants who had remained until the last moment loyal to Batista. Lieutenants Pérez San Román and Oliva were not and had never been henchmen or assassins, but they had been officers of a recent tyranny that was repudiated by all. And they were lieutenants, just lieutenants. Martín Helena was a colonel.

Pérez San Román and Oliva weren't henchmen or assassins, but there were henchmen and assassins in the Brigade 2506. Three, exactly three. What could they possibly have contributed to a force of 1500 men but disrepute? On the other hand, the three were grist for the mill of *fidelista* propaganda, especially one named Calviño, an incredibly sinister-looking character who reminded me of Nietzsche -- not on account of any philosophical bent, but because he seemed the embodiment of Nietzsche's "blond beast." In truth, there are American officials who are renowned for their intelligence and paid good money for it. Nevertheless, they don't even know where their noses are.

It's true the plan wasn't worth much. It was not its conceptual defects that bothered Kennedy but its frankly interventionist character, which kept the president awake at nights (although his insomnia wasn't enough for him to veto the invasion). He didn't know what to do with those 1500 trained Cubans, armed and ready for combat, and since he didn't know what to do with them, he sent them into battle.

One of the fundamental premises of the operation was the preemptive destruction of Fidel's tiny air force before it got off the ground. This would enable the invasion forces' B26s to fly the Cuban skies unmolested. Otherwise the slowness and unmaneuverability of these obsolete aircraft would turn them into flying coffins. Fidel's aerial bases were bombed; some planes were destroyed, but not all. A few Sea Fury helix fighter planes and one or two T-33 combat jet planes were saved. They were enough.

Brigade 2506, equipped with a few Sherman tanks, 50-caliber machine guns and 20mm anti-aircraft guns, was routed by horde after horde of thousands of resolute *milicianos*, who eventually obtained an 8:1 numerical superiority. The brigade was pounded by *fidelista* artillery, which had guns of up to 100mm and one first-class artilleryman, José "El Gallego" Fernandez. It was assailed by the *fidelista* air force -- while it had at its disposal only a few old fighter planes, it was no less awesome when viewed from the ground, shooting down, one by one, the Brigade's even older and slower B-26s. By the way, one of the pilots who contributed so much to Fidel's victory, would, in the fullness of time, embitter *El Comandante*'s old age. The name of that pilot was Rafael del Pino. (That was also the name, incidentally, of a man who spent eighteen years in prison for illegally entering Cuban territory with objectives he was not able to realize. Turned into a human wreck by the wounds he received when he was captured, that del Pino committed suicide. According to Fidel, it was because he lacked the character to serve his full sentence).

Only one thing could have saved the Brigade 2506: U.S. air support. But John F. Kennedy wasn't about to do such a thing. He didn't want any American to take part in an action planned by the CIA and ordered by him because such participation would constitute a flagrant imperialist intervention. Eisenhower had armed and trained the Brigade 2506 and Kennedy had sent it into combat, but the presence and participation of U.S. airmen in U.S. airplanes on U.S. aircraft carriers was something that Kennedy could not have ordered without violating his principle of non-intervention in the internal affairs of other countries. Kennedy's hypocrisy, his incredible pharisaical hypocrisy, is what drives me crazy. In the end, the hapless Bay of Pigs invaders were left to face defeat and ridicule alone.

127

That was Kennedy's doing. The same committed non-interventionist sent 16,000 American troops to Vietnam and started the most absurd and catastrophic war of modern times before an assassin's bullet pierced the back of his cranium -- not his heart -- and ended his life.

Vietnam? Where the hell is that? Is there any American who hasn't at least heard about Cuba or who doesn't know that it lies 90 miles off Florida? Even the dumbest among them could point to it on a map. Kennedy couldn't be persuaded to dispatch a few aviators to the near, familiar, and important Cuba. He did, however, send thousands of American soldiers to the remote, unknown and in no way important Vietnam. Fifty-five thousand Americans died there until Nixon, who lost the 1960 election by a hairsbreadth, put an end in 1973 to that calamitous war.

Well, let's return now to the Bay of Pigs fiasco, or as it is also known, the victory of Playa Girón. Recently, the former lieutenants Erneido Oliva, a veteran of the defeated Brigade 2506, and Rafael del Pino, a veteran of the victorious *fidelista* air force -- the one now a general in the U.S. army and the other until recently a general in Cuba -- met and embraced each other in reconciliation. This was very commendable. The past is past. Enough of hatreds. How beautiful if someday these two generals could embrace a third, perhaps General Leopoldo Cintras, who was for a time the Cuban commander in Angola and is still loyal to Fidel. Beautiful, but not very likely.

Fidel was victorious at Playa Girón. He would triumph, also, over another internal insurgency, though this victory would not be achieved so quickly. It would occupy him not for seventy-two hours but for seven years: I speak, of course, of the struggle against the guerrillas in the Escambray mountains.

They were guerrillas in every sense of the word, but they were never called guerrillas. Now men who rose against the government and took refuge in the mountains were called "bandits." The first took arms in late 1960. By 1962, Fidel ordered the Escambray to be "decontaminated," and since Fidel's orders are always obeyed and never questioned, the Escambray was "decontaminated." Except that something apparently went wrong, because the last of these "bandits" weren't killed or captured until 1967.

They were called the "Escambray bandits," but there were men-in-arms in many different places and provinces, though the principal force of this movement remained always in the Escambray. There the first rebels rose, and there the last fell.

I know little about these men, and what little I know, comes from official propaganda. In movies, television and literature, the *fidelistas* have invariably presented them as clumsy, cruel, rapacious and bloodthirsty. They are accused of making war relentlessly on peasants, stealing their crops, raping their wives and daughters, and murdering anyone who stood up to their violence. They are also accused of murdering young teachers and "alphabetizers" (those sent to the countryside to teach the peasants to read).

Undoubtedly, murders of alphabetizers did in fact occur. It seems probable that the Escambray guerrillas may have confused the alphabetizers for soldiers, since they also sometimes wore uniforms. In any case, there is no excuse for these crimes, and whoever is responsible for them did grievous injury to the cause of the insurgents. Years later, other enemies of Fidel who were not precisely mountain hicks, placed a bomb in a Cubana airlines plane, which exploded while in flight near Barbados. There are means that vilify even the best ends, and these are good examples. It doesn't matter that the *fidelista* press lavishly praises Muammar Qaddafi, who has financed similar terrorist acts. The *fidelistas* have a very peculiar ethic whereby an act is reprehensible if it is committed by an enemy, but meritorious or at least excusable if the work of a friend. As for Qaddafi, he is just a Bedouin. If American and British companies had not discovered oil in the sands of his country, he probably would be robbing desert caravans and pulling lice from his hair. We Cubans, whether we be physicians or peasants, belong to a civilized people. We can't kill teachers, even if they teach Marxism, or blow-up

129

airplanes in midair, even if they are filled with Communists. All is permissible in love and war, except crime.

I have made my feelings clear regarding the killing of teachers, but I have not said all there is to say about the Escambray. There are gaps and inexplicable particulars in the official history. The struggle lasted seven years; seven years is a long time to hold out against the hostility or even indifference of the local peasantry; ask Guevara and his guerrillas, who barely lasted months in Bolivia. One of the leaders of these so-called "bandits" spent four years in arms against the government before being captured thanks to the cunning of an able infiltrator. Some died or were captured, but others soon took their place. At one time, the government deployed a force of fifty thousand men in the Escambray -- about twelve men per square mile. Such a concentration of troops had not been hurled against insurgents in our country since Maximo Gómez faced the full wrath of Spain during our War of Independence. It is well to remember also that the combined forces of the army, navy and national police under the Batista regime amounted to 45 thousand men. And coming at this argument from another direction, we must not forget the strange customs of the peasants that lived in the Escambray, who fed their tormentors and misled the soldiers and *milicianos* that were pursuing them. To cure them of this madness, many of them were stripped of their lands and sent to faraway places like Sandino City, at the extreme western end of the island.

I repeat that all the information at my disposal comes from films, television serials and books written with the cooperation and under the supervision of the Interior Ministry. *All is Secret Until the Day Comes* is the title of one of the books I have used. Let us hope the title is prophetic.

Fidel's anti-guerrilla fighters were elevated to the category of heroes. I remember one in particular, Gustavo Escandon (a beautiful name), dubbed the "Steed of Mayaguara," who was the subject of many very readable books. I hope someday everything will be revealed about the Escambray so that we might learn the real character of the men Escandon faced; men with names sometimes as euphonic as his own: Tomás San Gil, Edel Montiel, Blas Tardío and Julio Emilio Carretero.

While the government was cracking down on the Escambray guerrillas, where were the July 26th Movement and the Revolutionary Directorate, which had done so much to overthrow Batista? They had begun to melt away and vanish. According to Guevara's theories, the *guerrilla foco* is what's fundamental; everything else, even the terrible struggle in the cities, is mere support.

These organizations, decimated by repression, dwindled down to nothing. Meanwhile, the old Communists' Popular Socialist party (PSP), intact, disciplined and ready for any shady deal, continued its unceasing advance. The PSP was intact because its participation in the insurrectional struggle against Batista had been small and wretched. First, it had harshly condemned the assault on the Moncada barracks; then it had opposed the armed struggle advocating instead something called "the struggle of the masses." Moreover, this armed struggle had as its object Batista, who the PSP had praised so lavishly only a decade earlier. Batista was no longer their ally, but he was still the same old Batista, the same murderer and thief of old.

The leaders of the PSP were also the same men: Blas Roca, Lazáro Peña, Joaquín Ordoqui, Juan Marinello, Carlos Rafael Rodríguez. Rodriguéz was sent by the PSP to the Sierra Maestra in the final months of the insurrection. There he fired not a single shot, but grew a little beard which, the truth be told, suited him rather well.

Aníbal Escalante, another of the old time Stalinists of the PSP, was to become the black sheep of the red flock. In late 1961, the powers that be decided to merge the July 26th Movement and the Revolutionary Directorate with the PSP to form a unitary group called the Integrated Revolutionary Organizations (IRO). This was to be the embryo of the future one-and-only Cuban Communist Party. Anibal Escalante was named Organizing Secretary of the IRO.

I myself was appointed secretary of the IRO chapter at the company where I then worked. In our workplace and everywhere else, an activist from the PSP -- in our case, a woman -- designated those tapped to leadership positions. I was chosen secretary because I belonged to the July 26th Movement even though, like General José Abrahantes, my comrade in the ill-fated Miret-Arcos expedition, I had never fired a shot or placed a bomb in my life. I was chosen because I was a *miliciano* (militiaman) in a combat battalion; because my knowledge of Marxism was then rather extensive; because I was a youth of some culture and well-behaved and personable when I was in good humor, (which wasn't always the case); and above all, because they said so.

One night, all the secretaries and organizers of the IRO were summoned to the Payret theater to listen to Fidel give a speech. I was seated in the second row. When the curtain was lifted, there seated at the presidential table among a dozen government officials, was *Comandante* Guevara, conspicuous on account of his serene countenance, and *Comandante* Escalona, conspicuous on account of his big ears.

El Comandante then made his entrance and the whole auditorium went crazy. Everyone, bigwigs and small, got on their feet and started to applaud. We applauded and applauded. Suddenly, some began to clap in unison, and soon we were all clapping in unison. Filled with good will and the spirit of cooperation, I also was applauding in time, but after a minute or so of this I began to feel like an idiot. This sentiment was not shared by my fellow secretaries, who seemed to be having a grand time. After two minutes, I just couldn't take it anymore. I started an improvised search for something I had lost or forgotten; I fumbled in one pant's pocket and then the other, those in front as well as back, but the clapping continued inextinguishable and implacable. I appealed to my fertile imagination and decided to search the floor for what I had supposedly lost. I got down on all fours between the theater rows and searched feverishly, but those damned bastards didn't know when to stop. What the hell, I thought. Seized by an uncontrollable rage, I got on my feet and crossed my arms on my chest, but not without feeling some apprehension about my political future. Fortunately, no one seemed to notice my heresy. All were enchanted. Finally, after I had lost all notion of time, the torrential clapping ceased and I fell exhausted into my seat.

The IRO, with its interminable and absurd meetings, was wrecking my life when Fidel came to my rescue. It turned out that Anibal Escalante, Stalin's disciple, wanted to follow in the footsteps of his guide and mentor, that astute and implacable Caucasian whom our black bard, Nicolás Guillén, placed under the protection of the African gods in one of his poetic effusions. As Lenin's health declined, Stalin devoted all his energies to co-opting the Bolshevik party apparatus while Trotsky was either indifferent to it or underestimated its importance. The brilliant intellectual didn't know that culture means nothing when one isn't shrewd.

I don't know what Fidel thinks of these matters. It is clear to me, however, that there is no such thing as a small enemy as far as Fidel is concerned. This, by the way, worries me to no end. Suspecting that Anibal was about to do to him what Stalin did to Trotsky, Fidel again appeared before his beloved television cameras; he fulminated against the ambitious Anibal, disbanded the IRO and restored my peace of mind. I know he didn't do it as a favor to me, but in any case I am grateful to him.

Not long afterward, *El Comandante* was almost at the point of giving us all peace and quiet, but of a very different kind: the peace and quiet of the grave.

IX. The Crisis of October

By late 1962, the IRO had suddenly disappeared and the troubles in the Escambray continued. Nothing seemed to matter anymore. That was the least that could be expected given the circumstances, for early in October President Kennedy condemned the installation in Cuba of medium and long-range Soviet missiles armed with nuclear warheads. He demanded that they be removed immediately and ordered a naval blockade of the island until the Soviets complied.

The propaganda war began. The leftists and so-called progressives took the field to combat this new imperialist lie. Others, on the other hand, believed Kennedy's affirmations. The arrogant and resentful General Charles de Gaulle, who felt he had been mistreated by the Americans during World War II, refused to look at the evidence presented to him by the American ambassador; it wasn't necessary, he said, to see the evidence to know that Kennedy was telling the truth and he supported him without reservations.

Leftists and imperialists agree on one thing: the world has never come closer to a nuclear war. Unfortunately for the leftists, the science of high-altitude aerial photography had advanced surprisingly, and the photographs taken over Cuba by U-2 recognizance flights, clearly demonstrated who was telling the truth and who was not.

Negotiations commenced between the two superpowers. Naturally, Cuba was not included in these negotiations. Cuba was only

134

a pawn in that deadly chess game. In chess, as we know, it is the queen, the rooks, the bishops -- that is, all the long-range pieces -- that decide the contest. The pawns participate, but are almost always sacrificed and never play a decisive role in the game. Neither do knights. In Spanish, knights are called *caballos* (horses). Fidel is also nicknamed *el caballo*. In this game of chess, "el caballo" was little better than a pawn himself.

[margin handwriting: Castro just a pawn]

Fidel, who was beginning to get a bit mad, ordered the shooting down of one of those U-2 planes that had shown him up. Nevertheless, the negotiations continued without him. Nikita Khrushchev, the stubborn and uncouth Ukrainian who made history at the United Nations with his shoe, proved a more capable and astute politician than the Boston golden boy. He agreed to withdraw the missiles in exchange for a pledge from the United States to abstain from attacking Cuba.

[margin handwriting: Withdrawl]

Like more than ninety percent of Cubans who reside on this island, I am very badly informed. I don't know, among other things, the exact terms of that pact. I don't even know if it was a secret protocol or a gentlemen's agreement, or whether Kennedy swore on a Bible or by the Druid deities of his Celtic ancestors. What I do know is that the Soviets won. They lost nothing that they had any reason to expect would be theirs permanently or for very long, and gained immunity for their weak ally. It's true that withdrawing under pressure is never elegant, but the Soviets are professionals, not swaggerers. It is possible that the Soviets don't even know what a swaggerer is, since this is a typical product of the underdeveloped Third World.

That the Soviets won is my opinion. It also must have been Khrushchev's, but it was not Fidel's. The superpowers had excluded him from their deliberations, and without even consulting him had agreed to remove Soviet missiles from Cuban territory. This constituted an offense toward Cuba, which is the same as saying an offense against Fidel.

[margin handwriting: Fidel was offended]

The tantrum that ensued was huge even by Fidel's standards. The Soviets sent one of their top men, Anastas Mikoyan, to Cuba,

135

but it was impossible to placate Fidel. Mikoyan wasted a trip, his time, and even missed his wife's funeral. A period of anti-Sovietism was beginning that would last six years in Cuba.

Having discussed the reasons for Fidel's tantrum, I will now detail the reasons for mine. I know that I am an unimportant man, an ordinary citizen, but I assert my right to protest and be angry. I asked myself then and I ask myself now: by what right did Fidel presume to turn our country into the primary target of a nuclear war? By what right did he involve our country in a contest of superpowers? What authority did he have to place the lives of all the inhabitants of our island in danger? Who conferred on him that authority?

The University battalion to which I belonged was stationed somewhere between Caimito and Guanajay on the outskirts of Havana. We had been there no more than a few days before we all understood from the constant comings and goings of uniformed Soviet personnel that the other side of the low and steep hills by which we were encamped --very near our position -- there was an important military installation. Years later, in a book by Robert Kennedy on the crisis, I saw a map that showed the locations of each and every missile base in Cuba. There, precisely between Caimito and Guanajay, and on the other side of those rocky heights, was located the only emplacement of Soviet long-range missiles capable of reaching any point in the continental United States. That was the first site that the Americans would have struck if war had broken out. And I was there, but a few hundred feet away!

Perplexed, I asked myself, what could Fidel Castro, or his brother, Raúl, Minister of the Armed Forces, have been thinking about when they placed a battalion composed of college students at the point of maximum danger, condemning us all to extermination in case of a nuclear attack?

I don't know if we were the best students of Havana University, but we were certainly the most resolute in our determination to defend the Revolution with our very lives. We also were future doctors, architects, biologists, engineers, and intellectuals -- in sum, the future of our country, a strategic reserve for its development or

136

reconstruction. Why, then, condemn us all to certain death in case of a nuclear attack? The answer is very simple: if there was a war, there would be no future for our country. The Castro brothers knew it. And Ernesto Guevara also knew it.

In his farewell letter to Fidel, *Comandante* Guevara asserts that never has a statesman reached such brilliant heights as Fidel during the Missile Crisis. It worries me to have to disagree completely about something with so celebrated and venerated a man. I think that on the contrary, Fidel behaved then so irresponsibly that his conduct can only be described as criminal.

I at last awoke to the truth. But the Revolution had been and remained for me a dream so beautiful that I just couldn't renounce it. I have always found it difficult to renounce my dreams, precisely because of the beauty with which my imagination endows them. But I never forgot what I learned then: for Fidel, Cubans are a herd that he can send to slaughter any time he desires.

The Missile Crisis was over, and so was our honeymoon with the Soviet Union. Fidel decided then, or perhaps he had already decided, that Cuba should become a beacon of liberation to all the peoples of the world oppressed by imperialism. And so began the great epoch of guerrilla warfare: guerrillas in Guatemala, guerrillas in Nicaragua, guerrillas in Venezuela, guerrillas in Colombia (although it wasn't necessary to foster guerrillas in that country, since they had been part of the national life for one and a half centuries), guerrillas in Peru, guerrillas in Argentina, guerrillas in Brazil, and guerrillas in Bolivia and in the Congo.

[handwritten margin notes: Honey moon w/ USSR over; After October missile Crisis relations bt Soviet Union + Cuba deteriorated.]

137

X. Trials

Venezuela was Fidel Castro's top-priority target of opportunity. There died Antonio Briones, one of my companions in adversity in Mexico, though I can't say that we had much else in common. Briones did not see combat because he died in the landing, but Arnaldo Ochoa did participate in the fighting. Ochoa was then a young officer and a veteran of Camilo Cienfuegos' march through the plains. I have heard several interesting anecdotes about Ochoa's escapades in Venezuela, but I think it best not to relate them lest I be charged with spreading false reports. Fidel and Raúl Castro, who know precisely what happened there, may tell what they know someday, if they think it convenient.

The guerrillas fought not only Yankee imperialism, but also Soviet hegemony over the worldwide Communist movement. This resulted in misunderstandings, disagreements, ruptures and excommunications. The political leaders of the Latin American Marxist parties, besides having been programmed to accept as the absolute truth only such plans as originated in Moscow, suffered also from an absolute incapacity to practice violence or to confront the consequences of a Communist-led guerrilla movement in their own countries. Fidel openly repudiated these Communist politicians and hurled at them this war cry: "It is the duty of every revolutionary to make revolution." That is to say, it is his duty to fight. But that was too much to ask of them.

As might be expected, this wave of repudiation eventually reached Cuba's pre-revolutionary Communists. Lázaro Pena was relieved of his duties as Secretary General of the Cuban Federation of Workers, Juan Marinello was forced to retire as rector of Havana University, and Blas Roca was relegated to writing a new Constitution and told not to be in any hurry about finishing it. Carlos Rafael Rodriguéz was removed as Minister of Agriculture, and appointed Minister of Government, that is to say, a minister without portfolio, the same post that he had held in Batista's cabinet in the early Forties. This Fidel is the devil's own!

Nonetheless, *El Comandante* got the old Communists out of a very tight spot when the Revolutionary Directorate, or what remained of that organization, went on the attack in 1964. The Directorate, then led by Faure Chaumont, had been able, after much laborious investigation, to uncover the identity of the informer who betrayed the whereabouts of Fructuoso Rodriguéz, José Westbrook and other members of the Directorate murdered by Colonel Ventura in an apartment on Humboldt Street. The informer was Marcos Rodriguéz, who worked for the Our Times Cultural Society, an adjunct of the PSP. Marcos Rodríguez was a friend and protégé of two influential old Communists, Joaquín Ordoqui and his wife Edith García Buchaca. Marcos Rodríguez's connections served as the basis for the implicit accusation that the PSP had knowingly shielded an informer.

But Fidel intervened and the old party emerged unharmed from the incident. Marcos Rodríguez was sentenced to death, however. But to assuage the old Communists, Jorge Valls, their chief accuser, was also punished.

Ironically, Valls had something in common with the old Communists. He also abhorred violence, but unlike the Communists, he did not predicate it. "Violence is the locomotive of history," Marx said. Or did he say, "midwife?" Well, I don't remember and I really don't care. Whatever the metaphor, the fact is that Marxists have always predicated violence, though many of them (including Marx) have refused to practice what they preached. They have always predicated violence, until the Soviets of all people, in our own day, abandoned Marx's teachings on class struggle.

Jorge Valls neither preached nor practiced violence. He was, however, capable of standing up to it. He proved it when, as a witness at Marcos Rodríguez's trial, Valls testified that he believed the PSP had used the defendant's friendship with Westbrook to infiltrate the Directorate and consequently was at least indirectly responsible for Rodríguez's betrayal and the death of the Humboldt martyrs (though he did not discount the possibility that they may have been directly responsible). Twenty years of imprisonment was the price Valls paid for his honesty and serene valor.

Two years later there was another trial, but now it was the members of the Directorate who were the accused. The principal figure at that trial was Rolando Cubelas. Cubelas had returned to finish his studies at medical school when the University of Havana resumed classes after the fall of Batista. He was elected president of the Federation of University Students (FUS) over Pedro Luis Boitel. (Boitel was imprisoned shortly thereafter and died as a consequence of a hunger strike. He was allowed to die. This reminds me of the confrontation between Mella and the tyrant Machado, although the outcome was very different.)

Cubelas also remembered Mella and seemed to want to emulate him. Mella, founder and first president of the FUS, was an outstanding athlete, who, among other feats, led his team to victory in a famed four-sculls rowing competition. Like Mella, Cubelas was on the crew of a winning University rowing team. Among his crew mates were the doomed twins, Patricio and Antonio de la Guardia, which made their champion canoe the most tragic in the history of competitive rowing in Cuba. I should advise the other members of that canoe of the doomed, the oarsman Roberto Rumbau and the steersman "Púa" Rosello, if they are still alive, to proceed with extreme caution.

Cubelas completed his medical studies but never practiced medicine. Instead, he re-entered the army, though he was more interested in partying with his fellow *comandante* Efigenio Ameijeiras

140

and other friends from his rebel days than in military activities. But Cubelas didn't only party; he also conspired with the CIA, or so it was alleged. The object of this conspiracy was no less than to assassinate Fidel Castro. Cubelas himself was supposed to execute him with a long-range rifle.

The plot was uncovered and the conspirators arrested. Everyone expected Cubelas to be given the death sentence, which would have been in accordance with current law and a new but already established tradition. But Fidel magnanimously intervened, rendering his opinion that the rebellious reveller's life should be spared. Naturally, the court heeded Fidel, setting aside capital punishment, and sentenced Cubelas to twenty-five years in prison. Many years later, the twins who rowed with Cubelas weren't even that lucky. Tony de la Guardia was sentenced to death for drug trafficking, a crime that, under the Penal Code, carries a maximum sentence of fifteen years. Patricio, because he knew of his brother's activities and did not turn informer against him, was given thirty years.

In view of the Cubelas case, I came to believe Fidel might commute Arnaldo Ochoa's sentence. Of course, it goes without saying that I am as great a believer in the magnanimity of *El Comandante* and the generosity of his Revolution as I am in the divine powers of Changó or Pallas Athena. I hoped, rather, that Fidel would make the mistake of equating the two cases. But this man, cursed be his name, never makes mistakes, or at least not the kind that might endanger his power. Cubelas' life was spared because Fidel understood that he wasn't a dangerous man and wouldn't be in the future.

One final trial before I am through, for I am also sick and tired of these farces. Aníbal Escalante, the daring Stalinist dreamer, started to backslide again. This time he attempted to exploit differences between Fidel and the Soviets, and egged on perhaps by Soviet Intelligence -- with which he had many contacts -- he vaguely embarked on what appeared to be a conspiracy. But this time, however, Fidel completely lost his non-too-plentiful patience and sent Aníbal to prison. Also arrested were such veteran Communists as Arnaldo Escalona, and newcomers such as Ricardo Bofill, the

141

professor of Marxism who many years later would establish the Cuban Committee for Human Rights.

The trial of Aníbal Escalante was a minor but instructive chapter in Fidel's political and ideological conflict with the Soviet Union. Fidel also was at odds with the Chinese. The disciples of the celestial Mao, intolerant even by Communist standards and absolutely inept at exerting economic pressure, had provoked Fidel's righteous ire by shortchanging him on deliveries of rice. The Soviets, on the other hand, were not completely inept at exerting such pressures; they have rarely proved completely inept at anything that relates to international politics.

Speaking of international politics, two important conferences were held in Havana in 1966 and 1967. The first was the Tricontinental Conference, which brought together Marxists and progressives from Asia, Africa and Latin America, very few of whom were followers of the Moscow line. The second was the Conference of Latin American Solidarity, with similar tendencies. These conferences gave birth to several organizations that did not amount to much but did serve to reaffirm the schism that had developed within the Marxist Church, which now had three apostolic sees: Moscow, Peking and Havana. One cannot help being struck by the differences in size, population and resources between two of these pontifical states and the third.

A few months after the second of these conferences had concluded, there occurred an event that was to prove catastrophic for the guerrilla movement in Latin America: Ernesto Guevara, pursued relentlessly, encircled and captured by Captain Gary Prado and his men in what was undoubtedly an impressive display of military prowess, was later stupidly assassinated by order of the generals who ruled Bolivia.

Ernesto Guevara is admired, idolized and even loved by many different sorts of people. One of my dearest friends, then incarcerated on the Isle of Pines, caused a riot by asking for a moment of silence in memory of the fallen Guevara, a suggestion that was not well received by many of his fellow inmates and companions in adversity. Carlos Alberto Montaner, one of the most implacable critics of the regime, has said that Guevara was intellectually superior to Fidel, which seems to me a repetition of the error Trotsky committed when he confused intelligence with culture.

I must confess that I feel no sympathy or admiration for this man. I cannot forget his hostility toward those who fought in the urban underground and the rancor with which he attacked Faustino Pérez on account of the failed April 1958 general strike. I remember also the role that he and his theory of the *guerrilla foco* played in the destruction of the democratic wing of the Revolution and the implementation of a totalitarian regime in my country. For this is my country. I am not a Cuban by adoption or decree, nor even by accident, for my parents were born here, as were my grandparents, my great-grandparents and almost all my great-great grandparents.

I can never forget Guevara's disastrous stewardship of our economy, which gave him an opportunity to put in practice his absurd neo-Marxist economic theories, such as budgetary allotments to state enterprises that removed all incentive for profit, and moral incentives for workers that killed off productivity. These ideas are now again held up as Cuba's answer to other Socialist voices in other Socialist countries that clamor for a little rationality, realism and common sense.

The most symbolic illustration of Guevara's ineptitude as an administrator can be found (or once was found -- I haven't been there in years) on the highway connecting Nuevitas and Camagüey. I am speaking of two factories that were constructed there in the early Sixties when the Argentine physician was in charge of Cuba's industrial development. The buildings are not unattractive, for they were constructed at a time when the *fidelistas* had not yet been seized by that strange passion for architectural hideousness that is the hallmark of all their public works today. One building was planned as a factory for processing cotton. The adjoining structure was to be a refinery for cottonseed oil. What is nowhere to be seen in that vicinity, what has never been seen, and what will never be seen there, is cotton. Only bleached palm trees, pine-cane shrubs and a hard grass called esparto, the typical vegetation of a barren savannah. Nothing else can grow on the thin layer of dirt that covers its serpentine rocks. Effort and money wasted.

Ernesto Guevara reminds me of his famous colleague, Dr. Frankenstein. He manipulated forces of Nature that he did not understand (or at most understood only partially) and was destroyed by his own creature. Guevara's "Frankenstein's monster" was his theory of the *guerrilla foco* as the basic factor of the Revolution. While fundamental to the Revolution, it functioned almost autonomously from the Revolution. One of Guevara's followers, the Frenchman Regis Debray, went so far as to maintain that the struggle in the cities, the really terrible life of the urban resistance fighter, softened revolutionaries and turned them into bourgeois, whereas the hardships of guerrilla life tempered and fortified the spirit. I detest dilettantes as much as I detest sharks.

In relation to the economy, Guevara was a dilettante. But he was no dilettante when it came to the revolutionary struggle. Still, he did not conceal his satisfaction when the Bolivian Communist party refused to recognize his leadership of the revolutionary struggle in their country and withdrew all material support. He didn't seem to care if he was left without uniforms, boots or medical supplies, and deprived even of the drugs he desperately needed to control his chronic asthma. Nor did he mind if he was cut off from sources of information on the movement of government troops or not supplied with arms, even defective arms, such as the shipment Rene Ramos Latour sent him when he was in the Sierra Maestra (this annoyed Guevara greatly then, but arms, even defective arms, are better than no arms at all). Finally, Guevara was not in the least concerned that there was no urban resistance in Bolivia to attack the government in the cities and disengage part of its forces. It didn't bother him at all going without the support that he had received in the Sierra Maestra thanks to the July 26th Movement.

No, I cannot sympathize with *Comandante* Ernesto Guevara. Nevertheless, I must and do recognize that he left some good legacies: his willingness to die for his ideas and for what he considered the truth, *his* truth; his austere conduct and indifference to comforts and material goods; his words against those rulers who have at their disposal goods and comforts that are not within the reach of those they rule; and his condemnation both of those who make a public display of their wealth and of those who though they may not flaunt it, possess it nonetheless. For that reason and that reason alone, I respect the man known to his friends and admirers as "Che."

XI. The Beginning of Ruin

Ernesto Guevara swept over the economy of our country like a monsoon. But sooner or later it stops raining, and the level of the river recedes though its waters are left murky. But Fidel is no mere monsoon; he is the Great Flood personified. It's not that I am complaining that it pours and pours and pours, just that it never stops. Not content merely to dedicate himself to the liberation of oppressed peoples at our expense, Fidel invents new and original theories on the construction of Socialism to test on us, and the most depressing thing about it is that his powers of invention are seemingly inexhaustible.

The Socialist countries, since the early days of Lenin, have based their plans for economic development on the industrial sector, and primarily on heavy industry. Fidel decided that the best thing for us was to begin our industrialization through agriculture. What he meant, of course, was that we could propel Socialist development by concentrating our primary efforts on the production of sugar, which is far from just an agricultural activity (sugar is not sugar until it has been refined). At the time, "agriculture" was believed to be the magic word that would open the entrances to all of the caves filled with treasure.

Unfortunately, the production of sugar proved too complex a task for the heads of enthusiastic *fidelistas*. It was particularly complex for the heads of those who had never set eyes on the inside of a sugar refinery, (or in some cases had not even seen the outside

146

of one). Yet these individuals, who couldn't tell a sugar refinery even if they were standing in front of one, were appointed to administer and run these enterprises.

One phrase sticks out in my mind from those days: "Plan Fidel." Back then, El *Comandante* didn't believe in the old and expired modalities of centralized planning. Fidel's own plans were . . . . Come to think of it, why should I be the one to explain his ideas? In recent years, several high-level functionaries in the economic sector have managed to defect, recovering their sanity with their freedom. Negrete, Sanchez Pérez and Pérez Cot know much more than I ever could about the chaos in the *fidelista* economy.

What can I say? What could I possibly add to such a discussion? Perhaps I should tell the story of an eight hundred acre farm that was planted as a vineyard in the vicinity of Jiguaní?

Yes, that's what I said. A vineyard. An eight hundred-acre vineyard with sunken concrete poles to train the vines; 2500 poles per one hundred acres, a total of twenty thousand at five dollars per pole (not counting labor). Total cost of poles: $100,000. One hundred thousand dollars invested in poles to grow grapes in a tropical climate!

But not only grapes. If one fruit of the frigid zone fails in a tropical climate, who is to say that other cold weather fruits also will fail? Not Fidel. He planted strawberries and apples in Banoa, a valley in the Escambray mountains. Fidel claimed to have discovered a microclimate (a zone of cold air in an otherwise warm region).

Should I tell the story of a caravan of trucks climbing up and down the steep inclines of the Sierra de Nipe to bring tons of fertilizer to the tablelands of La Mensura? Fidel -- that Christopher Columbus of microclimates -- had discovered yet another of these wonders of nature. Here he did not plant fruits, but special grasses and forage to tempt the demanding palates of his prized herd of Aberdeen Angus cattle.

And speaking of bovines, have I the heart to tell the sad, sad story of "International Black Velvet," the champion bull that won blue ribbons at all the Canadian cattle shows, and cost us (cost all

Cubans, including me) $50,000? That was in the Sixties, when that was real money. Only an expert stockbreeder would have purchased a bull with absolutely no interest in the sweet mechanics of reproduction to service cows that had probably been rendered infertile for want of their native fodder.

But all this is minutiae. To describe the disaster that Fidel has wreaked on the Cuban economy, the colossal waste of resources --human, material and financial -- for which his crazy ideas are responsible, is a job not for me (or even Superman) but for those fugitive economists who were close to the center of power when Fidel committed all his blunders. Forward, then, gentlemen, and good luck.

I do, however, want to talk about The Ten Million Ton Sugar Harvest (that's right, put it all in capital letters). It was the culmination of the Sugar Crusade to which Fidel had summoned the Cuban people. This long march, this economic epic, called for the production of eight million tons of sugar in 1968 and nine million tons in 1969, quotas that were not even remotely reached. But the ten million tons planned for 1970 were going to be reached.

"The ten million goes ahead as planned." "It goes and have no doubt it goes." "On my word as a Cuban, the ten million goes." It goes, goes, goes, goes. It seemed like a Western -- *The Searchers, Rio Bravo* or something of that sort; the only thing that was missing was John Wayne. Hour after hour, day after day, month after month came that demonic and merciless monosyllabic cry. Meanwhile, the entire economy and the resources of the nation were subordinated to the whim of one man and used to advance his political interests and personal prestige.

I can remember it as if it were yesterday. It is 1970 again. I can see and hear Manolo Ortega on television, speaking with the same conviction with which he once hawked Hatuey beer in the bad old capitalist days. Now he was working for a nobler cause: "On my word as a Cuban" (here he pauses -- Ortega is an excellent announcer) "the ten million goes." Again, it was that omnipresent phrase that would not go away. Manolo Ortega wasn't lying. He believed what he was saying, because Manolo was a *fidelista* and *fidelistas* are capable of believing anything that their well-beloved leader tells them.

Fidel is not a *fidelista*. Fidel is Fidel. Therefore, he knew the real situation. But he waited. Through March and April he waited, even though by then the fate of the sugar harvest was already decided as it is by that time every year. In May, some blockheads from Miami provided Fidel with the opportunity he was waiting for, when they hijacked a Cuban fishing boat with eleven men aboard. Fidel, quick as a tiger, threw together one of his mass demonstrations, and the world forgot momentarily about the sugar harvest (except for those still breaking their backs in the canefields). When the fishermen were set free and returned to Cuba, *El Comandante* used the occasion of their reception ceremony to announce the failure of the 1970 sugar harvest.

"The Ten Million Ton Sugar Harvest" was actually the eight and one-half million ton sugar harvest. In the twenty years since the harvest of 1970, we have yet to reach nine million tons.

What is the legacy of this catastrophe? I'll leave that to the fugitive economists to decide. As far as I am concerned, the only good thing that came out of it was a musical group founded at that time by the bassist Juan Formell who, naturally, called his ensemble the "Goes-Goes." The group sounded good then and sounds even better today.

Fidel, although he is a lawyer, is not a man of laws. He is, however, in the words of Pancho Villa, "a man of much law" (i.e. a huckster). To demonstrate that, with or without the ten million tons, he was still the man in charge, Fidel abolished Christmas. Christmas, he said, was an imposition of the Spanish conquistadors who had subjugated our country and forced on us their customs and traditions. He seemed to forget that, according to the last census, sixty-four percent of the citizens of our country (or seventy-four percent, if we count Cuban citizens in exile that the census doesn't) are descendants of Spanish conquistadors or other Spanish emigrants who came to Cuba during the Republican era. Another twenty-four percent -- those called mulattos -- are descended, in part, from the Spanish. But, most importantly, Fidel forgets that the last of the indigenous population of Cuba died out three hundred years ago. We have no "indigenous traditions or customs" to follow, and we are not and never have been, a conquered people. All the world knows it but I want to repeat it: Fidel's father was a Spaniard and his mother was the daughter of Spaniards.

Of course, Fidel did not abolish Christmas just to defend our national identity (although defending our national identity occupies him day and night). He abolished the December 25 holiday because its celebration interrupted the work of the sugar harvest. In those bygone days when sugar refineries actually made a profit, it was customary to begin harvesting sugarcane in January, when the stalks are at their most saccharine and the syrup from which the sugar is made most copious. Only then is it profitable to harvest and refine sugarcane, not before. By abolishing Christmas, Fidel got a head start on the sugar harvest. But it was all for nothing.

Fidel did away with our joyous Christmas and got away with it. If to break the spirit of a once rebellious people constitutes a success, and if to subjugate is to rule, then there can be no doubt that Fidel has been a successful ruler.

Carried away by my recollections of the destruction of Cuba's economy, I have neglected certain important events that I don't want to leave out. Let us first examine the activities of the enemy.

While Fidel was sponsoring the guerrilla movement in Latin America, what was the CIA doing? What was the sinister, treacherous and, in this case, uproarious CIA up to? Among other things, it was inventing a leader, a conductor of men who would liberate Cubans from Fidel's tyranny. His name: José Elias de la Torriente. His age: 64 years. His previous political experience: none. In fact, in 1967, when he was anointed as liberator by the tutelary gods of Langley, Virginia, Torriente had been an American citizen for almost thirty years and had not set foot in Cuba in twenty. To attempt to turn a man with such qualifications -- or, rather, no qualifications -- into a leader (and not just a leader, but one capable of challenging Fidel), is something beyond all my powers of comprehension. Neither do I understand how any country can amass so much wealth and power yet appoint to high government office individuals as stupid as those who conceived Operation Torriente.

Fidel's friends were also fighting among themselves. This squabble likewise culminated in a fatality: Nikita Khrushchev's political career. In 1964, he was replaced by Leonid Brezhnev, a Stalinist bureaucrat who wasn't in the least captivated by Fidel's personality. The consequences were slow in coming but they came: Brezhnev steadily and ominously began to turn the economic screws on Cuba.

Was it before or after the Prague Spring? Anyway, Brezhnev also wanted to put Fidel's house in order, but Fidel would have none of it. *El Comandante* ordered the suspension of talks then underway in Moscow on the provision of oil to Cuba because, as he stated at the time, the Soviets were conducting these negotiations in a manner injurious to the dignity of our people.

The Prague Spring was a crucial moment in the recent history of our country. The sentiments that the reform movement awakened in Fidel are reflected today in his rejection of perestroika. But Fidel -- perhaps because one good turn deserves another -- ordered the *fidelista* press to cover with absolute impartiality the events in Czechoslovakia, giving both the Soviets' version of events and the Dubcek reformers'. Even after the invasion of Czechoslovakia by forces from the Warsaw Pact, the Cuban press continued for the first few days its evenhanded reporting. But then, suddenly, Fidel Castro, the great champion of self-determination who was willing to fight to the death so that all the peoples of the world might enjoy that right, declared his unequivocal support for the invasion of a small country by a superpower and its allies.

Stupefied, frantic and in the grip of one of the worst rages that Fidel Castro has ever inspired in me (and that's saying a lot), it was then that I decided that I did not want to continue living in a country that was ruled by such a man. In reality, I did not decide but propose. Man proposes and God disposes. But in my case, it would

151

seem that the devil has had the final word, because I am still here today, August 30, 1989.

The invasion of Czechoslovakia was the beginning of the end of Fidel's first anti-Soviet period. Later would come another, but we'll get to that sometime, as my grandmother María Borja used to say. There was still room for an occasional outspoken remark by Fidel (Alexei Kosygin had to put up with a tantrum now and then as Mikoyan had before him), but the future of Cuban-Soviet relations was inexorable. With his absurd, anarchistic and crazy style of government, Fidel had transformed Cuba -- which once produced so much wealth for Spain and profits for American businesses -- into a country that was no longer able to support itself.

Rubén Martínez Villena, the Communist poet of the Twenties and Thirties, asked the people in one of his verses "to charge the lazy and kill them" so that, among other things, "the Republic may learn to rely on itself." The Republic, poet, was self-sufficient in your day because there was no other state to subsidize it. Now that is no longer so.

"All is vanity," said Solomon. Marx proclaimed all to be economics. And Freud discovered that all was sex. It is undeniable that vanity, economics and sex all play an important part in the lives of men and women. Of Fidel's vanity, I am not going to speak because I am a prudent man who avoids unnecessary problems. As for his sex life, it does not interest me in the least. I am, however, very interested in his knowledge of economics, because that affects us all. And how!

After holding a 30-minute interview with Fidel in 1959, Richard Nixon told President Eisenhower that the Cuban leader was, of all the celebrated politicians he had met, the one who understood government and economics the least. The perspicacity that some people demonstrate at times is truly incredible. It took me years to understand what Nixon grasped in only half an hour. Of course, I was then immersed in that "sleep of reason" to which Francisco Goya alluded.

In 1959, *El Comandante* knew nothing about economics. Thirty years later, he still knows nothing. I would dare to predict that he never will understand economics. "When a line is drawn and sums are added, he turns idiot," said a popular philosopher when assessing Fidel's administrative skills or lack thereof. Juanito was wrong, very wrong; because he's dead, I can't even disabuse him of his error. But I can assure the living that Fidel doesn't have an idiot bone in him, on the contrary possessing a brilliant intellect. It's just that he dedicates it to the only thing that interests him, or has ever interested him: power. To win power, to maintain power, and to die in power.

Fidel has a brilliant mind, but his mind is affected by an ever expanding egoism. The terrible economic crises that have beset our country throughout his rule have never threatened to topple his government. Stalin, the perverse Stalin, abolished rationing in the Soviet Union five years after the conclusion of a devastating war. But we Cubans have endured rationing for twenty-seven years in a country that has not been devastated by war, a country that is intact, except for the havoc that Fidel himself has wreaked upon it. Fidel tells us that our country is about to be invaded at any moment. Although the invasion never comes, the privations of war are always with us.

We await that attack while standing in food lines; *El Comandante* feasts on lobster on the grill, joined sometimes by Friar Betto, a red priest who doesn't resemble in the least Vivaldi. The great Venetian would, between masses, compose beautiful Baroque music. This unworthy Brazilian cleric composes, between banquets, spurious doctrines and silly apologetics for an enemy of religion. It's a pity that excommunications are no longer fashionable, at least in the Church. Still, John Paul II, because he is a Pole, is well acquainted with that class of rulers who generate poverty but refuse to share in it.

Fidel despises all economic laws, regardless of whether they regulate free markets or centralized economies. All laws are the drivel of armchair intellectuals. Fidel knows that the key to economic development lies in slogans, voluntary labor and the revolutionary

153

consciousness of the "New Man." There is no way to make Fidel understand that if uncompensated labor and longer working hours were decisive factors in productivity, no economic system could compete with slavery.

Fidel's economic theories have not threatened his power. On the contrary, they have strengthened it: Cubans must of necessity dedicate the greater part of their lives to running from one place to another trying to resolve "problems" that are problems only in a country governed with absolute incompetence. On the other hand, the same economic theories have done serious damage to Fidel's dream of international leadership. So to insure his power at home, which for Fidel is what's fundamental, he had to sacrifice (or postpone, because his optimism is indestructible) his dream of worldwide power, submitting instead to Soviet hegemony after a decade of blunders left the economy of the island in shambles.

Brezhnev came to the rescue. Soviet aid began to flow in ever larger quantities until it reached almost incredible proportions. Treaties were signed whereby the Soviet Union agreed to buy Cuban sugar at three, four and even five times the world market price. If Cuba consumed ten million metric tons of petroleum annually, wasting it as everything else here is wasted, the Soviets would send us several million more, at cost, which we in turn re-sold to third countries at a profit. As for the imbalance of payments that resulted from our trade with the Soviet Union, the sums were written on ice.

Let's talk like Marxists. Don't Marxists hold that a country's economy determines its fate? Well, then, how can a country be independent whose economy is dependent on subsidies from another country? It can't be. Independence, under such circumstances, is impossible. The *fidelistas* and their predecessors, the old Communists of the PSP, emptied rivers of ink and felled entire forests, writing against Cuban dependence on the United States. Nevertheless, the United States never subsidized our economy; it made profits off it. Never was our country so dependent as it is now under Castro.

And so ended Fidel's dream of world leadership and also his outspoken criticism of the Soviet Union. There would be no third

Rome. His guerrilla adventures were also at an end, or at least considerably curtailed. And the Soviet model of a centralized planned economy was instituted in Cuba.

So began in Cuba a period of outrageous adulation of the Soviet Union, which came to an abrupt end in our own day for reasons that no one then could have imagined. The Soviets were called "a nation of giants" by Fidel. The Soviet Union was named in the preamble of our new Constitution and our friendship and alliance with that country became part of our Fundamental Law. When Fidel, as chief of state, swore allegiance to the Constitution of 1976, he was, in fact, declaring his allegiance to a foreign state.

Words are picked up by the wind and carried away for ever, but stones are heavier and much more difficult to move. Next to the Mediodia Freeway, a luxurious mausoleum was erected (with an eternal flame and everything) as a final resting place for Soviets killed in Cuba while carrying out their peaceful missions of collaboration. A new embassy was constructed for the Soviets in Havana, taller and more extensive than any Cuban government ministry (with the exception, of course, of the Armed Forces ministry). A gigantic park was dedicated to Lenin, and in it was placed a gigantic statue of this most gigantic of a race of giants. By comparison, the statue of the father of our country, Carlos Manuel de Céspedes, located in the Plaza de Armas, seems almost a miniature. That little statue, however, is very important in my life. I have spent many happy moments and some not so happy by its side.

But let's return to words. As part of the frenzied worship of all things Soviet, Russian language classes were offered on radio and television, and thousands of *fidelistas* racked their brains with the Cyrillic alphabet, the absence of definite and indefinite articles, and the cursed declensions of Russian. Finally, the story of two Russian youths who served briefly in the rebel ranks during our War of Independence received the enthusiastic attention of journalists and official historians. This is a subject that fascinates me, though I am not so sure that it will interest my readers. Nonetheless, I can't help speculating what fuss would have been made about the "Inglesito" --

Henry Reeve, a Brooklyn-born teenager who reached the rank of general in The Ten Years' War and died in battle at age 24 --if he had been named, say, Alexander Mikhailevich Lukin, and been born in Grozni, Jerson or Piatigorsk.

Under no pro-American Cuban president, not even Batista, was the United States made an object of adulation in our country to the extent that the Soviet Union has been lionized by the government of Fidel Castro.

The renewal of the love affair between the Soviets and the *fidelistas* had other consequences: the old Communists were again returned to their former haunts of power. Lazáro Pena was reinstated as secretary general of the Cuban Federation of Workers; Blas Roca was named president of the new National Assembly of the People's Power; Carlos Rafael Rodriguéz was relieved of his post of minister without a ministry (which inevitably smacked of his Batista past) and named vice president of the Council of State; and Isodoro Malmierca replaced the raving and spent Raúl Roa as minister of Foreign Relations.

XII. Internationalism

There is a certain resemblance between dignity and arrogance, but they are not, by any means, the same thing. Fidel, an arrogant man if there ever was one, doesn't like in the least to sing the praises of others. Still, there are rewards. I do not mean the title of "Hero of the Soviet Union" or the medal of the Order of Lenin, which Brezhnev conferred on him. *El Comandante* is interested in power, not in the colored ribbons that sometimes come with it. I am speaking of the role in world affairs that the Soviets offered him. He may be a supporting player, but he is by no means an insignificant character.

The instrument that made this role possible -- a role that has meant so much to Fidel -- was his army. From 1959 to 1974, the *fidelista* armed forces, founded with guerrilla contingents from the Sierra Maestra and organized by Soviet military advisers, was almost from the first steadily accumulating armaments and men. But above all, its officers were acquiring expertise and experience until it transformed itself into the most magnificent war machine that Latin America has ever known. (God may be Argentine or Brazilian, but the armies of Argentina and Brazil combined would be no match for Fidel's).

Like the officers of our first republican army, the *fidelista* officer corps studied constantly and participated frequently in maneuvers. Naturally, those pre-1933 military men studied for the "love of the art," and prepared for battles that they well knew would

157

never come about. Moreover, no superpower ever took an interest in their preparations.

Those of Fidel's officers who demonstrated the most talent and aptitude were sent to the Soviet Union for courses in military strategy. Some like Ochoa and Raúl Díaz Arguelles (who came from the Directorate) also participated in internationalist adventures. What transpired was something like a process of natural selection that -- paradoxically -- weeded out for one reason or another, all the most distinguished guerrilla *comandantes*. Camilo Cienfuegos died and so did Guevara. Juan Almeida and Guillermo García were completely incapable of understanding the complicated military techniques of modern warfare. Delio Gómez Ochoa fell in disgrace. Ifigenio Ameijeiras and Dermidio Escalona were shunted aside because of their uncontrollable addiction to revelry. Huber Matos and Cubelas were jailed. Among the *comandantes*, only Abelardo "Furri" Colomé, Raúl Menéndez Tomassevich and Díaz Argüelles ever became distinguished generals.

And Raúl Castro? When I speak of distinguished generals, I mean those who have actually commanded troops. Since 1959, Fidel's brother has been nothing more than a military bureaucrat. As for José Ramón Fernández, the expert artilleryman who knocked to bits the Brigade 2506 at the Bay of Pigs, he was retired prematurely from the army for reasons that I do not know and that do not interest me. By the way, things have not gone at all badly for him; for many years now, he has been Minister of Education.

As early as 1963, the new *fidelista* army became involved in its first extra-continental conflict: the brief border war between Morocco and Algeria, in which Cuban tanks under the command of Ameijeiras tipped the balance in favor of the Algerians. I have heard it said that another detachment of tanks under Nestor López Cuba participated in the Yom Kippur War (naturally on the side of the Arabs -- more precisely, the Syrians). Could it be true?

In 1975, twelve years after the Algerian baptism under fire, Fidel could count on at least five first-class generals: Díaz Argüelles, Ochoa, Colomé, López Cuba and Leopoldo Cintras. Back then they were still called *comandantes*, but they were really generals and nothing less than generals. *El Comandante* put them into the Angolan war, which was to be the longest military conflict in our history. There in Africa, on the other side of the Atlantic, thousands of miles from home, Fidel let loose his foxes of war.

"Hounds of war" is the correct expression popularized by Frederick Forsyth, but I, with my customary prudence, prefer to use "foxes," because "hounds" means dogs, and I want to avoid all malicious and dangerous interpretations.

The episodes in Algeria and Syria (if this last indeed happened) were only dress rehearsals. The real debut of the military machine assembled by Fidel and the Soviets was Angola, which had just been granted its independence. It was in truth a successful debut. The Cubans repulsed a South African invasion, pushing them back across their border. They broke up the forces supported by Zaire and commanded by a gentleman who seemed to have his name backwards -- Holden Roberto. They successfully defended the small but rich Cabinda oil fields. Finally, they cornered the forces of Jonas Savimbi. Thanks to these Cuban victories, the Communists under Agostinho Neto were able to remain in power in Angola.

A Colombian battalion fought in the Korean War under the flag of the United Nations and some Mexican and Brazilian aviators flew in World War II. Latin Americans can be quite bellicose when it comes to fighting one another, but that was the extent of their involvement in foreign wars until Fidel came along. Of course, this can't compare with sending an army thousands of miles across an ocean. However, Fidel's feat would not have been possible without the political and logistical assistance of the Soviet Union.

Not everything went Fidel's way in Angola, however. Many Cubans died, including Raúl Díaz Argüelles, the first commander of the expeditionary force and a very able military man. He was blown up by a land mine. The Directorate no longer existed, but death continued to trail its former members. Of course, war is war, and there is nothing extraordinary about generals dying in battle, especially Cuban generals.

159

"Furri" Colomé was the principal architect of that victory, a brilliant and seemingly conclusive victory. But no, it wasn't a victory. Jonas Savimbi was cornered, but he wasn't beaten. Savimbi, who had fought with Guevara in the Congo, was not only a hard bone to crack, but a bone that could crack the hardest teeth. A war had just started that would last thirteen years.

In 1978, not long after the start of the Angolan war, Somalia attempted either to grab or to recover the Ogaden territory from Ethiopia (depending on which account you credit). Another war erupted, and Fidel (with the Soviets' consent) sided with Ethiopia, sending a new Afrika Corps under the command of General Ochoa. Ochoa made fast work of the brave and tough Somalis. This was indeed a conclusive victory, if anything can really be called that in this life.

I now can say with absolute certainty that Generals Colomé and Ochoa commanded, respectively, the Cuban expeditionary armies in Angola and Ethiopia. At the time, however, I couldn't confirm it since it was only a rumor. It was not until 1983, on the occasion of the thirtieth anniversary of the attack on the Moncada barracks, that the exploits of the two generals were at last made known, when both were invested with the title "Hero of the Republic."

This reminds me of a book about World War II (known in Soviet historiography as "The Great Patriotic War," as if the Soviets alone had fought the Nazis). The author, a certain Deborin, lists the three divisions of the Red Army that marched on the Third Reich and gives the names of their respective commanders. The first was under the command of Marshal Koniev, the second under the command of Marshal Rokosowski and the third. . . . Well, apparently, it commanded itself; or if it did have a commander, Deborin doesn't name him. Of course, it had a commander. Marshal Zhukov was not only in charge of the third division but was the supreme commander of all Soviet troops advancing on Berlin. But when Deborin wrote his history of "The Great Patriotic War," Zhukov was in disgrace and could not be mentioned. Stalinists are that way.

At the end of the Seventies, neither Colomé nor Ochoa were in disgrace, but their military successes had so eclipsed those obtained in skirmishes against Batista's troops by their political superiors thirty years before, that someone thought it inconvenient to publicize their exploits.

In the first days of the Angolan war, Juan Benemelis and I, two rather intelligent chaps if I may say so, and both experts in international politics and baseball, met by chance on the corner of 30th and 31st Streets in Almendares. We examined exhaustively the consequences that the African adventure could entail for the future of our country. After a careful analysis of all the incisive factors of that conflict, we both arrived at the conclusion that it would end in disaster. Fidel, we agreed, had gone out of fashion and simply refused to face up to it.

Apparently, even intelligent chaps can be wrong, because Fidel not only stayed in fashion, but transformed himself into a major player in world politics. As a result of the Angolan war, Cuba -- which is to say, Fidel -- was elected to the presidency of the Non-Aligned Nations. That this movement is a circus controlled by a club of dictators was never more evident than when it elected as its leader one of the most aligned nations in the world, the chief satellite of one of the superpowers: Fidel Castro's Cuba.

During Cuba's stewardship of the Non-Aligned Nations there occurred an incident that I would characterize as "embarrassing" if I believed it were possible for anything to embarrass so shameless an organization. The Soviet Union, one of the two superpowers, invaded a member state, Afghanistan, imposing on it a puppet Marxist government and initiating a military occupation that would last nine years. They say that Marxism, an absolutely materialist and therefore atheistic political doctrine, represents, above all, the interests of the proletarians. How, then, can Marxists pretend to establish the rule of the proletariat in a country almost devoid of proletarians? How can atheists govern a people that adheres totally to Islam? Whom do these Afghan Marxists represent?

161

Years later, Mikhail Gorbachev, the man who buried Stalinism in the Soviet Union, declared the invasion of Afghanistan to have been a "sin." A sin it certainly was, but the Non-Aligned Movement, so enthusiastic in its condemnation of U.S. intervention in Vietnam, did not condemn the Soviet invasion and occupation of Afghanistan, and its president, Fidel Castro, defended in cloak-and-dagger style the sinner Leonid Brezhnev.

But I am leaving the decade of the Seventies behind, and I haven't yet discussed two important events. Apparently, Fidel is not the only disorganized individual in this country.

The first of these occurrences was the rise to power in Chile of Salvador Allende, who was a Social Democrat and a fervent *fidelista* at the same time. Despite his devotion to Fidel, Allende did not enjoy the complete approval of his idol, owing to the Chilean's penchant for elections. Fidel was then going through the final phase of his guerrilla fever, which is, I may add, a recurring illness. Fidel's disdain for elections notwithstanding, Allende won with a coalition of social-*fidelistas* and Communists and assumed power in Chile. His victory was due entirely to the absurd Chilean electoral system, which does not provide for a second round of balloting in case no candidate receives a majority of all votes cast. Allende, who garnered just thirty-five percent of the vote, would have had no chance whatever of winning a second round of elections against a united right-centrist candidacy.

But what matters is that Allende won. With the approval of a little more than a third of the voters, he embarked upon the socialization of his country. Relations between Cuba and Chile became, as was perfectly natural, extremely fraternal, although some sparks flew when the poet Pablo Neruda (who had been excommunicated from the ranks of the *fidelista* faithful) was named ambassador to Paris. Then there was that little fracas caused by the friendship of the Chilean charge d'affaires in Havana with another poet, the dissident Heberto Padilla.

162

But this is all insignificant. Generally, relations between these two governments were as cordial and close as one might expect, although they were short-lived.

Allende tried to follow in the footsteps of his scolding mentor. The results are known to all. During those terrible days following the fall of Allende, Patricio La Guardia, a Cuban general who had been sent by Fidel to advise the Chilean president, wandered the streets of Santiago de Chile, gun in hand. Or was it his twin brother, Antonio? I never could tell them apart.

Just before Salvador Allende was toppled by the military, Fidel made a marathon visit to Chile. There he met a certain General Pinochet, who later would become a ruler as authoritarian as he but a much better administrator. On his way back, Fidel had an interview with another general, who was much more to his liking, Juan Velasco Alvarado, the president of Peru. On another technical stop, this time in Quito, he met the president of Ecuador, José Velasco Ibarra. The three presidents visited by Fidel lost their offices soon thereafter. *El Comandante* casts a bad shadow, some doubtless will think. Still, Latin American presidents don't appear to be superstitious. They still invite Fidel to their inaugurations despite these evil omens and other things.

Well, you win some and you lose some. Fidel lost Chile but won Nicaragua. The failure of Marxism in Chile wasn't really Fidel's failure, however. He never trusted in legalistic means of achieving power, not even when these were at his disposal during Prío's democratic government. On the other hand, the victory in Nicaragua was really *his* victory. At long last, after twenty years of failed attempts and disasters, Fidel succeeded in mounting another guerrilla movement that was able to seize power by defeating a regular army. The army the Sandinistas defeated, however, was not even remotely like Batista's. Somoza's National Guard was not short of officers who wanted to fight. What it did lack, however, was ammunition. President Jimmy Carter, about whom we shall speak more later, declared an arms embargo on the old Somoza dictatorship. That brought down the regime, Carter having decided that although Anastasio Somoza,

Sr. may have been Franklin Roosevelt's "son of a bitch," Anastasio Somoza, Jr. was by no stretch of the imagination his. By the way, I haven't yet been able to see the advantage in sponsoring the overthrow of a right-wing dictatorship so that a left-wing dictatorship can come to power. They say that in the months preceding Somoza's fall, several Cuban officers were seen travelling in Nicaragua. If such a thing is true, I should like to know their names.

Nicaragua's Sandinista dictatorship has always enjoyed an ample supply of arms, as has also the Salvadoran guerrillas, who seemed on the way to power when, to their misfortune, Carter lost his bid for re-election.

Well, I've already discussed all the significant events of the Seventies. The moment has come to speak of something that fills me with the greatest disgust and repugnance, but that I must nonetheless address. I mean, of course, the events of 1980, that most terrible year of the *fidelista* era, though I very much fear that worst are to come.

XIII. The Emigration

I started this book by alluding to the tragedies that Fidel Castro's government has prompted with its restrictive emigration policies. By 1979, twenty years after Fidel seized power, a million Cubans had already left a country where they were known as "worms" to settle in lands where they were still considered human beings. During those twenty years, thousands died attempting to flee the island clandestinely; other thousands, caught in flight, ended up behind bars.

Thousands more did not die or know the death-in-life of Cuban prisons, but were condemned to waste years of their lives -- years that they could never hope to recover -- waiting to be awarded an exit visa. It was something out of medieval times. Cubans were serfs who needed the permission of our lord to move from one fief to another.

I am personally acquainted with some cases. For example, I know of Ernesto Raúl Luque Escalona, my brother, who spent twelve years in expectation of being emancipated by the lord of the manor. During that time he received no less than six "C-8" forms -- a scrap of paper that informs you that your application to emigrate has been rejected. Naturally, it offers no explanation. All things considered, he may not have been so unlucky after all; at least he was spared actually having to assume the condition of a peon on a great landed estate. "The road to Miami also winds through the fields," Fidel declared. My brother, who was then very "treacherous," refused to break his back and possibly lose his life at an agricultural labor camp. He waited. Twelve years he waited. He does not hold the record. I believe the record belongs to the singer José Manuel "Meme" Solis, who waited 18 years from the date of his application.

In 1978, Fidel's desire for those despicable and depreciable dollars drove him to commit an error. I've said that Fidel never errs, but that is only when confronting questions or situations that may threaten his power. In other matters he seems to have a strong vocation for blundering. Moreover, Fidel takes advice from no one. He is alone; he wants it that way. Well, then, Fidel decided in 1978 to prove his humanitarian spirit by signing a pact with selected representatives of what was now officially known as "the Cuban community abroad," under the terms of which he agreed to free many political prisoners (not all, of course) and to permit the exiles -- the stateless worms who had deserted their country in the hour of danger (for Fidel all hours are "hours of danger") -- to visit their relatives in Cuba. I almost forgot: Fidel publicly recognized the attachment of those stateless persons to the customs and traditions of our country. Indeed, it is hard to find a child of Cuban parents born in the United States who doesn't speak Spanish perfectly.

The "communitarians," as the exiles were now called, came and went. They were exploited in a merciless manner by *fidelista* tourist organisms, but still they returned whenever they could to see their folks, leaving tens of millions of dollars behind.

But happiness is never complete. It was not only dollars that the "communitarians" brought with them, but proof -- palpable and evident -- of the astonishing economic and social success of Cubans in the United States. Demonstrating a drive, ambition and entrepreneurial spirit reminiscent of Arango's nearly forgotten sugarcrats, Cuban-Americans had become the most successful immigrants in the history of that nation of immigrants.

But here was the topping on the cake. Sure, the doctors, engineers, sundry professionals and businessmen, who had been the first to go into exile, might reasonably be expected to have prospered in the United States. But what truly astonished the populace was the success of common laborers and *campesinos*, and even men without occupations or advantages of any kind, who returned to Cuba proudly exhibiting their newly-won prosperity. For years, the exiles had been writing letters to their relatives and friends on the island telling them stories of bonanzas. The stories were true, after all.

The prosperity of the visiting exiles had a degrading, corrosive effect on what the *fidelistas* call "the revolutionary consciousness of the masses," and led to an increased desire on the part of Cubans to emigrate. Many who had never before considered leaving their country gave serious thought to it now, blinded by the "lies" that the visitors told them about capitalism. And many did, indeed, decide to quit this paradise where education and medical care are free and within the reach of everyone, to try their luck, instead, in a society dominated by violence and drug-addiction (oh yes, drug-addiction!), a society divided into opposing classes with disparate interests, a society characterized by man's exploitation of man (where, incidentally, the greatest exploiters were doctors and dentists).

Consequently, attempts to abandon the country by clandestine means increased, and, what was much worse, so did attempts to obtain diplomatic asylum by crashing foreign embassies, particularly those of Latin American countries. To catapult across the wall of a foreign embassy was perhaps more dangerous than to plunge into the sea in makeshift rafts and dinghies. While the Cuban Coast Guard cannot continuously patrol the entire expanse of Cuba's territorial waters, Cuban policemen can be posted outside every foreign embassy with orders to shoot to kill, orders they carried out without batting an eyelash.

Despite the risk of death, there were several ambitious attempts in 1980 to penetrate foreign embassies. These shook Fidel out of his complacency. A cute idea worthy of a sorcerer's apprentice -- or so he must have thought it -- occurred to Fidel. He retired the guard from the Peruvian embassy, which had been the scene of a recent incident. He must have surely expected that the embassy precincts would fill with fifty, sixty, one hundred, perhaps even two

167

hundred asylum seekers, complicating the lives of the Peruvian diplomats and their president, for whom Fidel felt no particular affection.

But that soon turned into a political catastrophe. To Fidel's great amazement (which turned quickly to rage), thousands of people converged on the unguarded embassy in a human avalanche that transformed the Miramar diplomatic district into a place of pilgrimage for Cubans. By the time *El Comandante* ordered the police to cordon off the area, eleven thousand people had taken refuge at the Peruvian embassy in a public display of repudiation that brought to the surface the tiger lodged inside Fidel.

Hours and then days passed. Eleven thousand people -- men, women, children and even the elderly -- were crowded into a space no larger than 30,000 square feet. They were thirsty, hungry and desperate. But at the same time, they were filled with hope. Among the crowd were a few delinquents (or a great many, if you credit official propaganda). But delinquents are people too; they have the same needs as other human beings.

Then, with the usual rhetoric about the humanitarian character of the Revolution, the authorities began distributing food to the confined multitude. Something must have gone wrong in their calculations, because they allocated three or four thousand rations to feed three times that number. What followed always happens in desperate and hopeless situations: the strong overpowered the weak and seized the short rations. The law of the jungle was imposed, just as the authorities had intended. There was a little bit of everything within the precincts of that ominous embassy: murder, rape, beatings and abuses of all kinds. The government alleged, of course, that it was not a case of human beings cracking under unbearable conditions but rather was because these men, women and children were "scum."

But the worst was yet to come. The government announced that the asylum seekers could return home and quietly await permission to leave the country. It promised that they would not be bothered. It also declared that anyone else who wanted to leave the country was free to do so, since the building of Socialism was a voluntary endeavor. Those who did not wish to take part in that work should go.

James Earl Carter, who was elected president in one of those collective blunders that the American public is free to commit every four years, offered a haven to all Cubans that wanted to leave the island. In Miami, Key West, Port Everglades, and Tampa, Cubans started chartering boats of all kinds to rescue their relatives and friends in Cuba. The Cuban government chose the Port of Mariel as the place of embarkation.

"The biggest dog's life that any man can drag behind him in this worldly kingdom." The words are taken from a short story by Alejo Carpentier, a writer as difficult to respect as a person as he is hard to surpass as a wordsmith. What phrase could I compose that would better describe the situation of the asylum seekers at the Peruvian embassy? Many, indeed, a majority, believed the assurances of government spokesmen -- and, it is worth noting, Fidel's assurances as well -- and left their infernal asylum, fleeing the dog's life that they had been leading for several days that must have seemed years to them. Little did they imagine that "the dog's life in this worldly kingdom" had just begun for them. To follow was the most shameful chapter in our history: the so-called "acts of repudiation."

We Cubans have never been a cruel people. In *The Brothers Karamazov*, Dostoevski expresses his preoccupation with the tendency to cruelty demonstrated by Russians. Maxim Gorki does the same in his numerous works. In truth, we don't have to go as far as Russia for examples. I have spoken already of the ferocious cruelty shown by other Latin American peoples during their wars of independence. In contrast, no Cuban writer could have expressed concerns similar to those voiced by the Russian masters. I have also noted that in Cuba's wars of independence our soldiers fought like men not beasts. During those terrible days of 1980, the cruel, the spiteful, the cowardly and the vile -- in sum, all men who hate as a vocation -- took over our streets and assailed with all their malice not only the asylum seekers who had relied on Fidel's word and returned home, but also the tens of thousands of other Cubans who had availed

169

themselves of his offer to sign-up to leave the country via Mariel. In all the cities and towns of our country, thousands of men, women and children were insulted, beaten, spat upon and humiliated in countless ways, in what was undoubtedly the most repugnant demonstration of collective helotry in the history of our country.

The outrages perpetrated by the King's Cuban Volunteers during the first years of our struggle for independence were isolated incidents, the work of a small group of men in wartime. The atrocities committed after the fall of Machado were directed at Machado's henchmen. But these "acts of repudiation" that took place in 1980 were not committed by detachments of troops following orders, nor by "sunshine patriots" venting their anger on the goons of a deposed dictator whom they had never dared oppose when he was in power. The disgraceful hate campaigns of 1980 were carried out by tens of thousands of men and women for no other reason than ingratiating themselves to a tyrannic government. For a time, these individuals came to represent the public image of our people, when, in reality, *they* were the dregs of Cuban society, the worst of the bad.

To cruelty was added hypocrisy. "Scum, get out; we don't want you," cried the mob as it carried out its vile work. But they didn't just want to punish those who rejected their share in paradise and wished to be let out of it. Their exhibition of beastliness also was intended to dissuade the fence stragglers, those who wanted to leave but for one reason or another could not make up their minds. I, for one, didn't dare to confront those mobs. I had my wife to consider as well as my 15-year-old daughter, whose beauty would have been one more incentive for those rabid dogs to attack us. I also had a son, then 12, who was not in the least interested in going anywhere. They dissuaded me.

That divine judgement upon our people contained just about everything in the way of retribution, including deaths. Even racism played its part. In Miramar, on leaving work one afternoon, I saw and heard a Chinese Cuban with an impassive and scornful face called a "yellow cur" by a Cuban black.

In another incident, I was not only a witness but a participant. I heard a great commotion outside my house and went out to see what was happening. The mob was assaulting a couple who had just left the building at 257 O Street. The man did not defend himself (nor could he) but held his wife in an embrace, trying to shield her from the mob's blows. Then, to my surprise, two neighbors and some five or six strangers locked arms and formed a ring around the couple, cutting them off from the mob. I joined the circle that was protecting those poor people. I ask myself now, how were we able to protect them? Why didn't the mob also attack us? Because they didn't know who we were, what we represented or what we could represent. We were strangers to most of them. As for the three in the mob who were our neighbors. They didn't know us, either. Here no one knows who's who.

We took off down O Street, going as far as the small park where Rafael Trejo was gunned down. We then crossed Infanta unto Jovellar, with the mob following in tow waiting to entrap us. At my side was a ten-year-old boy, armed with a stick and ready to use it. A boy of ten filled with hatred!

Where were we going? Where could we go? We arrived at the corner of Jovellar and San Francisco Streets, and it was there that a miracle happened: a white Lada automobile honked its way through the crowd and stopped in front of us. The driver unlocked the rear door and said with authority: "Get in." The mob was paralyzed for a few seconds. That was enough. By the time the more aggressive among them were ready to react, the Lada was speeding away with the unfortunate couple.

Did the government, that is to say Fidel, order and promote these "acts of repudiation?" I can't prove it. I can't even suggest it without incurring the risk of being charged with contempt for authority, writing enemy propaganda and spreading false reports. But if one solitary man can paralyze a mob and abscond with its quarry simply because he drives a Lada (a car that few Cubans could own then or now), gives orders convincingly, and looks as if he has the backing of authority, then surely the government, with its tens of thousands

171

of uniformed and armed men in Ladas, should have had no difficulty containing the violence. I accuse, therefore, Fidel Castro of having permitted in a most callous manner the mistreatment and humiliation of 125,000 citizens who left the country via Mariel.

But there was still more to come, however incredible that may seem. The ragtag flotilla of small boats arriving in Mariel to pick up refugees whose families and friends had sent for them, were, in addition, filled to capacity with common criminals taken either directly from prison or from the streets.

Fidel, who put an end once and for all to a national tradition of amnesty for political prisoners of which he was himself a beneficiary, and who has kept imprisoned for nearly thirty years his erstwhile follower and comrade-in-arms, Mario Chanes, chose instead to free and send to the United States lawbreakers whose offenses were committed against the lives and property of ordinary citizens (but not against the interests of Fidel Castro). This maneuver had twin objectives. First, it got rid of vermin who had already done all the harm they could to their countrymen on the island and were now of absolutely no use to Fidel. Second, it unleashed that plague on the United States, where these thousands of derelicts could do considerable harm to the prestigious reputation of Cubans residing there. Fidel loaded the boats with vermin, filling them to the rafters.

I saw those boats. They showed them on a cinema newsreel. With only the space where they stood, unable to move in any direction, the emigrants were packed like cattle, for the hundred-mile voyage that, if they made good time, might take ten hours. Since all the boats were filled much beyond their limit of passengers (as well as their limit of tonnage), it was inevitable that some of these vessels would sink. Scores of passengers drowned. In an editorial so overbrimming with cynicism and shamelessness *it* almost drowned several readers, *Granma*, the official party organ, described that makeshift flotilla as "the safest and most reliable cruise line in the world." Goebbels lives!

And that's how 125,000 Cubans departed their country. I said earlier that all of them had been subjected to mistreatment and humiliation. I wish to correct myself. The common criminals were brought directly from their cells to the boats, without ever having to face the wrath of the mob.

Mobs are a diabolic invention. Some call their methods "fascist." I don't agree. The fascists may have used mobs efficiently, but they didn't invent them. Something so simple and yet so effective as mob violence cannot be of such recent vintage as the Twenties and Thirties. The world is very old, and cruelty is as old as the world. In any case, mobs were never used in Cuba as a systematic instrument of state repression until that terrible year of 1980. That was the first time, but it was not the last. They were used again in 1987 and 1988, although on a smaller scale, against activists in the human rights movement. The protagonists were the same: indignant citizens who could no longer contain their rage at the words and acts of certain "worms."

The mobs and their "acts of repudiation" are the great strategic reserve in the *fidelista* arsenal of repression. They were used then and they will be used again whenever Fidel thinks it necessary or convenient. Anyone who assumes a dissident political posture must be ready to confront them, or rather must try to preserve his dignity before them, which is all he can do. No defense is possible.

I am preparing myself now to meet the mob: I hope I can keep my dignity. Other things, however, such as my teeth, the five quarts of blood in my body, an eye or so, and the integrity of my bones, I am not so confident of preserving. I won't be able to do anything against those dogs -- not even call them "dogs" -- because their shouts will drown out mine. But while I can, I want to tell all those who have participated or will participate in those carnivals of vileness, that you are the most despicable and repugnant rabble that has ever plagued this island and that your mothers should be called whores just for having given birth to you. That's what I call payment in advance.

On July 26, 1980, precisely on the anniversary of the assault on the Moncada barracks, and just months after tens of thousands of *fidelistas* had shamed our country with their mass exhibition of hatred and barbarism, Haydée Santamaría, the most important female figure of the Cuban Revolution, committed suicide. She was in her fifties and had known every kind of misfortune in her life. She must have been 25 when she participated in the Moncada assault, but even then she did not have a youthful appearance. Still, there was something in her eyes, in her expression, that was timeless. The years did not rob her of that indefinable something, and I should like to think that her sad death did not deprive her of it. Whatever it was, it lives in my memory, and makes me write these words that may perhaps serve as a fitting epithet: "Rest in Peace, Forever Young."

XIV. Bad Times

The year 1980 was a bad year for all Cubans, though not quite as bad as for those that enjoyed official "acts of repudiation" during the Mariel exodus. It was bad even for Fidel: in November of that year, Ronald Reagan defeated Jimmy Carter in the presidential election.

Of the eight American presidents who have had to contend with Fidel, Carter was the "best." The best American president for Fidel, that is, but the worst for the United States. Jimmy Carter was a liberal, and I cannot speak of him with much sympathy. Liberals are part of the American tradition and they play an important role in U.S. politics. What filled me with anxiety was that one of Carter's ilk became president at the precise moment in history when he would confront cool, astute, and voracious Stalinist politicians, the most prissy of which could easily have devoured a Yankee (or Southerner) for breakfast.

I have no doubt that Carter was a good man -- "A jolly good fellow, which nobody can deny." But, I ask you, what good is a "jolly good fellow" when we are talking about leading a great superpower at a time as turbulent as ours? What good are joviality and bonhomie against the sophistry of a veteran Soviet politician, the fanaticism of an Islamic fundamentalist, or even the outspokenness and disobedience of a Mexican president? Of what use, of what

175

possible use, is such geniality against Fidel's messianic complex and his inextinguishable hatred of the United States?

No, none except Carter would have allowed his powerful country to be insulted, harassed and humiliated. The Soviets knew how to make the best use of him, always within the bounds of protocol. But Third World politicians, with their underdeveloped sense of limitations, killed the goose that laid the golden egg. There is too much hatred in the Third World, too much envy; and hatred and envy cloud judgement. But for that, Carter could have been elected to a second term. He was a likable man, whose face radiated kindness. Moreover, precedent was on his side: All liberal presidents from Franklin Roosevelt to the hapless Richard Nixon were re-elected to office (with the exception of John F. Kennedy, who would have been re-elected had he not been assassinated). But Fidel Castro and the Ayatollah Khomeini spoiled it for Carter.

Fidel Castro introduced into the United States, practically by force, several thousand delinquents. The Ayatollah, for his part, inspired a well-armed mob of self-styled students to seize the U.S. embassy in Tehran and take dozens of Americans hostage and abetted them in their irrevocable determination not to set the hostages free until Iranian funds in U.S. banks were unfrozen.

It was too much. Americans understood that what their country needed was not "a jolly good fellow," but a tough guy. And there was a tough guy in the wings; he had been trying for several years to become president and was elected in November 1980.

The effects were soon evident: the Iman's intransigent and uncompromising students, who had occupied the U.S. embassy and held its diplomats hostage for more than a year, released them the moment Reagan took office on January 20, 1981. The simple outcome of an election had restored the Iman and his followers to sanity. Not a dime of Iranian funds in U.S. banks was returned.

For Fidel, the bad times had just begun, though he would try to put the best face he could on the events of that year. His bellicose propaganda increased even more than I thought possible. Reagan, he declared, was a committed advocate of war, practically a fascist, who would inevitably attack our country. The only thing that could perhaps dissuade him was total mobilization. Consequently, Fidel created the Territorial Militia, and made all Cubans pay for it by contributing one day of our salaries per week, which was no easy thing for our pocketbooks, since we needed every penny to shop in the "parallel market," as the official black market in Cuba is called. At the same time, the Armed Forces Ministry launched a frantic race to build military fortifications: pillboxes, trenches, bunkers and bomb shelters. In fact, so many holes were dug into the ground that the whole country began to resemble a giant Swiss cheese. Steel, cement and human sweat were poured needlessly into the ground, because Reagan, no doubt to spite Fidel, did not invade.

Panama, with whose government Fidel maintained most cordial relations, is smaller than Cuba and has one-fifth our population. It has an army as weak and inept as Batista's. But Panama also has large contingents of the U.S. military stationed in the Canal Zone, and, of course, the Canal itself, which the United States considers vital to its national security. The U.S. could not long afford to have the Panama Canal in the hands of a ruffian, an indicted drug trafficker who would sell his own mother if the price were right. Apparently, however, it can still afford to tolerate Fidel. No, it was not Fidel's costly war preparations that dissuaded Reagan from invading Cuba. It appears that he never had that intention.

He did, however, attack Grenada, and he would have been a fool not to do so. Well, perhaps not stupid -- just another Carter. When the Communists who controlled the small island republic started killing one another, Reagan sent the Marines and removed the contending factions from power.

The island of Grenada is very small, but it is still large enough to contain Fidel's most catastrophic defeat. He lost not only the influence that he exerted over its government but the Cuban capital, machinery and workers that were employed in constructing an airport whose size and geographic situation would have made an ideal pit-stop for planes flying to Angola. (The war in Angola had not been won despite initial successes.)

177

He lost the influence, but, above all, he lost the airport. In his fury he made yet one more heartless decision: he ordered the construction workers to defend the airport against the advance of the Marines. The construction workers had undergone military training, as most adult Cubans must. But they were not soldiers, nor were they there to fulfill any kind of military mission, and the territory that they were asked to defend was foreign ground. Oh, but if they died, if they were annihilated by the Marines, they would at least be useful as a propaganda tool against Yankee imperialism and its aggressive president. An heroic resistance by civilians, armed, but civilians nonetheless, would also have served to divert the attention of the Cuban people from certain embarrassing questions, such as, what was Cuban Intelligence up to that it did not notice the struggle among Grenadian leaders, and why did it not intervene to save the "dear comrade" Maurice Bishop?

To reinforce Fidel's decision to fight to the last man, Colonel Pedro Tortolo, was sent to Grenada to lead the construction workers in battle. He was a distinguished military officer, and had the added advantage of being black, which Fidel thought an indispensable condition for transforming him into a hero and martyr for Grenadians. But Tortola, who up to this time had enjoyed a brilliant career, did not prove the right man for the mission entrusted to him, which was nothing short of a suicide mission. The young colonel was asked to face an invincible opponent, and, in the end, his instinct of preservation prevailed, aided perhaps by common sense. He could not resist the pressure and deserted his men on the battlefield, seeking refuge in the Soviet embassy. Without a leader, and overwhelmed by the 82nd Marine Infantry, as well as by the absurdity of the mission entrusted to them, the Cubans surrendered.

The *fidelista* press published a series of ridiculous lies extolling the "heroic resistance." Colonel Tortolo was likened to Antonio Maceo, the great mulatto hero of Cuba's 19th century wars of independence. He was personally received at the airport by Fidel on his return to Cuba. In present-day Cuba, the truth has to claw and shove its way to make any progress at all, and still, it rarely succeeds.

In this instance, however, the truth finally prevailed and the hapless colonel was demoted to private and shipped to Angola.

Grenada was the first and only time in thirty years of unremitting struggle against Yankee imperialism that Cuban and American troops faced each other in battle. I hope that it will also. be the last, because such a confrontation would be senseless. For Fidel, yes, it would make all the sense in the world; it is his manifest destiny, his raison d'etre. For that reason, I imagine Fidel has prohibited the use of the word "Grenada" in his presence, and may even have proscribed Agustín Lara's famous song, *Granada*, which refers not to the island of Grenada, but to the Andalucian city from which Columbus set out to discover America: the city on whose shores our history began.

But Grenada was not the only "dirty trick" that Reagan played on Fidel. One day -- one day in the 2,922 days that Reagan governed the United States -- a ship devoted to oceanographic studies broke down in the Caribbean. Cast adrift, it was carried by the currents into our territorial waters. The Cuban Coast Guard attempted to tow it to port, but the crew of the scientific vessel put up a stubborn resistance. And it did something more: the ship radioed for assistance to the nearest U.S. naval station. Perhaps it wasn't really an oceanographic exploration ship. What is certain is that the base contacted the Pentagon, and the Pentagon contacted the White House, and the president ordered the nuclear aircraft carrier *Nimitz* to leave its home port in Puerto Rico and proceed at full speed to Cuba, accompanied by its complement of cruisers, destroyers and submarines. "At full speed," in this case, means 35 knots per hour, at which rate the flotilla would have reached Cuban waters in 24 hours. But it did not reach its destination. Someone just as prudent as me ordered the release of the American explorer vessel, and the U.S. Coast Guard was allowed to penetrate Cuban waters and salvage the mysterious ship. The *Nimitz* then returned to its home base.

Meanwhile, the war in Angola continued, as did preparations for the imperialist invasion, which included spectacular war-games conducted in the very heart of Havana. It was then, incredibly, that the Cuban government signed an immigration treaty with the country that would supposedly invade us at any moment. This was, undoubtedly, a singular event in the annals of diplomacy. How right was the Communist poet, Manuel Navarro Luna, who advised us to be surprised at nothing!

Nevertheless, the shocking treaty was short-lived, because Reagan did it to Fidel again. Without so much as a "here it comes," he launched Radio Martí, the Voice of America's Cuban program, which busted up, perhaps for ever, the news monopoly that Fidel had enjoyed for twenty-five years. In response, Fidel -- coming unhinged --suspended the Immigration Treaty, and renounced the tourist dollars that members of the Cuban community abroad brought to Cuba (as well as the headaches that the exiles' prosperity also brought him).

"Fidel, for sure, strike the Yankees hard!," was shouted again and again by the *fidelistas*. Sometimes I wish they would "strike the Yankees hard," not because I share their hatred of the Yankees (personally, I prefer the Dodgers), but because it often happens that when they can't hit the Yankees, they turn on their own countrymen. It's been four years since they've let me see my daughter.

While Reagan continued to push the world toward war, which was, after all, to be expected, given his perversity, there occurred in 1988 an extraordinary event, one more surprise in a decade of surprises, not all of which were unpleasant: the aggressive and bellicose president, the biggest warmonger of all the American presidents since Teddy Roosevelt, signed the only nuclear arms reduction treaty with the Soviets that actually reduced the number of nuclear arms in the world. Naturally, in order to speak of that treaty, we must refer to another pleasant surprise. It has a name, a patronymic and a surname: Mikhail Sergeyevich Gorbachev.

Brezhnev, whose style of government has been justly called "stagnationism," died in 1982. It was no coincidence that Brezhnev got along so well with Fidel. *El Comandante*, like a bank robber, always seems to be saying : "Nobody move." Brezhnev was succeeded by Yuri Andropov, a former director of the KGB, which naturally did not seem very propitious for future world peace. We never did learn Andropov's true character, because he died only a few months after assuming power. He was followed by Konstantin Chernenko, a veteran apparatchik, who looked as senile as Brezhnev in his last days. Appearances were not deceiving: in short order he occupied his niche along the Kremlin Wall. Then came Fidel's worst hour: Mikhail Gorbachev was chosen president of the Soviet Union. I tell you truly that misfortune lurks where one least expects it.

"Stagnationism" -- that's what I call a defining word. In 1985, when Mikhail Gorbachev assumed power, Cuba and The Soviet Union were both stagnant countries. Nonetheless, there was at the same time a fundamental and paradoxical difference: Cuba could afford the luxury of stagnation; the Soviet Union could not. The USSR did not have anyone to support it who could buy its exports at three times the world price and send it millions of barrels of oil over and above its domestic needs to resell for hard currency. It had no benefactor to underwrite year after year its balance of payments deficit. In other words, the Soviet Union had to -- and still has to -- support itself by its own efforts.

Moreover, it would be impossible, in the long run, to maintain military parity with the West when the economic disparity between East and West is so great and growing. We are talking about a matter of survival that goes beyond any doctrinaire rhetoric.

And, lastly, Gorbachev realized that in the world in which we live in the waning days of the 20th century, great territorial expansions and plentiful natural resources, have taken a back seat to the rapid advance of technology. To understand this truth one has but to glance at a map and compare the two principal capitalist economic powers, the United States and Japan. The latter is virtually without natural resources. Technological development is the product of human thought and cannot reach its full potential without freedom of expression. Modern society needs liberty as flowers need bees. Gorbachev understands this too well: he is a citizen of a country that has no one to subsidize it.

A centralized economy never works. It is absolutely incapable of competing with a free market economy, or of generating wealth at an equal or comparable level with modern-day capitalism. If Karl Marx were alive today, I imagine he would refute my affirmations with his powerful dialectic and his limitless rage, which was the fundamental trait of his disagreeable personality. But it so happens that Marx is dead and at long last buried. Lenin would also refute me if he could; but he can't. He died 65 years ago, before Gorbachev was born. Marx and Lenin are men from a different world and time. They cannot serve as guides to so changing and dynamic a world as ours in a time so unlike the one they knew.

The dire and undeniable necessity of keeping the Soviet Union economically in step with the other industrialized nations of the world, and the impossibility of accomplishing such a thing without first insuring certain liberties, gave rise to that which can be summarized in two Russian words that have in record time circled Eastern Europe and the world: perestroika and glasnost. They are but troublesome specters for some; such a one is Fidel.

The Chinese leadership realized many years ago the necessity of reforming its inoperative centralized economy, and took the required steps to do so. Unfortunately, the mandarin mind was able to grasp only half of the equation: the other half, democratization, was too much for it. The massacre at Tiananmen Square was the tragic result of doing things only halfway.

But Fidel won't even go *that* far. Bound to his stagnant world where everything has gone well for him from the first, Fidel looked unfavorably, even disdainfully, at reforms in the Soviet Union. With his customary perspicacity, he understood that these reforms, unlike those undertaken in the past by the Soviet Union or by Deng Xiaoping's gerontocracy, implied a surrender of bits of power and, therefore the disappearance of absolute power. For Fidel, if it's not absolute power, it's not power. Only one voice should be heard -- his; and if not his voice, then the voice of those who speak in his name.

Fidel confronted perestroika with his own "rectification program" consisting above all, of suppressing the few and limited means still available to us for liberalizing our country's economy,

182

such as the farmer's market. He met the winds of reform with the ancient worn-out theories of Ernesto Guevara that had wrecked the Cuban economy in the early 1960s -- theories that even Fidel had buried but now resurrected.

All things considered, Guevara's theories were not all absurd. I remember now one of his lapidary maxims: "Product quality is respect for the people." I recall it because the tension of writing this book has caused me to smoke like a condemned man. Well, as a habitual smoker I can attest that the *fidelista* entrepreneurial state cannot in this day and age manufacture matches whose use is not a dangerous adventure. There is no respect for the people, *Comandante* Guevara.

As for political liberalization, who now at the center of the Cuban government would dare suggest such an unstable and counter-revolutionary idea? Recently, several ordinary Cuban citizens who were most assuredly not at the center of government, but at the center of the enslaved Cuban people -- dissidents who, incidentally, did not seem to get along very well with one another -- waged a campaign to obtain for the Cuban people the rights enshrined in the U.N. Human Rights Charter to which Cuba is a signatory. At first, their protests were met with a certain indifference. But when their actions increased in audacity and appeared to gain the attention of the Cuban people, the regime unleashed on them brutal "acts of repudiation," and revived the old *fidelista* method for dealing with the opposition -- incarceration.

Such human rights campaigns are without a doubt meritorious and they have not been entirely fruitless. But there is something ingenuous, unreal and surrealistic in expecting that a totalitarian regime should respect human rights inherent in mankind. I have become an enemy of prophecies by reading Karl Marx, who was so enamored of them. However, I am going to try my luck as a prophet: Given the nature of the regime that he has imposed on our country, his years in power, the ideology to which he is bound and his own personal characteristics, I would dare to predict that Fidel would

183

respect human rights only when he is named caliph of Baghdad and protector of the faithful. That is to say, never.

In the end, there will be no perestroika or glasnost for Cuba. *El Comandante* does not want it, but I do. We Cubans want economic reforms and freedom of speech and press. We have proved it by making Soviet publications (that before perestroika were allowed to turn yellow from age on the news stands) the most eagerly sought, read and debated on the island. These were recently prohibited by Fidel, the same Fidel whose regime had for years represented everything that originated from Moscow as marvelous and unsurpassable. In any case, it will be a futile proscription. Radio Martí will see to it that we are told how the Soviets are demolishing the sinister Stalinist foundation of their country and building something new, better and more hospitable: a place where one may live in peace and without fear.

XV. High Treason

More than 30 years have passed since Fidel seized power. He is getting old. For the first time since 1959 there is a man much younger than him at the head of the Soviet Union. The *Comandante* is getting old, but he is not yet old, at least not old for a dictator: he has just celebrated his 63rd birthday. For those guilty of the twin sins of optimism and pessimism, I should like to remind everyone that life expectancy in Cuba is 74 years. Kim Il Sung, at 80, exhibits a vitality that is enough to make one cry. Mao died at 82 and in the last stage of his life involved the Chinese people in a whirlwind of madness and barbarism. At 85, Deng Xiaoping, though weakened by age and cancer of the prostrate, summoned enough strength to kill thousands of students in Tiananmen Square. Tito lived until he was 86 and the Ayatollah Khomeini died at 89, dictating to his last day death sentences against his enemies in the name of Allah, the Clement and Most-Merciful.

I have already made one prophecy and I do not intend to make another. I just want to say that Fidel's appearance and the resistance that he has shown throughout his life to disease, make me think (I almost said "dread") that he will live many more years. I also believe that he will not improve with age; he has not so far. The passage of time brings many disagreeable things, though sometimes these are accompanied by certain virtues that a long life affords: more serenity and self-control. But life has not given these gifts to *El Comandante*.

During a press conference held when Gorbachev visited Cuba in 1989, Fidel's tantrums and gestures were in marked contrast to the Soviet leader's serene joviality. But he was worse -- much worse than ever I have seen him -- when he was interviewed by Maria Kennedy Shriver of the tragic Bostonian clan. A question from the journalist touched off one of *El Comandante*'s many sensitive buttons and he lost all control: his face was contorted into a furious mask, his tiger eyes went in and out of focus, his hands alternately affirmed, denied and repudiated, he was so much out of control in all that frenzy of gesticulating, that one of his hands even came to rest on Maria Shriver's thigh. What kind of behavior was this for a statesman with more than thirty years experience in public life? There is something wrong, very wrong, in the spirit of a public figure when a simple question can unman him. Maria Shriver is, in truth, exasperating, but in a sense very different.

At the rate he is going, Fidel would tax the patience of Job if he were brought back to life just for that purpose. I myself was sent into a paroxysm of anger by him the day Blas Roca died. The old head of Cuba's pre-revolutionary Communist party had expressed a wish to be buried in the earth, not in those crypts and mausoleums that Cubans favor. Fidel honored Blas Roca's last wish and ordered that he be buried at the Cacahual Memorial beside Major General Antonio Maceo, and his aide-de-camp, Captain Francisco Gómez Toro, son of Generalissimo Maximo Gómez. Maceo and the younger Gómez were killed together in battle in 1896 and buried by the generalissimo at a hill near Havana called the Cacahual.

When the Cuban Republic was established in 1902, this hill was dedicated as a memorial to the two heroes and all who fell in battle for Cuba's independence. Around their simple memorial was constructed a great parade grounds, where military reviews were conducted in their honor. The Cacahual is our national sanctuary, reserved for those who gave their lives for our country. It is on that sacred ground that Fidel ordered Blas Roca buried.

186

The Popular Socialist Party -- predecessor of the Cuban Communist Party -- has provided us with as many myths as Castroism itself: the "political talent" of Carlos Rafael Rodriguéz, the "intellectual brilliance" of Juan Marinello and the "kindness" of Blas. Rubbish! How can a man like Blas Roca be called "good?" He served three dictators: Stalin, Batista and Fidel. What Communist didn't serve Stalin while that diabolic man lived? That Blas Roca also served Fidel may be of merit to the *fidelistas*. But to have served Batista was not like serving Stalin or Fidel, because no one was *compelled* to serve Batista. Both of Batista's two periods in government were marked by crime and corruption. Blas Roca was neither a criminal nor corrupt, but he was an accomplice to crime and corruption because he praised, applauded and adulated Batista, a corrupt and criminal ruler against whom the entire youth of our nation would rise less than ten years after Blas had declared Batista a "wellspring of Cuban democracy." The youth of Cuba took arms against Batista in 1953 without Blas Roca's approval.

We should not forget -- I will never forget -- Blas Roca's praise for Batista, uttered in 1944, when Batista had already assassinated Antonio Guiteras (the architect of social reform in Cuba after the 1933 Revolution), suppressed with great bloodshed the sugar workers' strike of 1935, and stolen millions in public funds.

Today, when Cuban soldiers return from Angola, they are taken to the Cacahual, which is no longer merely the place where General Antonio Maceo, and his faithful assistant, Captain Francisco Gómez Toro, rest. Now, it is where General Antonio Maceo, Captain Francisco Gómez and Comrade Blas Roca rest. It is almost as if Fidel had buried Batista himself with Cuba's greatest heroes. Shame!

Thirty years are a long time. More than thirty years have passed since New Year's Day 1959 when reason slept and the young hero promised us peace. During his first speech in Havana, hundreds of doves were released, and after flying about as birds are wont to do, one came to rest on Fidel's left shoulder as birds do not ordinarily do. But as we all later had occasion to learn, man cannot put his trust in animals: not in sharks, which are a symbol of voraciousness;

187

nor in doves, which are a symbol of peace. Neither can one trust tigers, that is, if one lives long enough to learn not to trust them.

The young *comandante*, with the dove perched on his shoulder, offered us peace. Almost three decades later, a war that had lasted thirteen years and that was fought thousands of miles from our shores, finally came to an end. The Angolan war -- in which 300,000 Cubans served -- ended thanks to two fortunate occurrences. One was an attempt by the South Africans to seize the strategic town of Cuito Cuanavale. The South Africans attacked, the Cubans defended, but where were the Angolans? Very well, thank-you. The troops in the field were commanded by the able General Polo Cintras; the supreme commander of all troops in Angola was General Arnaldo Ochoa, who was transformed into a living legend, not by official propaganda, which was never copious in respect to him, but by his deeds. A year after his victory he would be a dead legend.

The other event that ended the war in Angola was Gorbachev's decision to scrap the Brezhnev Doctrine. Thus ended the Soviet Union's imperialist adventures, which Fidel dubbed "internationalist actions." The Soviets had decided to put an end to their war in Afghanistan. They also decided to end the Angolan war, which in a way was also their war. The victory at Cuito Cuanavale saved the prestige of *El Comandante* and threw a smoke-screen around promises that Cuban troops would remain in Angola until apartheid was abolished in South Africa.

Talks were held here and there, but never were any talks conducted without the presence of a Soviet adviser to put his nose in everything. Fortunately, the Soviets were able to apply the brakes to the ever-renewable bellicose instinct of the *fidelistas*. At long last an accord was reached whereby Cubans and South Africans would withdraw from Angola, and Namibia would be granted its independence. This was linkage, clear and simple. Fidel, who had for years haughtily rejected Pretoria's offer of a joint withdrawal, was forced, in the end, to accept linkage.

It's said that sometimes one misses the forest for the trees; just as often, however, one looks at the forest and cannot distinguish between trees. I, for one, did not notice that General Ochoa was missing from the delegation that travelled to the United Nations to sign the peace treaty; more than a dozen generals were present, but not Ochoa. Although, to think of it, there was no reason for Ochoa or Polo Cintras to be present, because neither Ochoa, supreme commander of Cuban troops in Angola, nor Polo Cintras, head of the Southern Front, had anything to do with this "victory:" it was all the work of Fidel.

El Comandante's personality cult is so pervasive in Cuba that it is difficult to avoid idolizing him. The night I heard Fidel explain how *he* had led the troops to victory at the battle of Cuito Cuanavale -- Fidel, who had never set foot in Angola -- I could not help comparing him to a hero of the *Iliad*. Homer was in the habit of giving his heroes sobriquets: Achilles, "the fleet-footed," Hector, "the manslayer," Odysseus, "the hairsplitter." Fidel is no longer light on his feet (if he ever was), and although he has sent many men to their deaths and split every hair in the country, I would not compare him to Achilles, Hector or Odysseus. It seems to me that he is most like Agamemnon, "he that commands from afar."

Poor Agamemnon! How his hapless soul, in whatever regions it is confined, would envy the possibilities that technology offers the modern man. He would no doubt think that if he had been given the means at Fidel's disposal, he, too, would have vanquished the Trojans without having to stir from Mycenae, thereby sparing himself the disappointments and calamities that befell him in the *Iliad*: the hardships of a long campaign (not as long as the war in Angola, but long enough); the rows with the irascible, undisciplined and self-sufficient Achilles; the longing for his children; the infidelity of his wife; even his own premature death at the hands of she and her lover. All this he could have avoided. In truth, there are few who agree with the Spanish poet Jorge Manrique that "any time is better than the present," but among those unhappy few is a majority of the Cuban people.

And since we are talking about ill-starred warriors and heroes, let us not forget General Arnaldo Ochoa, once a "Hero of the Republic," who was recently executed for high treason stemming from his alleged involvement in drug trafficking.

High treason! What did it consist of? Ochoa was accused of having "committed hostile acts against other countries by helping to introduce drugs into those territories." The plural -- "countries" -- is superfluous, since everybody knows that the drugs that passed through Cuba were destined for only one country -- the enemy of choice in the *fidelista* global mindset. How can a hostile act against an enemy -- the United States -- be called "high treason?" And if Ochoa could be convicted by Fidel of "high treason" against the United States, why wasn't he also charged with "high treason" against Venezuela, where in the early 1960s Ochoa tried unsuccessfully to foment a revolution? Isn't that a hostile act against another nation? And, for that matter, why weren't the three survivors of Guevara's misadventures in Bolivia also tried for "high treason?" Better late than never.

Ochoa guilty of "drug trafficking?" What means did Ochoa have at his disposal in Angola to facilitate the vile work of the narco-smugglers in the Western Hemisphere? One who did have such means, and, apparently, also the inclination, was Rear Admiral Aldo Santamaría, erstwhile head of the Cuban navy, who was indicted of drug trafficking by a grand jury in Miami. The same Aldo Santamaría with 46 other generals and admirals comprised the so-called "Tribunal of Honor" that demanded the death penalty for their comrade-in-arms. All demanded it. All but one.

There were those in Cuba, then as now, that had the wherewithal to support drug smuggling: the Navy, the Air Force, the Coast Guard, the omnipresent State Security Service, the Military and CounterIntelligence Agency, and the Interior Ministry's mysterious Department MC, run by Colonel Tony La Guardia. The Army did not. And it was to this branch of the Armed Forces that Ochoa always belonged. From adolescence, he had worn an Army uniform.

Did Ochoa's lieutenant really meet with a powerful godfather of the Medellin drug cartel? Did Ochoa really contemplate assisting the narco-traffickers or had he stuck his nose in affairs that were none of his business? Arnaldo Ochoa and his lieutenant were *fidelistas*, and *fidelistas* have a way of looking at life, morals, and ethics that is completely alien to me, despite my long and involuntary cohabitation with them. Let us not forget that the drugs were destined for the United States, the focus of all the evil in the world. Surely the evil would disappear once that country was destroyed -- from without or within.

When the United States -- this malignant giant, the brains, arms and maximum expression of imperialist capitalism --falls at last, exploitation, misery and war will disappear from the world; workers will receive just compensation for their labor; blacks and women will not be denied equal rights; children will no longer die of curable diseases and all will have teachers and schools; men will no more fight other men in insane fratricidal wars (for all men are brothers); women will not have to mourn the tragic and useless death of their men; education, science and culture will be the patrimony of all humanity, and all will be able to satisfy fully their spiritual and material needs. In short, when the United States is out of the way, "life will flower and sorrow will die," to paraphrase Gardel's famous tango.

Naturally, poisoning such a merciless and selfish society with drugs would necessarily mean the deaths and degradation of millions of innocents -- for not all Yankees are bad people. But it would also save millions from the evils afflicting them, and insure the happiness of the world (or at least the Third World). It is a numerical, quantitative question.

The fairy tale that the reader has just been told is an article of faith for *fidelistas*. With such a perspective on things, it is no surprise that someone should have thought up the idea of drowning the United States in cocaine in order to advance peace and world liberation and insure the well-being of all men (well, most men). In fairness, not all of Fidel's followers are capable of participating in something so repulsive as narco-trafficking. If Ochoa did so or

191

conceived the idea of doing so, and took the first steps to realize that idea, how was it possible that Raúl Castro, Ochoa's immediate superior, did not charge him accordingly when he announced the decision to prosecute Ochoa?

To contemplate the commission of a crime is not the same thing as committing it. In any case, the maximum sentence for drug trafficking under the *fidelista* penal code is 15 years, not death.

Prosecutor Escalona did not sound entirely convincing to me. As for the defense counsel, I should prefer not to speak of them. Doesn't the government realize that Cubans have seen countless American and English films that culminate in court trials, and, therefore, even the youngest among us know what a defense attorney is? No, I will not mention Ochoa's attorneys, nor the attorneys of the other defendants. I prefer to speak of Prosecutor Escalona, who belongs to a tribe that is not very numerous elsewhere in the world, but that, in Cuba, is reproducing like rabbits. One finds them everywhere.

The trial was a mere formality: the important thing was that Ochoa should die. Why? The real motives were given by Raúl Castro the night he announced the court martial of the disgraced general. Raúl had with him a prepared speech, but in a rapture of inspiration for which I am very grateful, he decided to improvise. I don't think that Fidel was grateful, however.

In his improvisation, which was not published in the Cuban press, but which was recorded and aired by the sharp boys at Radio Martí, Raúl did not once mention narco-trafficking. He spoke rather of Ochoa's "populism" (did he mean "popularity?"); of Ochoa's criticisms of how the war in Angola was being conducted and of the war itself; of Ochoa's supposed opposition to the *fidelistas'* plans and dreams in the field of public health; and in particular of Ochoa's objection to .making Cuba a "medical superpower." Finally, Raúl alluded to Ochoa's "jokes and harangues" (about what or whom?). He spoke of all that, and, even more importantly, he lashed out against unnamed "idiots" who question Fidel's leadership, and invited those who were not happy with how Socialism was being built in Cuba to move to Poland, Hungary or Armenia (that is, the Soviet Union itself).

I have never considered Raúl a talented man. He is mediocre, and barely even that. Still, I never thought he would be capable of such a blunder as he committed that night. He spoiled everything with his extemporaneous remarks, which made it abundantly clear that Ochoa was being prosecuted for political dissent, not drug trafficking. Political dissent from the likes of Ochoa is punished with death in Cuba. And he died, though other factors also contributed to his demise.

Raúl Castro has played two very important roles in the travesty of the Revolution. First, he has assumed direct control over military affairs. These do not seem to interest his older brother much, despite Fidel's strong attachment to the vocation of war, the fact that he has worn fatigues these last 33 years, and his parapsychological gift for personally directing battles such as Cuito Cuanavale from thousands of miles away. Secondly, Raúl has acted, and very convincingly too, the role of the "evil brother," the more radical Communist, in fictitious and threatening contrast to Fidel the charismatic, who is portrayed as more benign and thoughtful.

A farce is a farce, even if it has been kept up for 30 years. A farce could be kept up forever, but that still wouldn't make it true. If someday, God forbid, I were asked to choose between the two Castros (two persons, but one "Big Brother"), I should unhesitatingly pick Raúl.

Let us continue now with more theater. The scene shifts now from the "evil brother" to the hapless Ochoa, who is about to exit the stage before the firing squad. The general confessed his crimes, which of course means nothing after the confessions of Bukharin, Radek and Kamenev, among others. These victims of Stalinist terror accused themselves with far greater enthusiasm than Ochoa, and their murders were later inscribed by the Soviets themselves in the annals of universal infamy. To the detriment of official propaganda, Ochoa exhibited a marked change in attitude between his appearance at the "Tribunal of Honor" and his court-martial: the apathetic, depressed and taciturn man who was shown at the first trial did not resemble in the least the man we saw at the court-martial where he was sentenced to death. There he demonstrated his true character, which had made him Cuba's most distinguished soldier since the War of Independence (1895-98). Such was his conduct on that occasion that even now that he is dead it continues to irk the big-wigs of the regime.

Stripped of his rank and decorations, and dressed in civilian garb, Ochoa impressed his countrymen with his cool indifference before the fate that awaited him, his dignified bearing, his handsome appearance, and his slow and deliberate speech. Peasants always face death like men, whether they be generals, presidents or baseball players.

There was more to this trial, much more, than what we were shown on television. The government, which did not air the entire trial but only edited portions, is unintentionally responsible for the many rumors that now circulate about Ochoa's courtroom demeanor. When the prosecutor questioned him, Ochoa is said to have answered, "Escalona, we know each other well." Could it be true? How could we find out? But remember: everything is a secret until the day it's made known. Bukharin's trial was once also a secret, and a secret it remained until the day that *Sputnik* (or was it *Moscow News*?) revealed the truth.

Still, what we already know is enough. Public opinion did not support the death sentence for Ochoa. For the first time that I can recall, Fidel (who always speaks in the name of all the people and always uses that collective "we" when referring even to himself) acknowledged that he was acting without even the implied consent of the people by adopting the first person singular ("I") to indict Ochoa.

Why, then, did he condemn to death his comrade-in-arms, his samurai, a man who had followed and served him for thirty-two years, for all his adult life and even as a boy? Why didn't Fidel forgive Ochoa as he had Rolando Cubelas, a man who not only was neither his comrade nor his follower (and never had been) but also had tried to assassinate him? Because Ochoa, unlike Cubelas, was dangerous!

Who can tell what thoughts passed through Ochoa's mind during his imprisonment? How his spirit may have been affected by the recollection of his humble beginnings in the revolutionary struggle as a soldier of Fidel, his first battlefield promotion, his march through the plains of the hinterland with Camilo Cienfuegos' column, his guerrilla ádventures in Venezuela (following this time not Fidel's steps but his ideas), his military studies in the Soviet Union, his efforts to overcome his lack of a formal education, his academic successes, his wars, his battles, his victories, and his enemies.

Conversely, what did an imprisoned Ochoa mean to Fidel's own enemies in the government? What projects would they have carried out that depended on the general? And what of the army, soldiers and officers? Ochoa was loved and admired by his subordinates; perhaps too well loved and too much admired for his own good. Camilo Cienfuegos and Ernesto Guevara were also loved and admired by their men. But their military feats were comparable to Fidel's, while Ochoa's were incomparably superior.

Napoleon, who was not a fan of executions despite his familiarity with death, did once lose his patience and ordered the execution of the duc d'Enghien. In response, Talleyrand, that shameless politicaster, coined one of his brilliant phrases: "It was not a crime, it was a blunder." The death of Arnaldo Ochoa was no blunder.

The trial of the general, the brothers La Guardia, and the rest of the officers accused of narco-trafficking, was the greatest political catastrophe ever suffered by Fidel. He lost what was left of his international prestige and what little credibility he had in the eyes of his people.

The trial was a disaster because of the vagueness of the accusations against Ochoa, because of the judicial irregularities that were committed, and because of the behavior of the defense counsel, who were shown as mere understudies for the prosecutor. Lastly, it was turned into a sham by the prosecutor himself. I admit that my animus

195

toward the prosecutor may also have been fueled by factors beyond his control. Despite his undeniable knowledge of jurisprudence, and a certain histrionic eloquence that every good prosecutor must possess, it was difficult for me to take General Juan Escalona seriously: he just looked too much like Louis de Funes.

The worst thing of all was that it was impossible to believe that the drug-smuggling activities described at the trial could have been carried out without the knowledge and consent of the highest authorities in the country. Please don't take offense, Fidel and you other gentlemen, but believe me: it would be impossible. You, Fidel, have taught us to regard the organs of State Security as thoroughly efficient. You have portrayed them as such in films, books, interviews, and a television series that we have all seen. You have conditioned us to believe that State Security is everywhere, that it watches everything, that it supervises everything, that it never rests, that it never rests on its laurels, and that it never lets down its guard. You have even convinced us that Cuban Intelligence has infiltrated the CIA, that it has countless agents in the United States, many of them in Miami, the "capital of Cuban exiles."

What the hell have Reinier and David, the two invincible heroes of the espionage serial, "It Had to Be in Silence," been doing all this time? How could it be possible to realize drug-smuggling activities -- not via remote airports like San Julian at the desolate Western tip of the island but via Santa Clara and Varadero in Havana itself -- without State Security or Military Counter-Intelligence knowing of it?

What say the officers now who divorced their wives when apprised by Counter-Intelligence that they were unfaithful? Could the sexual lives of these ladies be more important than the smuggling of drugs through national territory?

Fidel himself, on the night that he announced his decision not to commute Ochoa's death sentence, complained bitterly and in harsh language of the perfidy and ingratitude of the Americans, who had not informed him of the activities of Tony La Guardia, although he, Fidel, had informed them of a plot to assassinate Reagan. According to Fidel, Cuban Intelligence is so active and efficient that it can pick up radio signals transmitted by a would-be assassin somewhere in the vast territory of the United States, but at the same time is unable to discover that Varadero, Cuba's busiest tourist resort, was being used to smuggle drugs into the United States!

For many years, the United States has alleged that Cuban officials were directly implicated in drug trafficking and had indicted four in absentia as long ago as 1982. That question posed by Maria Shriver that so irritated Fidel, did it not have to do with just such allegations? My memory fails me; it happens to all of us from time to time.

Cubans here are not just convinced that the government's Intelligence and Counter-Intelligence services are very efficient. We also believe with absolute certainty, because we have been given cause to believe, that Cuban Intelligence is unconditionally loyal to Fidel. With such efficiency and loyalty, how was it that they failed to see everything that was happening? And if they did notice, how was it that they failed to inform *El Comandante*? Could that be possible? In any case, it's not believable.

Could General Ochoa have saved himself? No, I do not think so. His talents like Generalissimo Gómez's were those of a soldier; he lacked the political acumen necessary to understand Fidel's complex personality (the only personality in our country). Moreover, Ochoa was a *fidelista* all his life. He proved it when he affirmed before the "Tribunal of Honor" that his dying thought would be of Fidel. I was not in the least amused. However, it was undoubtedly something a follower of Fidel would say. General Rafael del Pino had much better luck. He served a quarter of a century in Fidel's Air Force, where he showed the same loyalty and competence as did Ochoa in Fidel's Army. But General del Pino is not and never was a *fidelista*. He demonstrated his independence as early as 1963, when he was chief of the aerial base at Holguín. When a cyclone laid waste to the province of Oriente in that year, destroying the Holguín barracks and leaving his men in the cold, he treacherously purloined by cover of night, the only wood left in the whole province to reconstruct his barracks, wood that had been destined for some pet project of Fidel. By laying his sinful hands upon that sacred wood, Rafael del Pino showed himself to be an iconoclast, which is something incompatible with *fidelismo*. One day, many years later, he flew a plane with almost his entire family and escaped to the United States. He still lives.

Had Ochoa been of a similar mind, he would have remained calm and quiet, keeping to himself all his criticisms and objections. At the very least he should have kept calm and quiet long enough for his appointment as chief of the Western Army to become effective. He then could have deposed Fidel by a coup d'état, for he lacked neither the daring nor prestige to do so. In any case, if a coup proved impossible, he would have been able to flee with his family, as did del Pino.

Nothing else remains that I would like to talk about. The trial of José Abrahantes, the Minister of Interior, does not much interest me. Abrahantes, unlike Ochoa, was a mere *arriviste*. While public opinion was opposed to Ochoa's execution, it was decidedly favored that of Abrahantes. When the former police chief was not executed, the government was obliged to offer explanations. Abrahantes headed for decades Fidel's secret police. But he had to be sacrificed (though his life was spared) because Fidel needed someone sufficiently high in the power structure to blame for his regime's failure to expose in time the scandal of the Cuban Connection. The whitewash of Fidel was accomplished at Abrahantes' expense.

Abrahantes, who 31 years and 7 months ago had gone to fetch me at my hotel in Mexico City and conducted me to the apartment barracks of the July 26th Movement, was now more useful to Fidel in prison. *El Comandante* is a pragmatic man, not much given to sentimentality. It is said that Abrahantes was supposedly sympathetic to perestroika and glasnost; but though we can believe that of Ochoa, it would be impossible to believe it of Abrahantes. As for a power struggle between Raúl Castro and Abrahantes to succeed Fidel, such speculations are scarcely worthy of comment. Raúl Castro is not what one would call a talented man, but neither is he a neophyte.

Ochoa's martial feats in Angola overshadowed Fidel's skirmishes with Batista. Abrahantes, who had no battlefield experience, posed no threat to anyone.

And, again, why all this talk of succession? I have already mentioned Fidel's age and his probable life expectancy. Yes, Fidel could die tomorrow, like any man born of woman; but he could also last 25 years or more (God forbid!). In the end, no one will succeed Fidel, not permanently or even provisionally. Fortunately for Cubans, Fidel is a unique phenomenon in our history. No one will be able to fill the void left by his death or his disappearance from the political life of our country. His regime is an edifice constructed on one pillar. It cannot stand once the pillar has fallen.

XVI. The Judgment of History

I have already mentioned Carlos Alberto Montaner's thesis that Fidel has been able to do everything that he has done only because there was a revolution in Cuba, or, more specifically, because he evolved in a revolutionary atmosphere. I agree. In fact, the Cuban Revolution has soured me on all revolutions past or future, and that includes any hypothetical anti-Castro revolution. What have all revolutions been but great massacres? Massacres all: the English Revolution, the French Revolution, the Haitian Revolution, the Mexican Revolution, the Russian Revolution, the Chinese Revolution, the Cuban Revolution, the Nicaraguan Revolution and the Iranian Revolution. Our neighbor to the North calls its war of independence a "revolution." But the "American Revolution" was not really a revolution, because it lacked the violent social changes that always characterize and accompany every revolution: scaffolds and firing squads.

When one fights in a revolution every dream is beautiful: it is like being in love. Afterwards, when those who survived the war seize power, they bring always with them despotism --not enlightened despotism, just despotism. A Mexican whose name I can't recall put all this into eight words: "this revolution has degenerated already into a government." Love, despite its many disappointments, is not as thankless as revolution.

A revolution is the rule of violent, merciless men whose affections are weak if they have any at all. "At the risk of sounding foolish," *Comandante* Guevara said, "let me say that a revolutionary is someone motivated by great feelings of love." The author of this bold assertion knew well what it was to risk his life, but he did not know anything about love.

There can be no doubt that the Revolution opened the way for Fidel Castro, but it was his personal characteristics, the combination of good and bad qualities that form his peculiar personality, that enabled him to take full advantage of the possibilities that a revolutionary climate afforded.

"Render unto Caesar what is Caesar's," counselled Christ. This is sage advice, because when not given their due, Caesars frequently will take it by force -- and in passing break the heads of the defaulters. I then, will give our Caesar his due: Fidel is, to begin with, a man of notable intelligence and prodigious memory. All his considerable mental faculties are guided toward one end: the acquisition of power. His disastrous conduct as a ruler has caused many to question his ability, but such doubts are born of incomprehension. They misjudge Fidel because they don't understand the man or what really interests him.

One of Fidel's other notable characteristics is his talent for histrionics. I don't say this with the least intention of belittling him, because I have only the greatest respect for the acting profession. I truly believe that if Fidel had dedicated himself to the stage he would have attained fame comparable to that he now enjoys -- except without hurting anyone. I do not doubt that he would have equalled the celebrity of a Lawrence Olivier or a Jack Nicholson, an Yves Montand or a Marcelo Mastroianni. Fidel is capable of transmitting his feelings and moods to any audience that hears him. I have seen him do it many times, more than I care to remember. He is also capable of depicting convincingly a character or a situation that is alien to his own real personality or circumstances. Such are the qualities that go into making a great actor.

201

I remember one of his appearances before the General Assembly of the United Nations. On that day (I do not know why) Fidel decided that he should appear humble before his audience. So at the conclusion of his speech, he quickly sat at a chair near the podium provided for the next speaker, who with the rest of the audience was on his feet applauding Fidel. Timidly, uneasily and a bit surprised, his knees pressed together like those of a schoolboy and his speech neatly folded on his lap, Fidel listened to the thunderous ovation, demonstrating his evident desire that the applause should end, so that he could escape from that embarrassing situation. Bravo!

Intimately bound to his histrionic capacity is his unflappable aplomb, which he loses only when someone contradicts him or asks him a question relating to a subject about which he does not care to speak. Fidel can say the most incredible things as if the whole world would believe them, and as if he himself believed them.

He also possesses charm, a good appearance, and a voice that was initially deficient but has been perfected into an effective instrument. Finally, he is possessed of audacity and a boundless ambition. His profound knowledge of human nature enables him to detect dangerous men (in this he sins sometimes by excess, but never by omission). Some of his personal traits are not exactly virtues but they serve his ends just the same: an absolute egoism and a lack of strong affections, roots, mercy or love. He also lacks any respect for tradition, friendship, loyalty or family values (having abolished the family in a systematic manner). For him, the fatherland is a mere base of operations.

There are no limits for Fidel or soft spots in his character. I have said that Guevara didn't know anything about love, and felt no compassion for his enemies. Nevertheless, I should have preferred that he rule Cuba today rather than Fidel. In such a hypothetical, (or rather impossible) situation, I think that had I behaved bravely, Guevara might perhaps have allowed himself to be impressed with my courage. Had I showed myself to be intelligent and cultured, he might have been impressed by my intelligence and culture. But nothing impresses --nothing ever can impress or move -- Fidel.

202

All this goes into making a monstrous personality without precedent in the history of our country. It was not by accident that Fidel embraced Marxism, an ideology that upholds absolute power like no other, and that is superior in that respect even to the divine right of kings. Nor should it surprise that today he so tenaciously defends the purity of Marxist tenets. This preoccupation with the purity of ideologies, whether political or religious, is unmistakably reminiscent of the Medieval Scholastics. It is very typical among engorged men whose every material want has been amply provided for.

"Mao's well-fed cadres," is a phrase used by John Le Carre. It is possible that the master of the thriller may not even remember having written it, for those words cannot have the same significance for him that they have for me. Those who have been born in Anglo - Saxon countries see the Great Khan and other rulers of the same species as something remote, exotic. It is only natural: it has been more than three centuries since the corpse of the last English dictator, Oliver Cromwell, was flung into a sewer.

Fidel the Marxist fears -- and not without good reason -- that in a few years, when the people hear Marx's name, they will think first of Groucho and his brothers. I have a vaguely similar problem with names and surnames. As everyone doubtless has noticed by now, I count myself among Fidel's detractors. I am sure it will cost me dearly. It so happens that all my colleagues refer to Fidel by his last name, while I have always called him just Fidel. I want to make it clear -- lest it become the subject of twisted interpretations -- that my calling him Fidel is no mark of love, respect, or admiration. It is not due to any positive feeling on my part for him. Rather it is due to the fact that the word "Castro" does not mean Fidel to me. When I hear "Castro," what comes immediately to mind is not *El Comandante*, but Juan Castro, the best catcher that I have ever seen in action.

Incidentally, both Castros have a lot in common: they are both tall, strong, authoritarian and proud, and both have been greatly assisted by television. Fidel Castro, because he knows how to use it

203

to the fullest as an instrument of power; Juan Castro, because a camera shot from center-field displays most strikingly his skills as a catcher. I think not without sadness how different our lives would be if Fidel had been capable of governing with something like the solid and serene mastery with which Juan Castro plays baseball.

The surname Castro is of Galician origin. I believe, though I may be mistaken, that in the Galician language it means "a fort or military camp," which reminds me of the legend of Robin Hood, and in particular of his foe, the evil Norman baron Isambard de Bellame. The fort or "castro" in which the evil Isambard lived was known to the Saxons as "Evilhold," a word that I reproduce in the original English and that prudence alone prevents me from translating into Spanish.

As if I didn't have enough problems in my life, these damned literary allusions will not let me work in peace. I should make an effort to write with more serenity and coherence, especially now that I am at last coming to the end of this long six-weeks march.

In fact, what is happening is that I have just one more thing to say, and like Bartleby in Melville's story, "I would prefer not to." This is the third time that I cite Melville, and since four can fit as well as three, I will quote him once more, though I promise this will be the last. Besides, this quotation from the sermon pronounced by Maple's father is really worthwhile: "Delight is to him -- a far, far upward and inward delight -- who against the proud gods and commodores of this earth, ever stands forth his own inexorable self."

Probably, you have all noticed already that I need to fortify my spirit. Believe me, I have reasons enough. You may have noticed also that I am obsessed with the narrative history of *Moby Dick*, because of the resemblance between our country and the SS *Pequod*, a ship that sailed to its final destination under the command of a mad captain. At last, we Cubans have set out on that voyage of no return.

"I proclaim this fatal truth: Louis must die for France to live!" No people have a greater capacity for composing historic phrases than the French. I also will proclaim a fatal truth, though I very much fear that this time it will not be the king's head that will roll. This is my truth: "Fidel Castro must leave because it is necessary that our country survive."

He must go because no arrangement, no serious negotiation, no attempt at national reconciliation is possible with him, because the only language he speaks is force and violence. He must go because he is blocking the way of an entire people, like a fish bone stuck in the throat of a hungry man. He must go because it is imperative that we reform the absurd, inoperative and crazy economic system that he has created after his likeness and image, and that he will never reform (because to reform that system would be to repudiate himself). He must go because the Communist system in Cuba survives only with subsidies from the Soviets, who cannot combat the irrationality and inefficiency of that system in their country while at the same time subsidizing the identical system in ours. He must go because his personal interests are at odds with the interests of the nation.

The bunker mentality that Fidel has demonstrated recently is typical of a man who is obsessed with power and lives only for power. With that same mindset, Hitler caused the destruction of almost all of Germany. When the Soviets penetrated the Northern borders of Germany and the Americans crossed the Rhine, there really wasn't anything more for the Allies to do: the German armies had already been decimated on the Eastern Front, and Germany's industry crippled by continuous U.S. and British aerial bombardment. But Hitler ordered a fight to the last man, and predicted that Berlin would be a mass grave for the Red Army. A grave it was, except that Hitler was mistaken about the cadaver. Hitler decided to die, for life without power did not interest him; and if he had to die, he decided that the German people should die also. Mussolini, when he was defeated, attempted to flee. He loved life and wanted to preserve it. He was a bad man, but at least he was a man. Hitler loved only power; he was a monster.

In Cuba we hear the same voices that must have resounded in that Berlin Bunker in the Spring of 1945: "Marxism-Leninism or Death!" Why? Why must we die in the name of a doctrine, a doctrine that we don't even share, and that not even one-third of our population claims to profess? "We would rather let the island sink in the ocean than return to capitalism." Why? Drown yourselves, *fidelistas*, this island does not belong to you! "We will resist even if not a drop of oil, not a grain of wheat, enters our country." What do they want to turn us into? A tropical Albania, perhaps? We are not a nation of mountain goats.

Fidel must go and take his brother with him (though even that isn't important, since the brother won't count for much after Fidel is gone). The other members of the present leadership are to Fidel what Mussolini was to Hitler. They are not good for much of anything; they are inept and corrupt, and live like bourgeois in the midst of our poverty. While enjoying all kinds of material benefits, they speak to us of austerity, effort and sacrifice, widening ever more "the gulf that exists between the everyday reality of workers and the pompous lifestyles of managers," as Gorbachev puts it. But Fidel's underlings, though bad, are men. We can deal with them, and perhaps there may even be some among them who can contribute something positive to the nation.

Fidel can go to North Korea, perhaps, where he can reunite with his spiritual twin, Field Marshal Kim Il-Sung, after having settled past differences on the conduct of the Angolan conflict. Or perhaps he can go to Afghanistan, and lend his services to his brother Afghans, who were abandoned, according to Fidel, by the Soviets. Libya, however, is not a possibility, because Qaddafi is an unpredictable man and may order Fidel thrashed as an infidel -- and I don't want anything bad to happen to him, I just want him to leave. Now, come to think of it, the best place for him to go would be Angola. If Fidel was capable of directing and winning from Havana the battle of Cuito Cuanavale in the Angolan war, what might he not be able to accomplish if he ever actually got near the scene of battle? A five- or six-weeks campaign should suffice to bring Savimbi's head to Luanda impaled on a tribal lance, for the greater glory of folklore.

Many years ago, while he was still fighting Batista in the hills, Fidel confided to Celia Sánchez in a now-famous letter that his real destiny was to fight the United States. I believe every man has a right to choose for himself the primordial destiny of his life. It is possible that to combat the United States is, indeed, Fidel's destiny; but I am sure that it is not my destiny or the destiny of my country. Let Fidel fulfill or attempt to fulfill his destiny, but without using the Cuban people as an instrument for his personal aspirations.

Perhaps he should forget about all the other places that I have with every good intention suggested to him, and go instead to the United States. That's it. He should penetrate the entrails of the imperialist monster, and once there, issue a call to all who are oppressed by its unjust capitalist system -- the blacks, the Chicanos, the Puerto Ricans, the Sioux, the Cheyenne and the Comanches -- to gather in the Appalachian Mountains, the Bighorn Mountains (where Chief Crazy Horse once fought), or the Sangre de Cristo Mountains, for one last uprising against the white man. This crazy *caballo* [horse] can do anything that occurs to him, as long as he leaves the Cubans in peace.

Without him we could reform our social system and make it more viable, more human. We could be a bridge of friendship between the United States and the Soviet Union, since no other country has had such close relations with both superpowers. We could stop quoting Martí and begin to apply his teachings, such as creating a republic "with all and for the good of all." We could achieve a national reconciliation based on mutual respect of one another's opinions. We could have a country where jails are not filled with men who are guilty of no crime. We could have a country where fear is not an everyday habit, distrust is not systematic, and hypocrisy is not a part of everyone's daily routine. We could be a country no one would want to escape.

But Fidel will not leave. Not of his own free will. A long chain of deeds and circumstances have led us -- he as well as we -- to this present situation. It all started five hundred years ago with the early demise of liberty in Spain. It seemed at first that we were destined to escape the despotic fate common to all Hispanic countries. But we did not escape, and all seems to indicate, that we shall be the last to be free of despotism. Cuba's magnificent 19th century culminated in the frustration of a mock-independence. Later came a dictatorship that begat a worse one that in turn opened the way for the one afflicting us today; before and in between the dictators, there were presidents who respected our liberties but who contributed with their venality to the fall of democracy. And death thwarted us time and time again; it struck us in a very selective, indeed, maliciously selective way. Is there any other country in the world where so many essential men have died prematurely?

And so it was, maestro Lezama, that we came to be in this blind alley, without a glimmer of hope, and surrounded by death. But if there is no escape, if there is no hope, what do any of us have to lose? What can *I* lose who have nothing? I will speak then with all frankness, and with absolute liberty, as if all of my being were free, when, in fact, only my spirit is free.

I, Roberto Luque y Escalona, one man, just one man, a citizen of the Republic of Cuba by birthright and a spokesman by choice for the most silent of majorities -- a position to which I have not been elected, and which I will gladly relinquish or share with any other candidates who should appear -- I challenge you, Fidel, to call a plebiscite to decide our future and yours. I assure you that you would lose. We are fed up with you, your despotism, your irresponsibility, your incompetence. Your rhetoric can only fool those who need to believe your lies. The children who survived the tiger's kill are now men and women. And they know how to distinguish objects, persons and animals. They know that what moves with slow and silent grace, what so dazzles the eye with its beautiful display of colors, is a tiger.

Havana, July 25 - September 7, 1989

Epilogue

Havana, 7 October 1991

It has been exactly two years and one month since I finished a book entitled *The Tiger and the Children*, and one year and sixteen days since *Fidel: the Judgement of History* appeared in bookstores. When I am a big boy, nobody will change the titles of my books -- I swear. This is not to say that *Fidel: the Judgment. . .* is bad -- many people have liked it. It is only that this has nothing to do with me. Besides, the principal ideal that I have tried to express is contained in the original title.

In these two years, sorrow has caught up with the tiger. Socialism, which official propaganda had announced as the absolute master of the future, hardly has a present these days. In Europe and the Americas, in Africa and Asia, where it was in power and where it threatened to take power, socialism is in retreat and is falling to pieces. Only China, that marvelous country where sexagenarian politicians are considered young, and North Korea, whose beloved leader already is over eighty and is beginning to worry about his solitude, accompany Fidel in the insane, vain, and (why not?) criminal effort to save the most inhuman, oppressive and inefficient social system the modern world has known.

"Whatever happens is positive," says a Cuban politician who loves serenity more than himself. I do not share that philosophy. I think that when what happens is positive, it means that we are not where we should be. Nothing that has happened in the world during the past two years has been positive for Fidel Castro.

209

One has to begin somewhere, so we shall begin with Manuel Antonio Noriega, the insolent General of Dignity. Although Noriega lost his generalship, he did not lose his dignity only because he never had any. He was Fidel's last friend in Latin America -- a friendship sustained by shared hatreds and loves: hatred for the Yankees and love of dollars.

The events of Eastern Europe were a chain of nightmares, with Germany, Romania and Czechoslovakia providing particularly chilling scenarios. In the German Democratic Republic, the solid GDR of propaganda, symbol and shop window of socialist prosperity, people began to flee to the other Germany not in crude rafts with whatever they can carry with them but in their own cars -- of bad quality but cars nonetheless. It was something never seen before: the well-off fleeing to where they have nothing. Later the wall would be taken down, reduced to small chunks and sold to tourists. In Romania, the beloved Ceaucescu, firm and intransigent, lost his firmness and his intransigence before a volley from a firing squad. He already had lost the love. In Czechoslovakia, something less spectacular but equally abominable occurred: a writer assumed the Presidency of the Republic.

Like a virus, like a plague of old, like whatever you want, the plague has extended beyond Europe, crossing the Mediterranean and the Sahara and penetrating Africa, site of the greatest feats of *fidelismo*. The tribal chiefs disguised as Marxist leaders shed their costumes. Mengistu Haile Mariam has fled Ethiopia without waiting for the second anniversary of the death of the man who might have been his savior, General Ochoa. The upstart king of Ethiopia now rests from his labors in luxurious exile.

And last but not least, Angola. The Angola of Augustinho and of Savimbi, of Dos Santos and Argüellos, of Colomé and Centras -- and of Ochoa (again that peasant adventurer). No country --except for Spain and the United States -- is more closely linked to our history. Only in the United States are there more dead Cubans than in Angola; one and all died and were buried on foreign soil because of the deeds of Fidel Castro.

210

"How Savimbi runs!" sang Carlos Puebla fifteen years ago, that Communist troubadour who ruined the digestion of the patrons of the *Bodeguita del Medio* restaurant. Savimbi runs no more. Now

"How Savimbi runs!" sang Carlos Puebla fifteen years ago, that Communist troubadour who ruined the digestion of the patrons of the *Bodeguita del Medio* restaurant. Savimbi runs no more. Now he strolls in triumph, acclaimed, through the streets of Luanda, capital of a country that is the symbol and sum of the failure of a man who thought himself great.

Enough about Africa; let's go to the Middle East, to the Persian Gulf. There Saddam Hussein awaits us, the Father of all Ridiculous People; there in the sands of Kuwait, are buried (we continue with the subject of tombs) some of the fondest hopes of Fidel. May all the devils take them.

The last, fondest hope of this enemy of strangers' hopes died in Moscow. The Russians, famous and unknown alike, those round-headed Russians whom Fidel detests so much, destroyed his last hope when they squashed the intended coup by *El Comandante's* friends. Stalinism has died. Its burial shall be in St. Petersburg. And please, no flowers because it doesn't deserve them.

Nor did Pepe Abrahantes deserve them, he who died in prison in an odd manner. Fidel's has been a life full of deaths, almost all for his gain. Celia Sánchez is the exception. Abrahantes, on the other hand, is one of those who leads the squadron of conveniently dead. Of course, perhaps Patricio de la Guardia should also have died. It seems to be a dangerous subject.

So then, while Fidel accumulates failures, submerges the country in misery, and prepares his 110,000 square kilometer funeral pyre, what has become of the author?

Let's see: he carried out two hunger strikes, both failing in their objectives. During the first and immediately after the second he was betrayed by those whom he had considered his friends (which doesn't say much for his wisdom). As if failure and betrayal were not enough, he is as a result of the hunger strikes pretty battered: permanently thin, emaciated, with his hair on the retreat. He is no longer "a charming and tough little man" like Chandler's Harry Jones.

Yet not all was failure and betrayal. His book was published, sold, and discussed; it was among the best-sellers in Miami for

211

thirteen weeks. A successful writer? If so, he would be the poorest successful writer in the world, a sort of Van Gogh of political literature, although it is improbable that he would cut off an ear and even less probable that he would give it to anyone.

As was to be expected, he had to sample one of the specialties of the house, the so-called (by the *fidelistas*) "act of repudiation." But it was quite a moderate one, as though the dogs understood that although it is still safe to bark, it already is dangerous to bite. A minor tale of corruption and decadence: the man who led the *Fidelista* mob this time was one of those who in 1980 had helped to save the cornered couple.

At 54 years of age, and not without a certain feeling of surprise on his part, the author experienced prison. "Better late than never," the saying goes. "Better never than late," say I in this case. We will go on with the sayings for the sake of history: "you suffer but you learn," written by an anonymous would-be philosopher on a wall of Cell 33 of the jail at 100th Street and Aldabó. Certainly the author learned something: when Miriam and Ernesto visited him for the first time, he realized that it is possible to be happy in jail. Of course, happiness is not lasting there; but is there any place where it is? In jail he tasted the pride of the strong when the official who had thought he could break the author called him a bully. In jail he suffered the pains reserved for the unbelievers and the forgetful, failing to believe in the spiritual strength of the Russian people and forgetting a well-respected saying by Martí ("Man loves liberty even though he may not know it"). Thus when a jailor brimming over with joy told him that Gorbachev had been overthrown, he felt as though the sinister building that had provided him with temporary shelter was coming down on top of him. Stalinism was in power again; Fidel had saved himself one more time.

But he didn't save himself. Nothing and no one can save him now. The supply of miracles is exhausted. Myths and magic words have lost their effectiveness, their hallucinogenic and stupefying power. Fidel can still practice his vocation for destruction, his love of death. But he no longer can conquer. That is all.

212

Dalton wrapped his arms around her waist and pulled her close. "You deserve a proper thank-you for taking care of me," he whispered as his mouth found hers.

His lips were warm and held a hint of whiskey. They were perfect. Her heart beat at record time. Her hands slid up to hold the ridge of his shoulders as Dalton pulled her tighter and the pressure of his mouth increased. Her body heated as if she were basking in the sun.

His tongue traced her lips. Her fingers seized his coat and she moaned. More…she wanted more. She returned his kiss.

Melanie had no idea how much time had passed by the time Dalton released her. Dazed, it took her a few seconds before she realized that someone was clapping.

"I think we're making a scene," Dalton said as he picked up his bag and took her arm, leading her toward the door.

She glanced around to see a family grinning at them. "I guess we are…"

The words came out sounding shaky. The warmth of his lips still lingered on hers. She still tingled all over. Not thinking about what she was doing, she ran her tongue along her bottom lip. His taste still lingered.

Dalton groaned. "Please don't do that."

"What?"

He leaned in close. "Lick your lips. If you do it again I might *really* make a public scene."

Dear Reader,

During the fall months of the year the focus in my house turns to American football. We spend hours watching and discussing it. We even attend games. While the males in my family are concerned with only what is happening on the field, I often think about what goes on behind the scenes. Who takes care of the players? What happens when a player gets hurt? During one of those games I wondered what it would be like if the team doctor was a woman, and how it would be for her to work in that man's world…

This is just what my character Melanie does in this story. For her, the game of football is a family affair. And when she has to call in an orthopaedic surgeon who cares nothing about the game for a second opinion, the fireworks explode.

I hope you enjoy reading my book as much as I enjoyed writing it. I love to hear from my readers. You can contact me at susancarlisle.com.

Susan

ONE NIGHT BEFORE CHRISTMAS

BY
SUSAN CARLISLE

MILLS
BOON

First published in Great Britain 2015
By Mills & Boon, an imprint of HarperCollins*Publishers*
1 London Bridge Street, London, SE1 9GF

Large Print edition 2016

© 2015 Susan Carlisle

ISBN: 978-0-263-26095-3

Susan Carlisle's love affair with books began when she made a bad grade in maths in the sixth grade. Not allowed to watch TV until she'd brought the grade up, she filled her time with books and became a voracious romance reader. She still has 'keepers' on the shelf to prove it. Because she loved the genre so much she decided to try her hand at creating her own romantic worlds. She still loves a good happily-ever-after story. When not writing, Susan doubles as a high school substitute teacher, which she has been doing for sixteen years. Susan lives in Georgia with her husband of twenty-eight years and has four grown children. She loves castles, travelling, cross-stitching, hats, James Bond and hearing from her readers.

Books by Susan Carlisle

Mills & Boon Medical Romance

Heart of Mississippi
The Maverick Who Ruled Her Heart
The Doctor Who Made Her Love Again

Snowbound with Dr Delectable
NYC Angels: The Wallflower's Secret
Hot-Shot Doc Comes to Town
The Nurse He Shouldn't Notice
Heart Surgeon, Hero...Husband?
The Doctor's Redemption
His Best Friend's Baby

Visit the Author Profile page at millsandboon.co.uk for more titles.

To Lacey.
Thanks for loving my son.

**Praise for
Susan Carlisle**

'Shimmering with breathtaking romance
amid the medical drama, spectacular
emotional punch, a believable conflict and
vivid atmospheric details, *NYC Angels:
The Wallflower's Secret* is sure to thrill
Medical Romance readers.'

—Goodreads

CHAPTER ONE

DR. MELANIE HYDE stood with the other chauffeurs waiting and watching passengers outside the security zone at the top of the escalators. Overhead the notes of "Jingle Bells" were being piped via speakers throughout Niagara Falls International Airport in upstate New York. She wiggled the small white sign she held back and forth. Written on it was *Reynolds*.

She was there to pick up the "go-to" orthopedic sports doctor. He'd been flown in on a private jet paid for by the Niagara Falls Currents, the professional football team and her employer. Her father, the general manager, had sent her on this mission in the hope that she might, in his words, "soften the doctor up."

Melanie had no idea how she was supposed to do that. She would have to find some way because she didn't want to disappoint her father. Long ago she'd accepted what was expected of her. Not that she always liked it.

Maybe the one physician to another respect would make Dr. Reynolds see the team's need to get Martin "The Rocket" Overtree on the field for the Sunday playoff game and hopefully the weeks after that.

As club physician, Melanie had given her professional opinion but her dad wanted a second one. That hurt, but she was a team player. Had been all her life. Just once she'd like her father to see her for who she really was: a smart woman who did her job well. An individual.

In the sports world, that orthopedic second opinion came in the form of Dr. Dalton Reynolds of the Reynolds Sports and Orthopedic Center, Miami, Florida.

She'd never seen him in person but she had read plenty of his papers on the care of knee and leg injuries. "The Rocket" had a knee issue but he wanted to play and Melanie was feeling the pressure from the head office to let him. More like her father's not so gentle nudge.

Having grown up in a football-loving world, she knew the win and, in major-league ball, the money, was everything. The burden to have "The Rocket" on the field was heavy. On the cusp of a chance to go to the Super Bowl, the team's star player was needed.

She shifted her heavy coat to the other arm and scanned the crowd of passengers streaming off the escalators for a male in his midfifties and wiggled the sign again.

A tall man with close-trimmed brown hair sporting a reddish tint, carrying a tan trench coat and a black bag, blocked her view. He was do-a-double-take handsome but Melanie shifted her weight to one foot and looked around him, continuing to search the crowd.

"I'm Reynolds," the man said in a deep, husky voice that vibrated through her. The man could whisper sweet nothings in her ear all day long.

Jerking back to a full standing position, she locked gazes with his unwavering one.

"Dr. Dalton Reynolds?"

"Yes."

His eyes were the color of rich melted chocolate but they held none of the warmth. He wasn't at all who she'd anticipated. Old and stuffy, instead of tall and handsome, was what she'd had in mind. This man couldn't be more than a few years older than her. He must be truly brilliant if he was the most eminent orthopedic surgeon in the country at his age.

"Uh, I wasn't expecting you to be so...young," she blurted.

He gave her a sober look. "I'm sorry to disappoint."

She blinked and cleared her throat. "I'm not disappointed, just surprised."

"Good, then. Shouldn't we be getting my luggage? I'd like to see the patient this evening."

With it being only a week before Christmas, he must be in a hurry to return home to his family. After a moment's hesitation she said, "I don't know if that'll be possible. The players may have gone home by the time we get back."

"I didn't come all this way to spend time in my hotel room. I have a practice in Miami to be concerned with." That statement was punctuated with a curl of one corner of his mouth.

He had a nice one. Why was she thinking about his mouth when she should be talking to him about Rocket? The off-center feeling she had around this stranger unnerved her. She worked in primarily a man's world all the time and never had this type of reaction to one of them.

They started walking toward the baggage area.

As they did, Melanie put the sign she was still carrying in a garbage can, then pulled her phone out of her pocket. "I'll try and get Coach. Have him ask Rocket to hang around. But football players sometimes have minds of their own."

"I can appreciate that, Ms…?"

Melanie stopped and looked at him. He faced her, his broad shoulders blocking her view of the other people passing them.

She raised her chin. "I'm Dr. Melanie Hyde."

A flash of wonder flickered in his eyes.

Good. She'd managed to surprise him.

"Dr. Hyde, if Mr. Overtree expects my help he'll need to be examined as soon as possible. I have patients at home who are trying to stay out of wheelchairs."

With that he turned and walked toward the revolving luggage rack.

Melanie gaped at him. So much for "smoothing him over."

Dalton had little patience for silly games. Even when they were played with attractive women. He'd been astonished to find out that the team doctor was female and the person who had been sent to pick him up. Usually that job fell to a hired driver or one of the team underlings. He had to admit she was the prettiest chauffeur he'd ever had.

As far as he was concerned, he was here to do a job and nothing more. He wasn't impressed by the game of football. The only aspect that drew him in was that he cared about helping people who were hurting. He'd been called in to examine an injured player at great expense. The money he earned, good money, from making these types of "house calls" was what he used to support his foundation. It oversaw struggling foster children with physical and mental issues, giving them extra care so they had a chance to succeed in life. He would continue to do this job as long as the teams paid him top dollar. However, he didn't buy into all the football hype.

He knew from experience that not everyone was cut out for games. He'd left that far behind, being constantly teased for being the "brain with no game." It had taken time and work on his part but he'd overcome his childhood. Now he was successful in his field, had friends and a good life. He had proven anyone could overcome their past. That was why he'd started the foundation.

To give other kids a step in the right direction so they didn't struggle as he had.

The tall, athletic-looking doctor came to stand beside him. She almost met him eye to eye. He liked women with long legs. Glancing down while watching the baggage conveyer as it circled in front of him, he confirmed the length of her legs. She wore a brown suit with a cream-colored blouse. There was nothing bold about her dress to make her stand out. Still, something about her pricked his interest. Her features were fine and her skin like porcelain, a complete contrast to her all-business appearance. Not of his usual fare—bleached blonde and heavy breasted—she looked more of the wholesome-girl-next-door variety. Under all that sweetness was there any fire?

He looked at the bags orbiting before him. *Football was still such a man's world, so why would a woman choose to become a football team doctor?*

His black leather duffel circled to him. He leaned over and picked it up. Slinging it over his shoulder, he turned to her. "I'm ready."

"This way, then." She pulled on the large down-stuffed coat she'd held. As she walked, she wrapped a knit scarf effortlessly around her neck and pulled a cap over her hair. He followed her.

There was a nice sway to her hips. Even in the shapeless outfit she had a natural sex appeal. He shouldn't be having these sorts of thoughts because he wouldn't be here long enough to act on them.

The automatic glass doors opened, allowing in a blast of freezing-cold air that took his breath and made his teeth rattle. "Hold up." He stepped back inside.

She followed. He didn't miss the slight twitch at the corner of her full lips. She was laughing at him. He didn't like being laughed at.

He plopped his bag on the floor and set his shoulder bag beside it before putting on his trench coat.

"Is that the heaviest overcoat you have?" she asked.

Tying the belt at the waist, he looked directly at her. "Yes. There isn't much call for substantial clothes in Miami."

"I guess there isn't. Would you like to stop and get a warmer one on our way to the practice field?"

He shook his head as he picked up his bags again. "I don't plan to be here that long."

Again they headed out the door, Dalton tried

to act as if the wind wasn't cutting right through his less-than-adequate clothes. Even with a shirt, sweater and coat he was miserable.

"Why don't you wait here and I'll circle around to get you?"

"No, I'm fine. Let's get moving." He bowed his head against the spit of icy rain.

Dalton had spent a lifetime of not appearing weak and he wouldn't change now. As the smart foster kid, he hadn't fit in at school or in the houses he'd been placed in. With a father in jail and a drug addict for a mother, he'd been in and out of homes for years. It wasn't until his mother died of an overdose that he'd stayed in one place for any length of time. At the Richies', life had been only marginally better before he was sent to another home.

He'd had plenty of food and clothes, but little about his life had been easy. When all the other kids were out playing, he was busy reading, escaping. The most miserable times were when he did join in a game. He was the last one chosen for the team. If finally picked, he then had to deal with the ridicule of being the worst player. He learned quickly not to show any weakness. As a medical student and now a surgeon, the honed trait served him well.

Football, freezing weather and a laughing woman, no matter how attractive she was, were not to his taste. He needed to do this consultation and get back to Florida.

Melanie couldn't help but find humor in the situation. Dr. Reynolds' long legs carried him at such a brisk pace, she had trouble staying in the lead enough to show him where the car was parked. He must be freezing. Niagara Falls was not only known for the falls but for the horrible winter weather. What planet did he live on that he hadn't come prepared?

She pushed the button on her key fob, unlocking the car door as they approached so that he wouldn't have to wait any longer than necessary outside. Minutes later she had the car started and the heat blasting on high. She glanced at her passenger. He took a great deal of space in her small car. Almost to the point of overwhelming her. Why was he affecting her so? Melanie glanced at him. Judging by the tenseness of his square jaw, he must be gritting his teeth to keep them from chattering.

"I'm sure it'll be warm in a few minutes."

An *mmm* sound of acknowledgement came from his direction as Melanie pulled out into the evening traffic on the freeway.

Her phone rang. "Please excuse me. This may be the office about Rocket." She pushed the hands-free button. "This is Mel."

"Rocket is on his way back." Her father's booming voice filled the car.

"Great. I'm sure Dr. Reynolds will be glad to hear that. We should be there in about thirty minutes." Her father hung up and she asked her passenger, "Have you ever been to Niagara Falls?"

"No."

"Well, the falls are a beautiful sight any time of the year, but especially now with the snow surrounding them."

"I don't think I'll be here long enough to do much sightseeing."

"It doesn't take much to say you've seen the falls. They're pretty large."

"What I came for is to see Mr. Overtree, so I imagine I should focus on that." Obviously he wasn't much for small talk or the local sights. Melanie stopped making an effort at conversation and concentrated on driving in the thickening snow and slow traffic. With her heavier clothes on, she began to get too warm but didn't want to turn down the heat for fear Dr. Reynolds needed it.

They were not far from the team camp when he said, "I don't think I've ever met a female team doctor before."

She'd long ago become used to hearing that statement. With a proud note in her voice she said, "As far as I know, I'm the only one in the NFL."

"What made you want to be a sports doctor?"

His voice, she bet, had mesmerized more than one woman. Where had that idea come from? What was his question? "I wanted to be a part of the world of football."

What it did was make her feel included. She'd grown up without a mother, a coach for a father and three brothers who now played professional football. In her family if you didn't eat, drink and live football you were left out. As a girl she couldn't play, so by becoming the team doctor she took her place as part of the team. Even when it wasn't her heart's desire. "Team means every-thing, Mel," her father would say. "That's what we are—a team." He would then hug her. To get his attention she learned early on what she needed to do as part of the team. As she grew older the pressure to be a team member grew and became harder to live with.

She often wondered what her father would say if she confessed she didn't want to belong to a team any longer. Sometimes she'd like to just be his daughter. She was afraid of what the repercussions might be. Still she would have to say she was happy, wouldn't she?

Melanie pulled the car into her designated parking space in front of the two-story, glass-windowed building. "Leave your bag in the car. I'll take you to the hotel after we're through here."

Dr. Reynolds nodded and climbed out. He wasn't large like some of the players but he did look like a man who could hold his own in a fight. With those wide shoulders and trim hips, he appeared physically fit.

"This way," she said as they entered the lobby. The space was built to impress. With hardwood floors, bright lights and the Currents' mascot and bolt of lightning painted on the wall, the place did not disappoint. No matter how many times Melanie entered this direction, she had a moment of awe. She enjoyed her job, liked the men she worked with and loved the passion of the crowd when the Currents took the field to play.

Dr. Reynolds followed her through security and down the hall to the elevator. There they waited in silence until the doors opened and they entered. She pushed the button that would take them to the bottom floor where the Athlete Performance Area and her office were located. When the elevator opened she led him along a hall painted with different football players making moves. "Rocket should be back here."

The team had a state-of-the-art workout facility, from whirlpool and sauna to a walking pool and all the other equipment on the market to help improve the human body. She was proud of the care she was able to provide for the men. Two years ago she had instituted a wellness program for retired players who continued to live nearby.

She pushed open the double swinging doors and entered her domain. Here she normally had the final say.

Rocket was already there, sitting on the exam table. Wearing practice shorts and a T-shirt with the sleeves cut out of it, he looked like the football player he was. What didn't show was the injury to his knee and his importance to the Currents winning a trip to the Super Bowl.

She pulled off her coat. "Rocket, sorry to pull you back in but Dr. Reynolds wanted to see you right away." Turning to Dr. Reynolds, she said, "This is Rocket—or Martin Overtree. Rocket, Dr. Reynolds."

The two men shook hands.

"Thanks for coming, Doc," Rocket said. "Mel says you're the man to help keep me on the field."

"I don't know about that. I'll need to examine you first." Dr. Reynolds pulled off his coat.

"I'll take that," Melanie offered and draped it over a chair in the corner.

The doctor rolled up his shirtsleeves, revealing tanned arms with a dusting of dark hair. Using his foot, he pulled a rolling stool from where it rested near the exam table. He straddled it and rolled to the end of the table. "I'm going to do some movements and I want you to tell me when or if they hurt and where."

Melanie watched as the doctor placed his large hands on either side of the huge running back's dark-skinned knee. With more patience than he'd shown at the airport, he examined it. Rocket grunted occasionally when Dr. Reynolds moved his knee a certain way.

The doctor pushed with his heels, putting space between him and the patient. "Now, Mr. Over-tree—"

"Make it Rocket. Everyone else does."

Dr. Reynolds seemed to hesitate a second before he said in a stilted tone, "Rocket, I'd like you to lift your foot as far as you can without your knee hurting."

Rocket followed his instructions. The grimace on the player's face when his leg was almost completely extended said the knee might be in worse shape than Melanie had feared.

Dr. Reynolds placed his hand on the top of the knee.

She'd always had a thing for men's hands. To her they were a sign of their character. Dr. Reynolds had hands with long tapered fingers and closely cut nails that said he knew what he was doing and he could be trusted. Melanie liked what they said about him.

He moved his fingers over Rocket's knee. "That's good. Have you had a hard hit to this knee recently?"

Rocket made a dry chuckle. "Doc, I play football. I'm getting hit all the time."

"Yeah, I know who you are. But has there been one in particular you can remember?"

"A couple weeks ago in the game I was coming down, and the safety and I got tangled up pretty good."

Melanie had learned early in her career as a team doctor that many of the players, no matter how large, were deep down gentle giants. Often they had a hard time showing weakness and fear. Rocket was one of those guys. Melanie was grateful to the doctor for his compassionate care.

"Any popping sensation, swelling or pain?"

"Not really. If Doc here—" Rocket indicated Melanie "—hadn't pulled me off the machine the other day I wouldn't have really noticed. Players are in some kind of pain all the time if they play ball. We get to where we don't really notice."

Dr. Reynolds gave him a thoughtful nod and stood. "I'd like to get some X-rays and possibly a MRI before I confirm my diagnosis."

"I'll set them up." Melanie made a note on the pad at her desk.

The double doors burst wide open. Her father entered. In his booming voice he demanded, "Well, Doc, is Rocket going to be able to play on Sunday?"

Melanie flinched. Based on what she knew about Dr. Reynolds in their short acquaintance, he wouldn't take kindly to being pressured.

Reynolds looked her father straight in the eyes. "It's Dr. Dalton Reynolds." Not the least bit intimidated, he continued, "And you are?"

Her father pulled up short. Silence ping-ponged around the room. Few people, if any, dared to speak to her father in that manner. When he was a coach he had insisted on respect and as general manager he commanded it.

"Leon Hyde, general manager of the Currents." He offered his hand.

Dr. Reynolds gave her a questioning look, then accepted her father's hand. The moment of awkwardness between the two men disappeared as the doctor met her usually intimidating father toe to toe.

She couldn't remember another man who hadn't at least been initially unsettled by her father. Dr. Reynolds's gaze didn't waver. Her appraisal of him rose.

"So, Dr. Reynolds, is Rocket going to be able to run for us Sunday?" her father asked with a note of expectancy in his voice.

"I need to look at the X-rays and MRI before I can let you know."

"That'll be in the morning," Melanie said.

"Good." Her father turned to her. "Mel, we need Rocket on the field."

"I understand." She did, but she wasn't sure her father wasn't more concerned about winning than he was Rocket's health. She just hoped it didn't come down to her having to choose between the team and her professional conscience. "But I must consider Rocket's well-being. I won't sign off until Dr. Reynolds has made his determination."

Her father gave her a pointed look. The one she recognized that came before the team player speech.

Instead he continued, "You'll see that Dr. Reynolds gets to the Lodge and is comfortable, won't you?"

As always, it wasn't a question but a directive. She nodded. "Yes."

"Good." He looked at Dr. Reynolds. "I anticipate a positive report in the morning."

The doctor made no commitment.

Her father then gave Rocket a slight slap on the shoulder. "Go home and take care of that knee. We need you on the field Sunday."

Melanie watched the doors swing closed as her father exited. She was impressed by Dr. Reynolds's ability not to appear pushed into making a decision. Her father was known for being a persuasive man and getting what he wanted. He wanted Rocket to play Sunday. Dr. Reynolds didn't act as if he would be a yes-man if he didn't feel it was safe for Rocket to do so. On this she could agree with him.

Still, it hurt that her father didn't trust her opinion.

Dalton pulled the collar of his coat farther up around his neck and hunched his shoulders. They were in her car, moving through what was now a steady snowfall. It was unbearably cold. Even the car heater didn't seem to block the chill seeping into his bones.

Dr. Hyde leaned forward and adjusted the thermostat on the dashboard. "It should be warm in here soon."

He wasn't sure he'd ever be comfortable again. Thankfully, a few minutes later he began to thaw. She maneuvered along the road with the confidence of a person who had done this many times.

"We should be at the Lodge in about half an

hour. Would you like to stop for something to eat? The Lodge does have an excellent restaurant if you'd rather wait."

He looked out the windshield. "I don't think I'm interested in being out in this weather any longer than necessary."

"It does require getting used to."

He couldn't imagine that happening either. "Why is Mr. Overtree called The Rocket?"

She glanced at him and chuckled lightly. "You apparently have never seen him play. He's fast. Very fast."

"I've never seen a professional football game."

Melanie looked at him. The car swerved for a second before she corrected it.

"You might want to watch the road."

She focused on the road again. "You've never seen one in person? Or on TV?"

"Neither. No interest. I have a busy practice."

"You have to be kidding! Football is America's game." She sounded as if she was going to get overly excited about the subject.

"I think it's baseball that's supposed to be the 'all-American game.'"

"It might have been at one time but no longer."

The words were said as if she dared anyone to contradict her.

He couldn't help but raise a brow. "I think there are a lot of people who love baseball that might disagree with you."

"Maybe but I bet most of them watch the Super Bowl."

Dr. Reynolds gave a loud humph. "I understand that most watch for the halftime show and the commercials." He didn't miss the death grip she had on the stirring wheel. She really took football seriously. It was time to move on to a new subject or ask to drive. "The general manager's name is Hyde. Any relation?"

"My father."

"Isn't that a conflict of interest?"

She glanced at him again. "Normally, no. We're so close to going to the playoffs that everyone on the team, including my father, is wound up tight. Anyway, most of my work is directly with the coach."

Based on the way her father spoke to her, she'd agree with him if Dalton declared Rocket shouldn't play. His being asked to consult seemed necessary just to make the team look as if they were truly interested in the player's health. So far, all he could tell they were concerned about was winning the next game.

"What made you decide to be a team doctor?"

"With brothers playing in the NFL and a father who coached, it's the family business. I always wanted to be a doctor and being a team doctor gave me a chance to be a part of football," she said in a flat tone.

Was there more going on behind that statement?

The concept of family, much less a family business, was foreign to him. His family's occupation had been selling drugs and he'd wanted to get as far away from it as he could. He'd been a loner and alone for as long as he could remember.

Thankfully she turned into a curving road lined with large trees and had to concentrate on her driving. A few minutes later, they approached a three-story split-cedar building. She pulled under a portico with small lights hanging from it. Two large trees dressed in the same lights with red bows flanked the double wood-framed doors.

"This is Poospatuck Lodge. I think you'll be comfortable here. The team keeps a suite."

"Poospatuck?" When had he become such an inquisitive person? Usually on these trips he did what was required without any interest in the area he was visiting.

"It's an Indian tribe native to New York."

As she opened the door Dalton said, "It's not necessary for you to get out."

"I don't mind. I need to speak to the management and I can show you up to your suite."

Dalton grabbed his two bags from the backseat and followed her through the door into the welcome heat of the lobby. Large beams supported the two-story ceiling. Glass filled the wall above the door. The twinkle of lights from outside filtered in through the high windows. Flames burned bright in a gray rock fireplace taking up half of one wall. Above it was a large wreath. Along the mantel lay greenery interspersed with red candles. A grand stairway with an iron handrail led to the second floor.

Christmas had never been a big holiday for him. As a small child, it had just been another day for his parents to shoot up and pass out. In fact, the last time he was taken from his mother had been the day before Christmas. It hadn't been much fun spending Christmas Day at a stranger's house. Being a foster child on that day just sent the signal more strongly that he wasn't a real member of the family. Some of his foster parents had really tried to make him feel a part of the unit but it had never really worked. Now it was just another day and he spent it on the beach or with friends.

Dr. Hyde walked toward the registration desk located to the right of the front door.

The clerk wore a friendly smile. "Hello, Dr. Hyde. Nice to see you again."

"Hi, Mark. It's good to see you also. How's your family doing?"

"Very well, thank you."

"Good." She glanced back. "This is Dr. Reynolds. He'll be staying in our suite. I'll show him up."

"Very good. It's all ready for you."

She turned to Dalton. "The elevator is over this way but we're only going to the second floor if you don't mind carrying your bags."

"I believe I can manage to go up the stairs."

She gave him an apologetic look. "I didn't mean to imply…"

"Please just show me my room." Dalton picked up his bags off the floor where he'd placed them earlier. He didn't miss her small sound of disgust as she turned and walked toward the stairs. He followed three or four steps behind as they climbed the stairs. He enjoyed the nice sway of her hips.

At the top of the stairs she turned left and continued down a wide, well lit hallway to the end.

A brass plaque on the door read Niagara Currents. She pulled a plastic door key out of her handbag. With a quick swipe through the slot, she opened the door. Entering, she held the door for him.

He stepped into the seating area. The space had a rustic feel to it that matched the rest of the building. The two sofas and couple of chairs looked comfortable and inviting.

"Your bedroom is through here." She pushed two French windows wide to reveal a large bed. "This is my favorite part of the suite."

He didn't say anything. She turned and looked at him. Dalton raised a brow. A blush crept up her neck.

"Um, I like the view from here is what I meant to say. The falls are incredible."

Dalton moved to stand in the doorway. A large window filled the entire wall. He could just make out the snow falling from the light coming from below.

"There's an amazing view of the falls from here. Now you can say you saw the falls."

"So do you stay here often?"

She glared at him. "What're you implying, Dr. Reynolds?"

"I was implying nothing, Dr. Hyde. I just thought you must have stayed overnight if you were that well acquainted with the view."

"This suite is sometimes used for meetings. Now, if you'll excuse me, I need to be getting home. I'll be here at eight-thirty in the morning to pick you up."

"Why not earlier?"

"Because the X-rays won't be ready until nine. So just enjoy your evening. If you need anything, ask for Mark."

"I shouldn't call you?" he said in a suggestive tone, just to see how she would react. Dr. Hyde pursed her lips. Was she on the verge of saying something?

After a moment, she looked through her handbag and pulled out a card. She handed it to him. "If you need me, you may. Good night."

The door closed with a soft click behind her.

Why had he needled her? It was so unlike him. Maybe it was because she'd questioned his clothing decisions. She'd been polite about it but there was still an undercurrent of humor. Could he possibly want her to feel a little out of sorts too? He had to admit it had been interesting to make her uncomfortable.

CHAPTER TWO

MELANIE PULLED IN front of the Lodge at eight-thirty the next morning. The snow had stopped during the night but the sky was overcast as if it would start again soon. She'd left last night uncomfortable about Dr. Reynolds' suggestive manner. She wasn't feeling any better about being his hostess this morning.

When his dark shapely brow had risen as if she were proposing she might be staying the night with him, she'd been insulted for a second. Then a tinge of self-satisfaction had shot through her that a male had noticed her. She'd had her share of boyfriends when she'd been young but recently the men attracted to her had become fewer. They seemed frightened by her position or were only interested so they could meet either one of her famous brothers or one of the Currents players. The one that she had loved hadn't truly cared for her. She'd known rejection and wanted no part of it.

There had been one special man. He was a law-

yer for a player. She couldn't have asked for someone who fit into her family better. He lived and
breathed football. They had even talked of mar-
riage. It wasn't until he started hinting, then asking her to put a good word in with her father when
an assistant manager's job came open that she realized he was using her. When she refused to do
so, he dumped her. It had taken her months after
that to even accept a friendly date. After that experience she judged every man that showed any
attention to her with a sharp eye. She wouldn't go
through something like that again. Dr. Reynolds
might flirt with her but she would see to it that
was all that would happen. A fly in, fly out guy
was someone she had no interest in.

She entered the lobby to find Dr. Reynolds
waiting in one of the many large armchairs near
the fireplace. Was he fortifying himself for the
weather outside? She smiled. He had looked rather
pitiful the night before in his effort to stay warm.

This morning his outfit wasn't much better.
Wearing a dress shirt, jeans and loafers, he didn't
look any more prepared for the weather than he
had yesterday. In reality, it was unrealistic to expect him to buy clothes just to fly to Niagara Falls
to see Rocket but he would be cold. However, he

was undoubtedly the most handsome man she'd ever met. His striking good looks drew the attention of a couple of women who walked by. He had an air of self-confidence about him.

His head turned and his midnight gaze found her. His eyes were his most striking attribute. The dark color was appealing but it was the intensity of his focus that held her. As if he saw beyond what was on the surface and in some way understood what was beneath.

His bags sat on the floor beside him. She didn't have to ask if he had plans to return to the sun and fun as soon as possible. If Rocket needed surgery he would have to go to Miami to have it done. She hoped that wouldn't be the case but feared otherwise.

"Dr. Reynolds, good morning," she said as she approached.

He stood, picked up his shoulder bag and slipped it over his neck. Grabbing his other bag, he walked toward her.

Apparently he was eager to leave. She stepped closer. "Have you had breakfast?"

"I ate a couple of hours ago."

So he was an early riser. "Then we can go." Melanie turned and headed back the way she had come. By the time she settled behind the steering wheel, he'd placed his bag in the backseat and was buckling up.

As she pulled out onto the main road, he said, "Well, at least it isn't snowing."

"No, but the weatherman is calling for more. A lot more."

"Then I need to see Mr. Overtree's X-rays and get to the airport."

"Only eight more days. You must be in a hurry to get home to your family for Christmas."

"No family. I'll be working."

"Oh." Despite her family's year-round focus on football, they all managed to come together during the holidays. Sometimes it was around Christmas Day games, but they always found a time that worked for all of them. Her brothers had wives and children, and the crowd was rowdy and loud. She loved it. Melanie couldn't imagine not having any family or someone to share the day with. Even though much of the work fell to her. The men in her life expected her to organize and take care of them. She'd never let them know that sometimes she resented them taking her for granted.

They rode in silence for a while. He broke it by asking, "How much longer?"

"It should be only another ten minutes or so."

The sky had turned gray and a large snowflake hit the windshield. By the time she pulled into the team compound it had become a steady snow shower. Instead of parking in the front, this time she pulled through the gate to the back of the building and parked in the slot with her name painted on it. Thankfully, her spot was close to the door so they wouldn't have far to walk.

Dr. Reynolds huddled in his coat on their way to the door. With his head down, he walked slowly as if in an effort not to slip on the ice and snow. Melanie stayed close behind him. She had no idea what her plan was if he started to go down. Inside, they both took off their jackets and shook them out.

"I'll take that," Melanie said. Dr. Reynolds handed her his overcoat. Their hands brushed as she reached for it. A tingle of awareness went up her spine. Shaking it off, she hung their coats up on pegs along the wall and headed down the hall. "This way."

"I assume Mr. Overtree's X-rays will have been sent to your computer in the exam room. The MRI as well."

"Yes."

She made a turn and went down another hallway until she reached the Athlete Performance
Area and pushed open one of the swinging doors
and held it. She let him have the door, then continued into the room. Rocket, Coach Rizzo and
her father were already there.

Her father gave her a questioning look. She
shrugged her shoulder. Surely her father wouldn't
push Dr. Reynolds to agree to let Rocket play
if the test indicated that he shouldn't. As team
doctor, she had the final say anyway. She would
refuse to be a team player if it came down to
Rocket's long-term health. Moving on to her desk,
she flipped on the computer. She pulled up Rocket's chart. "Dr. Reynolds, the X-rays from last
week and his most recent ones are ready for your
review."

Giving her what she could only describe as an
impressed look, Dr. Reynolds seemed to appreciate her being efficient and prepared. For some
reason that made her feel good. The kind of respect she didn't feel she received from her father.
She stepped away from the desk to allow him
room. When the other men moved to join them,
she shook her head, indicating they should give

Dr. Reynolds some space. Despite that, her father still took steps toward her desk.

"Thank you, Doctor. You've been very thorough," Dr. Reynolds said to her.

It was nice to be valued as a fellow medical professional who was more interested in the health of the player than whether or not the team won. She and Dr. Reynolds were at least in the same playbook where that was concerned.

In her mind no game was worth a man losing mobility for the rest of his life. A player's heath came first in that regard. She was sure her father and the coach didn't feel the same. More than once she'd been afraid that there might be repercussions from them if she placed a player on the disabled list. Even the players gave her a hard time about her being overly cautious. As their doctor, the players' health took precedence over winning a game. Rocket had his sights set on being the most valuable player. He might agree to anything to get it. Even playing when he was injured. Sometimes she felt as if she had the most rational mind in the group.

Dr. Reynolds took her chair. He gave that same concentrated consideration to the screen as he seemed to give everything. With a movement of one long finger, he clicked through the black-and-white screens of different X-ray angles of Rocket's knee. He studied them all but made no comment.

He turned to her. "Did you have a MRI done?"

She nodded.

"Good. I'd like to see it."

She moved to the desk and he pushed back enough to allow her to get to the keyboard. As she punched keys she was far too aware of him close behind her. Her fingers fumbled on the keys but seconds later she had the red-and-blue images on the screen.

Minutes went by as Dr. Reynolds moved through the different shots.

"Well?" her father snapped.

"Let him have time to look," Melanie said in an effort to placate him. Her father shot her a sharp look.

Dr. Reynolds continued to spend time on the side views of the knee. The entire room seemed to hold their collective breath as he spun in the chair. His gaze went to Rocket. "It looks like you have a one-degree patellar-tendon tear."

That was what she had been afraid of. "That was my diagnosis."

Dr. Reynolds nodded in her direction.

"We still needed a second opinion," her father said as he stepped back.

For once it would be nice for her father to appreciate her knowledge and ability.

"Can he play?" Coach Rizzo asked.

"The question is—*should* he play?" Then, to Rocket, Dr. Reynolds said, "Do you want to take the chance on ruining your knee altogether? I wouldn't recommend it. Let it rest, heal. You'll be ready to go next year."

The other men let go simultaneous groans.

Rocket moaned. "This is our year. Who's to know what'll happen next year?"

Her father looked at Rocket. "What do you want to do? Think about the bonus and the ring."

How like her father to apply pressure.

Dr. Reynolds looked at him. "Mr. Hyde, this is a decision that Rocket needs to make without any force."

Her father didn't look happy but he also didn't say anything more.

Rocket seemed not to know what the right answer was or, if he did, he didn't want to say it.

"Hey, Doc, what're the chances of it getting worse?" Rocket asked.

"If you take a hard hit, that'll be it. Your tendon

is like a rope with a few of the strands frayed and ragged. You take a solid shot and the rope may break. What I know is that it won't get any better if you play. One good twist during a run could possibly mean the end of your career."

Her father huffed. "Roger Morton with the Wildcats had surgery and returned better than ever."

"I'm not saying it isn't possible. However, not everyone does that well."

Coach Rizzo walked over to Rocket and put his hand on his shoulder, "I think 'The Rocket' has what it takes to play for us on Sunday."

Dr. Reynolds stood. "That'll be for Mr. Overtree to decide."

"You can't do anything more?" Rocket asked Dr. Reynolds.

He looked as if he wanted to say no but instead said, "I'd like to see you use the knee. See what kind of mobility you have."

Before Rocket had time to respond, Coach Rizzo spoke up. "Practice starts in about ten minutes."

"Mel, why don't you show Dr. Reynolds to the practice field?" her father suggested.

"Okay." Once again, she wasn't sure how being tour guide to the visiting doctor fell under her job description but she was a team player. She would do what she was asked. As she headed out the door she said over her shoulder, "Rocket, be sure and wear your knee brace."

She looked at Dr. Reynolds. "The practice field is out this way."

Dalton followed Melanie out a different set of double doors and into a hallway. At the elevator they went down to the ground floor. Once again she was wearing a very efficient-looking business suit. With her shapely, slender body it would seem she'd want to show it off; instead, she acted as if she sought to play down being a woman.

Her father sure was a domineering man. She seemed to do his bidding without question. He was afraid that if he hadn't been brought in for that second opinion, her father would have overridden any decision she made about Rocket. For a grown woman she seemed to still be trying to make daddy happy.

"We aren't going outside, are we?" he asked.

She grinned. "No. We have an indoor practice field. A full stadium without the stands. You should be warm enough in there."

"Good."

Melanie led them down a hallway and through two extralarge doors into a covered walkway. Seconds later they entered a large building.

They walked down one of the sidelines until they were near the forty-yard line. A few of the players wandered out on the field and started stretching. They wore shoulder pads under practice jerseys and shorts.

"Hey, Doc," a couple of the players yelled as they moved to the center of the field.

She called back to them by name. Dalton wasn't used to this type of familiarity with his patients. As a surgeon he usually saw them only a couple of times and never again.

It was still cooler than he liked inside the building. Dalton crossed his arms over his chest, tucking his hands under his arms.

Dr. Hyde must have noticed because she said, "It's not near as cold in here as outside but we can't keep it too warm because the players would overheat." Not surprisingly Melanie didn't seem affected by the temperature.

Rocket loped on the field from the direction of the dressing room. Dalton studied the movement of his leg and so far couldn't see anything significantly out of the norm.

Melanie leaned toward him. "They'll go through their warm-up and then move into some skill work. I think that'll be when you can tell more about his knee. In the past he seemed to show no indication there might be a problem until he was running post plays."

"Post plays?"

"When they run up the field and then cut sharply one way or another."

He nodded and went back to learning Rocket's movements. *Rocket.* He shook his head. It seemed as if he was picking up the slang of the game.

Would Dr. Hyde agree with him if he said that Rocket didn't need to play? As a medical doctor, how could she not?

They had been standing there twenty minutes or so, him watching Rocket while Melanie spoke with every one of the big men who passed by. The staff along the sidelines with them did the same. She was obviously well liked.

The next time a guy came by her, Dalton asked, "You have a good relationship with the team. Does anyone not like you?"

A broad smile came to her face. "We're pretty much like family around here. We all have a job to do but most of us are really good friends. I work at having a positive relationship with the players. I try to have them see me as part of the team. I want them to feel comfortable coming to me with problems. Men tend to drag their feet about asking for help." He must have made a face because she said, "Not all, but I want them to come to me or one of the trainers before a problem gets so bad they can't play."

Dalton had nothing to base that type of camaraderie on. Long ago he'd given up on that idea. Unable to think of anything to say, he muttered, "That makes sense."

She touched his arm. Her small hand left a warm place behind when she removed it to point at Rocket. "Watch him when he makes this move."

The hesitation was so minor that Dalton might have missed it if he hadn't been looking as she instructed.

"Did you see it?"

"I did. It was almost as if he didn't realize he did it." He was impressed that she had caught it to begin with.

"Exactly. I noticed it during one practice. Called him in and did X-rays. Dad insisted I contact you. We can't afford for Rocket to be out."

He looked at her. "Afford?"

She continued to watch the action on the field. "Yeah. This is big business for the team as well as for all these guys' careers."

He looked at Rocket and made no effort to keep the skepticism out of his voice when he asked, "No life after football?"

She stepped back and gave him a sharp look. "Yes. That's the point. A successful season means endorsements, which means money in their pockets. That doesn't even include the franchise."

"And all this hinges on Rocket?"

"No, but he's an important part." She looked around and leaned so close he could smell her shampoo. "The star—for now."

He wasn't convinced but he nodded and said, "I think I get it."

Melanie's expression implied she wasn't sure he did.

They continued to watch practice from the edge of the sideline. The team was playing on the far end of the field.

"How long has Rocket...?" he began.

She turned to look at him.

Over her shoulder he saw a huge player barreling in their direction. His helmeted head was turned away as he looked at the ball in the air. Not thinking twice, Dalton wrapped his arms around Melanie and swiveled to the side so he would take the brunt of the hit. Slammed with a force he would later swear was the equivalent of a speeding train, his breath swooshed from his lungs. His arms remained around Melanie as they went through the air and landed on the Astroturf floor with a thud. The landing felt almost as hard as the original hit. He and Melanie ended up a tangle of legs and arms as the player stumbled over their bodies.

There was no movement from the soft form in his arms. Fear seized him. Had she been hurt? A moan brushed his cheek. At least she was alive. He loosened his hold and rolled to his side but his hands remained in place. Searching Melanie's face, he watched as her eyes fluttered open. She stared at him with a look of uncertainty.

"What…what happened?"

Dalton drew in a breath, causing his chest to complain. He would be in considerable pain in the morning. "We got hit."

"By what?"

"Doc Mel, you okay?" a player asked from above them.

Dalton looked up to find players and staff circling them.

A large man with bulging biceps sounded as if he might cry.

"I'm sorry, Doc Mel. Are you okay? I tried to stop." If that had been his idea of slowing down, Dalton would have hated being on the receiving end of the player's full power. Dalton returned his attention to Melanie. One of his hands rested beneath her shoulder and the other on her stomach. Her cheek was against his lips. "Do you think you can stand?"

"Why did you grab me?"

"Because you could have been hurt if I hadn't." Didn't she understand he might have just saved her life?

"Hurt?" She turned her head toward him. Her eyes were still dazed. "You have pretty eyes."

Dalton swallowed hard, which did nothing to ease the pain in his chest. She must have a head injury because he couldn't imagine her saying something so forward.

"Lie right where you are," one of the people above them commanded. "An ambulance is on its way."

Dalton shifted. "I don't think that's necessary."

The trainer said, "Yes, it is. You both need to be checked out."

"Look, I'm a doctor. I would know if I need…"

"Now you're a patient." A man with a staff shirt said, "Mel, where do you hurt?"

Dalton's hand moved to her waist and gave it a gentle shake. "Dr. Hyde, can you move?"

"Melanie…my name is Melanie," she murmured.

Three of the trainers shifted to one side of her and placed their arms under her, preparing to lift her enough to separate them.

"Melanie, they're going to move you." Dalton took his hands away.

She nodded then made a noise of acceptance and the trainers went to work. Dalton started to rise and a couple of the trainers placed their hands on his shoulders, stopping him.

A few minutes later the sound of the ambulances arriving caught his attention.

Melanie wasn't clear on all that had occurred before she woke up in the brightly lit emergency room.

"What's going on?" She looked at David, one

of the trainers, who was sitting in a chair across the room.

"You were in an accident on the practice field."

Before David could elaborate, a white-haired doctor entered. "So, how are you feeling?" He stepped close to the bed and pulled out a penlight.

Slowly the events came back to her. She started to sit up. "How is Dr. Reynolds?"

The doctor pushed her shoulder, making her lie back. "First let me do my examination, then you can go check on him."

She settled back.

"I'll be in the waiting room," David said and went out the door.

"Now tell me what happened," the doctor said as he lifted one of her eyelids.

Melanie relayed the events she recalled and finished with "and Dr. Reynolds took the impact of the hit."

The doctor nodded thoughtfully. "That he did."

"How bad is he?"

"If you'll give me a few minutes to finish my exam you can go see for yourself."

Melanie's chest tightened. She hoped he wasn't badly hurt. Thankfully, the doctor pronounced her well enough to go. The time that she waited for the nurse with the discharge papers only made her anxiety grow. Because of her, Dalton was hurt.

"What exam room is Dr. Reynolds in?" Melanie asked as she pulled on her shoes.

"Next door." The nurse indicated to the right.

"Thanks." Melanie rose slowly, still feeling dazed. She sat on the edge of the bed for a few seconds. Her body would be sore tomorrow.

Minutes later, she knocked on the glass sliding door to the exam room. At a weak, "Come in," she entered. Dalton still wore his slacks but no shirt. He had a nicely muscled chest. She groaned when she saw the ice pack resting on his left rib cage. His eyes were glazed as if he were in pain and his lips were drawn into a tight line. Guilt filled her.

Another one of the trainers stood in the corner of the room, typing on his cell phone. When she entered he slipped out, giving her the impression he was relieved to do so.

"Hey," she said softly.

Dalton's response came out more as a grumble than a word.

Melanie stepped farther into the room. She had to let him know how much she appreciated what he'd done. "Thank you."

He nodded but his jaw remained tight.

"How are you?"

"I've been better." The words were uttered between clenched teeth.

A stab of remorse plunged through her. He was here because of her. She approached the bed and moved to put her hand on his shoulder, then stopped herself. That would be far too personal. "Don't talk if it hurts too much."

A nurse entered.

Melanie didn't give her time to pick up the chart before she asked, "How is he?" She had to find out something about his injuries without him having to do the speaking.

The nurse looked at him. "Do I have permission to discuss your case?"

He nodded.

"The doctor has some bruised ribs. He'll be sore for a week or so but nothing more serious."

At least that was positive news. Melanie was already guilt ridden enough. "Then he will be released?"

"He'll be released as soon as he has someone who can take him home and stay with him. He isn't going to feel like doing much for a few days."

"I'll see that he gets the care he needs," Melanie assured her.

Dalton's eyebrows went up. "Plane..."

The nurse placed the blood pressure cuff around his arm. "You don't need to be flying. I don't think you could stand the pain."

There was a knock at the door and Melanie looked away from Dalton to find John Horvitz, her father's right-hand man, standing there.

"How're you both doing?" Obviously he would be concerned about the visiting doctor being hurt on team time.

Melanie gave John a brief report. "He's in so much pain, it's difficult to speak." Dalton gave her a grateful look.

John focused his attention on her. "Your father wanted me to check on you both. He had a meeting. I'll be giving him a full report."

And he would. That was always the way it had been. Her father sent someone else. When he'd coached, team issues took precedence. As the general manager, it wasn't any better. His concern had always come through a subordinate. What would it be like to have him show he really cared?

"He'll call when the meeting is over," John finished.

"Who hit us?" she asked.

John grimaced. "I was told it was Juice."

"He must have been flying!"

"Not 'Freight Train'?" Dalton mumbled.

Melanie laughed. The poor guy. Maybe he did have a sense of humor. She wrapped her arms around her waist when the laughter led to throbbing.

"Are you sure you're okay?" John asked her.

"Sore, but nothing that I can't stand. Dr. Reynolds is the one we should be worried about. I think we would both like to get out of here."

As if on cue, the ER doctor came in. "If you'll give me a few minutes, I'll see you have your discharge papers. There will be no driving or flying for two days."

Dalton partially sat up, "Two days!" As if the effort was too much for him, he fell back, closing his eyes.

She owed him for making sure she hadn't really got hurt but this was a busy time of the year and adding the Currents' play-off game didn't make it better. Now she was being saddled with taking care of him for two more days.

"The team will see that you are as comfortable as possible," John assured him.

Dalton's eyes opened but he said nothing.

John continued, "There's a driver and a car waiting to take you both home. I have notified the Lodge to do everything they can to make your stay comfortable."

"I'll see that he's well taken care of. Thanks, John," Melanie said.

Half an hour later, Melanie sucked in her breath when she looked out the hospital sliding glass door. Snow fell so thickly that she could just make out the cars in the parking lot. "The snow has really picked up."

Their driver waited under the pickup area with the engine running. Dr. Reynolds, always the gentleman, allowed her to get in the backseat first. Wincing as he bent to climb in, he joined her. He reached out to pull the door closed and groaned.

"Let me help." She leaned across him. Her chest brushed his as she stretched. His body heat mixed with the air blasting out of the car vents, making her too warm. He smelled like a fir after a misty rain. She stopped herself from inhaling. Using her fingertips, she managed to pull the door closed. His breath brushed her cheek as she sat up again, causing her midsection to flutter.

The windshield wipers swished back and forth in a rapid movement but the snow continued to pile up on the glass. She glanced at Dr. Reynolds.

His shoulders were hunched and he was peering out with a concerned look on his face.

"Normal?" The word came out with a wince.

"We get a lot of snow here. We're used to it. Looks like we'll have a white Christmas, with it only being seven days off." She tried to make the last sentence sound upbeat. In pain, he took on an almost boyish look that had her heart going out to him.

He leaned back and closed his eyes. "Only thing white at Christmastime where I come from is the beach."

That didn't sound all that festive to her. Snow, a green tree, a warm fire and people you loved surrounding you was what she thought Christmas should be. She loved this time of the year.

The driver had the radio playing low and after the song finished the announcer came on. "Fellow Niagarans, it's a white one out there. The good news is the roads are still passable and the airport open. But not sure it will be tomorrow. The storm isn't over yet."

Dalton moaned.

"I'm sorry for this inconvenience, Dr. Reynolds. Maybe in a few days you'll be up to going home," Melanie said in a sympathetic tone.

And she wouldn't be nursemaiding him anymore. She needed to talk to her father about what her duties as team doctor entailed. It would probably be a waste of time; he'd never listened to her in the past and wasn't likely to do so now.

Dalton questioned if the stars were aligned against him. He was stuck in Niagara Falls longer than he'd planned. Too long for his comfort. The driver pulled under the awning of the Lodge. Dalton opened the door despite the pain it brought and climbed out. It wasn't until he turned to close the door that he saw Dr. Hyde getting out.

"What're you doing?" he muttered through tightly clamped teeth.

"I'm going to stay and see about you tonight."

"What?"

"Didn't you hear the doctor? You need someone to check on you regularly over the next twenty-four hours."

"I'll be fine."

"For heaven's sakes, can we go inside to argue about this?"

Without another word, he turned and pulled open the door to the Lodge. He had to admit it required a great deal of effort to do so.

She came to stand beside him. "You obviously need help. I feel guilty enough about you getting hurt. The least I can do is make sure you're okay."

His look met hers for the first time since they'd left the hospital. He wasn't used to seeing concern for him in anyone's eyes. He tried to take a deep breath. Pain shot through his side. He reluctantly said, "I would appreciate help."

"Then let's go try to make you as comfortable as you can be with those ribs. The elevator is over this way." They walked across the lobby.

"Not going to make me climb the stairs?" Each word pained him but he couldn't stop himself from making the comment.

She glared at him. "I thought your ribs hurt too much to speak."

He started to laugh and immediately wrapped his arms across his chest.

They rode the elevator up and walked to the room. At the door Melanie took out a room key.

"You have a key to my room?" Dalton asked with a hint of suspicion.

"I was given one when we knew you were coming so I could check on the room before you arrived." She slid the plastic card in the slot and opened the door. "I'm sure you're ready to lie down. I'll call for some food."

"Are you always so bossy?"

Melanie dropped her pocketbook into the closest chair. "I guess I am when it comes to taking care of my patients."

Dalton started toward the bedroom. "I'm not one of your patients."

"You are for the next twenty-four hours."

He wasn't pleased with the arrangements. Still, something about having her concerned for him gave him an unfamiliar warm feeling. He'd never had anyone's total focus before. Mrs. Richie had been the only foster mother who came close to doing that, but he hadn't been there long before he heard her telling the social worker that it would be better for him to move to another house. After that he'd never let another woman know he hurt or see him in need. He made sure his relationships with women were short and remained at arm's length. All physical and no emotional involvement was the way he liked to keep things.

Dalton crossed the living space and circled one of the sofas that faced each other on his way to the bedroom on the left. There was another room on the opposite side of the large living area. He would leave that one for Melanie. Giving a brief glance to the minibar/kitchen area on the same side of the suite as the extra bedroom, he kept walking.

He ached all over. His jaw hurt from clamping his teeth in an effort not to show the amount of pain he was in. He'd learned as a child that if you let them see your weakness, they would use it against you. Now all he wanted to do was get a hot shower and go to bed.

Kicking off his shoes, he started to remove his knit pullover shirt and pain exploded through his side, taking his breath. For once in his life he had no choice but to ask for help. When his breath returned he opened the door and said, "Dr. Hyde?"

Melanie jumped up from the chair. She must have been watching for him. Hurrying toward him, her eyes were filled with concern, "Are you all right?"

"I need help with my shirt."

She stepped close. "Why do you need to take it off? You could lie down with it on."

"Shower."

"Oh."

"Help?"

"Sure. Sure." She didn't sound too confident as

she followed him back into the room. When he stopped at the bed she reached for the hem of his shirt. Her blue eyes met his. There was a twinkle in her eyes when she said, "You know I'm usually on a first-name basis with people I help undress. You can feel free to call me Mel."

Was she flirting with him? "You said Melanie." She gave him a questioning look.

"That's what you told me to call you after we were hit. You can call me Dalton."

"Dalton—" she said it as if she were testing the sound of it on her lips "—hold real still." She gathered the shirt until she had it under his arms.

Pain must have really addled his brain because he liked the sound of his name when she said it. He was just disappointed he didn't feel well enough to take advantage of her removing his clothes.

"Raise your hands as high as you can. I'll be as careful as I can but I'm afraid it's going to hurt."

He followed her directions. She wasn't wrong. It hurt like the devil as she worked the sleeves off. Sweat popped out on his forehead.

"I'm sorry. I'll get you something for the pain as soon as I'm done."

Dalton was exhausted by the time she finished.

"Let's go to the bathroom to remove your pants."

"I can do that."

"What's wrong? You afraid you have something I haven't seen? I'm a doctor for an all-male football team. I think I can handle removing your pants."

"You're not my doctor."

"Just as I expected. The double whammy. Who makes the worst patient? A male doctor."

He sneered, then walked gingerly into the bathroom and closed the door.

"Just the same, I'll be right out here if you need me," she called.

If nothing else she was tenacious. With more effort than he would have thought necessary, he managed to get his pants down. In the shower he stood under the hot water until he was afraid he might need Melanie's assistance to get out. That would be the ultimate humiliation—having to ask for help again. He already looked feeble as it was.

His clothes were not right for the weather, he was hurt and now he needed her help to undress. He had to get a handle on the situation.

He turned the water off and stepped out of the shower. Melanie opened the door and entered just as he pulled a towel off the rack.

He stood motionless. "What're you doing here?"

She met his gaze with determination. "I'm going to help you dry off. There's no way you can handle that by yourself. If you're afraid I'll look, keep that bath sheet and I'll use one of the others."

Their standoff lasted seconds before he handed her his towel. He wouldn't be intimidated. Standing proudly in front of her, he didn't blink as she took the rectangular terry cloth. She circled behind him and ran the fabric across his shoulders then down his back.

His manhood twitched.

Melanie continued down his legs and up the front before she stepped around to face him. "Lean your head down."

Her voice sounded brisk and businesslike, as if she dried men off all the time. He rather liked having a woman dry him. Despite the pain he experienced with each breath, his body was reacting to the attention. Melanie briskly rubbed his hair, then went over his shoulders and down his chest. When she passed over his ribs, he hissed.

She gave him a sad look. "I'm sorry. I'm trying to be careful."

Going further south, her hands jerked to a stop and it was her turn to release a rush of air.

"I guess you weren't careful enough," he smirked.

Her wide-eyed gaze met his.

"I think I can finish from here." He didn't miss her gulp.

With a shaking hand she handed him the towel and left with the parting words, "There's a robe hanging on the back of the door."

Well, he'd won that standoff. Melanie wasn't as unaffected as she would like to make out. He let the towel drop to the floor. No way was he going to make the effort to put a robe on when he was just going to crawl into bed.

Melanie wasn't in the bedroom when he came out and he didn't pause on his way to the bed. The effort alone had his side aching. He managed to cover his lower half before there was a light knock on the door. He was in so much pain he didn't even make an effort to answer.

She pushed the door open enough to stick her head in. "You need help?"

He hated to admit again that he did. "Would you put some pillows behind me?"

Melanie hurried to him. She went around the bed, gathered the extra pillows and returned, placing the pillows within arm's reach.

Dalton groaned as he tried to sit up.

"Let me help you." Melanie didn't meet his look as she ran her left arm around his shoulders to support him. With her other hand, she stuffed a couple of pillows behind his back. The awkward process put them close. Too close for his comfort. His face was almost in her breasts. She smelled sweet. Nothing like the aroma of disinfectant their profession was known for. Too soon she guided him back against the pillows so that he was now in a half-sitting position. "Is that better?"

He nodded and made an effort to adjust the covers so that his reaction to her assistance wasn't obvious. Why was his body reacting to her so?

"Good. I'll get you that pain reliever." She stepped out of the room and soon returned with a bottle of tablets and a glass of water. Shaking out a couple of pills, she handed them to him, then offered him the glass of water.

Gladly he took the medicine and swallowed all the water. Closing his eyes, he was almost asleep when the covers were pulled up over his chest. He was being tucked in for the first time in his life…and he liked it!

CHAPTER THREE

MELANIE SETTLED IN to the overstuffed chair closest to the door to Dalton's bedroom. Dalton. She liked the name. He wasn't as much of a stuffed shirt when he was hurt. She would never have dreamed she would ever be babysitting the world's foremost orthopedic surgeon. Here she was spending the night and him really just a stranger. That might not be technically accurate after she'd toweled him dry. She'd been aware he was a man before, but she was well aware of how much man he was now.

Heavens, after those eventful moments in the bathroom she was almost glad he was hurt. She wasn't sure what she would have done had he leaned over and kissed her. Shaking her head, she tried to get the image out of her mind but it didn't seem to want to go. Being a professional, she shouldn't have been shocked or affected by his nakedness but somehow his body's reaction to her ministrations made her blood run hot. What was she thinking? She wasn't even sure she liked him. He'd made it clear he cared nothing about football and her life revolved around the game.

Her cell phone rang.

"Yes, Daddy?"

"How is Dr. Reynolds?"

Just like him not to ask about her. Tamping down her disappointment, she answered, "He's asleep and not too happy with having to be here longer than he planned."

"Well, try to keep him happy. We need him to sign off on Rocket."

"Dad, I wouldn't count on him doing that." Or her, for that matter. But that wasn't a battle she would have over the phone.

"Well, you never know. Since you're going to be spending some extra time with him, try to sweeten him up some."

That she *wouldn't* be doing. "I'll let you know if anything changes."

Her father hung up. She shifted to get more comfortable but that didn't seem to happen. Dalton might have taken the majority of the hit but she could tell that she hadn't escaped unhurt. She would like to sleep but she was waiting for one of the girls in the office to bring her some clothes.

While Dalton had showered, she'd called one of her friends and asked her to pack a bag and bring it by the Lodge. As soon as it arrived she would get a bath in the other room and then a nap.

As if thinking about it made it appear, there was a knock at the door. It was the bellhop with her bag. After thanking and tipping him, she closed and locked the door. She needed to check on Dalton before seeing to herself.

She set the bag on the floor next to Dalton's door and then pushed it open. It wouldn't pay for him to think she was sneaking a peek at him. She went to his bedside. He slept making a soft, even snoring sound. The covers had slipped down, leaving his chest bare. It was well developed as if he was used to physical activity. There was a smattering of hair in its center.

"Like what you see?"

Jerking back, heat rushing up her neck, her gaze flew to Dalton's face. "I was just checking on you."

"That's what they all say." His eyes closed again.

She left the room, hoping he wouldn't remember her visit.

A noise woke Melanie from where she slept on one of the sofas. She'd chosen to rest there so she could hear Dalton if she was needed. The extra bedroom was too far away.

She sat up. A fat ray of light came out of the open door. Dalton stood silhouetted in it. She sighed. At least he was wearing the robe.

"How're you feeling?"

"Hungry." His breathing still sounded difficult.

"I called for sandwiches earlier. They're in the refrigerator in the minibar. I'll get them." She stood. Pulling on the matching robe over her tailored-shirt-and-pants pajama set, she flipped on a lamp.

Giving her a critical look, he followed her to the bar. There he took one of the high stools. Melanie flipped on the light over the bar and pulled the tray of sandwiches out of the refrigerator, placing them on the bar. "What would you like to drink?"

Dalton glanced out the window. Following his gaze, she saw that the lamps lighting the falls made it easy to see snow falling.

He looked back at her. "Coffee?"

"Coming right up." She prepared the coffee machine and started it. While it bubbled and dripped she pulled out her own sandwich. "Cream and sugar?"

He shook his head.

"Does it still hurt to breathe?"

He nodded.

Pouring his coffee, she handed it to him. "Would you like more pain reliever?"

"Yes."

"I'll get you some after we eat." Despite his injury, she had a feeling he used as few words as possible all the time. She opened the refrigerator, pulled out a soda for herself and walked around the bar. Taking a stool, she made sure it wasn't the one right next to his.

They ate in silence. When Dalton finished he pushed the plate away and limped toward the window. He stood staring out. Melanie joined him. From this position the falls could be seen but it wasn't the same magnificent view as from his bedroom.

After a moment she murmured, "I want to thank you again for protecting me. I know getting stuck here wasn't what you planned."

"Not your fault."

"Still, I feel bad."

"Don't."

Neither one of them said anything for a few more minutes. Melanie was surprise by how comfortable it was to just stand next to him and look out at the snowy night. When was the last time she had spent a moment or two just being with someone?

Not that she was attracted to Dalton. She stepped away. "I need to clean up."

While she was busy behind the bar, Dalton went into his bedroom. Finished with putting everything in its place, Melanie went to Dalton's room to see about giving him some medicine. She found him sitting on the edge of the bed.

Melanie picked up the pain reliever bottle she'd left on the bedside table. Shaking out a couple of pills, she handed them to Dalton. She picked up the glass left there earlier. "I'll get you some water."

As she went by, his fingers circled her wrist, stopping her. His hand was warm on her skin. "Thank you for taking care of me."

Melanie could see the effort the words cost him, both physically and mentally. Had no one ever cared for him? Surely as a child his mother had nursed him when he was sick?

"I'm glad I could help."

He let go of her and she continued to the bathroom to fill the glass. When she returned he was already asleep. The robe he'd worn lay on the end of the bed. He must have taken the pills dry. She left the glass on the table and adjusted the covers around his shoulders. After turning off the bedside lamp, she left the room, leaving the door cracked so she could hear him if he called.

Dalton woke to the sun streaming through the large window and the roar of the falls. He rolled over and let out a loud groan. He'd heard that having bruised or broken ribs was superpainful. What everyone said was right. If he had to sit up on a plane for three hours he wouldn't be fit to do anything for a week. Thankfully, he didn't have any cases waiting. He looked at the snow piled on the windowsill and shivered. Cold was just not his thing.

The door opened and Melanie's head appeared around it. "You okay in here? I heard you call out."

"Yes."

"You hungry again?"

He nodded. "What time is it?"

"Almost eleven."

"That late?" When was the last time he'd not been up at six?

Melanie glanced out the window. "How about some hot cereal?"

"Okay."

"Cream of Wheat okay?"

He'd not had Cream of Wheat in years. Mrs. Richie had served it almost every morning. It was a cheap way to feed a large number of children. The thing was, he didn't really mind. He, unlike most of the other children, liked the cereal.

"Sounds good."

"You seem to be breathing easier. Has some of the pain gone away?"

He shrugged. "Not really."

"I'm sorry to hear that. I'll call for some breakfast." She left, pulling the door closed.

Dalton struggled to stand. The pain was excruciating, but he couldn't lie there all day. That certainly wouldn't make it any easier to get around. He also didn't want Melanie to come back and start helping him dress. If she saw him in the nude again it had better be for his benefit as well as hers. *Damn*, where did that thought come from?

He had no interest in Melanie. Then again, he was stuck here for a few days. He had time to kill and he was attracted to her. But they really had nothing in common outside of their profession. Last night had been a normal male reaction to a woman toweling him dry and nothing more.

With great effort and teeth-gritting pain, he managed to get his clothes on. He was grateful for his loafers because those he could at least slip his feet into, even if they were inadequate for the weather.

He joined Melanie in the living area. She was dressed in another well-cut suit. The only concession to her being a woman was the ruffles down the front of her shirt.

There was a knock at the door and she went to answer it. The bellhop pushed a cart in. Melanie smiled and called him by name. How like her to have made a friend. Dalton thought how it had taken years for him to cultivate the friends he had.

After tipping the bellhop, she closed the door, then pushed the cart toward the bar area. "I thought you might like a real pot of coffee and maybe some eggs with the cereal."

"That sounds good."

She started setting food on the bar. He went to help and she said, "No. I'll get it. You're still not in very good shape."

"I need to move some or I'll get so stiff that I can't." He took the same stool as he had the night before.

"Give it a few more hours before you start getting too energetic." She poured a cup of coffee from a carafe and placed it in front of him.

"You do remember I'm a doctor?"

"I do. And I'm one too, well aware of the kind of care you need. I also feel very responsible for what happened to you. So please humor me for a little while longer." She set the food out and removed the covers. "You'll be on your own soon enough."

"How's that?"

She joined him, taking what he now considered her stool. "I work at the local hospital one day a week and today is that day."

"Really?"

"Yes, really."

He picked up his spoon. "It's just that I'm a little surprised. So you're going to trust me here by myself?"

"I think your ribs will keep you in line."

He looked out the window. The idea of being stuck in the suite all day by himself with nothing to do might be more painful than trying to breathe.

"Mind if I tag along?"

Melanie viewed at him as if he were a bug under

a magnifying glass. Was he not welcome? "You want to go to the hospital with me?"

"I think it'll be a pretty long day if I stay here."

"Are you sure you feel up to it?"

"I'll make it." He took a sip of his coffee. "I'll have pain pills."

"Okay. If that's what you want to do."

Half an hour later they were getting their coats on. Melanie stepped over and helped him pull his collar up around his neck when he couldn't bring himself to attempt it. Melanie seemed to know he needed assistance without him asking. She was no doubt a caring and thoughtful doctor. Somehow it was getting easier to accept her help. "Thanks."

She smiled and headed toward the door. "If you stay around much longer you're going to have to buy some clothes or you'll freeze to death."

Dalton huffed, which brought on a stab of pain. "Would we have time to stop somewhere before going to the hospital?"

She opened the suite door. "No, but we can afterwards."

Her eagerness to get to the hospital intrigued him. The fact she made a point to work at a hospital each week was interesting. There was more to Dr. Hyde than met the eye.

The same driver who had brought them to the hospital was waiting on them in front of the Lodge. He drove them to Melanie's car at the Currents' complex. It had been sitting outside and she removed snow from the windshield before leaving. The inside of the car was so cold it seemed to never warm up. Dalton could hardly wait to buy some heavier clothes.

Melanie wasn't sure that bringing Dalton along to the hospital was such a good idea, but she didn't have the heart to leave him alone all day. Even if she had to have a shadow, it was better than leaving him behind. She'd had no idea that her assignment to pick him up at the airport would lead to her entertaining him for days.

"So where do you work when you go to the hospital?" Dalton asked.

"In the peds department."

"Wow, that's a big difference from working with the team."

"Not really. Both come in with stomachaches and injuries. The size is the only difference."

"I guess you're right."

They entered the Niagara Hospital through a staff door near the Emergency Department.

Melanie loved the old stone building. There was nothing chrome and glass about it, yet it offered state-of-the-art medical care. She enjoyed her work with the Currents, but her heart was with the kids.

Heat immediately hit her in the face and Melanie started removing her outer clothes. Dalton unbuttoned his thin overcoat. She continued along the corridor to the end where the service elevator was located and he followed. As they started upward, she said, "This hospital cares for about seventy-five percent poverty level patients. Most can't pay outside of government assistance. Many only come in after they have no choice because their problem is so bad."

Dalton looked at her. "So how does the hospital stay open?"

"By support of the people who live around here and fund-raising. The Currents do a fund-raiser in the off-season each year. A get-to-spend-the-day-with-a-pro-player type of event."

The elevator door opened and they stepped out. Dalton asked, "Is it successful?"

"Very. People come from all over the world to see their favorite player. Rocket earned the most in the bidding last year." Melanie turned to the left and walked down the wide hallway. She went by the patient rooms and stopped at the nurses' station. All the while she was conscious of Dalton beside her. He would be taking in the place with perceptive eyes. She'd seen his intense evaluation of Rocket and had no doubt he would do the same here.

The clerk sitting behind the desk said, "Good morning, Dr. Hyde. Marcus has been asking for you."

Mel chuckled. "I'm sure he's looking for a piece of candy. I'll start my rounds with him.

"Lisa, this is Dr. Reynolds. He's going to be doing rounds with me today."

Lisa gave Dalton a curious look. "Nice to meet you, Doctor."

Dalton nodded. Melanie was confident he was out of his medical element. She'd seen pictures of his shiny new clinic set in the South Beach area of Miami. No doubt he would have a hard time identifying with the type of patients this hospital typically saw.

"Well, I guess I better get started since Marcus has been looking for me." She turned and headed along another short hall. Over her shoulder she said to Dalton, "We can leave our coats in an office down here."

A few minutes later Melanie knocked on Marcus's room door and pushed it open.

"Dr. Mel!" The eleven-year-old boy had big eyes and a wide smile.

"Hi there, Marcus." She walked to the bedside and Dalton came to stand at the end. "How're you feeling today?"

"Pretty good. Are the Currents ready for the game on Sunday?"

Melanie looked at Dalton. "This guy is a walking encyclopedia of Currents statistics."

"That's impressive." Dalton sounded sincere despite his disinterest in football. She appreciated him being positive for the boy.

"This is Dr. Reynolds, Marcus. He's helping me out today."

The boy looked at Dalton. "Hi, Doc. You like the Currents?"

Dalton shrugged. "I did meet Rocket Overtree yesterday. He seemed like a nice guy."

Marcus lit up like a Christmas tree and started asking questions at a rapid pace.

Finally Melanie held up a hand. "I think that's enough questions. I need to check you out."

"Aw, come on, Dr. Mel. I want to hear about Rocket."

Dalton smiled. "We should let Dr. Mel do her thing. She might be feeling left out."

Melanie gave him an appreciative look and pulled her stethoscope from around her neck. "Okay, let me give you a listen."

Marcus swung his legs around to sit on the edge of the bed.

Melanie leaned toward him. "Heart first."

"Dr. Mel, I know the drill by now." Exasperation filled Marcus's voice.

She smiled. "I guess you do."

Melanie always hoped when she put her stethoscope to the boy's chest she wouldn't hear the swish and gurgle that said he had a bad valve. Marcus's family couldn't afford the medical care he needed. To her great disappointment, the sounds were just as strong as ever.

"Okay, deep breath time." She moved her stethoscope to his back.

Marcus filled his lungs and released them a couple of times.

"Well, you sound good," she lied. He did for someone in need of heart surgery. With every week that went by he was getting weaker.

Dalton moved to stand beside Melanie. "Marcus, do you mind if I listen to you also?"

"Sure. If you want to."

"Mind?" He indicated her stethoscope.

Pleasantly surprised that he was showing this much interest in Marcus, Melanie handed the instrument to him. She'd figured all he would do was follow her around killing time and have no direct interaction with her patients. Since his specialty was adult medicine, she'd thought he'd have no interest. Her primary practice had to do with grown men but she looked forward to the one day she spent on the pediatric floor. Difference was that he'd probably had the opportunity to choose his area of medicine while she had been told she would be a team doctor.

Melanie watched Dalton's face. His mouth tightened. He must have heard what she did. Dalton looked at her with concern showing in his eyes.

"Thanks, Marcus." Dalton handed the stethoscope back to her.

Melanie took it and wrapped it around her neck. To Marcus she said, "I'll stop by before I leave today. I forgot I have something for you. I left it in the office."

"Okay. But don't forget."

Melanie laughed. "I won't."

"I won't let her," Dalton added with a smile as he followed her out. When the door was closed between them and Marcus, Dalton demanded, "Why hasn't he had surgery?"

"Because his parents can't afford it. A couple of doctors are getting together to try to work something out. Have him moved to a children's hospital and find some financing."

"He's not going to be able to wait long."

She glared at him and worked to keep her voice even. "Don't you think I know that? I've been seeing him on and off for months. I'm well aware of how far the damage has progressed."

His expression turned contrite. "I'm used to fixing problems right away. I didn't mean to imply that you weren't doing all you could."

Was that his way of saying he was sorry? "I might have overreacted. I know we aren't supposed to have favorites, but Marcus is mine."

"That's understandable. He's a nice kid. Seems smart too."

She walked down the hall to the next room. "He's managed to have excellent grades despite being in and out of here."

"So who do we see next?" Dalton asked.

Over the next hour they fell into the routine of stopping outside the room door of the next patient while Melanie gave him a brief medical history. They saw children from two to eighteen years of age.

Only a couple of times did Dalton wince when he made a move, otherwise Melanie would have never known he'd been injured. The man sure could hold his emotions in check.

"This is our last stop. Josey Woods is a teen who has just finished chemo. She's made good progress but has pneumonia. She was admitted for a little support since she couldn't seem to shake it on her own. If all goes well she'll be going home tomorrow."

Dalton nodded and they entered the room. A young girl sat in a chair watching a music video on the TV hanging on the wall. There was a blanket lying across her legs.

"Hello, Josey. I'm Dr. Mel Hyde. You can call me Dr. Mel and this is Dr. Reynolds. We're going to be checking on you today."

"Hi," Josey said softly, not making eye contact. Blond fuzz covered her bald head.

"I hear you're feeling better and ready to go home." Melanie stepped closer.

The girl nodded.

Dalton hung back near the door. Apparently he was sensitive to the shy patient, whose mannerisms indicated she might have "white coat syndrome." Melanie was glad that neither she nor Dalton were wearing their lab jackets.

"I'd like to listen to you, if I may?" Melanie asked.

Josey leaned forward as if she was resigned to having no choice. She, like Marcus, had been in the hospital for far too much of her childhood.

"I see you like Taylor Swift," Melanie said as she prepared to place the stethoscope on Josey's thin chest.

"Yes, she's my favorite."

"I like her music too." Melanie listened to the steady thump, thump, thump of her heart. It sounded good.

"You do?" Josey seemed to perk up. She leaned forward.

"I do. Take a deep breath." Melanie glanced to where Dalton leaned against the wall just inside the closed door. He had a slight smile on his face.

Josey eagerly announced, "I have her autograph."

"You do? Another breath. I'd love to see it."

A few seconds later Josey said, "I'll show it to you." She pushed the blanket off her legs and rose. Dressed in a long-sleeve T-shirt and flannel pants, she moved around the bed. There was a limp to her stride. She took a glossy photo off the bed tray and came back to Melanie, handing it to her.

"I'm so jealous." Melanie smiled at the girl and handed the picture back.

"Taylor is too girly for me. I'm a bigger fan of CeeLo Green," Dalton said, having stepped toward them.

Josey looked at him. "I like him too."

"I'd bet you like Justin Timberlake too." Dalton's voice held a teasing note.

Josey's cheeks turned pink. "Yes. I like his music."

Dalton looked from first Josey to Melanie. "All the women I know like his looks."

"Hey, don't pull me into this conversation," Melanie protested.

Dalton came to stand beside her. To Josey he said, "Would you mind if I looked at your legs?"

She acted unsure but then she said, "I guess that would be okay. I've been told there's nothing that can be done about them."

"I'd just like to look. I promise not to hurt you."

Melanie had to give him kudos for his bedside manner with the girl. He'd found common ground before he approached the skittish patient. The man had skill.

"Josey, would you please walk to the door and back this way for me?"

She nodded and did as he asked.

When she returned Dalton said, "Please sit on the edge of your bed. I'm going to feel your legs. If at any time you are uncomfortable let me know and I'll stop."

"Okay."

Dalton went down on his heels. He felt her feet and moved along one leg and then the other. The look on his face was the same one he'd worn when he examined Rocket. Dalton used his fingers to tell him what he needed to know. A few minutes later he stood.

"I'm sorry to have to ask you this but I need you to remove your socks and pants so I can see your knees. If you have some shorts to put on that would be fine."

Josey looked at Melanie, who gave the girl a re-assuring smile.

"Okay."

"We'll step out into the hall. Just call when

you're ready." He started toward the door and Melanie followed.

She closed the door behind them. "I had no idea about her limp. It wasn't on the chart."

"My guess is that she and her family have just accepted it."

A faint, "I'm ready," came from inside the room.

Dalton went in ahead of Melanie this time. He was in his element and seemed eager to see if something could be done for Josey, who was already sitting on the side of the bed with the sheet pulled over her waist.

"I'm ready."

"Great. I'm going to do something similar to what I've already done. All you have to do is sit there. If what I do hurts, just let me know."

Dalton put his hands on her right knee and manipulated it. He then moved to the left, the one with the limp. A few minutes later he stood and backed away. "I'd like to look at your left hip. All you have to do is lie on the bed and let me move your leg back and forth. You can tell me 'no' and I'll understand."

"Okay."

Just like a teen, she used only one-word answers. Josey scooted back on the bed, lay down and adjusted the sheet. Melanie worked to control her smile. A girl was modest at that age, even around a male doctor. Melanie looked at Dalton. Especially one as good-looking as him. She couldn't blame Josey. She'd have felt much the same way if she was half-clothed in front of Dalton.

"I'm going to raise your leg up. Tell me when I've gone as far as I can." He lifted her leg slowly.

Thankfully the range of movement looked fine.

He brought the leg out to the left and then across her other leg. "Good. You can sit up." He offered his hand to Josey. She took it and he pulled her upright. "I'm glad you are doing so well and getting to go home tomorrow."

"Me too."

"We'll let you get back to your videos," Melanie said as she followed Dalton out the door as the sound of a popular song on the TV grew.

Dalton stopped when they were well out of hearing distance from anyone who might be in the hall. "I would like to see X-rays of her knee, both front and side view. I would also like to see the MRI."

"I doubt either have been done."

"You have to be kidding. Why not?" He paced

three steps up the hall then turned and came back to her.

"Because there was no reason to. She is being treated for an infection as a complication to chemo. There would be no reason either should have been ordered. Here—" she gestured around her at the building "—we are treating her cancer issues. The leg issues were not on the staff radar."

His sound of disgust rubbed her the wrong way. She wasn't to blame here. If it were up to her these children would all have the finest medical care money could buy. For people like Josey and her parents it was an everyday worry about how they would pay for Josey's needs.

"Then they should be ordered," Dalton said sharply.

Now he was starting to tell her what to do. "That's easier said than done."

He glared at her. "Why is that?"

"The X-rays are doable but the MRI is a problem."

He stepped forward, his frustration written all over his face. "And I ask again—why is that?"

"Because there is no MRI machine here. She would need to be transferred to another hospital to have it done."

"Then do it."

She pulled him into an empty patient room. "Now wait a minute. You don't give me orders. You're not even on the staff here. So don't start throwing your ego around!"

Dalton looked at her calmly but the tic in his jaw gave his irritation away. "You don't want to help the girl?"

Melanie stepped back as if she had been slapped. "Of course I do."

"Okay, then. The first step is seeing that we get X-rays of her knee and a MRI if possible."

"I can order an X-ray. I'll have to see how best to proceed with the MRI."

"Good. Let's go do it."

When she didn't move Dalton took her elbow and gave her a little nudge.

Melanie pulled her arm out of his grip. Head held high, she walked down the hall. Had she ever been this angry? Who did he think he was, telling her what to do? Making demands. And, worse, implying she didn't care enough to do everything that could be done for Josey.

Stalking to the nurse's station, she went to one of the computer stations and typed in her password. She pulled up Josey's chart and ordered an X-ray with anteroposterior and lateral views.

"I'd like a skyline as well."

She looked up. Her face was inches from his. Dalton's arms were braced on the back of her chair as he leaned over her, looking at the screen.

She snapped, "You do understand that you don't have privilege at this hospital?"

"That's why I'm asking you to request one."

"Request? I missed that part." She was starting to sound childish even to her own ears. Thankfully no one was in the charting room to overhear.

Dalton sat in the empty chair next to her. He grunted as he did so, which reminded her that he still hurt. "Look, I'm sorry if I sound as if I'm telling you what to do, it's just that I think I can help Josey. Sometimes I get high-handed in my excitement." His fingertips touched her arm for a second. "Would you please also request a skyline view?"

She wasn't sure she liked his manipulation any better than being told what to do. What she did appreciate was his passion about helping Josey. He saw a problem, believed he could fix it and wouldn't stop until he tried. If only all that just didn't come with his general barking-orders attitude.

She gave him a sideways look intended to show him that she knew he was managing her, then typed in the order.

"When should those be back?" Dalton asked, standing.

"Tomorrow at the earliest. They are not a priority, so she won't have them done until morning." When he started to say something, she put up a hand to stop him. "You will just have to accept that. I will not push anymore."

"If I get a flight out tomorrow will you see they are sent to me?"

Melanie pushed away from the computer. "I will. Despite what you might think, I'd like to see Josey walk without a limp."

A heart-melting smile came to his face. "I never thought any different."

"You sure implied it."

"How about I buy you dinner tonight to make up for that?"

Melanie met his gaze. "Now you are using bribery to get your way."

He shrugged. "You have to eat, don't you?"

She did, but not necessarily with him.

"So what's next?" Dalton asked.

"I have to do some dictation. See that charts are up to date."

He groaned. "I think I'll find the cafeteria and get a bad cup of coffee. That sounds like more fun."

It hadn't been as uncomfortable as she'd anticipated to have Dalton around but it was nice to have a few minutes to herself.

For the next few hours Melanie worked her way through the charting and made sure orders were posted. While she did so she overheard a number of the nurses talking to each other about Dalton. More than once a comment was made about how good-looking he was, followed by the question of whether or not he was married, then giggles. If they knew what a stuffed shirt he was, how demanding he could be, or that he hated sports and snow, they might not have been so impressed.

But he had been chivalrous when he protected her from getting hit, had been fair with Rocket and almost warrior-like with Josey. Maybe there was something more socially redeeming in him than she cared to admit.

She hadn't seen Dalton since he'd left for coffee. Where had he gotten to? Great, now she'd have to go hunt him down. Melanie glanced at the computer. Marcus's chart was still up. Before leaving she needed to go by and give him his present.

Returning to the office where she and Dalton had left their coats, she looked through her pocketbook and pulled out the tickets to the Currents' Sunday afternoon playoff game. She went down the hall and stopped at Marcus's door. The music from what sounded like an adventure movie came from inside the room. She knocked and received no answer. That didn't surprise her. Pushing the door open just far enough to call Marcus, she waited for an answer and heard none.

"Man, that's the best. Luke made him pay," Marcus's voice carried.

"Darth Vader is a villain's villain."

That was Dalton. Even in a few short days she had his voice committed to memory.

Melanie pushed the door open to find Marcus sitting up in bed and Dalton reclined in a chair next to him. Flashing on the TV was a Star Wars movie. A loud swish and boom filled the air. Neither male gave her any notice as she walked farther into the room.

"What's going—?"

"Shh, this is the best part," Dalton said, not even bothering to look her way.

Melanie moved around behind him and regarded the screen. Two people using light sabers slashed at one another.

Marcus leaned forward. "Wow, look at how he makes that move."

Obviously the two males had found something to bond over. She didn't say anything again until the fight was over. Even then she spoke softly to Dalton. "I'm ready to head out when you are."

He glanced at her. "This is almost over."

From that statement he left no doubt he wasn't leaving until then. Against the wall on the other side of the room was an extra hardback chair. She circled the bed toward it. Dalton and Marcus both groaned as she walked between them and the TV.

"Aw, come on, Dr. Mel," Marcus whined as he put his head one way then the other to see around her.

"Hurry up, Dr. Hyde." Dalton shifted in much the same manner as Marcus had.

She hurried by them. While pulling the chair in the direction of the bed, it made a scraping noise on the floor. Both movie watchers glared at her for a second before they returned to viewing the action.

"Sorry," she said contritely before picking up the chair. She placed it on the floor next to Marcus's bed and primly sat on it. Did she dare disturb them?

Less than half an hour later the movie ended.

"No matter how many times I see it, it's great. A classic." Dalton stood with effort and a slight grimace.

"You're right, bro, one of the best movies ever." Marcus brought his legs to the floor.

Melanie looked from one of them to the other. "Who are you two?"

"We're Star Wars fans." Marcus acted as if that was a badge of honor that had bonded him and Dalton together forever.

She nodded as if she understood what that meant. "Well, it's time for Dr. Reynolds and me to go. I just came down to bring you what I promised. It's not a trip to a Star Wars convention so I hope you still like it."

Marcus looked at her eagerly. "What is it?"

"How about box tickets to the Currents' playoff game on Sunday?"

His huge white smile stood out in contrast to his dark skin. "Man, really? Box seats! How cool."

His smile suddenly faded.

"What's wrong?" Melanie asked.

"I'm stuck in here." He looked at his bed.

"I fixed that too. You have a pass out for the day as long as you do exactly what you're told."

Marcus's smile grew again. "You can count on that." He turned to Dalton. "Will you be there?"

"No, I'll be leaving before then. But I'm sure you'll have fun."

"I can't wait. I just hope 'The Rocket' will play."

Melanie looked at Dalton, then said, "We'll have to see about that. There'll be a car here to pick you up on Sunday. You can bring one person with you. I'll stop in and say hi when you get to the stadium."

"Thanks, Dr. Mel. You rock."

"You're welcome. See you then." Melanie turned toward the door.

"It was nice to meet you, Marcus. I hope you're out of here soon." Dalton offered his hand.

Marcus placed his thin one in Dalton's and they shook.

"Later, man." Marcus put large headphones over his ears and picked up an iPad.

"That was a nice thing you did for Marcus," Dalton said.

Melanie shrugged. "No big deal. They were offered to me and I gave them to him."

"I have the feeling that you do whatever you can to make these kids happy. You have a big heart, Melanie."

She had to admit it give her a warm feeling to have him notice how much she cared. Her family wasn't even aware of where she spent her days off. She'd let this stranger into her world without even thinking. Even so, she didn't plan to let him too close—she'd seen what happened when she allowed that. Her work with the kids was her private domain.

Why had she shared it with him?

CHAPTER FOUR

IN THE PASSENGER seat of Melanie's car as they left the hospital parking lot, Dalton asked, "Where're we headed now?"

"I thought the mall might give us the most choices for men's shops." She looked over and grinned. "I didn't think you'd want to get out in the weather any more than necessary. At least in the mall it'll be warm between stores."

"You're enjoying my discomfort."

She glanced at him with a grin on her lips. "Enjoy may be too strong a word. It's more like I find it humorous."

Dalton watched as her grin transformed into a smile. Melanie's lips were full, with a curve on each end as if they were always waiting to lift in pleasure. What would it feel like to kiss them? Would they be as plush as they looked? He'd see to it she smiled with pleasure.

Where had those thoughts come from? He shifted in his seat. No doubt it came from the attraction he felt for her. "What's so entertaining about it?"

"That a man of your intelligence would come this far north in the middle of winter without the correct type of clothes."

He smirked and chuckled. "You're right. Put that way, I don't sound too smart. My only defense is that I hadn't planned to stay so long."

They both laughed. Snow continued to fall and the traffic increased. He sat in silence as Melanie concentrated on driving.

"I hope you weren't too bored today." Melanie pulled out into the traffic along the major freeway.

"No, it was fine." Dalton hadn't spent a more satisfying day in a long time. Despite the fact that his whole body hurt, he had enjoyed working with the children and seeing different medical issues. He'd spent so long in the adult-care world, and focused on bones and tissue, it was refreshing to think small and broader.

He'd found out he and Melanie shared a common interest in children. That had come as a surprise. She kept doing that. First she was a female team doctor working in the NFL. Melanie also wasn't easily deterred from what she believed was her duty, which showed in her insisting she take care of him. And now he'd found out her real love was children. He'd never met a more fascinating woman with such diverse interests. It would be exciting to discover other aspects of her personality. At least while he was stuck there.

They hadn't traveled far when Melanie exited the freeway. She drove down a side road and turned into the parking area of a shopping mall. The lot was full and they rode up and down the aisles looking for a spot. "People are out Christmas shopping. With only six days left, the mall is packed."

"You don't Christmas shop?" He understood that women lived to shop.

"I did mine months ago. I don't like to wait to the last minute."

"I'm impressed."

Melanie turned to him. "So how about you? Do you have all your shopping done? Do you need to do some while we are here?"

What should he tell her? He didn't have anyone to buy for? "My secretary handles that for me."

She glanced at him. "Really?"

Dalton chose to ignore the question in the hope she wouldn't pursue it.

She found a parking spot about as far away from

the entrance as possible. He wasn't looking forward to the frigid walk. The sun was setting and the temperature dropping. Bundling up as best he could, he started across the parking lot beside Melanie.

"I should have dropped you off at the door and then parked," she said apologetically.

"I wouldn't have allowed you to walk across this large lot by yourself." He stuffed his hands in his pockets as the wind picked up. "Not safe."

"Your mother must have taught you to be a gentleman."

Despite all the years that had passed, his chest tightened. He let her push through the revolving door first and then followed in the next partition. He said, more to himself than her, "No, that's one thing she wasn't guilty of."

"There's a men's shop down here on the right that should have what you need. I'm sorry you're having to buy clothes you won't have much use for later."

"It's better than being in the hospital for frostbite. Besides, I'm sure this won't be my only trip up north."

"Well, there is that." Melanie headed into the mall and he fell into step beside her.

They walked past the glass-fronted stores and around the next corner.

"I love to come here during the holidays. The decorations always put me in the holiday spirit." Enthusiasm filled her voice.

"I've never really thought about it."

She pointed up. "Where in the world can you see ornaments larger than a person? Or such beautiful trees?"

The wonder in her voice was almost contagious.

"You said you always have your shopping done early. Does that mean you just come to the mall to get in the middle of thousands of people because you like the decorations?"

"I do. As long as I don't have to fight over gifts I like being in the middle of things."

"Then I'll make sure I hold you back while I'm trying to buy clothes. I wouldn't want you to get in a scuffle."

She laughed. "Thanks, I'd appreciate that. I wouldn't want to reflect poorly on the Currents' name."

"Do you always think about the team first?"

She shrugged. "I guess that's how I was raised."

"It seems to me you should think about yourself first every once in a while. I've not known you long, but you're quite a unique person. There's a lot more to you than your work with the team."

Melanie stopped walking to look at him. "Thank you—that was nice of you to say."

Her admiration made him uncomfortable. "Don't sound so surprised. I can be nice."

"Here's the shop I told you about. I think you'll find what you need in here."

"You're not coming in? What if I don't get the right stuff?"

"I was just going to wait out here for you, but if you'd like my help…"

"I could use it." He could decide on his own clothes but he enjoyed seeing her flustered. He liked teasing her and he never teased.

"Okay."

He went through the open doors of the store and she followed.

Dalton looked around. "So what do you recommend?"

She said without hesitation, "You need a couple of flannel shirts, heavy sweater, cord slacks and thick socks."

"Wow, I'm almost sorry I asked."

"You really should have a jacket but, since you aren't going to be here long, I hate for you to spend that kind of money. Especially when you might not wear it again anytime soon."

"Can I help you?" a blonde saleswoman wearing a tight dress and a smile asked.

"Yes. I'm interested in a couple of warm slacks, two shirts and a sweater."

Her smile grew. "Well, you're in the correct place. Come right this way."

Dalton glanced at Melanie and caught her rolling her eyes. She didn't seem impressed with his reception. Interesting.

Melanie tagged along behind Dalton as he followed Miss Fresh and Perky toward the back of the store. He seemed more than willing. Why it mattered to her, she had no idea.

"Right, here is our slacks selection." The clerk waved a hand toward a rack of pants, then pulled a pair out. "I think these would look great on you. I'm guessing a thirty-four/thirty-four."

Dalton nodded and smiled as if she'd given him a compliment.

No wonder her brothers said this was their favorite place to shop.

Dalton felt the material. He looked at her. "What do you think?"

Melanie was surprised he remembered she was there. She stepped forward and rubbed the pants leg. "They should do."

"Why don't you try them on so your wife can see them?" the saleswoman said.

"She's not my wife," Dalton said.

At the same time Melanie said, "I'm not his wife."

The saleswoman's smile brightened. "I'm sorry. My mistake. The dressing rooms are this way."

"Melanie, while I'm trying these on, would you mind picking out some shirts? A sweater, if you see one you like," Dalton called over his shoulder; he seemed far too eager to follow the saleswoman.

If Melanie didn't know better she would say she was feeling jealous. That wasn't something she made a habit of. Why would she care if a saleswoman flirted with Dalton? He was nothing to her. Still, he knew more about her than her own family.

She walked to the other side of the store to where the shirts hung and picked out a couple that would look nice on Dalton. Nearby on a shelf was a stack of sweaters in multiple colors. She pulled out one in burgundy and held it up. With Dalton's coloring it would suit him. Making her way back to where Dalton stood talking to the saleswoman, she joined them. They were both laughing.

"I found these. Do you want to try them on?" she said in a sharper than normal tone.

With a raised brow, Dalton asked, "What size are they?"

She told him.

"Those will do. How about a sweater?"

Melanie held it out for him to see.

"That color is perfect for you," the saleswoman cooed.

"Then I'll take it." He grinned at Melanie.

She'd had all she could take. This obvious flirtation was starting to make her sick. Why it mattered Melanie couldn't fathom, but it did. Outside of that one time in the bathroom when he'd handed her the towel, he'd treated her like a colleague. But wasn't that what she was? Why did she want him to flirt with her the same way?

Because it would be nice to feel like a woman. In her world, both at work and with her family, she was treated like one of the boys. Was she guilty of letting them do so?

The saleswoman took the clothes. "Is there anything else I can get you?"

Dalton's far-too-syrupy grin had Melanie walking off. "I think you can handle the rest without me."

Fifteen minutes later Dalton exited the store. Melanie sat on a bench in the middle of the mall, waiting. When he joined her, she said, "You seemed to be enjoying your shopping trip."

He grinned. "I was. What about a coat?"

"If you really want one there's a store down this way." She stood and started walking down the mall. "It carries a good line of coats. There may not be a salesperson in a tight dress, though."

"Do I hear a touch of jealousy in there?"

"You do not. I just don't think clerks have to wear skintight clothes to sell men's clothing."

"What should she wear? Something functional like your suits?"

"What's wrong with my suits? They're business-like. Professional looking." She raised her voice.

"I think you can be professional and look like a woman too."

She turned to him. "Are you saying I don't?" Her anger grew. People were beginning to look.

"You can dress anyway you wish."

"You're right—it's none of your business." Melanie stalked ahead of him.

By the time he had reached her side, they had arrived at the coat store.

"I don't think you'll need my help here. I'm going to look next door. I'll meet you right here when you're finished."

Melanie didn't give Dalton time to answer before she walked on. She needed to get away from him for a few minutes. Stopping at the show window, she looked at the mannequins dressed in glitzy dresses in seasonal colors. Did she really dress unfemininely? Here she was, carting him around, seeing he had warm clothes, and he was giving her fashion advice. How much nerve could the man have?

She looked down at her high-quality tailored suit. These were the kind of clothes she'd always worn. That wasn't true. Her mother had dressed her in frilly dresses, especially on holidays.

When her mom died, her father had spent little time worrying about how Melanie dressed. He'd handed money over to the housekeeper or baby-sitters and asked them to buy her clothing for special occasions. As she grew older her father gave the money to her. Melanie was a tomboy and that was encouraged. She looked up to her brothers, so she tended to choose shirts and jeans to wear like them.

For the prom, her friend's mother had taken her and her friend to buy their dresses. It was one of the few times she had female help with picking out clothing or with any of the other rites of passage most girls shared with their mother. A few times she'd cried herself to sleep when she heard about events like a Mother/Daughter Luncheon or when her friends talked about spending a day shopping with their mothers. She had long ago moved past feeling sorry for herself and compensated by making herself needed by her father and brothers. That was where she found her security. It would be wonderful to feel appreciated, just the same.

Why had Dalton's one comment got under her skin? Had she forgotten how to dress like a girl? Had she been living in the world of men so long that she'd given up even trying to act like a woman? When was the last time she'd bought something lacy and girly? She did like sexy underwear but few had seen that side of her.

"So which one do you like best?" Dalton's deep voice said beside her.

She jerked around. He'd caught her looking at

the dresses. Now he would be pleased that what he'd said had got to her. To cover her embarrassment, she asked, "Did you find a coat?"

"You answer my question, then I'll answer yours."

She huffed. The man exasperated her. "The red one, if you must know."

The dress was mid-thigh-length and had a scooped neck. It fit tightly down to the waist then flared out into a full skirt. She'd seen fewer dresses prettier.

"Are you going to try it on?"

"You haven't answered my question."

Dalton held up a sack. "I did get a coat. I bought it on sale so you don't have to worry about me spending so much money. So are you going in?"

"No. I don't need a dress like that."

He seemed to give that remark some thought, then looked at her. "Shame. I think you'd look very pretty in it."

Melanie didn't want to admit the glow of warmth his words created.

As if he'd forgotten what they had been talking about, he said, "Hey, I'm hungry. Is there a decent restaurant here?"

"There's one down the next wing."

They made their way through the growing crowd to the restaurant. In front of the brick-facade pub, they stopped and he gave the girl standing behind a podium his name.

"Why don't we wait at the bar?" Dalton suggested.

Melanie nodded.

They took stools next to each other.

"Would you like a drink?" Dalton asked.

She ordered wine and he a whiskey.

"I haven't asked in a while, but how are you feeling?" Melanie fingered the stem of her glass.

"Let's just say that I know where my ribs are located."

"Maybe you should have stayed at the Lodge and rested."

"Are you kidding? If I had done that I wouldn't be moving now. How about you? Feeling any aftereffects?"

"When I turn a certain way I know something has happened."

Dalton nodded.

The hostess approached and said their table was ready.

Dalton placed his hand at her waist as she slid off the high stool. His fingers were warm and firm but soon fell away. She was far too aware of him following her as they maneuvered between the tables, trailing the hostess, carrying their drinks with them.

The girl seated them beside the roaring fire in the center of the dining area. The table was covered in a white cloth and a small lantern burned in the center. It was far too romantic a setting for Melanie's comfort.

"Is this table okay with you?" Dalton asked.

"Uh, sure."

"You don't sound very confident."

The man was perceptive. She'd have to watch her facial expressions around him. "No, no, it's fine."

Dalton helped her with her chair, then took the one beside her, facing the fire. His knee touched hers under the table and she shifted away.

"You have enough room?"

"I'm fine."

"I have a feeling you've said that most of your life." He picked up the menu that the hostess had left on the table.

What did he mean by that statement?

Dalton flipped through the menu. "Have you ever eaten here? Do you know what's good?"

"I've had lunch a few times. I always have either a salad or burger. So I'm not much help on the other stuff."

"I want something warm. Go-down-into-the-bones warm."

She grinned. "Now that you have clothes you're going to feel much better."

"I'm counting on that. I going to start with some soup and have a steak. How about you?"

"I'm going to have a salad and roasted chicken."

When the waitress came, Dalton gave her their order.

Dalton had been asking her questions regularly and Melanie was determined to take advantage of this time to ask a few of her own.

"So tell me, why did you become an orthopedic doctor?"

He took a sip of his drink, then placed the glass carefully on the table. Did it make him uncomfortable to answer personal questions? He certainly didn't seem to mind asking them.

"I was a good student. I took a biology class and was hooked on science. Medicine just seemed like the natural progression."

"So why orthopedics?"

"When I did that rotation, there was this man

who had been crippled for most of his life. He agreed to a new procedure and now he's walking. I wanted to make that possible for people."

That answer she liked. She was glad to know he hadn't got into it for the money. With his fancy practice, she'd wondered what motivated him.

He continued, "I have a talent for what I do. The next thing I knew, I was being asked to evaluate athletes. One thing led to another."

"Seems like you have a high-pressure practice."

"It can be but I have a great staff and a couple of other doctors working with me."

"So what do you do to blow off steam when it gets to be too much?"

"Why, Melanie, are you trying to find out about my private life?" There he was with the uncomfortable questions again.

"I am not. I'm trying to have pleasant conversation over dinner."

Dalton's hand came to rest over hers for a second. "It's pleasant being here with you."

"I think you're trying to dodge the question."

Grinning, he nodded. "Maybe a little. I'm a pretty private person. I like to spend the day at the beach, swimming. I bike to and from work. I read mysteries and have been known to go to

South Beach clubs on occasion. I work more than anything."

"I can't imagine biking to work. That must be nice."

"Most days it is. The weather does get hot in midsummer, but I go in so early it doesn't much matter."

The waitress returned with their soup and salad. Their conversation turned to the books he had read. Many of them she had appreciated as well. They debated the pros and cons of the plots.

By the time they'd finished their meal, Melanie found she rather enjoyed Dalton's company. He had a way of drawing her out. Really listening to her opinions. She'd felt invisible for so long, it was nice being the center of someone's focus.

He paid for their dinner and they walked back to the mall door they'd entered.

"Time to bundle up." Melanie stopped beside a bench and began putting her coat on. Dalton placed his bag on the seat and helped her when she missed a sleeve with a hand. He then pulled his new jacket out of the large bag. It was a black wool pea jacket with a double row of buttons down the center. He slipped it on.

"Looks nice. But I would suggest that you not

wear the tag." Melanie removed the paper hanging from under his arm. "You'll be much happier now."

"Wait—there's more." He dug into the sack again and pulled out a red and black scarf. Wrapping it around his neck, he flipped the ends over his shoulders and smiled broadly.

Melanie laughed. "Nice choice, but I don't think it'll keep you warm that way. Let me show you." She took the material and looped it around itself and pulled it up close to his neck, then she tucked the ends inside the lapel of his coat. Patting his chest with both hands, she met his gaze with a grin. "There."

Dalton wrapped his arms around her waist and pulled her close. "You deserve a proper thank-you for taking care of me," he whispered in a sandpapery voice as his mouth found hers.

His lips were warm and held a hint of whiskey. They were perfect. Her heart beat at record time. Her hands slid up to hold the ridge of his shoulders as Dalton pulled her tighter and the pressure of his mouth increased. Her body heated as if she were basking in the sun. His tongue traced the seam of her mouth. Her fingers seized his coat and she moaned. More, she wanted more. She returned his kiss.

Melanie had no idea how much time had passed before Dalton released her. Dazed, it took a few seconds before she realized that someone was clapping.

"I think we're making a scene," Dalton said as he picked up his bag and took her arm, leading her toward the door.

On unsteady legs, she went with him. *Wow! What a kiss.*

She glanced around to see a family grinning at them. "I guess we are." The words came out sounding shaky. The warmth of his lips still lingered on hers. A tingle lingered from his touch.

Dalton stopped on the sidewalk. "One more thing." He dug into the bag and came out with gloves.

"You thought of everything."

Pulling them on, he then stuffed the bag into the nearest trash can. He returned to her.

Not thinking about what she was doing, she ran her tongue along her bottom lip. His taste still remained.

Dalton groaned. "Please don't do that."

"What?"

He leaned in close. "Lick your lips. If you do it again I might really make a public scene."

Melanie felt hot despite the temperature being low enough for snow to fall. Dalton had been as turned on as her. "We should get out of this cold."

"I'm ready when you are."

Something about his last statement made her think it might have a deeper meaning. One she wasn't sure she was prepared to deal with.

An hour later when Melanie pulled under the portico of the Lodge, Dalton still hadn't recovered from kissing her. He wanted her.

When she'd looked at him with that sparkle of mischief in her eyes and the smile that made her lovelier than any other woman he'd ever seen, he couldn't help himself. He had to taste her. She had no idea how desirable she was. Now, he wanted more than a kiss. If that one was any indication, the electricity between them would be powerful. Why couldn't they enjoy each other while he was here?

"How about coming up?"

"I don't know…"

"Come on. We could watch a movie." He wasn't

interested in a movie but he would do whatever it took to spend some more time with Melanie.

"Do you feel up to having company? I would think you'd be tired and hurting."

He was hurting but it had nothing to do with being hit. "I am but I would be doing that anyway. The pain relievers have helped. So come on."

"Okay." She pulled on through the entryway and found a parking spot nearby.

At the door of his suite she hesitated. "Maybe—"

"Look, you didn't have a problem coming in when you insisted that you needed to be here for me. There shouldn't be any big deal to spending an evening watching TV with a friend."

She stopped short.

"Don't look so surprised. I think we've become friends after today." That had been more than a friendly kiss. But he wasn't going to mention that and scare her away.

"I guess we have."

"What's the problem? Don't you think we can be friends?"

"No...yes. I don't know. I just don't spend a lot of time in men's hotel rooms."

"You could have fooled me. You were here all last night."

She pursed her lips. "You know what I mean. I think you're making fun of me now." She started down the hall toward the stairs.

He grabbed her arm, stopping her. "Maybe a little bit. Come on in. I can use the company. After all, I don't really know anyone else in town."

"Now you're playing on my sympathy." She hesitated another moment. "Okay, for just a little while."

Dalton let go of her arm and then unlocked the door. Melanie stepped into the suite. He joined her and closed the door. He walked to the coffee table and picked up the remote control to the large-screen TV and handed it to her. "Here, pick out something you'd like to watch while I put up my new clothes."

He came out of the bedroom a few minutes later, and found the TV off and Melanie sitting in one of the swivel chairs facing the window with the view of the falls. She didn't even react to his presence until he sat in the matching chair, and then only to glance at him. Neither of them said anything for a long time.

"I love the falls," she murmured. "They're so beautiful, but when the snow is on the ground and ice forms…it's magical."

"Have you always lived in Niagara Falls?"

"Heavens, no. I've lived in a number of places. You go where the football job is. Most coaches don't last but a few years if they aren't winning and only a few more if they are. Only when Dad became the general manager and I got the team physician position have I managed to stay in one place for a while."

"I hated moving around as a kid."

What had made him say that? He didn't talk about his childhood. That was a dark time in his life. Somehow Melanie made him feel safe to do so.

"I know what you mean. I don't know if I'll ever move away from here. Anyway, you can't get this just anywhere." She indicated the falls.

"You're right, but there are other wonderful places to live. Next to the beach, for example."

"It has been so long since I've been to the beach I can hardly remember what it's like."

"You're welcome to visit me anytime. My place is just across the road from the water. Take your towel and spend the day."

She looked at him for a second. "I'm sure I would interfere with your lifestyle."

"Is that your subtle way of asking if I'm dating someone?"

"Maybe. I'm not used to men inviting me to stay in their homes. I wouldn't want to step on some woman's toes."

Dalton glanced at her. He dated but never seriously. In fact, she was the first female he'd ever invited to spend any length of time in his home. With Melanie he was making a number of firsts. "I was just making a friendly offer. No pressure. You could always stay at a hotel if you wanted to."

"And I would bet you're counting on me not showing up."

"I'd have to admit I would be shocked if you did."

They sat in silence for a few minutes. Dalton found it rather interesting that he wasn't uncomfortable just sitting there. Had he ever spent time with a woman appreciating a view? He did dinner, movies, clubs and sex but never looking at something as simple as water falling. He'd never given much thought to connecting to a woman on a level as simple as enjoying her presence because he didn't want to. They met each other's mutual needs and he was gone. He always made that clear up front. Being around Melanie was doing something strange to him.

She stood. "Thanks for the offer of a movie but I'm tired and I think I'd better go. One of us slept on the sofa last night."

"That was your call, not mine. There's a big nice bed in both the rooms." The chair rocked softly as he stood.

"I guess I'm not going to make you feel guilty." Melanie moved toward the door.

"No, that's not going to happen. If you leave, who's going to make sure I can undress myself?"

"Now who's making who feel guilty? I think you'll manage."

"Is there no way I can talk you into staying?" Dalton moved closer, taking one of her hands.

"Dalton, I'm not sure what you're trying to talk me into here."

He reached an arm around her waist and pulled her close. His hand went behind her neck, bringing her face to his. "I've been thinking about nothing but kissing you again since we left the mall."

His lips found hers.

After a second her hands came to rest at his waist and started up his sides. He groaned.

She jerked away. "I'm sorry. I forgot."

"It doesn't matter." He brought her back to him. His lips found hers again. Melanie's hands went up his arms to grip his biceps. Her chest pressed against his as she leaned into him and returned his kisses. He teased her mouth and she opened for him. Their tongues mated and drove his desire for her higher.

Dalton pulled back and whispered, "Stay."

"Why?"

The question punched him in the gut. How did he answer that? *Because I want your body. Because it would be a way to pass the time.* What could he say that Melanie might accept?

She was no doubt looking for more than he was willing to take a chance on. He had only the truth. "Come on—it's not a big mystery. You're a healthy woman and I'm a healthy man. We're attracted to each other. Our kisses proved it. I thought we might have a good time together."

"So you've decided that since you're stuck here that I might be a little entertainment."

That statement didn't make him feel any better. Short-term was all he could offer. "That's not exactly accurate."

"Dalton, I'm flattered by the offer, I really am, but I'm not someone's one- or two-night stand. Let's not mess up what's becoming a nice friendship. I'll call you in the morning and see if you feel like you can fly. If so, I'll see about getting you a flight out."

Had he just been shot down? Dalton wasn't pleased with this twist of events. Melanie had turned the tables on him and taken the upper hand, made his suggestion sound like an insult. He had lost control of the situation. "Now wait a minute, Melanie, I think you've got this all wrong."

"No, I think I understood clearly. I'll call you in the morning."

She was gone before he could comprehend what had happened. If their kiss was any indication, she'd enjoyed it. But she was running from anything more. Maybe it was just as well. He wasn't looking for permanency and she'd all but told him he wouldn't do.

He'd learned long ago that having someone in his life to care and be around wasn't in the stars for him. They would only leave. He'd taken control of his life. Had built one that didn't depend on anyone but himself. Melanie didn't fit into the world he'd created for himself. Still, he enjoyed her far more than he'd liked any woman in a long time.

So why did it hurt so much when Melanie closed the door behind her?

CHAPTER FIVE

MELANIE RELIVED HER and Dalton's kiss over and over during the night. She'd been kissed before but never with the same breathtaking power, leaving her weak-kneed, heart pounding. Still she didn't know what he wanted from her.

She'd been mistaken about him when they'd first met. But she'd been wrong about another man and that mistake had taken her months to recover from. She couldn't trust her judgment, especially when Dalton's kiss had left her breathless. Her emotions had been played with once before and she refused to let that happen to her again.

When Dalton had arrived she'd questioned if he would be supportive of player care or succumb to pressure from the management to put Rocket back on the field. Thankfully, they were on the same side about what Rocket should do.

All the worrying and the angst didn't matter anyway because Dalton would be gone soon. They lived the length of the country from each other.

Their paths weren't any more likely to cross than they had so far.

The wind howling made her question how bad the weather had become. Getting out of bed, she went to the kitchen and started the coffee machine before clicking on the TV. Pushing the button on the remote, she located the weather channel. A storm was affecting the entire east coast. Dalton wouldn't be pleased—he wouldn't be leaving today.

She called the Lodge and asked for his room. A few minutes later a drowsy-sounding Dalton struggled to say, "Hello?"

"I'm sorry but I have some bad news for you."

"Good morning to you too, Melanie." His voice sounded clearer. "You kept me up last night."

How could the man manage to get her heart pounding with a few simple words? It was nice to know that their kisses had disturbed him as well. She needed to get things back on a business level.

"Uh, I hate to tell you this but you're not going to get a flight out today. There's a major weather front coming in."

Melanie was surprised when there wasn't a large groan of disappointment on the other end of the line. She would miss him when he was gone.

"I figured that might be the case when I looked out the window this morning."

Imagining him still in bed with the covers tangled around his waist, his bare chest dark against the white sheets and the snow falling, had her wishing she wasn't talking to him over the phone but in person.

"So if I can't go home today, what're we going to do?"

The vision of him in bed popped into her mind again. She needed to stop thinking of him that way. They wanted two different things. "Well, I'm going to practice in a few hours. I have a couple of the players to check in with and preparations to make for the game tomorrow. Also I need to double-check Rocket."

"I think I'll go along. Better than being stuck here."

With a note of humor in her voice she said, "I missed the part where you were invited."

"Come on, Melanie, you know you enjoy having me around."

She huffed. Admitting he was right wasn't something she was prepared to do. Even after spending three full days with him, she found she'd missed him last night. "How're you feeling, by the way?"

"Stiff, but I'll live. A hot shower will help with that. Want to come over? I might need help drying off."

Now she was really having a hard time concentrating on what she had to say. "If you're going with me, be ready in an hour."

His soft chuckle filled her ear before she disconnected the call.

Dalton liked watching Melanie work. She had a real rapport with the players and staff. There was a firm but gentle manner to her care. A couple of times she'd even asked him if he was willing to give his opinion. He'd gladly done so.

It shocked him that he wasn't more upset about not being able to get a flight home. In fact, when Melanie had picked him up she'd told him he might not get out until after Christmas. He wasn't pleased but what could he do? With the snow and the holiday plane traffic, he'd be here at least another four days. More time to get to know Melanie. He'd flown in with every intention of leaving within twenty-four hours and here he was, almost glad he was stuck in Niagara Falls.

One of the players came in. "Hey, Doc, can you give my neck a look?"

"Sure, Crush, have a seat." Melanie directed the huge man to a stool.

Dalton assumed she'd asked him to sit there because she wouldn't be able to reach his neck otherwise. Melanie wasn't a tiny woman but around all the extralarge men she was dwarfed in comparison. Still she had an air of authority.

Fifteen minutes later Crush had been put under the care of a trainer for a heat compression to his neck.

"What's the deal with everyone having a nickname?" Dalton asked. "Is that the thing to have if you play football? There's Rocket and Crush and you are even called Mel instead of Melanie. Doesn't anyone go by their real name?"

She shrugged. "I don't know. In some cases it's someone's ability, in others a sign of affection and others it could be something embarrassing they have done in the past and now it's just part of them. Why? You don't like nicknames?"

He knew what it was like to have a past filled with negative names. "No, I don't."

Melanie stopped what she was doing and looked at him. "Why not?"

"I guess I was called an ugly one too many times as a kid." There he was, doing it again. He'd never told anyone that. Saying it somehow made it not feel so heavy anymore.

"I'm sorry."

"Nothing for you to be sorry about. It was a long time ago. I've gotten over it."

Melanie looked at him for a moment. Did she believe him?

A few more players came in with complaints. She checked them out and sent them to the trainers to use the exercise bikes to warm up.

At one point Rocket entered the room. "Hey, Doc Mel. Hello, Dr. Reynolds."

"You here to have your knee wrapped?" Melanie asked.

"Yeah. Not having any problems but I'm doing as you say."

"You can't be too careful," Dalton said. "Take care of it. You don't want it to get worse. I'm still unsure about you playing tomorrow."

"I've got this, Doc. I'll be fine. The team needs me."

"Tomorrow, before the game, I want you at the stadium early in the morning," Melanie said.

"Will do," Rocket said over his shoulder as he pushed through the training room doors.

Melanie looked at the wall clock. "I'm headed

out to the practice field. I'll understand if you'd rather stay here."

"Are you implying I might be scared?" Dalton had long overcome being intimidated by people playing games.

"Well…" she said with a grin.

He stood. "I can handle it."

Melanie gave him a sharp look. "Okay. Come on."

They walked the same pathway as they had two days earlier and entered the practice area. Again Melanie went to the midfield line and stopped. A number of players spoke to her as they jogged onto the field.

"Hey, man, I'm sorry."

Dalton looked at the gigantic man standing beside him. "What?"

"I'm the one who blindsided you and Doc Mel the other day. Man, I'm sorry. I was looking for the ball. Are you okay?"

"I'm fine. Doc Mel is also."

The man studied Melanie. "You sure?"

She placed her hand on the player's arm. "We're both fine, Juice."

The man's concern showed in the seriousness

of his eyes. "Good. I sure was worried. I'm sorry that happened."

"It was an accident. I know that." Mel smiled at him.

Juice gave Dalton a questioning look.

Dalton offered the player his hand. "No hard feelings, I promise."

Obvious relief covered his face. "Thanks, man, I really appreciate that."

"Juice, let's go," Coach Rizzo called from the center of the field.

Dalton watched as the player loped out onto the field.

"Thanks for being so understanding. Juice is one of those tender-hearted guys I was talking about. I'm sure he lost sleep over what happened."

Dalton faced her. "Hey, I understand when accidents happen. I'm not such an ogre I can't accept that."

"I wasn't so sure about that a few days ago," Melanie murmured.

"How's that?"

"You acted pretty uptight when you first arrived."

Had he come over that way? Despite being in control of his world, owning his own practice and being a sought-after surgeon, any time the idea of a game being more important than a person came up it put him on edge. He just didn't place the same value on winning that others did. "I was that bad?"

"You were pretty inflexible."

"You still think that about me?"

Melanie smiled. "I'm learning to appreciate other aspects of your personality."

Why did he all of a sudden want to thump his chest?

For over an hour they watched the players move around on the field without any close calls.

Finally Melanie said, "I've some paperwork to take care of. So I'm going to my office for a while."

"Since I'm staying here for a few more days I need to make some calls, change around my schedule. Is there a place where I can use a computer and talk in private?"

"There's an office next to the Performance Area that isn't in use. You're welcome to it."

"Great."

He made his calls. One to an associate at his practice, telling him to request Josey's records.

If they showed what he thought they would, he believed he could help the girl.

An hour later Melanie knocked on the door of the office Dalton was using. "I have to do some shopping for my family's Christmas dinner. With the game tomorrow and Christmas Eve a few days after that, I won't have another chance. Do you want me to drop you off at the Lodge or arrange for you to get a ride back?"

Dalton couldn't remember the last time he'd been to a grocery store. Most of his meals were eaten in the hospital cafeteria or at a restaurant. Something about going to one with Melanie made it sound intriguing. It certainly sounded better than sitting in his room watching movies. "Mind if I come with you?"

Her look of shock was almost comical. "You want to go to the grocery store with me?"

"Don't act so surprised. I eat too."

She put her hands on her hips and glared at him. "When was the last time *you* went to the grocery store?"

"Okay, maybe I don't go often but it would be better than sitting in my room by myself."

"So I'm a step better than boredom."

He held her gaze. "I find you far from boring."

The air suddenly held an electric charge. "Um, you can go if you like but fair warning—it'll be a madhouse so don't expect it to be fun."

"I think I can handle it."

Melanie had to admit that Dalton was good help with grocery buying. He'd insisted on pushing the cart while she gathered the supplies she needed. It was a rather odd feeling to be spending an afternoon hour in the grocery with a man. It wasn't something she'd ever done before.

"You cook dinner for your entire family every Christmas Eve?"

"My sisters-in-law help. I do the majority of the meal but they bring the sides and desserts."

"Sounds like work."

"Not really. I enjoy it. Especially when I'm not pressed for time. This year, with the Currents in the playoffs, it will be more difficult. But I'm tickled to have the Currents doing so well. What do you usually do for a Christmas meal?"

"I go to a restaurant close to my condo for a meal with a few friends and then we spend the afternoon on the beach or beside a pool. Sometimes I'll have friends in for a catered meal but mostly it's a quiet day."

She looked at him as she placed four cans of beans in the cart. "You don't get together with family? What about your parents? Brothers and sisters?"

He was starting to think coming here with her might not have been such a good idea. "No parents. No siblings."

"I'm sorry."

"No need to be sorry. It's just the way it is."

That sounded rather sad to her. "It isn't quiet at the Hyde house. With seven kids running around, the TV on full volume, and my brothers and father armchair coaching. It is loud."

At least she wasn't asking him any more about his family.

"If you don't get to leave before Christmas you are welcome to join my family."

"I'll think about it."

Melanie moved around the turkeys, looking for the perfect one. Having picked one out, she lifted it toward the cart.

"Let me have that." Dalton took the turkey from her and placed it with the other food.

Melanie continued around the store until she had everything on her list. They loaded the groceries into the car. She offered to take Dalton back to the Lodge, but he insisted that he should help unload the groceries. She agreed. Melanie wasn't sure she was comfortable having him in her small condo. Could she resist him if he kissed her again?

By the time they had unloaded the bags at her condo, they were both cold.

"I don't see how you stand living in this winter." Dalton joined her at her door for the second time with bags of food. "I know why we have so many snowbirds now."

"I have to admit this is rather extreme." Melanie pushed the door open and went down the short hallway to the kitchen.

After Dalton had dumped his bags on the counter he stood looking at the space beyond, which was her living area.

What did those perceptive eyes see? "Is something wrong?"

"No, I was just thinking how much this place looks like you. I like it."

Her sitting room was filled with overstuffed furniture so that it was warm and comfortable. Bright pillows in red, green and yellow were situated on the couch and chairs. Books lined one wall. A couple of floor lamps sat so they hung over one end of the couch and a chair. Modern art pictures of flowers hung on the walls. A small tree with multicolored bulbs sat in a corner. Surrounding it on the floor were presents of all shapes and sizes.

"Thank you. I spend a lot of time here so I want it to be as inviting as possible." Stepping over to the tree, she plugged the lights in. She stood looking at them for a few seconds before she walked to the kitchen. There she started taking food items out of bags. "Why don't you sit down and I'll get us something warm to drink."

"Why don't you tell me where to find the coffee—?"

"I was thinking hot chocolate."

"Okay, hot chocolate. Then we both can sit down and rest for a minute."

"If I do that I might not get up again."

"I'll see that you do. So where's a pot and that hot chocolate?"

Melanie pulled packets of hot chocolate out of the cabinet behind her. "The teapot is in the cabinet beside the oven. You can heat water in it."

Dalton found it and had water heating with the same efficiency he did everything else. While he did that, she stored away most of the food. They were still waiting on the water to get hot when she pulled out an onion and began chopping it for the dressing.

"Hey, what're you doing?"

"I can't waste time. I need to get busy with cooking this food."

"I think you can take five minutes for yourself. Go sit down. I think I can handle the hot chocolate."

She had to admit that it would be nice to sit, drink a cup of hot chocolate and close her eyes. "Okay, since you put it that way."

Melanie went to the couch, curled up in the corner, pulled her feet up and laid her head back. Her eyelids started to droop. She'd just close them for a minute.

She woke to warmth. There was a blanket covering her. The sun had set. A single lamp shone across the room. Dalton sat on the other end of the sofa reading a book. "Why did you let me go to sleep?"

He looked at her and closed the book. "Hey, I don't control that."

She threw the blanket back. "I've got to get busy."

"What's the hurry?"

"I've got food to prepare."

"What happens if you don't?" he said in a tone that implied she was overreacting.

"Then we won't have enough for the Christmas meal." She stood.

"And this would be the end of the world?"

Now he was starting to make her mad. "My family expects me to fix the turkey and dressing."

"And you wouldn't want to disappoint them." He made it sound as if her family was taking advantage of her. He put his book down. "To keep you from going into a panic, I'll help. Just assign me something easy."

"You don't have to."

"If it will stop you from feeling guilty over a nap, then I can help out."

"How about cutting onions?" she asked, heading for the kitchen.

"Why?"

"For the dressing. I wish you had woken me."

He joined her. "You needed to sleep. Between your job with the team, working at the hospital and taking care of me, you haven't had much downtime in the last few days. I kind of liked listening to you snore."

"Hey, I don't snore!" She gave him a light swat on the forearm.

"I think the lady doth protest too much, especially when she does."

They both laughed. She'd not had this much fun in a long time. She would miss Dalton when he was gone. Too much, she was afraid. "You're so bad."

"Thank you."

"That wasn't meant as a compliment." She turned and pulled a cookbook off a shelf. "The onions are in a bag under that cabinet." Melanie pointed just past him. "Here is the knife and cutting board." She pulled them out of a drawer.

Dalton took the items from her. "I hope you don't expect my chopping to be perfect."

She met his gaze. At least he'd offered to help—something that her father or brothers wouldn't think to do. "I can't imagine you not being confident about your ability in anything."

Dalton's eyes darkened for a second, then cleared. Had she said something wrong? "I'm going to start making the cornbread." She pulled the cornmeal out from under the cabinet.

A few minutes later he ran a finger down her cheek when she came to check on his progress.

"Please don't."

Why had his simple touch made her want to lean into his heat and not leave?

"Are you scared of what I might do or is it because you're afraid of what you might do?"

If she was truthful, it was both, but she couldn't say that. "I thought we were going to keep things between us friendly."

"I was just getting your attention to ask if you had given any thought to dinner."

"No."

"Then it's a good thing that I have. I found a magnet stuck to your refrigerator with a pizza place on it while you were snoring. I ordered cheese and pepperoni. Should be here soon. I hope that's okay with you."

Melanie stepped back before she did something she might regret. Like hugging him. "Sounds perfect." Surprisingly, she was finding more and more things about Dalton that were perfect.

An hour later Dalton pushed his chair back from Melanie's café-style table and said, "It's been a long time since I've had a pizza that good."

"It's my favorite. I lived off pizza when I was a kid. The only thing my father knew to do for meals was cook frozen pizza or order in."

"It isn't easy to lose a mother when you're young."

"No. You sound like you understand."

He wasn't sure he wanted to discuss his mother in general and certainly not in particular. "I have a pretty good idea."

"You said your parents were gone. How old were you when they died?"

She wouldn't let it go. Would it really hurt him to tell his story? "Only my mother has died, as far as I know. I have no idea about my father."

"But you said—"

"They are dead to me. My father went to prison when I was a couple of months old. I never really knew him. I was taken from my mother when I was six. She died a couple of years later in jail." It wasn't as painful to tell Melanie as he'd thought it might be. Something about her made him believe she wouldn't judge.

"I'm sorry. We have more in common than I thought. We both lost our mothers."

This was getting far too personal for his taste. She made it sound as if they had a bond that would always bind them in a special way.

"So where did you live?"

"Foster homes. More than one, actually."

"That couldn't have been easy. At least I had

my father and brothers. Even though they weren't around much. Mostly it was just Coach and me."

He liked that she had turned the focus off of him. "Your father wasn't around much either, was he?"

"No. But I always knew he cared about me."

"That was a good thing." He had been thirteen or fourteen before he'd thought someone actually cared about him. Mrs. Richie had been that person but she'd soon pushed him away as well. Trusting a person to have his back was something he had a difficult time doing.

She nodded. "It was. There were times I wished he understood me better. But my dad was more about guys than girls. I don't even know why I'm telling you this."

Dalton knew what it was like not to be understood. He took another swallow of his drink. "What're friends for?"

"It's not to dump the past on. I do know that." She rose and started cleaning the table. "I hate to put a man out in the cold but I need to take you to the Lodge. I have to be up early to get ready for the game."

"Do you mind me going with you? Since I'm here I might as well check on Rocket if he plays."

"No, I'd be glad to have you on the sideline but I want to warn you it'll be freezing. There's supposed to be some sun but only in the late afternoon."

"Great. I'll be looking forward to it." There wasn't much enthusiasm in his words.

"You don't sound like it. I'll stop by Coach's house early and get a few of my brother's old gloves and a hat for you. See if I can find some boots."

"Maybe that way I won't freeze."

"There are warmers you can stand beside so that doesn't happen."

When was the last time he'd not been prepared for what life brought him? Long ago he'd learned the importance of being ready. If you were prepared, then you were in control of what happened. Nothing about this trip, outside of caring for Rocket, had gone as he had planned. To his astonishment, it didn't seem to upset him as much as it should have. He was learning to appreciate the wonder of what might transpire.

His friends in Miami would hoot when he told them he'd gone to a pro football game. And probably fall on the floor laughing when they found out he'd stood in the snow on the sideline. Dalton smiled to himself. He should give some thought to whether or not to tell them about this trip. The teasing might be more than he could take.

"Come on, I'll take you to the Lodge," Melanie said as she picked up her coat off the chair where she'd left it earlier.

"Gee, I thought I might get an invite to stay the night." His tone was flippant but he wouldn't hesitate to take her up on the offer if she made it.

"Dalton—" Her voice sounded unsure.

"I'm just kidding. I wasn't planning to spend the night." Her apparent relief pricked his feelings. "I'll call a taxi. No need for you to go out." He pulled out his cell phone and searched for a car service.

"I don't mind taking you."

"It's not a problem." He dialed the number of the service and spoke to them. After disconnecting he said, "They should be here in about fifteen minutes."

"Okay." Melanie sounded sad. She dropped her coat on the chair again and stepped toward him.

His look locked with hers.

"I'm sorry, Dalton. I'm not a very good flirt. Not like the saleswoman. I've seen too many women make fools of themselves over players. Even my own brothers. I'm not that kind of person. I don't invite men to stay. I'm not a short wow person. I'm more of the cautious, get-to-know-you-slowly type."

Dalton came closer and cupped her face. His thumb caressed the curve of her cheek. "Short wow, huh? I've not heard that before. I really was teasing about staying. There's nothing for you to feel bad about. If it isn't for you, it isn't for you."

A few minutes of uncomfortable silence filled the space between them. Why had he asked about staying? He wanted that easy interaction between them back. His phone buzzed and he answered it. "I'll be right out." To her, he said, "Taxi's here." Turning away from Melanie, he pulled his coat on, wrapped his scarf around his neck the way she'd shown him. "What time will you pick me up in the morning?"

"Eight."

"I'll be waiting in the lobby. Don't come in. I'll watch for you." He went to the door.

"Dalton..."

He turned to find Melanie right behind him. She grabbed the lapels of his coat, stood on her toes and brought her mouth to his. Her lips were damp, as if she'd just run her tongue across them with indecision. They quivered slightly. The kiss was sweet, sensuous and sincere. And entirely too short.

"See you tomorrow." She sounded a little breathless.

Wow. He had a feeling he was headed in a direction he hadn't planned to go and wasn't sure he could control.

CHAPTER SIX

MELANIE PULLED HER car into the slot designated as hers at the stadium. The other spots were slowly filling up as the players and staff arrived.

Dalton had been waiting in the lobby, just as he'd said he would. Her face turned warm as she watched him walk toward the car. That was all it took for her body to hum. It was becoming more difficult for her to keep her distance. Being impulsive was so unlike her. She still couldn't believe she'd kissed him after she'd told him they should only be friends. Had she opened the door to rejection again? Thank goodness he seemed at ease as they drove to the stadium. She was relieved he didn't mention the kiss.

Pulling a bag along with her medical one out of the backseat, she joined Dalton at the front of the car. She handed the bigger one to him. "Your warm clothes."

"Thanks." He glanced at the sky, where gray clouds gathered. "I'm going to need them."

She nodded.

"What's going on with you? It's like there is a hum of electricity about you."

"I guess it's excitement." Great—he'd noticed. This was a healthy direction. She led him through a large roll-up door opening big enough for a transfer truck to completely enter.

"What are we in, a wind tunnel?"

Melanie pushed her hair out of her face. "It's like this all the time. Even in the summer. It's caused by the air coming off the field though the tunnels."

They took a ramp and entered another door into a warm, long hallway. Melanie walked ahead of Dalton but she was aware of him close behind her. Too aware.

Never a forward person where men were concerned and still not sure she wasn't making the wrong step, Melanie was still glad she'd kissed him. When she'd told him he wasn't invited to stay she hadn't missed that dark look of rejection in his eyes. Something about his expression made her think it was a deep-seated emotion that Dalton felt more than the average person. She didn't want him to leave her place thinking she wasn't attracted to him. Who was she kidding? She wanted him on a level she'd never felt before but she had no doubt he would break her heart. They didn't want the same things in a relationship.

Today she had a job to do and thinking about Dalton wasn't the best way to do a quality one. Treating him like the visiting professional was what she needed to do.

At another door, she turned the knob and opened it. "This is the Currents' locker room."

This was her space. Next door was the training room and beyond that the dressing room. She placed her bag on the desk. "You can leave that—" she indicated the bag Dalton carried "—on that chair. Most of my time will be spent next door until the game starts. Then I'll be on the sideline. I'd be glad to have someone take you up to the Manager's box if you'd like."

"No, I'd rather see what you do."

Melanie liked the idea of Dalton being interested in her part of the medical profession. She'd had the impression when they'd first met that he didn't think too highly of it. Maybe today he'd completely change his opinion.

"Well, just know the option is always there. It's warm and there's food."

"Please don't tempt me." He grinned.

"It's time for me to check in with the trainers. They'll already be taping some ankles and caring for knees of the players that arrived early."

"I'd be interested to see how that's being done. I'm only involved in the surgery when a repair is needed, never on the preemptive side. It would be beneficial to watch it done."

"Help yourself. You can see plenty of it today."

Dalton left her for the training room. A couple of times when a player pushed through the doors to her office Dalton's voice carried as he questioned someone about why they were doing it that way. Once his laugh mixed with one of the player's.

It fascinated her that he seemed to interact with the players so well when he had no interest in the game. Or at least that was what he'd claimed. She hadn't thought he'd be comfortable with the players. Now he seemed interested in at least getting to know the team on a medical level.

Soon it was time for the team to go out on the field for the pregame warm-up. She joined Dalton in the training room.

"While they're out doing warm-ups I'm going up to say hello to Marcus. Would you like to come?"

"Sure. Do I need to put on my warmer layer?"

"That's not necessary. We'll be in the building the entire time." She went out the door and Dalton followed her. When he'd arrived less than a week ago she would have never believed she'd still be entertaining him. It was funny how life took twists and turns. Dalton might be hanging out with her because he had nothing better to do, but she was enjoying having him around. Especially when he kissed her. Melanie glanced at him. That was something she was better off not thinking about.

They took an elevator that dropped them off in a concourse carpeted in black and yellow—the Currents' colors.

A security guard stood just outside the elevator. "Why, hello, Doc. I haven't seen you in some time. It's good to see you."

"Hi, Benny. Nice to see you too. How's that new grandbaby doing?"

"Growing like a weed. Growing like a weed."

"That's great."

As they walked away Dalton asked, "Do you know everyone?"

"Don't you know the people where you work?" Surely he was on friendly terms with the people in the hospital where he did surgery. This was her place of work, just like that was his.

They walked on until they came to the Currents' staff family box that was on the forty-five-yard line.

Melanie pushed the door open and Dalton followed.

The back of Marcus's dark head was all she could see. She smiled. He had his nose pressed against the glass. A fog ring had formed in front of his mouth.

Snow fell outside to the point that in order to see the lines on the field, the snow had to be blown away.

"How's the front-row seat, Marcus?" At her question, the boy turned around.

There was a large smile on his face. "This is awesome. Thanks, Dr. Mel."

She took the chair next to him while Dalton stood nearby. On the other side of Marcus sat an older woman with gray in her tight curls. Melanie smiled at her.

"This is my grandmother," Marcus offered. "She's a big Currents fan."

The woman smiled at Melanie. "I'm Lucinda

Abernathy. Thanks for doing this for Marcus. He'll remember it forever."

"You're welcome. I'm glad I could. Marcus, look who came with me?" She glanced back at Dalton.

Marcus smiled. "Hi, Doc."

"Hey, Marcus. How're you feeling?"

"Much better since I've been let out of the hospital for a while."

"I can understand that. It's been rather nice for me not to be in one all the time too."

Melanie looked at him. That was an interesting statement. He couldn't get back to Miami fast enough the other day and surgeons were known for spending large amounts of time in an OR.

She spoke to Marcus and his grandmother. "Have either of you tried the buffet?"

"Is that for us too?" Marcus asked as if he thought it might be too good to be true.

"Sure it is. Do you mind if Dr. Reynolds and I eat lunch with you and your grandmother?"

"No."

"Then let's eat." Melanie moved so that Marcus and his grandmother could come by her and be first in line. She said to Dalton, "This is our chance for a meal. We don't get another until well after the game."

"I'm hungry so this is a great time." He leaned in closer as if he didn't want anyone else to hear. "Without you spending the night and telling me what to do, I didn't get up in time to have breakfast."

"Shh," Melanie hissed as she walked to where the food was being served. Dalton was teasing her but still it made her blood flow warm just to think about *what if.*

He stood close behind her. His breath ruffled her hair when he whispered, "I'm really hungry."

Melanie poked her elbow in his ribs.

"Aww," he grunted.

She whirled around. "I'm so sorry. I forgot." She took his arm that wasn't holding his side. "Sit down. Sit down."

He settled into a nearby chair. "I'm fine. Really."

"I hurt you." She went down on a knee so she could see his face.

"I got what I deserved for picking at you."

"Are you hurt, Doc?" Marcus asked as he and his grandmother stood staring at them with full plates in their hands.

"I'm fine. Juice used me as... What are those things called that football players hit?"

"A blocking dummy," Marcus said with complete confidence. "You got hit by Juice? How cool."

"It wasn't so cool at the time." Dalton groaned as he turned in his chair. "Not so cool at this minute either."

Melanie's heart tightened. She'd have to put Dalton on the plane soon before she managed to beat him to death. "I'll get you a plate."

"I'm not going to argue."

Melanie was afraid she might cry. Dalton took her fingers in his and gave them a squeeze. "I'm going to live. Just give me a minute to catch my breath."

"Okay."

"Now, I'm going to move over to the table with Marcus and his grandmother. We'll save you a seat."

She gave him a weak smile. "Do you like your burger all the way?"

"Everything but onions. I might get up close and personal with someone before the day is out."

Melanie was glad that their lunch partners had found the table set up in the back of the room. "Do you need help getting there?"

"Melanie, I feel emasculated enough without you making me an invalid."

She bit her lip. Was she making it that bad? "All right. I'll try to show you as little concern as possible."

"Hey, don't go overboard. I like your attention."

She gave him a wry grin. "I think that's what got you into this situation."

Dalton had the good grace to give a wry smile. "That it did."

"I'll get your burger. You get yourself to the table." Melanie turned her back to him. It was tough to resist helping him, but maybe he was right, she was fussing too much.

Dalton remained at the table with Marcus when his grandmother and Melanie went to pick out desserts. "So you didn't have any guys begging you to bring them to the game?"

Marcus shrugged. "Sure, but I rather they come because they are my friend not just because I had cool seats for the game."

"So you think your friends might be using you?"

"When you're a sick kid you learn real quick who your friends are. I have a couple of good ones and couldn't bring them both. My grandmother watches every Currents game. I had to bring her or she would have killed me."

Dalton chuckled. "I guess you didn't have a choice."

"Naw."

"So when you grow up, what do you want to be?"

"I'd like to be a history teacher."

Dalton nodded. He hadn't expected that as an answer. "That sounds like a good plan."

"I like to read about history and go to forts and museums. Some of my friends make fun of me, but my grandmother says not to pay them any attention."

"Some guys just don't get it. You grandmother's right. I'm glad you have her. You'll end up being the smart guy who teaches those guys' children."

Dalton knew well the importance of having someone to cheer you on. He hadn't had anyone. Yet something deep inside him still wanted to make Mrs. Richie proud. "Keep up your studies and make your grandmother happy."

"I will."

Melanie and Marcus's grandmother returned. Placing a plate with three different desserts in front of him, Melanie then sat in the chair next to his. "I've got to go in a few minutes. If you'd like to stay here and watch the game with Marcus you're welcome to."

"Are you trying to get rid of me?"

"No, but you may wish you had by halftime."

"If I'm going to really keep an eye on Rocket, then I need to be on the field."

"That's true."

They made their way back to the Currents' locker room area. This time Dalton didn't follow. He walked confidently beside Melanie. When they arrived at the office again, Melanie said, "I keep the clothes I need in a locker in the bathroom. I'll lock the doors and you can dress in here. I found some of my brother's old long underwear. I think you'll be glad I did. Be ready to go in a few minutes."

Her tone implied that if he wasn't he'd be left behind.

He was tall enough that the snow suit she'd brought him fit well when it was zipped up the front. The boots were large but not so much so they were clown size and difficult to walk in. They were well lined and he was positive he would be glad to have them on.

Melanie came out of the bathroom dressed much

as he was. "We need to get moving. It's time for the team to go to the field."

The wind pushed them backward as they made their way out of the tunnel behind the team. They ran onto the field while he and Melanie walked to the sideline.

"Feel free to stand by the warmers but don't get too close because they can melt your overalls."

By the middle of the second quarter of the game, Dalton was stomping his feet and standing beside a warmer. Snow blew as the wind picked up, producing mini tornados around his feet. Still the stands were filled with people shouting as the players moved the ball first one way and then another. He didn't understand all the penalties or the nuances of the game but he had to admit it was easy to get caught up in the excitement. He marched up and down the sideline beside Melanie as the team changed ends. She was completely into the game. Occasionally, she would holler and jump up and down. What would it take to have her that enthusiastic about him?

Rocket played well and there was no indication that his knee was giving him any problems. After a play, one of the men didn't immediately get up. Melanie and a couple of the trainers wearing medical packs around their waists ran out on the field. Soon the player was being helped to the side as Melanie gave him her complete attention.

At halftime they went into the locker room with the players. He was thankful for the warmth. The only problem was that it didn't last long enough. They had to return to the field about the time feeling returned to his toes. He hated this weather.

Melanie grinned as they made their way up the tunnel. "You sure you wouldn't rather be in the heated, glassed-in box with Marcus?"

He groaned. "Please don't tempt me." Dalton kept walking. He was determined to impress her by sticking out the game.

It was the middle of the third quarter and the Currents were winning when another player was injured. Melanie jogged onto the field once again. A group of players and staff surrounded the man lying on the ground.

For a few seconds there was complete silence in the stadium. Melanie stepped outside of the circle and waved him toward her. She didn't wait on him to arrive; instead, she returned to the center of the circle. Hurrying as fast as he could without slipping on the icy ground, Dalton made his way halfway across the field. It was much farther than it looked. As he reached the group, they opened for him.

Melanie was on her knees beside the groaning player. She saw Dalton and moved so that he could kneel beside her at the player's thigh. His cleat had been removed. A plastic sheet was beneath him. A blanket had also been thrown across the man's shoulders.

"What do you think? Broken or fractured Lisfranc joint?" Melanie asked, looking at Dalton.

"Hey, Doc," the player called, "it hurts but I can play."

Dalton and Melanie ignored the statement. He placed the palm of his hand over the top of the foot and found it was already swelling. Moving over and around Melanie, Dalton went to the feet of the player. "We need to cut the sock off."

Melanie was handed scissors by one of the trainers. With efficacy of movement she had the sock removed. While she was busy doing that, he took off his gloves. Before he touched the player Dalton rubbed his hands together to make them as warm as possible. Placing his fingers on either side of the foot, he worked his way over the bones. As he touched the top of it the man winced.

Melanie was right. "I think it's a fracture, but we need an X-ray to confirm."

"Call for the cart," she said loudly and a couple of the staff broke away from the group to do her bidding.

Dalton stood and Melanie did too as the cart arrived. She oversaw the player being loaded. When he was ready to be taken off the field, she said to Dalton, "I'm going with Mitchell to the locker room to see that he's taken care of until the ambulance arrives."

"I'll come along." Dalton started to add *if you need help*, but she wouldn't. Melanie had handled the situation with professionalism and quality of care. He'd been impressed. There was more to being a team doctor than he'd believed.

She'd seen to it that the ankle as well as the leg had been immobilized when they reached the medical area. Few he'd seen could have done it better. While she worked, the TV mounted high on the wall blared the game.

There had been another couple of touchdowns and the faint roar of the crowd reached them under the stands. Everyone, except him, reacted outwardly to each of them. He had to admit there had been a wish to throw his hands up as the

Currents crossed over the line and a tug of disappointment when the other team took the lead again. By the time the ambulance arrived, there were only a few minutes left in the game and the Currents had the ball.

"Come on, Doc," Mitchell said to Melanie as she gave her report to the EMT, "let me stay until the game is over." He'd been give pain medicine and was feeling better.

"We have it on in the wagon," he heard one of the EMTs assure Mitchell.

The player was being whisked out the large roll-up door Melanie and he had walked through that morning. The TV was still on and a couple of the staff had stopped what they were doing to stand looking up at it. Melanie joined them and he stood beside her.

The Currents were on the two-yard line. If they made this play they would win the game. A thud from the pounding of feet came from above. It seemed as if everyone in the room held their breath.

The quarterback handed off the ball to number twenty-one, who Dalton had learned was Rocket. He made a move to the left, not being caught by the two men chasing him, then he cut to the right to dodge another man. He jumped a pile of men tangled up on the goal line and fell into the end zone. The crowd erupted into a roar as the last second ticked off the clock. The Currents had won the game.

"We won. We won." Melanie jumped up and down and then threw her arms around Dalton's neck and kissed him.

His arms circled her waist and he passionately returned her kiss.

Melanie broke away. "I'm sorry. I got carried away."

"I'm not." But next time he wanted her to kiss him because of him.

They looked at the TV again. His team members were slapping Rocket on the back. When they finally climbed off him and let him stand, Rocket struggled to do so.

In unison Dalton and Melanie said, "His knee."

CHAPTER SEVEN

MELANIE SHOVED THROUGH the doors and started running up the tunnel toward the arena. Dalton was right behind her. As they approached the field, people started coming in the other direction. Soon they were fighting against the tide. Dalton went past her and created a path for her to follow. It was nice to have him looking after her.

They finally made their way to the bench on the sideline where Rocket was sitting. A number of players, staff, Coach Rizzo, her father and some of the media stood close by. A couple of the heaters had been moved to either side of him and his winter game cape had been placed over his shoulders.

"Rocket, we saw it on TV. How's your knee feeling?" Melanie asked in a panting voice.

"Hey, Doc. Doc Reynolds. I thought you might be showing up."

"So how is it?" Dalton was already down on a knee in front of Rocket.

Melanie had forgotten to put on her outer clothes. Dalton wasn't wearing his coat, hat or gloves either. He must be cold. She sure was. But Dalton didn't show it. His concern was focused on Rocket.

"I'm going to have to put my hands on you. I'm afraid they aren't warm," Dalton told Rocket.

"Don't worry. I'm so cold that I probably can't feel you anyway."

"I'll make it quick. Then we'll *all* go inside."

Dalton did the same type of exam he'd done at their first meeting. Except his face grew more thoughtful this time.

Finished, he stood. "I don't want you walking on this leg. You need to have an X-ray and MRI ASAP."

"Let's get the cart back out here," Melanie told one of the staff.

"I really did it this time," Rocket said.

"I'm afraid today might be it for you this year." Dalton put his hands under his armpits and stomped the ground. One of the trainers put a blanket over his shoulders and also handed her one.

"We need him for next week," Coach Rizzo protested. "Even bigger game than this."

Her father glanced at the media, busy flashing pictures. "We don't need to make that decision until after the tests are done. This is something better discussed when we have all the information."

Dalton looked at her as if expecting her to disagree with her father.

"That sounds like a wise plan. We won't know anything for a couple of days," Melanie offered in a conciliatory tone.

Dalton gave her a disappointed look, then headed for the tunnel leading to the locker room.

The cart pulled up close to Rocket and Melanie stayed with him until he was being driven off the field. While the trainer prepared Rocket for his trip to the emergency room, she went to her office to change.

Dalton was sitting in a chair with one ankle over a knee, his outer clothes already removed. His look met hers when she entered.

"I'm freezing. That's the last time I'm running out without at least my overcoat." She pulled the blanket closer around her.

"I'm almost warm. But my toes are still burning," Dalton said flatly.

"We'll be out of here soon. I have to go to the

hospital to check on Mitchell and see that Rocket gets those tests run. I'm assuming you want to go with me."

"Will you be taking any of my advice if I do?"

She stopped halfway into the bathroom. "What does that mean?"

"It means you know that Rocket shouldn't play in any more games until that knee heals. Why didn't you say so?"

"Because we don't know that for sure until after we do the tests and because you never make those type of statements in front of the media. The Currents are in the playoffs for the first time in franchise history. Rocket is an important part of making that happen. If the other team thinks Rocket won't be there, it might not give them a physical advantage but it will certainly give them a mental one. The same goes for our team. We can't have them believing Rocket is out before it's a fact. It affects them mentally as well."

"You have to be kidding. One player carries that much weight?"

"I'm not and he does." She continued on into the bathroom. Why couldn't he believe that winning the game was important?

Melanie stepped out again and looked at him.

"Didn't you see how the fans reacted today? Hear Marcus talking about his grandmother's love for the Currents?"

"But is a win worth the price of a man being crippled for the rest of his life?"

What kind of a person did he think she was? "No, it isn't. I don't think so as a person and I certainly don't believe that as a doctor. All I'm saying is that we need to take it slow, know what we're talking about."

Dalton seemed to consider that. He uncrossed his leg and put his hands on his knees. "I can agree with that. As long as I know whose side you're on."

"Side? What side?"

"Rocket's or the team's."

One of the trainers opened the door and stuck his head in, preventing her from commenting. "The hospital called. They have the X-rays on Mitchell and Rocket ready."

"Good. Please, let them know I'm on my way."

She didn't have time to return to her argument with Dalton. There were patients to consider. He'd been asked here to give a second opinion and he had. Now he was butting into what he didn't understand. It insulted her that he questioned her ability to put the players' health above the team's need.

Dalton was waiting with his new overcoat on and the bag of clothes she'd brought him by the time she'd stored her game clothes and picked up her purse. "I don't have time to drop you off at the Lodge. They are expecting me at the hospital."

"I already said I was going to the hospital with you."

Melanie started out the door. "Then you need to keep in mind that I'm the team doctor and I have the final say."

"I understand that. But, just so you know, I'll give my professional opinion as I see fit."

There was that tone she recognized from when they'd first met.

She wouldn't make any headway in this conversation so she kept walking toward her car. Snow had piled up on the windshield. "Would you hand me the scraper out of the glovebox?"

Dalton opened the passenger door. "I can do that—you go ahead and get in."

"Are you trying to tell me what to do again?"

His heavy sigh made a puff of fog in the cold air. "Melanie, I'm only trying to be helpful. Let's call a truce until we have both had some rest.

We've had a busy, cold day and it's not over yet. Why don't we plan to fight this out tomorrow, if we must?" He found the scraper and started removing snow as if he wasn't still sore.

Melanie settled in the driver's seat and turned the heat up high. It had been an emotional day and if the truth be known she wanted nothing more than a hot bath and bed. But that would have to wait a few more hours.

She watched Dalton as he worked. Despite their recent argument, he had been a trooper and good help during the game. She'd been glad to have him on the field to confirm Mitchell's possible diagnosis and be there with Rocket. Still, she didn't like Dalton questioning her motives.

Hours later, Melanie pulled in front of the Lodge. She'd reviewed Mitchell's and Rocket's X-rays and visited both the men in their rooms. Neither was happy about having to stay overnight, but their wives and families were handling keeping them happy. Dalton had remained beside her the entire time. They had agreed on their earlier diagnosis of Mitchell's foot and were waiting on Rocket's MRI. The hospital had promised to notify her if anything changed during the night.

She'd told the nurse she would be back first thing in the morning to check on them.

A groan coming from Dalton brought her attention back to the present.

"What's wrong?"

He pointed to a sign that read "No Water."

She couldn't leave him here. He deserved running water after the day they'd had.

He'd have to go home with her even if it strained her nerves to have him close all night.

"I guess you'd better come home with me."

"Don't sound so excited about the idea. I don't want to put you out."

"And I don't think I can take a long hot shower without feeling guilty if I leave you here. And I plan to have a long hot shower."

"So you're only being nice to me to ease your conscience?"

"Something like that."

He chuckled. "At least you're honest."

"I'll wait while you get the things you need."

"I don't have but one set of clothes really." He pulled at his shirt. "If you have a spare toothbrush I should be good."

She already knew he slept in the nude. Great. What was she getting herself into this time?

As she pulled out of the parking lot she said, "I hope they have the water on by tomorrow night because the Currents are having their Christmas party here."

Dalton was fairly sure that Melanie would have been perfectly happy to go home to an empty condo and have some time to herself. But he couldn't face a night without any water. He'd try to give her space and be as unobtrusive a guest as possible.

"Why don't you shower first? I have a few phone calls to make," she said as she removed her coat and hung it up on a peg just inside the door.

He put his jacket and the large bag with the extra clothes in it on a chair. "I can't take advantage of your hospitality by doing that. You have yours, then I'll get mine."

"When I get in I'm staying until the hot water is gone. If you want any, then you need to get it now." She walked into the kitchen.

"Okay, okay. I'll make it short."

Dalton tried to make it a quick shower but he stayed longer than he'd planned. The hot water felt so good, he couldn't bring himself not to enjoy it just a few more minutes. Forcing himself to get out, he toweled off. What was he going to wear?

He opened the door a crack and called, "Melanie!"

"Yes?" she answered a minute later from outside the door.

"I hate to ask you for anything more, but do you have any sweatpants or something else I can wear?" There was a moment of silence as if she were thinking.

"Wait a sec. I do have some old sweatpants somewhere that might fit you."

A moment later a hand thrust navy material through the crack. Dalton took it.

"Pass me your dirty clothes and I'll start them washing."

Scooping up the clothes he'd taken off, he handed them to her. Careful not to let her see him nude, he pulled on the sweatpants. They were smaller than he would have liked but at least he wouldn't be wearing just a towel.

Somehow her compassionate invitation tonight after their long day and fight made him resist applying any pressure to their wavering relationship. He wanted her to know that he respected her and appreciated her willingness to share her home.

What he felt now was an odd emotion. One he wasn't sure he was comfortable with.

What if he let go? Really invested himself in a relationship? He couldn't do that—she'd eventually leave, as everyone he'd truly cared about had. It wasn't worth chancing the heartache.

He entered the living area to find Melanie standing behind the bar that separated the kitchen from the larger space. The TV was on and tuned to a channel with a digital fire.

"Nice fire," Dalton said.

Her eyes went wide when she saw him and her gaze settled on his bare chest long enough that he almost forgot his resolve to keep it simple between them.

She looked away. "I, uh, needed warming up. I thought it might help."

"I left you some hot water."

"Good. I'm on my way to use it all up."

Thoughts of Melanie taking a shower had him wanting to join her. But tonight wasn't the time to push. No matter how his need for her was growing. It was becoming more difficult every second because she only wore a housecoat. For a fleeting moment he questioned whether or not she had anything on under it.

"I'm sorry I didn't have a T-shirt large enough for you."

Did she mean that? Her gaze seemed to dart down to his chest and away again every few seconds. Her interest was an ego builder.

She held a mug up. "Would you like some tea or coffee? I'm out of hot chocolate. You hungry? Want a sandwich?"

"Thanks, a sandwich and tea would be great."

"The kettle is hot. Bags beside it. You'll find sandwich meat, cheese in the refrigerator and the bread is right here." She patted the bag sitting on the counter. "I'm going to get my shower. I've put bed things out on the sofa. Sorry I can't offer you your own bedroom."

She sounded so formal. Was she nervous?

"Melanie, I'm sorry I've been thrown in your lap like I have for the last few days. I know you probably thought you would pick me up from the airport and then be done with me. I do appreciate your efforts to make me comfortable."

"You're welcome, Dalton. I feel bad that you've been stuck here."

But he'd started to enjoy it. He hadn't realized how much he needed a vacation away from his demanding practice. He'd learned a few things in the past few days, had a story to tell and met Melanie. All in all, it hadn't been that bad. In fact, he couldn't remember laughing or smiling more.

Melanie headed for her bedroom. As she went in she said, "Good night."

Dalton watched the door close between them. Disappointment filled him. He wouldn't be sharing a meal with her. The ambience of the fire and a hot drink weren't the same when the woman you wanted to share it with was in another room.

He looked at the pile of bedclothes, then back at the door. The sound of water running reached his ears and a vision of Melanie standing under a stream of steamy water had the front of the stretch material he wore tightening. Dalton sighed. He wouldn't be getting much rest tonight.

Melanie purposely pulled on the oldest and most unrevealing pajamas she owned. She was still cold after her shower and the temptation to go to Dalton and ask him to hold her was too strong. She huddled in her bed, wishing for kisses from him that she knew from experience would heat her to the core.

He'd made no advances or even said anything that could be misconstrued as an innuendo since they'd entered her home. It was as if he were putting her at arm's length. Had their fight turned his interest sour?

It was disappointing to think he no longer wanted her. When he'd walked into the living room wearing those too-tight sweats, revealing more than they should have, and his wide chest and muscular arms bare, she almost couldn't breathe. If Dalton had given any indication of interest, she would have stepped into his arms and asked if she could join him in his shower.

But he hadn't and she didn't. It was best left alone anyway. He'd made it clear any relationship between them would be strictly physical, no long-term emotion. She closed her eyes, pulled herself into a ball and shivered. Hopefully, sleep would come. Exhaustion must have finally taken over because she woke to the faint sound of movement in the other room. Who was that? What time was it?

Dalton. Morning.

Well covered in her pajamas, she opened the door to her bedroom and stepped out. Dalton stood in front of the kitchen stove. Much to her disappointment, he was wearing his own clothes. There was no bare chest for her to feast on this morning. His shirt tail was out and he'd only closed two of the buttons across his abdomen. It was a nicer view than the sun rising over the falls. She'd like to enjoy the view every morning. A wish that wouldn't come true.

"Good morning, sleepyhead."

"Hey." She moved further into the room.

"I thought I was going to have to come wake you."

Melanie tingled at the idea. What would it be like to be awakened by Dalton? Would he kiss her awake? Nuzzle her neck? Run a hand along her leg? A shiver went through her. She had it bad.

"Is something wrong? You have a funny look on your face."

"No, no, nothing's wrong." She had to change the subject. "What're you doing back there?"

"I'm making us breakfast."

"And what will that be?"

"Scrambled eggs and toast." He pushed the spatula around the pan. "Should be ready in a minute."

"I'll dress, then. I have to get to the hospital and then check on the Christmas party preparations."

Dalton gave her a quizzical look. "Since when does a team doctor become involved in Christmas party decorations?"

"Coach is the general manager of the Currents, remember? He asked me to make sure everything is correctly done."

"Have you ever thought about saying no?" He pulled bread out of the toaster.

"Why would I?"

Dalton shook his head and murmured, "I guess you wouldn't."

She stepped closer to the bar. "What does that mean?"

"Breakfast is ready. Why don't we eat it while it's hot?" Dalton scooped eggs onto plates.

He hadn't answered her question. Did she really do her father's bidding? She'd always done as he asked. Had wanted to help as part of the team. She was only being a good daughter.

"So the plan for today is to go to the hospital and then back to the Lodge?" Dalton asked as he placed the plates on the table.

"Yes, but I can drop you by the Lodge first if you would like."

"I'd like to see Rocket's MRI."

Hopefully that wouldn't bring another round of disagreement between then. She didn't doubt that they both wanted the best for Rocket but she had other issues to consider. Dalton didn't understand that. Probably never would. "You are welcome at the team party, if you would like to come?"

"I don't think so. I don't like to crash parties."

Her fork stopped halfway to her mouth and she gave him a peeved look. "You're not crashing if I invite you. If it'll make you feel better you can come as my date."

He smirked. "Why, Melanie, are you asking me out?"

The man was making an effort at humor now?

She glared at him. "I'm trying to be polite but if you're going to be a smart aleck about it, then spend the night in your suite watching TV. The guys are fun to be around. After yesterday's game they'll be in high spirits. If nothing else, the food will be worth it. We use the best caterer in town."

"Since you put the invitation so sweetly, how can I resist? Yes, Melanie, I would love to be your date for the Christmas party."

He made it sound like there would be more to it than a friendly outing.

After breakfast they visited Mitchell and Rocket. Both were clamoring to see their discharge papers, which would put them out of the hospital in time for the party. The MRI showed that Rocket's knee had become marginally worse. The decision on whether or not to let him play would be made closer to the game. Finished there, Melanie drove them to the Lodge.

In the lobby Dalton asked, "What time do I need to be ready?"

"I have to be here at seven," Melanie said.

"Then I'll be waiting in the lobby for you."

"Okay." She headed down the hall to the ballroom.

Melanie stopped. The realization of what she'd done dawned on her. She had a date with Dalton! The evening pantsuit she'd planned to wear wouldn't do, especially after his remark about her fashion sense. Suddenly she wanted to show him just how much of a woman she was. And she knew just the dress to prove it.

She checked on the party preparations and was headed to the mall by just after lunchtime. Hopefully, no one had bought that red dress. With it being two days before Christmas, it took her far longer than she would have liked to find a parking space. She walked to and through the mall at a quick pace as if someone might snatch the dress off the mannequin minutes before she arrived. Breathing a sigh of relief when she saw it still in the window, she entered the store. She went straight to the counter and waited in line. When it was her turn, she asked to try the red dress on.

"It's the last one we have," the saleswoman said as they made their way to the front of the store.

Melanie's heart plummeted.

"What size are you?"

She told her.

"I think you just might be in luck." The saleswoman smiled as she took the mannequin down and began undressing her.

A few minutes later, Melanie had the dress on and was smoothing it over her hips. She stepped outside the dressing room to look in a mirror.

"It's perfect," the saleswoman breathed.

Melanie turned one way and then the other. Smiling, she said, "It is, isn't it?" She studied her reflection. A dress was only the start. She touched her hair.

"Big Christmas party to go to?" the saleswoman asked.

"Yes. And I know this may sound like a strange question, but can you suggest some place where I can have my hair and makeup done? This afternoon?" She hated the desperation in her voice. Did the fact she was out of her element show?

"Let me make a couple of calls. My sister works

at a hair salon here in the mall. The department store at the end does free makeovers if you buy makeup. I have a friend that works there."

"Thank you so much."

Melanie had the dress off and paid for by the time the saleswoman had finished her calls.

She came to stand beside Melanie. "They are both expecting you. Ask for Heather at the salon and she will introduce you to Zoe for your makeup."

On impulse Melanie hugged her. "Thank you so much."

"Not a problem. My pleasure. Merry Christmas," she called as Melanie walked away with a spring in her step.

The salon was only a few stores down. Heather, a girl of about twentysomething with a blue streak in her hair, was waiting on her. "Mary said you were on your way. What would you like to have done?"

Melanie hesitated for a moment. "I'm not sure."

"Well, since you're going to a party, why don't we try a few different ideas and see what you like?"

Melanie nodded and followed. Two and a half hours later, she'd had a wash, trim and style. It was classic and perfect for her. She'd even had her nails and toes polished while having a facial. Already feeling like a different woman, it was now time for the makeup. That item was way out of her comfort zone.

Heather walked her down to the department store and introduced her to Zoe. In no time, she had Melanie in a chair and was showing her a makeup regimen. Forty-five minutes later, Melanie left with her eyes looking smoky and sensuous, her cheekbones accented, and her lips a pouty red. In her hand was a bag of makeup goodies to try on her own. She had never felt better about her looks.

On the way out of the store she passed the handbags. Unable to control herself, she bought a tiny sparkling red evening clutch and decided she also needed a pair of shoes.

As she drove home a ripple of insecurity raced through her. Would Dalton like her new look?

Dalton scanned the lobby for Melanie as he strolled down the stairs. Thankfully his ribs had improved each day. Now he could take a breath without a sharp pain. It was a good thing because the vest he wore would have hurt otherwise.

As Melanie had disappeared around the corner to see about the party room earlier, Dalton went over to Mark, the man behind the desk, and asked for assistance renting a tux. He had been very helpful.

Now Dalton was dressed in formal wear and he couldn't locate his date.

A woman wearing a red dress stood in front of the fire with her back to him. *Must be one of the players' wives or girlfriends.* They were known for having glamorous women on their arms.

He scanned the area again. Team members were filing though the door and the lobby was becoming more crowded by the minute. Where was Melanie? She wasn't usually late. Maybe she was busy in the ballroom. He was almost to the bottom of the stairs when the woman turned around. His breath caught. This time his heart, not his ribs, hurt. *Melanie.*

He'd never seen a more beautiful or alluring woman. Her hair was pulled up on the sides, accentuating her high cheekbones. Her eyes were skillfully highlighted and there was a tint of red on her lips. She looked nothing like the no-nonsense Melanie he'd become accustomed to. No woman in the nightclub scene in South Beach could have looked sexier.

His blood ran hot. She was *his* date tonight.

Melanie walked toward him in barely there shoes the same color as her dress. He almost missed the last tread of the stairs. Heaven help him, every fiber of his being screamed to forget the party and take her up to his suite.

"Hi, Dalton," she said in a soft, unsure voice.

"You look beautiful." He couldn't take his eyes off her.

"Expecting me to be in one of my masculine suits?" There was a teasing tone to her question.

"Well, actually, yes. But I find this a very nice change." Far too nice. He was in trouble. She tempted him already but as this gorgeous vamp, he was a goner.

"Thank you. Shall we go to the party?"

Dalton offered his arm. "Yes. I'll have the prettiest woman there on my arm. Just remember who brought you."

She giggled.

It was the first time he'd heard her do that and it reminded him of bells tinkling. He planned to make her giggle again. Soon.

They walked across the lobby. With the image

of Melanie in that red dress, he might start seeing the Christmas season differently. As they passed the front entrance a large man who could only be a player said, "Is that you, Doc?"

"Hi, R.J.," Melanie said.

The player stared at her. "It really is you, Doc. You look great."

A touch of pink brightened Melanie's cheeks. She stood so close, Dalton felt her stiffen. He squeezed her hand resting on his arm to reassure her. He was afraid she might bolt. She'd been invisible for so long, this amount of attention had to make her insecure.

"Thank you, R.J."

Dalton led her away and around the corner, following the other players and their women, who were dressed in festive clothes, down a wide hallway. They entered the darkened ballroom that twinkled with white lights. A huge Christmas tree stood in one corner, decorated in Currents colors and with Currents ornaments. Surrounding the dance floor were tables set for a meal with flickering candles and greenery in the center.

"Merry Christmas, Juice," Melanie said.

A quizzical expression came over the player's face. "Wow, Doc. You look sexy." Shock followed and his gaze dropped. "Uh, I'm sorry, Doc, I shouldn't have said that."

She smiled. "It's okay, Juice. Thanks."

"Why don't we get some seats at a table?" Dalton suggested.

"Okay." She led him to a table close to the dance floor. Another couple was already seated there. Dalton held the chair for Melanie and she sank into it. The man Dalton recognized as one of the trainers leaned across the table and leered at Melanie. "Doc Mel. Is that you? You look great."

"Thanks, David. Hi, Katie." Melanie introduced Dalton to both of them, then said quietly to Dalton, "This is embarrassing. I never would've worn this dress if I had known it would cause such a scene. Maybe I need to go change."

"You will not! You're a beautiful woman and it won't hurt to remind some of these people you aren't one of the guys."

She looked at him and smiled. "No, it won't."

The players and staff kept stopping by and speaking to Melanie. She seemed to take their admiration more in her stride as they commented on her looks. About thirty minutes after he and Melanie had arrived at the party, Rocket and Mitchell limped in with arms locked and their wives at their sides. There was a round of applause. The men smiled broadly and bowed.

Soon after, Leon Hyde walked to the middle of the dance floor. One of the hotel staff handed him a microphone. The crowd quietened.

"Welcome, everyone. I'll make this short and sweet so we can get down to the important stuff. Eating and dancing. Thanks for the part you play on the Currents team. You've gone above and beyond this year and we still have two more playoff games and the Super Bowl to look forward to. If they are anything like yesterday's, the road will be an exciting one. Enjoy your holiday and come back ready to work. Merry Christmas, everyone."

The crowd clapped. Soon afterward, the room became loud with conversation and music. Dalton and Melanie, along with the other couples at their table, lined up at the buffet to get their dinner.

They were still there when Melanie's father stopped to speak to them. "Mel, did you check on Rocket's test today?" he asked.

Dalton couldn't believe it. He was the first male in the room who hadn't commented on Melanie's appearance. Didn't he ever really look at his daughter?

"Yes," Melanie said.

"Well?"

He seemed impatient for her to expand on the answer, as if he were in a hurry to move on.

"Rocket needs to rest for a couple of days. Then I'll reevaluate him," Melanie hedged.

Her father didn't look pleased with her answer. "He has to play. The team needs him."

"I understand."

Dalton's hand tightened on the plate he held. Did her father always pressure Melanie like this? What kind of situation had Melanie grown up in? He hadn't had parents around but she had, yet was her father really there for her? Maybe their childhoods hadn't been that dissimilar after all. The difference was that Melanie stayed connected to people while he chose to keep anyone he might care about at a distance. Could he have done something different?

Leon Hyde extended his hand to Dalton. "Dr. Reynolds, it's nice to have you join us tonight."

"Thank you. I appreciate Melanie inviting me. Doesn't she look amazing?"

Her father regarded Dalton as if he were unsure about what to say, then look at Melanie and offered, "Very nice."

What was wrong with him? Couldn't he see that

Melanie was a beautiful young woman? Efficient, intelligent, capable, but a woman nonetheless.

When her father's attention was pulled away by another man, Dalton put a hand at her waist and gave her a light hug. "I'm hungry, how about you?"

She nodded and gave him a smile that didn't reach her eyes.

Melanie had excused herself to go to the restroom. She was making her way back up the hall on her way to the ballroom. A group of players and their dates stood outside the door. There they were able to talk without screaming over the music. As she approached, one of the players with his back to her said, "Can you believe Dr. Mel?"

"You're not kidding. I had to do a double take. I don't think I've ever seen her legs," another player added.

One of the women leaned in. "Hank talks about Doc Mel all the time. I always thought she was a he. After seeing her tonight I might be jealous."

Hank put his hand around her waist and pulled the woman close. "Hey, you don't have to worry about that. Everyone thinks of Doc Mel as one of the guys."

One of the guys. That was what she'd been, growing up. She'd even dressed the part. As an adult that hadn't changed. She had no idea she'd receive such a reaction by just wearing a dress and spending a little more time on her appearance.

She moved by the group unnoticed and stepped inside the room. There she stood to the side, watching the activity. The band had started playing and couples filled the dance floor. Other people talked in groups.

Dalton strolled toward her. He looked heart-stoppingly handsome in his tux.

"I've been looking for you."

That was all it took for her body to jumpstart to a hum.

"What's the most fascinating person in the room doing standing by herself?"

She gave him a bright smile. Dalton had always seen her as a woman. Even when he'd asked her about being a female team doctor. She'd never been one of the guys to him.

"She's waiting on the most handsome man in the room to ask her to dance."

Even in the dim light she could see his gaze intensify at her flirting. He took her hand securely in his and led her to the floor. A slow song had just begun. Dalton's arms circled her waist. Melanie placed her hands at the nape of his neck. His hair brushed against her fingers.

His mouth came closer to her ear. "You've been the talk of the party."

She looked at him. "I'm not sure I like that."

"That's because you've been hiding the fact you're a woman for too long."

He was right. She wouldn't be doing that any longer. Starting tonight.

Melanie stepped closer to Dalton, bringing her body against his. He tensed, then his arms tightened. He was warm. His breath brushed against her hair. She inhaled. *Dalton.*

The dance floor was crowded yet the only person she saw or heard was him. They were in their own world.

He kissed her temple. Her fingers teased his hair. Dalton brought his hips to hers. The ridge of his swollen manhood clearly made his desire known.

The song ended. He said, "Melanie, I think we'd better sit the next one out."

"I don't want to." Her hand caressed his neck.

"Neither do I but I don't want to embarrass you.

If I continue to hold you I'm going to start kissing you and I'm not going to stop."

Melanie liked the sound of that, but she did have a reputation and position to consider. "Okay."

They returned to their table. When they were seated Dalton took her hand and held it beneath the table. A number of the players brought their wives over to meet her.

The party started winding down none too soon for her.

"Do you have to stay and see about anything?" Dalton asked.

"I just need to check in with the person responsible for handling the party."

"When you are done, how about joining me for a view of the falls at midnight?"

She whispered in his ear, "Are you wooing me to your room, Dr. Reynolds?"

Dalton leaned back and captured her gaze. "Only if you want to be."

CHAPTER EIGHT

MELANIE'S FIST HESITATED for the second time in the air as she prepared to knock on Dalton's door. Just a few evenings earlier she'd spent the night in this suite. This time her hand shook as she went back and forth with indecision. If she stepped over the threshold she was afraid her life would change forever. Maybe she was making too much of the importance. After all, Dalton had been nothing but a gentleman. Why would he be any different now?

They could have a friendly cup of hot chocolate and look at the view. He'd mentioned nothing more. But the way he'd touched her earlier said he wanted everything she would give. If she took this chance, could she stand the hurt if he promised nothing more? What if she didn't go in? Would she always wonder what could have happened between them? Know that she could have taken a chance on love and hadn't because she was too afraid? Feared rejection too much?

Her skin heated. Dalton's desire for her while they were dancing had been obvious. Being wanted was stimulating. He'd made her feel like a woman. Something she didn't know she'd been missing until he'd come into her life. Even if she were to have just this one night, she wanted it with Dalton. As a female she had power and she wanted to use it, revel in it and savor it. Loving Dalton was worth the risk to her heart. All she could do was open it. It was up to him to accept what she was giving. If he didn't, then she had at least tried.

With head held high, she rapped on the door. It opened a second later as if Dalton were standing on the other side, waiting for her knock.

"Hi." She suddenly had a longing to flee. But she wouldn't. She wanted this. She wanted him.

Dalton had removed his jacket and taken off his tie. His vest hung loose. Could a man look sexier?

"Come in. Hot chocolate is almost ready. I was waylaid by Rocket when I crossed the lobby. Took me longer to get up here than I planned."

"Rocket does that sometimes." They were having a pleasant everyday conversation. What had she expected him to do? Pull her into the room, take her in his arms and slam the door? And to think she'd stood outside like a nervous virgin. She was over that. "I'm going to sit down and take these torture devices off my feet. If you don't mind?"

"Make yourself at home."

The only light burning in the room was the one over the bar area. She took a chair in front of the window. Sitting, she worked to release the strap of her shoe.

"Here, let me do that." Dalton placed two mugs on a nearby table and sat in the other chair. "Give me a foot."

Melanie swiveled the chair toward him and lifted a leg. He cupped his hand behind her ankle and rested it on his thigh. With the nimble fingers of a man who did delicate work for a living, he undid the strap.

"Other one."

His no-nonsense tone had her relaxing back against the chair. "Now this is the life. Beautiful view, hot chocolate on a snowy day and a man at my feet." She giggled. That sounded nothing like what she'd intended to say. Too suggestive.

Dalton's hand ran across the top of her foot, no longer encased. She looked at him. Their gazes met and held. He brought her foot to his mouth and kissed her instep. Her breath caught. Her heartbeat went into overdrive. He reached for one of the mugs and handed it to her. "Just relax and let's enjoy the view."

She looked out at the falls but not for long. Her attention returned to Dalton. He was the better view. His profile in the dim light reminded her of a sculpture she'd seen in a European museum once. Her gaze followed the line of his forehead, along his nose, to his strong chin. She watched him so closely that she saw the movement of his mouth before he spoke.

"You're staring at me."

She looked at the falls. "No, I'm not."

"You were."

"Are you calling me a liar?"

Dalton wrapped both her legs with an arm and with his other hand he started to tickle the bottom of her feet.

"Stop!" She laughed.

"Admit you're a liar."

"I'm not." She chuckled again and tried to pull her legs away but he held on tighter, continuing to run his fingers over the bottom of her feet.

"You were staring at me. Say it—'I was staring

at you.'" Dalton continued moving his fingers. She squirmed, causing her dress to inch up her thighs.

Melanie pulled at her hem, but it did little good. "I will not."

Dalton stopped and looked at her but still held her legs firmly. "You don't have to say it if you kiss me."

"That's blackmail!"

He cocked his head to the side and acted as if he was giving that statement a great deal of thought. "It is."

"You aren't worried about going to jail for coercion?"

He raised his chin and pursed his lips. His gaze captured hers. "You're not just any woman. So I'm willing to chance it."

"Okay, but you have to let me go."

"I don't think so." Dalton tugged her toward him. "I don't trust you." When she sat on the edge of the chair he reached an arm under her knees and one around her waist, then lifted her, bringing her to his lap. "Now it's time to pay for your lies."

He held her tightly.

Two could play this game. She shifted in his lap a couple of times, pulling on her dress as if she were trying to make herself decent. Done, she looked at him. His lips had thinned and his jaw was tight. He looked strained. She inwardly smiled.

Running her hands over his chest, she moved them up to his neckline. She slipped her fingers under the collar of his shirt. His intake of breath hissed. She brought her hands up to cup his face. Shifting again, her hip brushed against his hard length.

His eyelids lowered, hooding his eyes.

Melanie licked her lips. He groaned. She brought her face closer to his and whispered against his lips, "What was I supposed to say?"

Dalton's hands tightened on her waist as he growled, "Hell, it doesn't matter. Kiss me."

She did.

He gave her a moment of control before he seemed to lose his. His grip on her waist eased. One hand moved to the back of her neck. He pulled her lips more firmly into his. Melanie's hands went to his shoulders and gripped the fabric of his vest. Dalton eased the pressure as the tip of his tongue traced the seam of her lips. She opened her mouth and he thrust in.

Heat shot to her center. Blood pooled, hot and heavy. Her tongue met his with a confidence she'd never imagined. The man's loving was dangerous and exhilarating.

His lips left hers and moved to nuzzle behind her ear. She purred with pleasure. She offered him more access and Dalton's lips traveled to her collarbone. There the tip of his tongue outlined its distance. His other hand cupped the top of her knee then went to the exposed expanse of her thigh. He lightly brushed her leg as his hand journeyed toward her hemline, teasing it before it went down her leg again.

Melanie turned her face and kissed him. Giving him lingering ones, then pressing her lips to his cheek before placing a kiss on his neck. Her fingers fiddled with the second button of his shirt until she had it open. She leaned over far enough for her lips to caress the skin visible in the V of his shirt.

He shifted, making her more aware of his length resting at her hip. His hand left her leg to cup her breast. She couldn't have stopped the sound of longing she made if she'd wanted to.

"Like my touch, do you?" His deep voice had taken on a raspy note.

His lips returned to hers as his hand slipped

under the strap of her dress. When his fingers touched skin, she jerked.

"Shh," Dalton whispered against her lips. "You feel like warm silk."

Melanie relaxed. His hand at her waist slid up her back and pulled at the zipper. Slowly it came down as his lips found the ridge of her shoulder. With the zipper opened to the bottom of her shoulder blades, his hand returned to her neck. His fingertips tickled her skin as they trailed down her back. Melanie held her breath. Her skin was hot where he'd been, tingled where he touched and quivered in anticipation of his next move. She was a mass of sensations, all created by Dalton.

His mouth took hers in a honeyed kiss while his hand nudged her dress strap down her arm. She wore no bra, so his fingers were free to follow the same path back. Dalton's hand brushed the slope of her breast and rested there. His mouth left hers to place kisses across her cheek to her temple as his hand cupped her breast. The pad of his thumb teased her nipple until it stood rigid.

"Perfect," Dalton murmured. Using one of his fingers he started at the top of her breast and followed the slope down to circle her tip.

Melanie moaned as heat filled her and her core contracted.

"I want to see you." Dalton's fingers returned to the dress zipper and pulled it completely open. Using a hand on her shoulder, he leaned her back, supporting her across his arm. It left her open and vulnerable. Her arm went around his neck. He pushed her dress strap from her arm until her breasts were free.

His sharp intake of breath made the blood flow to her breasts, making them tingle with heaviness. She relished the fact that Dalton found pleasure in what he saw.

He cupped her breast again. As if weighing and committing it to memory, he fondled and caressed until she wriggled.

"Baby, you're killing me." He lifted his hip. "Have compassion."

Her hand rested over his bulge. "What's wrong?"

Dalton's fingers left her breast to remove her hand and place it in her lap.

"Not yet. I want to enjoy more of you."

His hand went to her breast again and lifted. She watched as his dark head came down to capture her nipple in his wet, warm mouth. Her eyes closed in pleasure as she soaked in every ounce of sensation.

Dalton's tongue swirled around her nipple, drawing and teasing until she writhed with need. Her hand flexed and released in his hair. Dalton growled low in his throat. He released her breast and kissed her neck. His tongue flicked out to taste her.

How much more of this could she take before she was consumed by the fire he created and stoked deep within her?

Dalton dragged her other strap down her arm until her dress gathered at her waist, leaving her breasts completely defenseless to his manipulations. His mouth found the neglected breast and made it feel as appreciated as he had the other one.

Melanie ran her hands through his hair, encouraging every tantalizing movement of his mouth. She had the fleeting thought that she should have been embarrassed by her wanton position both on him and in front of a public window, but all she could comprehended was her body's reaction to Dalton's ministrations. She'd never felt more free or more like a woman in her life.

One of Dalton's hands went to her thigh and slid under the skirt of her dress. His fingers skimmed her inner thigh and moved away. Slowly his hand moved up to the edge of her panties. One finger slipped under. It traced the line of her underwear toward her throbbing core. His mouth continued to do wondrously delicious things to her breast.

His finger made slow tormenting motions. Her muscles tensed. She parted her legs in invitation. He took it and grazed the lips of her opening. The ache curling in on itself became tighter. Panting in anticipation, she waited. Dalton was bolder this time. He pushed into her opening at the same time he tugged and swirled his tongue around her nipple.

Melanie arched like a bridge in his arms. With the power of the water flowing over the falls, she burst. For spectacular seconds she remained suspended in bliss before slowly returning to reality. Dalton was there to catch her. His arms circled her waist and his lips touched the top of her head.

Dalton had done many things in his life that made him feel successful but none had given him more satisfaction than watching Melanie come apart in his arms. He'd lifted his lips from her breast just in time to see her head roll back onto his shoulder, her eyes close and her lips part as she found her piece of heaven.

He'd been afraid that she wouldn't come to his room. Feared how badly he wanted her to. Felt foolish standing by the door like a kid waiting to get into a candy store. What was happening to him? He managed to keep women in their place, at a distance where he felt no real emotion, then along came Melanie. She had his feelings so twisted, he could think of nothing but her. He'd learned long ago that to care meant hurt. He was afraid things between them had already reached that stage. Could he walk away now? Would he want to?

He gazed at her, reclined in his lap, and smiled. She was stunning.

"Dalton, kiss me," Melanie whispered with her eyes shut and the sigh of release still on her lips.

He wouldn't turn that request down. His mouth found hers. She returned a tender kiss that made him even harder than he would have believed possible. If he didn't have her soon he would explode.

His look met hers. Placing a hand on her stomach, he made small circles over satiny skin. "You are so amazing."

"You're not half-bad yourself." One of her hands went to the opening in his shirt. She flattened her palm against his skin.

He loved her touch. Something that simple from her excited him.

"It's my turn."

"Oh?" He raised a brow.

She released another button of his shirt and ran a hand over his ribs. "Does it hurt much?"

He shook his head. "Only when I'm punched."

Melanie looked at him with troubled eyes. "I'm sorry I forgot." She undid another button. "Maybe I can make it up to you." The last button of his shirt slid out of its hole. She pushed the fabric away, exposing his stomach and ribs.

She pressed her lips to his skin. His muscles quivered in reaction.

"Does it hurt here?" Her mouth touched a rib. "Or here?" She found his skin again. Moving farther around to his side, her tongue darted out.

He flinched in reaction.

With a sound of satisfaction, Melanie said, "This must be the spot." Her hand dipped beneath his shirt and caressed his side while she continued to kiss him. Her breasts rested against his chest as she kissed his damaged body.

She looked up at him. "Better?"

"No," he ground out. "Because that isn't the part of me in pain."

"So where's your problem? Maybe I can kiss it and make it better," she said in a teasing tone.

The thought of that happening had Dalton ready to take her on the floor. Melanie deserved better than that, especially with it being the first time between them. He gave her a nudge from behind and she stood.

He wasted no time in standing also. "Heavens, woman, are you trying to kill me?"

She looked unsure, standing there with her dress circling her waist and her hair tousled.

He cupped her cheek and gave her a caressing kiss. "If you were to give me a kiss where I hurt it would be more than I could stand. Hold your hands above your head."

"Why?"

"Melanie, you can trust me."

Her arms went up. Dalton took the hem of her dress and pulled it off over her head. He dropped the material to the floor. His gaze met hers and held for a few seconds before it traveled down to her breasts. They were high and the nipples taut. Unable to resist, he reached out and took one in his palm. Releasing it, he watched it bounce gently. He'd never been more fascinated. His gaze moved down to her barely there panties to follow the length of her legs. "You have gorgeous legs."

"Thank you."

"No, thank you for sharing them with me."

"You're starting to embarrass me."

"Why? I'm admiring you. You're beautiful and should be admired."

"That, and I'm standing here with almost no clothes on while you're still dressed."

He grinned and took her hand. "That problem's easily solved. Come with me."

Dalton led her across the living area to his bedroom. He turned off the light over the bar before he joined her. The only light came from the lamps shining around the falls. Shadows played over Melanie's body, making her appear otherworldly. Maybe she was. She'd certainly placed a spell on him.

He stopped beside the bed and released Melanie's hand. Taking hold of his vest and shirt, he started removing it.

"Let me help you." Melanie rested her palms on his chest and fanned them outward, pushing his clothing away. She continued over his shoulders and down his arms until the items were a pile on the floor. Coming closer, she reached for the button at his waist.

He stopped her movements with his hand over hers. She looked up at him with questioning eyes. His mouth came down to hers in a searing kiss she eagerly returned. His arms wrapped around her waist, bringing her against the ridge of his manhood. She rubbed against him. He wouldn't last much longer. He lifted her so that her feet didn't touch the floor and carried her the few feet to the bed.

Bending a knee, he laid her down on the comforter. Melanie looked at him with half-lidded eyes. She reminded him of a woman waiting on her lover in one of the old masters' paintings in the Louvre. All flesh, light and desire.

Dalton had every intention of being that lover.

His hands went to his pants button and released it and then the zipper in short order. He pushed his pants and underwear down at the same time. Stepping out of them, he stood.

Melanie's intake of breath made his chest swell. She liked what she saw. Just as she had when she'd been toweling him dry.

He moved to the bed and looked down at her. "Melanie, when I touch you again I will have to have you. I won't make any promise for the future. If you don't want that, it will kill me to let you go, but I will."

She leaned up. Taking his fingers, she tugged. "I want you. Even if it is just for tonight."

She understood him.

He came down over her, his mouth finding hers. She wrapped her arms around him and held him tight. As they kissed he pulled the covers back and then rolled to his side, taking her with him. He released her lips and said, "Crawl under."

As she brought her legs up, Dalton reached for her panties and pulled. "It's time for these to go."

Melanie lifted her hips and he slid the panties down and off her feet, throwing them to the floor. He flipped the covers over them and brought Melanie close. They lay facing each other. His gaze met hers. Her eyes were deep and luminous.

Unable to resist any longer, he glided a hand over the curve of her waist to her hip and across her behind. She blinked.

Melanie was perfect. He'd implied she should show off more of her body but now that it was his he didn't like the idea as much.

His? When had he started to think of her as belonging to him? The second she'd so freely found her release in his arms. He hadn't planned this. Hadn't been looking for it, but he would embrace it while he could...while it lasted.

She ran her hand over his shoulder and down his bicep to his elbow. The back of her hand floated over his stomach and lower. One finger trailed the length of him. His need had become a gnawing animal within him.

He leaned away and found his pants on the floor. Pulling his wallet out, he located the foil square and opened it. After covering himself, he rolled back into Melanie's arms.

She lay on her back and moved between his legs. His mouth went to her tempting breasts before he kissed his way to her mouth. Her arms circled his neck.

Melanie whimpered and lifted her hips, bringing his erection into contact with her wet and waiting center. He requested she open her mouth for him and her tongue intertwined with his.

Dalton flexed his hips and entered her. He pulled back and Melanie's fingernails dug into his shoulders. She would leave marks that he would carry proudly. He lunged again. This time taking her completely. She stiffened. He pulled away but didn't leave her. She opened her legs wider and moved with him.

"Look at me, Melanie."

Her eyes flickered open.

He raised himself up on his hands and thrust again and again. He had to control her. Her body quivered, then tensed before she fell apart beneath him. Dalton leaned down and kissed her softly on the forehead. She would have no doubt who had brought her to ecstasy.

With another deep thrust, Dalton found his rapture as well. Maybe she had the control after all.

Melanie woke to the toasty heat of Dalton against her side. She snuggled closer. The arm around her waist tightened. He'd awakened her during the early hours and made fast, hot, passionate love to her. Had she ever felt more alive?

She'd known other men, but none had such power over her with a single kiss or had created such a driving need to have him near. Mercy, the man knew how to love.

Love? That was what it had been with Dalton— lovemaking. She was in love with Dalton.

How had that happened? When he'd been so great with Rocket and Marcus? When he'd respected her boundaries? When he'd made his desire for her known more than once last night? It didn't matter when. It just mattered that it was a fact.

She loved him for standing up to her father, for knowing his own mind, for caring about sick children, for his sensitive care of Rocket—the list went on. But mostly she loved him because he saw her. The person. Not as a team member but as a woman, unique in her own right.

Melanie smiled to herself. Seconds later it slowly faded. She couldn't let him know. He'd made it clear that anything between them should have no emotional attachments. She was destined for heartache, but she would accept that when the time came.

She placed her arm over his at her waist and laced her fingers with his. Taking what she could while she could would have to be enough.

"Good morning, sleepyhead," he said in a raspy voice.

"I wouldn't be such a sleepyhead if someone hadn't woken me in the middle of the night."

His manhood, firm and long, stood against her hip. "I must not have done a good job if you are complaining about losing sleep."

"Now you're fishing for compliments."

He nuzzled her neck. "Maybe I need to convince you a little more that I rate praise."

"That's a good start." She turned to face him, interlinking her legs with his.

He chuckled, bringing a hand to her breast. "Why don't I start with...?"

Sometime later, with the sun streaming through the window and the roar of the falls outside, Melanie sat next to Dalton with a sheet pulled over her breasts, eating a grape off their room-service brunch. The sight of the sun was bittersweet. He would be leaving soon. He'd said nothing about how he felt about her. But he wouldn't; he'd made that clear. She was just a distraction while he was stuck in Niagara Falls. No way would she ruin what time she had with him by worrying about the future.

Dalton leaned over and kissed her bare shoulder. "What has you so deep in thought over here?"

"Just thinking that I've always wanted to wake up to this view of the falls."

"Have I been used?" he asked in an innocent tone.

"No more than you wanted to be."

He grinned. "I could have been used more."

"Now who is complaining?" She acted as if she were in a huff, planning to get out of bed.

Dalton took her hand, turned it over and kissed her palm. "I don't care the reason why—I'm just glad you're here."

Melanie melted. The man could charm a snake out of a basket without a flute.

"What do you have to do today?" Dalton placed their tray on the floor and rolled toward her. The sheet slid low over his hips.

He seemed unaffected while her body heated. Did he have any idea how irresistible he was? Drawing her eyes away so she could concentrate, she said, "Nothing but a little more cooking for Christmas dinner preparations. The team has today, Christmas Eve and Christmas Day off. I don't have to be back to work until Friday."

"Great. Then we can spend the day together." He tugged at the sheet.

She held it tight against her. "That sounds nice to me."

"What would you like to do?"

The lump in her stomach eased. He wasn't talking about leaving. "If it was summer I'd say we should go out on the *Maid of the Mist*, but the river is too icy for that."

"*Maid of the Mist?*"

"The boat that goes out on the river and up close to the falls."

"I like the view from here." Dalton looked out the picture window toward the falls, then back at her. "This view is even better."

She leaned over and kissed his cheek. "I know what I'd like to do but I don't know if you would enjoy it. And it would be cold."

"What's that?"

"I'd like to go to the Festival of Lights and see the fireworks."

"That sounds like fun." Melanie's enthusiasm for the season seemed to be rubbing off on him. "If I may borrow your brother's clothes again."

"Of course." She gave him a quick kiss and started out of the bed, pulling the sheet with her.

"Where are you going?" He jerked the sheet out of her hands.

"Hey, give that back!"

"No."

"Why not?"

"Because I want to admire you walking across the room."

With great effort and heat on her cheeks, she strolled to the bathroom. Inside, she closed the door and leaned against it. Dalton was flipping her life over. She'd never lain around in bed with a man, and certainly not naked. But he had insisted that they have breakfast in bed. To walk in front of him, or any other man, without clothes on was far beyond her comfort zone. What would he have her doing next?

Minutes later she was in the shower soaping her body when the glass door was pulled open. He stepped in.

"Dalton!" This was another first—taking a shower with a man—one that thrilled and terrified her.

"Melanie."

"I'll be through in a minute."

"I thought I could help."

"Help?"

"Scrub your back. Then maybe you could dry me off." He wiggled his eyebrows.

"I don't think—"

He grinned. "Melanie, in some ways you're so naive. Turn around."

She did as he asked. "Why do you call me Melanie when everyone else calls me Mel?"

"Because everyone else does call you Mel. Melanie is a pretty name. A feminine name. It suits you." With soap in hand, he moved it over her right shoulder.

She turned around to face him with a smile on her face. "Thank you. That's the nicest thing anyone has ever said to me."

He slipped his arms around her and pulled her against his wet, slick body. As Dalton's lips came toward hers he said, "I meant every word."

CHAPTER NINE

DALTON WAS STILL reliving and looking forward to more hot passionate minutes in a shower with Melanie as they walked along looking at the bright flashing and twinkling lights of the Festival of Lights. Melanie was like a child, pointing and running from one place to the next in her excitement. Just watching her made him smile.

Melanie had managed to slip under his barriers. Being around her was infectious. She had a wide-open heart that embraced the young and old, the large and the small, no matter how much she had going on in her life. She had managed in a few short days to make him see the pleasure in life, find humor. Most of all she'd made him discover what he could receive in return if he trusted himself enough to open up to someone.

Melanie had a happiness in her that didn't seem suppressed by her childhood. She saw joy in a child's smile when he received tickets to a football game, or when one of the players called hello, or even in preparing supper for her family who paid her little attention. How did she come away with such a positive outlook? Could he have tried harder to fit in at his foster homes?

He had to admit the festival was rather fascinating with its blocks' worth of buildings, animal shapes and plants all outlined in lights. A number of them were synchronized to music. Even the falls' water and mist had been lit so it appeared to turn different colors. The season was beginning to grow on him.

It was past time for him to go home, but he wasn't ready. The practice was closed for the holiday and he could stay until after Christmas without ruining his schedule. A long-distance relationship would be difficult to maintain. Would they even have a chance or would she tire of him not committing? Would she be willing to even try?

They strolled hand in hand as they looked at the displays and discussed them. At a small café they stopped in to warm themselves with hot chocolate and a cookie.

"I'd like to go up on the Ferris wheel," Melanie said after taking a sip of her drink.

Despite the cold and snow, he couldn't deny her

anything. Plus the idea of huddling under a blanket, looking at the falls and stealing kisses from Melanie high up in their own private world had its appeal. He had it bad. "That sounds like fun."

She put her hand over his. "I think you'll be impressed."

"It'll be nice just to be with you."

She smiled, stood and started putting on her coat. "Then let's go."

He laughed. "You're more eager to go out into the cold than I am."

Melanie leaned down and gave him a quick kiss on the lips. "Who knows, if you're nice I might keep you warm."

His body fired at the thought. He stood. "Is that a promise?"

"Come on and see." She pulled on her knit cap.

Dalton enjoyed the banter between them. He'd never had that with another woman. Somehow Melanie brought out the impulsive side of him. That part of his personality had been buried until now.

They walked the two blocks to where the Ferris wheel turned. Each spoke and crossmember was decked out in white lights. After standing in a small line they were soon seated with a thick blanket over their laps and tucked around their feet. The chair rocked gently as they moved away from the ground. Melanie wrapped her arms around one of his, huddled close and laid her head on his shoulder. Dalton liked being the one she came to for comfort. Snowflakes drifted down around them. The lights grew smaller below them.

"Oh, look," Melanie whispered with amazement.

Dalton's gaze went to the falls, which were lit in the red and green of the season. "That is pretty amazing."

"I love it up here."

He kissed her.

"Hey, we better be careful—we might freeze together." She laughed.

"I wouldn't mind." He put his gloved hand over hers.

She clutched his arm tighter. "I wouldn't either."

They rode in silence for a few minutes, then Melanie said, "I can't believe tomorrow is Christmas Eve."

"I hadn't thought about it. I guess it is."

She shifted slightly and looked at him. "Would you like to come to dinner with my family tomorrow night?"

He'd never been very good at family celebrations. No real practice with them. He had no interest in being the odd man out. "I don't know. How would your family feel about me just showing up?"

"They'd be glad to have you. The more the merrier."

Something in him wanted to say yes while another part of him remained unsure. "Let me think about it. Christmas Eve isn't my favorite day of the year."

Melanie didn't say anything more for a few minutes. "Why not?"

"Because that's the day they took me from my mother and put me into foster care."

Her sniffle made him look at her. He brushed an icy tear from her cheek. "Hey, don't cry. Now, I have this time with you to replace that memory."

She kissed him and didn't say anything for a while. "Will you tell me about it?"

He didn't want to talk about his past but he was one hundred feet up. There was no easy way out.

"My parents were drug addicts." Her fingers pressed his arm in encouragement.

"My father went to jail a couple of months after I was born. When my mother went to prison, I didn't have anyone else to take care of me and I went into foster care. My foster parents tried, but I didn't fit in. I liked books. I was smarter than the other kids. And they knew it. I wasn't any good at what they liked to do. So I spent most of my time by myself."

"You said the other children liked to do things? Like what?"

"Like football, baseball, whatever game was in season."

"Oh. They must have made fun of the boy who read all the time."

"They did, but that's just how kids are. I understand that now. By the time I entered high school I was no longer that awkward kid anymore, but by then I was more interested in earning money to go to college than I was in playing sports."

"The kids called you names, didn't they? That's why you don't like nicknames."

Melanie was too smart. "It is."

A boom and the opening bulb of colored sparks raining down against the black sky drew their attention.

"Fireworks," Melanie said in awe.

Another round of light flashed in the night as they continued in a slow circle. Dalton placed his arm around Melanie's shoulders and pulled her close. They said nothing. Occasionally a soft "Oh..." came from her.

Talking about his past had been difficult, but sharing it with Melanie seemed to lift a weight from him. He appreciated the moments, just as he had when he'd spent time looking at the falls with her. Just being with Melanie seemed peaceful. He would miss that when she was no longer around. The thought saddened him more than he wished to admit.

He couldn't have planned it more perfectly when the grand finale of the fireworks went off as they came to the top of the wheel. Afterward they descended to unload. Offering Melanie his hand, she placed hers in his and stepped out.

"That was wonderful," she said. "Thanks for taking me up."

Dalton smiled. "You're right—it is fun. And I think you're the one who took me."

"You might be right. Uh, about dinner. Just know you're welcome. I'd like for you to be there, but only if you want to be. I can always bring you leftovers."

Dalton squeezed her hand. It might not be that bad to spend Christmas Eve with Melanie's family. They were an important part of her life. And she had become important to him.

They headed in the direction of where Melanie had parked the car.

"I didn't mean to put a damper on the evening by telling you my life's story," Dalton said after they had walked a block.

She took his arm again and hugged it close as they continued on. "No damper. I was just thinking about how much I would enjoy a hot shower."

"That sounds great. Mind if I join you?"

"I'd be mad if you didn't."

Melanie enjoyed their shower as much that night as she had earlier. Adding to the pleasure, she'd been toweled off by Dalton and she'd returned the favor. Now it was morning and she lay next to him, listening to his even breathing as he slept. He'd woken her in the early hours of the day and made love to her again. Instead of feeling tired, she felt invigorated. The man held a sweet power over her that she had no complaints about. Other than it wouldn't last.

A finger brushed the spot where her hip and leg joined. She looked at Dalton. His eyes were still closed but there was a hint of a smile around his lips. She made a move toward the edge of the bed. A hand clasped her wrist.

"Oh, no, you don't." Dalton tugged her back to him.

"I have to get going. I've dinner to finish. And I need to bake a cake."

"That can wait." He kissed the curve of her shoulder.

"I don't think so. I've already stayed in bed far too long." She tried to remove her hand from his grasp.

"What if I agree to help you? That would give you time for..." Dalton trailed off with a suggestive look at the bed.

"Don't tempt me."

His hand released her wrist and ran up her arm. "That's exactly what I'm trying to do."

"Well, as enticing as the invitation is, I'm going to have to take a rain check. I really must get moving."

"If I can't lure you into staying, then I guess I just need to go with you. Maybe if I help I can have a second helping of dressing."

Joy filled her. "You're coming to dinner?"

"Yes, thank you for the invitation."

She smiled widely. "Wonderful. I want my

brothers and their families to meet you. I would have hated knowing you were spending Christmas Eve alone."

"Wouldn't you have stopped by afterwards?"

"Absolutely."

He gave her a long slow kiss. "That's nice to know."

Hours later she and Dalton unloaded food from her car and carried it into her father's house. He'd called while they were at her condo to tell her that he was at the office and would be there in time for dinner. Her brothers and their families would be arriving soon. One had flown in and the other two were driving. Dalton had questioned her about their arrival, but he'd said nothing about the fact the airport was open.

"Just put it down wherever you can find a spot in the kitchen," Melanie said over her shoulder as she carried the dressing into her father's house.

Melanie glanced around the living area as she walked through on her way to the kitchen. Her father had a simple ranch-style home that was large enough to hold the entire family. It was done in dark colors with pictures of her father with teams he'd coached on the wall. Autographed footballs set under glass in several places. Thanks to the maid that came weekly, the place looked clean and tidy.

Every home she'd lived in growing up had looked very similar to this one. There was a marked contrast between her condo and her father's. There was nothing in her place that said she was a sports fan. Her personal space was warm and feminine, right down to the yellow throw pillows on her sofa.

Dalton followed her in and put the turkey on the counter. "I'll go get the rest of the dishes while you get things together in here."

"Thanks, Dalton. You're a great help."

He was. She was so used to doing everything by herself she'd never realized how much work it was.

"No problem. By the way, did I tell you how nice you look?"

"Thank you." He knew how to make a woman feel like a woman. In and out of bed.

She didn't have much hanging in her closet that she considered superfeminine. After searching long enough that Dalton called from the other room that he'd loaded the car, she'd decided on a blouse in a silk fabric, a sweater with pearl buttons she'd pushed to the back of the closet and her most fashionable shoes. At Dalton's look of appreciation she had no doubt she'd made the right choices.

Melanie closed the refrigerator door after putting the congealed salad inside and walked over to him. Going up on her toes, she kissed him. "You look nice yourself."

His hands tightened around her waist. She stepped back despite the longing to move closer. "I still have a lot to do and you're a distraction."

Dalton let her go. "Then I guess you better give me a job so I won't be tempting you."

"Okay. You can see about getting the plates, napkins and silverware set up on the table. We'll eat buffet-style. There are far too many of us to fit around Coach's table."

"Why do you call your father Coach? You did that at the party." Dalton looked at her with an odd expression.

"I guess that's all I really ever heard him called, so I started doing it also."

"Your father was okay with that?"

"I think he likes it, actually."

"If I ever have kids, they will call me Dad or Daddy."

What she'd seen of his interaction with kids, he'd make an excellent daddy.

Over the next half an hour she gave Dalton directions, and he followed them to the letter. It would be her guess that he didn't often relinquish control to others. It impressed her that he was willing to do it for her.

The outside door burst open and a gush of freezing air announced her oldest brother, Mike. "Hey, Mel. How's it going?"

Melanie squealed and stopped what she was doing to hug him, his wife, Jeanie, and their three children. "Mike, Jeanie, kids, I'd like you to meet Dr. Dalton Reynolds."

"You can call me Dalton." He extended a hand to Mike.

"Nice to meet you, man," Mike said. "Mel, you don't even have the TV on. What about the game?"

Mike took a seat in front of the huge TV in the living area. Jeanie came to the kitchen to help her, and the kids went to join their father. Dalton stood nearby with a bemused look on his face. A few minutes later, her youngest brother, Jim, came in with his wife, Joan, and not far behind him was her middle brother, Luke.

"Hey, guys, doesn't Mel look great? I don't know if I've ever seen you dressed so...girly," Luke said.

She gave him a slap on the forearm, then circled his neck with her arms, giving him a hug. "Good to see you too. Thanks for the compliment, I think."

Dalton looked more uncomfortable as her family grew. Had she made a mistake by asking him to come? The situation could quickly become overwhelming. While her sisters-in-law were busy in the kitchen, she slipped away to speak to him.

"Hey, how you holding up?" Melanie asked as she came up beside him where he leaned against the wall, observing the men watching the football game.

"I'm fine."

"They can be a little, uh, overpowering."

He nodded as the entire male part of the family jumped up when something happened on the TV.

She slipped her hand into one of his and squeezed.

He smiled. "Yeah, but they seem like really nice guys. I'm glad I've gotten to meet them."

Melanie let go of Dalton's hand, not wanting her family to start asking twenty questions about their

relationship. Melanie wasn't sure she could answer any of them. She had no idea where she and
Dalton were headed. He'd said he only did short-
term. If it was up to her she'd do whatever it took
to make it work between them. She'd had a full
life before Dalton arrived, she thought, but now
that he was in it, she wanted more. Her only hope
was that when he left town, it wasn't for good.

About that time her father came through the
door. Everyone but her and Dalton lined up to
either hug or shake hands and slap each other's
backs in welcome. With that done, her father
stepped over to them. "Glad you could make it,
Dr. Reynolds. Mel, I guess you have everything
ready."

"Yes. It'll be on the table at halftime."

"Good." He went to join the others, who had
returned to the game.

Dalton looked at her in astonishment. "Do you
always plan meals around football games?"

"Not always. But this year there's a special
Christmas Eve game on." Why did she feel as if
she needed to apologize? She looked at her family. Was their world too wrapped up in the sport?

One of her sisters-in-law insisted they turned
the TV off completely while they had their meal.

There was moaning and groaning, but when all the grown females agreed the TV went black.

While she and Dalton were standing in line waiting to serve their plates, Mike said, "So, Dalton, you're the guy our sister spent the night with?"

"Mike!" Melanie shrieked in embarrassment. Did he know about the past few days?

Dalton looked at her and grinned. "Yes, that was me."

"Dalton!"

He shrugged his shoulders. "Hey, I'm just telling the truth."

Mike laughed.

"Yeah, Dad told us about you getting hit by Juice. I've played against him and I'm impressed you're out of hospital," Jim said with a chuckle.

"Thanks for taking care of our kid sister." Luke wrapped an arm across her shoulders and squeezed. "We couldn't do without her."

"You're welcome," Dalton said. "She is pretty special."

"We would agree with that," said her brother from the other side of the table.

She and Dalton found places to sit beside each other on one of the two large couches. They held their plates in their laps. What room there was at the dining room table was given to the children.

"So, Mel, you going to sign off on Rocket playing on Sunday?" Jim asked.

She sat close enough to Dalton to feel him tense. Why had Jim brought up that subject?

"We—" she indicated Dalton "—still need to assess him again."

Her father returned from refilling his plate. "Mel's a team player. She'll see that Rocket is on the field."

Melanie felt Dalton's gaze on her, but she said nothing. She shifted on the couch cushion. Was she a team player anymore? Had she ever been? Maybe she'd just been playing the part her father wanted her to?

With the meal over as well as the game, everyone gathered around the tree. Presents were distributed. Melanie watched the look of shock on his face when her niece said, "Dalton. Who's Dalton?"

Her mother said, "Dr. Reynolds."

"Oh." Her niece carried the small present to Dalton.

He looked at Melanie.

She smiled. "Everyone gets a present under our tree."

"But I didn't—"

"That doesn't matter. Open it."

Dalton pulled the paper off and lifted the top. He reached down and picked up the lapel pin depicting the waterfall with "Currents" written across it. A smile spread across his face.

"Something to remember us by," Melanie said. She really meant *remember her by*.

"Thank you. I can't tell you the last time I got a Christmas present. I'm sorry I didn't get you anything."

She leaned close. "I'll take a kiss later."

He captured her gaze. "You can count on that."

Soon after the presents were all opened, her brothers and their families left to stay in rooms at the Lodge. She and Dalton were loading the last of the dishes into her car when her father said, "Mel, I've called a press conference for the day after tomorrow at nine a.m. I'll expect you to be there to reassure everyone about Rocket."

"Coach, I still need to reevaluate him." She wished she'd sounded firmer.

"Then have it done before the press conference."

"Mr. Hyde, with all due respect, I don't think it's in Rocket's best interest to even consider playing."

"Dr. Reynolds, I appreciate you coming all the way up here and I'm sorry that you've had such a difficult and long stay, but you've given your opinion. Mel has the final say as the team doctor."

When Dalton started to say more she placed a hand on his. "It's Christmas Eve. Let's not get into this tonight. Day after tomorrow will be soon enough."

Her father said, "Mel, I've taught you what's expected when you're a member of a team."

Melanie knew that all too well. *Do what's best for the team.* She resented the pressure he was applying. Was uncomfortable with Dalton seeing how her father treated her. Maybe she should be a team player and go along. She always had before. No, she couldn't face Dalton or herself if she didn't do what was best for Rocket. Disappointing her father would be hard, but lowering her medical and personal standards would be worse.

She kissed her father on the cheek. "Merry Christmas, Coach." The words were flat, even to her own ears.

Dalton said little on their drive back to her house and neither did she. The proverbial two hundred and fifty–pound football player in the car kept them quiet. That was pressure of its own. Now she felt as if her father was pulling her one way and Dalton the other. They carried in the dishes with few words spoken. Melanie went to the kitchen and started putting leftovers into storage containers.

"I'm glad you came tonight," she said as she cleaned out the dressing pan. She meant it, but would he ever be the kind of guy that would enjoy going to her family's get-togethers? "I know my family can be a bit much."

Dalton moved away from where he stood looking at her Christmas tree and came to stand on the other side of the bar facing her. "I'm glad I went. I better understand you."

She met his gaze. "How's that?"

He shrugged. "Just that now I know why you work with a professional football team but spend your days off at a children's hospital. Or why you were so surprised at the party the other night that they thought you are an attractive woman. And why you are letting your father manipulate you into doing something you know isn't right."

"My father is not manipulating me."

"You don't call what he said tonight manipulation? Your reaction was to say nothing. Classic control method. You didn't even tell him there's a good chance that Rocket will not play."

"I don't know that for sure." She was starting to get annoyed.

Dalton's chin went down and he gave her a look that said, *You have to be kidding.* "Oh, come on Melanie. You do too. You know as well as I do that it isn't in Rocket's best interest to play. You called me in as an expert when you already knew he shouldn't play. But you are letting you father push you into believing differently. It's more important to win than for a man to maintain his health and mobility. What it boils down to is, you want to make your father happy so he'll notice you."

"How dare you?" The spoon she held fell from her fingers and clinked on the floor. She ignored it. Anger fired in her chest.

"I dare because…"

"Because why?"

"It doesn't matter. It doesn't take much to see that your father has always treated you as one of the guys in your family instead of a daughter who needed a father's attention. That extends to your professional life and now he sees you as a puppet he can manipulate."

That was how her ex-boyfriend had treated her when he was trying to get a job with her father. She'd been his puppet for months. When he didn't get what he wanted he threw her away. Her fingers gripped the edge of the counter. "That's not true!"

"I disagree."

She hated the calm smug way he spoke to her.

"If I was willing to bet, I'd put my money on it that it wasn't your idea to become the team doctor."

He was right. It hadn't been. She wanted to be a pediatrician.

"I'm right. I can see it on your face. You care too much about what your family expects. Your father is so focused on football he hardly recognizes you as the wonderful, remarkable woman you are. In many ways you're guilty of fostering that. You wanted to be a pediatrician but did what would keep you included by the family and noticed by your father. You're a caring and bright doctor with a large heart, and you are all woman when you let it show. Stand up to your father. Stand up for Rocket and yourself."

Dalton watched as Melanie stood straighter. She

glared at him. The wild look in her eyes said he'd pushed too far. He'd almost told her he cared for her, but if she rejected him, he didn't know if he'd recover. Having gone years without letting someone have that kind of power, he couldn't risk doing so now.

"How dare you presume to tell me how a family works? You know nothing about family dynamics."

He flinched. She was cutting deep.

"What qualifies you to judge mine?" she all but spat.

He held up a soothing hand. "You're right—I don't know about families. But what I do know is medicine and knees. If you let your father or anyone else on the Currents staff pressure Rocket to play on Sunday, they are wrong. He could damage his leg permanently."

"But we don't know that for sure."

"I do."

"How, Dalton? Because you're the go-to man for leg injuries? Because you are all-knowing and all-seeing. You're not any better than you think my father is. You want to oversee every decision. Be the final word. You're so used to being right or having the ultimate say that you can't stand the thought that someone might disagree with you or want to do it differently."

"I'll have you know that I always put my patients first." Dalton stepped back. He was starting to lose control of the conversation and Melanie.

"And I always put my players first. Still, it's not as cut-and-dried as you think it is. You have a practice where you're the king of the mountain. You've spent all your life standing alone. Trying to prove to yourself and others that you're worthy of being wanted, or asked to join the team. Even when you could have been chosen you remain by yourself. You are so afraid of being rejected you are scared to let go. So don't tell me about what I should do when you have no idea what it's like to carry so many others on one decision."

What she said smarted.

"I think I should leave before either one of us says something they might regret."

"That figures."

"What?"

"Running and hiding when it gets too hard. Anytime you lose the upper hand or feel the situation slipping out of your control you leave. Is that what you have been doing all your adult life? That way you don't have to worry about ever feeling like you did as a kid. Of all people, you're the one telling me to stand up to my father. But you haven't left your past behind. It follows you like a chain with a ball attached. You even made it clear that what was between us would be only temporary because you were afraid you might feel too much. Might have to stay in one place and commit.

"You're highly successful, top in your field, yet you still think like the little boy who wasn't picked to play ball. You fear that anyone you have a real connection with will turn you away. Not want you. No one likes to be rejected. I certainly didn't."

"How is that?"

She glared at him. "My old boyfriend used me to get a job with my father. When I said I wouldn't help him, he dumped me. Everyone gets rejected, so don't think you are so special in that regard. How others feel and act isn't under your control. You're afraid they will disappoint you or hurt you. You don't give them a chance to show you anything different. It's time to trust you're worth having."

Now she was starting to throw mud. "Don't take the high road here, Melanie. I may have to be in control because of my past, but you're controlled in the present. I'm not sure one is better than the other. You think I can't say what I feel, but I can." He pointed to her and back to himself. "There is something special between us."

Her eyes widened.

"Don't act so surprised. You know as well as I do that what has happened over the last few days is rare between a couple. I wanted us to figure out how to make it work. Now I think that's not possible until you can make a decision for yourself, out from under you father's thumb."

"And I think you need to revisit your past so you can face the future. Learn to be a part of a relationship wholeheartedly. Find value in yourself, not through your profession."

Dalton shook his head. "I'm sorry things ended this way between us. It's not what I had hoped for. I'll call for a taxi and wait at the store down the street."

It took a few seconds before she sighed, then said, "Don't do that. I'll drive you to the Lodge." She walked to the coatrack.

He didn't argue. The idea of walking down the street in the cold did nothing to improve his spirits. They rode in silence to the Lodge. Dalton was afraid to say more for fear he'd make the situation worse. Melanie pulled to a stop at the front door.

He climbed out. "Goodbye, Melanie."

"Goodbye, Dalton."

CHAPTER TEN

MELANIE TOOK A deep breath and adjusted the collar of her shirt. Looking into the mirror in the bathroom of her office one more time, she saw only the red rimming her eyes. Hopefully the cameras wouldn't be on her that long. She had the press conference to get through, then she would have a few days to compose herself before the game. And she would collect herself—she had to.

It had been the longest drive of her life back to her condo after dropping Dalton off. Back home, she'd not even stopped to finish storing the leftovers from dinner. Instead, she'd gone straight to her bathroom and turned on the shower. Climbing in, she'd let her tears flow with the water until it was cold.

How had things turned so ugly between her and Dalton? She'd never spoken to another person with such venom before. Why him? Because she cared so much.

She'd called the Lodge the next morning, asking

for him. Mark was on duty and he told her that Dalton had already left for the airport.

Christmas morning. Merry Christmas. He must have been really angry with her.

Melanie had spent the rest of the day vacillating between wallowing in pity and eating every piece of candy she could find. By the middle of the afternoon, she'd called her father and told him she wouldn't be by, but would see him at the press conference. With her brothers in town, she wouldn't be missed.

She went over her conversation with Dalton again and again. Their upbringings had been miles apart—him by himself and her with people to answer to all the time. They were too different to understand each other. But they had no trouble communicating in bed. So much so that she missed him with a pain that was almost breathtaking. Surely with time that would ease. If it didn't, she had no idea how she would survive.

Now it was time to put on a happy face to the sports world. She'd done a few press conferences but they still weren't her idea of fun.

A knock came at her office door. "Hey, Doc, Mr. Hyde sent me down to tell you it's time."

"Thanks, I'm on my way."

Her father was eager for this press conference to go his way. There hadn't been time to do new tests on Rocket. She had spoken to him earlier that morning and he'd said his leg felt fine.

Ten minutes later Melanie was sitting at a table in front of the press with her father, Rocket and Coach Rizzo.

Her father started the conference by making a statement about his hopes for victory on Sunday. "And now we will take a few questions."

The people in the room all started talking at once. "Dr. Hyde, Dr. Hyde."

Her father recognized the man.

Melanie forced a smile. "Yes?"

"What is your professional opinion regarding Rocket playing this Sunday?"

She took a deep breath. "Rocket has been resting his leg. Closer to game day, I will put him through a battery of tests and make the final decision about whether he plays or not."

Her father leaned toward the microphone, "All plans are for Rocket to be on the field Sunday. I'm sure you agree, Dr. Hyde."

She couldn't believe that her father was now putting words in her mouth on national TV. Could he undermine her professionally any more effectively?

It seemed to take forever for the press conference to end. She spoke to Rocket, telling him she wanted to see him in her exam room in thirty minutes, and she left.

Dalton had been right. She was letting her father push her around about Rocket and that had to stop today. Back in her office, she called her father's secretary and asked to see him that afternoon.

Rocket showed up on time and she did her exam. She sent him for an X-ray and told him to spend some time with the trainers working on the machines. Rocket seemed upbeat and talked of nothing but playing in the game. Tension and excitement filled the building with everyone in high spirits about the Currents' chances of winning.

At the time slot Melanie had been given, she arrived at her father's office. She was announced over the phone by his secretary. Her father waved her into a chair in front of his desk as he continued his phone conversation. Just like at his home, football memorabilia filled every shelf. There were a few old pictures of her brother's children but nothing of the entire family together or of her.

A few minutes after she'd arrived, he hung up and said, "Mel, I think the press conference went well."

"Coach, that's what I want to talk to you about."

"Is something wrong?"

"I wish you hadn't said Rocket would be playing on Sunday. It isn't a sure thing. It's my job to make those determinations. I would appreciate it if you wouldn't put words into my mouth."

Her father leaned forward in his chair and gave her a pointed look. "And my job is to keep the franchise making money. Part of that is putting the correct spin on the situation. I want Rocket on the field. Give him steroid shots, pain relievers—I don't care what. But it's your job to see that he plays."

"That's where you are wrong, Coach. It's my job to see that the players remain in good health. That their lives now and later aren't put in jeopardy. I can't stand by while anything different happens."

"You will do as you are told."

Dalton had called it. She'd been so caught up in being noticed by her father she'd compromised who she was. She blinked. But no more. She would no longer be anyone's puppet. It was time for a drastic change. One that was overdue.

"Father—" at her use of that unfamiliar address

he cocked his head and gave her a questioning look "—I won't."

"Mel—"

"It's Melanie."

"What has gotten into you?"

"Nothing that shouldn't have happened sooner. I won't agree to Rocket playing on Sunday or any other Sunday until next season. His leg will not improve enough in the next few days for him to play. I'm not going to sign off on him. Dr. Reynolds was right and I should have agreed with him when he gave his opinion. The team will have to win without Rocket."

"Mel, you are part of the team. You need to act like a team member."

"No, Father, I need to do what is best for Rocket and that is for him not to play."

Her father stood. "This is more than just about one person."

"That's where you are wrong. It is about a person. You never have seen the individual. It has always been about the team—in your professional and private life. I no longer want to be a part of a team. I want to be your daughter. That is all. I love medicine but I have always wanted to work with kids. I'm thankful for all you have done for me but it's time for Melanie Hyde to be herself. I'll be turning in my resignation after the season is over."

"Mel, I think you should give this more thought." His voice rose.

"No, sir, I think that's the problem. I've been using my head instead of my heart for too long. I'm going with my heart now."

"Mel—"

"Melanie, please."

Her father's face had turned red. "Melanie, we'll talk again when you're more rational."

"I won't be changing my mind about Rocket or leaving. I love you, Father, but it's time for me to live the life I choose. Not the one chosen for me."

Her father wore a perplexed look on his face as if he hadn't comprehended a word she'd said. His phone rang and, to his credit, he paused a second before he answered it. As he did, she left the office.

Dalton flapped the file he'd been reviewing down on his desk. It had been two weeks since he'd left Niagara Falls. It was a new year but it hadn't been a good one. He missed Melanie to a degree he would have never thought possible. It was almost a physical pain that didn't seem to ease.

He fingered the file he'd just put down. It was Josey Woods's—one of the patients he and Melanie had seen on the day they went to the children's hospital. His colleague had spoken to him about Josey being a good candidate for a new procedure they were doing on children her age with long-term bone malformation. The only complication was her recent chemo. When she was far enough out, they would bring her in for the surgery. Josey was just one more reminder of Melanie. As if he needed one.

As soon as he had returned to the Lodge, he'd called to see if he could get a flight home. There had been one early the next morning. More than once he'd started to call Melanie but had pushed Off on his phone. As he'd watched her interaction with her family he'd felt her pain that they took her for granted. Worse than that—how could a man pretend to care about Melanie to get to her father? She deserved better. He was furious on her behalf.

What if he and Melanie had tried to make it work? Their backgrounds were so far apart, would they have made it a month, six, a year? Would he have ever fit into her family? Yet he and Melanie had been so close. Their bodies in sync with each other.

She'd accused him of running away. Maybe he had but he needed a chance to think. Give her space as well. It was time he went home anyway. He'd opened himself to her more than he had to anyone in his life. Even gone so far as to tell her he cared about her on a level he didn't clearly understand at the time. He'd returned to the world he knew and understood, yet he was out of control. Something was missing. That something was Melanie.

He'd unfastened the part of his heart he'd guarded so carefully for so many years and let her in. She'd ended up capturing his entire heart and he'd left it behind in Niagara Falls with her. He couldn't deny it. He'd fallen in love with Melanie.

But even that knowledge didn't make his life any better—if anything, it made it worse. He'd told her it was up to her to come to him. She had to break away from her father. See herself as Dalton did. As a strong woman who was special in her own right, not because she was just part of a group. It was for her own good. He only hoped she realized it before the pain of losing her killed him.

He'd watched the game on Sunday for two reasons. One—to see if Melanie agreed to let Rocket play. And the other—to see if he could catch a glimpse of her. To his displeasure, he hadn't seen Melanie. To his frustration and disappointment, Rocket was dressed in his game uniform ready to play. The sports announcers said that Rocket was being held in reserve in case he was needed. If the team fell behind, he'd be sent in. Because the Currents were winning for most of the game, Rocket never had a chance to play. The announcer went on to say that they were saving Rocket's leg for the Super Bowl. Still, Melanie must have given her okay for him to play or he wouldn't have been on the sideline in his uniform. Nothing had changed.

The Currents won the game, but Dalton didn't see it as a victory.

Now, he looked out the window of his second-floor office at the top of a palm tree that blew gently in the south Florida breeze. A statement that Melanie had made during their argument continued to haunt him. She'd said he needed to face his past, make peace with it so he could understand relationships. Was that what he'd been doing all these years—hiding from people? If his affair with Melanie was an example, hiding might have been a good thing. If you let go and showed weakness you could get hurt.

In his adult life he'd made sure he was always in control. While he'd been in Niagara he'd not had that luxury and he'd never been happier. Did he want to go back to being the old Dalton? Now that he knew what it felt like to have someone care about him, and to care about them in return, he wasn't so sure.

If Melanie came looking for him, would he be the man she wanted if he didn't reconcile with his past?

Three days later he turned right into the street where he'd lived when he was ten and eleven. He'd already visited two places of the five where he had lived as a child. One of the houses had been boarded up and the other had a different family living in it. He hadn't expected to speak to anyone when he'd started his road trip northward to a town in central Florida, but something pushed him to knock on the door.

Dalton drove slowly down the street, watching for the all-too-familiar yellow house in the middle of the row. He pulled to the curb across from it.

Toys still littered the yard. There was a car in the drive. Someone must be home. What was gone was the empty lot next door where everyone had gathered to play. Did his foster parents still live here?

He climbed out of his car and started toward the house. Some of his hardest years had been spent here. This was where he'd lived when he'd made up his mind he would be a doctor, make something of himself and leave who he had been behind. He'd managed to do that until Melanie came into his life.

Standing on the porch, he knocked on the screen door. He waited a few seconds and knocked again. The shuffle of feet came from inside and then the door was open a crack.

"Can I help you?"

"Mrs. Richie?" Dalton asked, peering through the screen to see the old woman's features.

"Yes."

"I don't know if you remember me, but I'm Dalton Reynolds. I lived here for a while. I was one of your foster kids."

She pushed the screen door open. "Dalton Reynolds! Of course I remember you. How're you doing?"

"I'm fine. I'm a doctor in Miami."

"Do tell. But I'm not surprised. I always knew you would make it. You were a tough one. Come in and tell me about yourself."

She turned and headed down the hall he remembered as longer and wider. Not given a choice, he followed her to the kitchen. It hadn't changed much. Some of the appliances looked new, but otherwise it was the same.

"Have a seat, Dalton. I'll get us some iced tea." She went to the cabinet and pulled two glasses out.

Dalton sat in the chair he had as a child. It creaked, just as it had then.

Mrs. Richie walked to the refrigerator, removed a pitcher and filled the glasses. She came to the table and placed one in front of him and the other down next to the chair she eased into.

"It's nice to hear you're so successful." She took a sip of tea.

"Why? You didn't think I would be?"

"Heavens, no. I could see you were smart. You made good grades even though you were so unhappy. You didn't let that stop you."

He met her look. "You knew I was miserable?"

"I could tell from our talks you were unhappy. I knew how the other kids treated you."

"Why didn't you do something to stop it?"

"Because it would have only made it worse. If I had stepped in for you every time it would have been harder for you when I wasn't around. I had confidence you would find a way around it. You did. You concentrated on being a good student."

"I read all the time."

"You did. I knew you were trying to escape, so I saw to it that there were plenty of books around on your level and above."

And there had been. Dalton had never questioned why there was a steady stream of books available to him. Or why Mrs. Richie loaded everyone up to go to the library every Saturday when he was the only one willing. In her own way she had given him a wonderful gift.

"But I didn't have any friends."

"That's why I suggested to your caseworker that you might be better off moving to another home. I could see things were getting hard for you around this neighborhood."

He'd seen the move as a betrayal when she'd been trying to help him. Life had been better for him in the next home. He'd stayed there until he'd graduated from high school. "Thank you, Mrs. Richie."

"You're welcome. Now tell me about your life. Do you have a wife and children?"

"No. But I hope to soon." Dalton spent the next few minutes telling her about himself. When he left, she made him promise to keep in touch, even if it was a yearly Christmas card.

"You're one of the success stories, Dalton. Be proud of yourself. I am."

Dalton wasn't proud of the way he'd left things with Melanie. That he planned to remedy right away.

Melanie didn't stay for the Super Bowl celebration. The Currents had won by a wide margin. Without Rocket. She'd already cleaned out her office and said her goodbyes. She would miss the players and staff. They had become like family, but it was time to move on and find another family. With any luck, maybe create one of her own.

She smiled as she stepped out of Miami Airport and the heat of the sun touched her face. Just a few hours ago she'd been knee-deep in snow. She was trading that for sand. Pulling the strap of her small bag over her shoulder, Melanie raised her hand for a taxi.

Two hours later, she stood in front of what she hoped was the door to Dalton's apartment. It had taken some web surfing, phone calls to colleagues and one heart-to-heart with Dalton's secretary to find out the address, but she hadn't given up. She just hoped another woman didn't answer the door.

Pushing the doorbell, she waited. Nothing. Pushing it again, she listened for footsteps. None. Fumbling around in her purse, she found her business card and a pen. On the back of the card she wrote: "Came for that visit. I'm at the beach."

She took the elevator down from the penthouse floor and crossed the street to the beach. Despite it being the middle of January, there were a number of people enjoying the water. Pulling her new towel out of her new beach bag, she laid it out on the sand near the water. She removed her cover-up and sat on the towel. It was a beautiful spot.

Looking over her shoulder, she searched what she believed were Dalton's windows for movement and saw none. Her nerves were getting the better of her. Would he be glad to see her? Worse, ignore her note? She just had to hope that she hadn't been imagining what had happened between them in Niagara. He had said he cared. Surely that hadn't changed in a month.

It was a workday, so he probably wouldn't be home for another two or three hours. She could enjoy the beach for a while and worry later. Pulling her bag to her, she reached in and brought out a romance novel she'd bought in the airport. It would have a happy ending even if she didn't get hers.

Melanie woke with a sense that someone sat beside her. She opened one lid to see a shadow across the bottom half of her body. It was a big person. She opened both eyes. It was a man, but she was looking into the sun and she couldn't see his face but she did recognize those shoulders.

"Dalton…"

"What are you doing here, Melanie?" He didn't sound excited to see her.

She sat up. "You said I should come visit."

He wore a shirt with a too-heavy-for-the-climate sweater over it and long pants, socks and boots. The man had a serious problem with wardrobe decisions.

"No, I meant here on the beach. You're burnt. You should know better than to stay in the sun too long when you're not used to it."

Melanie looked down at the tops of her feet. She would be unhappy soon as the sunburn set in.

Dalton stood in the shifting sand with all the grace that she'd remembered him having. He offered her his hand. "Come on—let's go get some aloe on you before you start hurting."

She took his hand and he helped her stand.

He handed her the cover-up. "Pull this on while I put the rest of your stuff in your bag." He picked up her book and raised a brow before placing it inside.

Melanie slipped on the oversize T-shirt. Dalton didn't seem pleased or upset to see her. She wasn't sure how to take that.

He carried her bag as they walked across the sand toward his place. Not once had he touched her. Fear started to seep in that he never would again. He was being too civil after all the harsh words she'd said. They seemed never to be on the same wavelength except in bed. Even now she was half-clothed and he was dressed as if he was headed to snow country. *Snow country*. Had he been coming to see her?

"Uh, Dalton, aren't you a little overdressed for this part of the world?"

He glared at her. "The only time I seem to have

the correct clothes on when I'm around you is when we are in bed…"

Thinking about Dalton in bed had her almost as hot as her burned skin. "Why do you have those on now? Going somewhere?"

"I was."

"Well, don't let me hold you up. I can take care of my burn myself."

"I'm not going now. There's no reason to."

"Why?"

They crossed the street and entered his building. "Because I was coming to see you. I was at the airport and I forgot something important. I had to come back and I saw your note."

She reached out to him as the elevator door closed with them in the car.

"Don't touch me, Melanie. If you do, I'll forget that we need to talk. And we *need* to talk."

Melanie let her hand drop. What exhilaration she'd felt at learning he was coming to see her died. This wasn't an open-arms welcome.

The elevator opened and they walked down the hall to his door.

"I know I said some hasty things to you and I'm sorry."

Dalton unlocked the door and pushed it back so

she could enter first. "I'm not sorry you did. They were things I needed to hear."

"Still, I didn't have to be so horrible when I said them." She looked around. His place was unbelievable. Ultramodern, with a one-eighty view of the ocean—it was like being outside all the time. One of the windows was a sliding door that was pushed back and a breeze flowed through.

Dalton went into the all-white kitchen and said, "Would you like a glass of iced tea?"

"That would be nice."

He fixed the drinks while she wandered around the living area. It was done in different shades of sand colors with an occasional pop of color.

"Nice place."

"Thank you. I don't spend as much time here as I would like to."

She turned to look at him. "Why is that?"

"It's not much fun to come home to an empty house. I hope to change that, though."

He was making her nervous. Was he trying to tell her that he'd found someone else?

"Look, Dalton, I just came by to say I was sorry about what happened between us. I tried to call you the next day but you were already gone. I just wanted to apologize. I won't keep you any longer." She started for her bag but he stepped between her and it.

"You said Rocket couldn't play."

She looked at him, surprised at the change of subject. "How do you know?"

"I watched the championship game. Even watched the Super Bowl."

"Wow! You have changed."

He moved closer. So close she could feel the heat of his body. "I was so desperate for a glimpse of you I'd sit through anything."

Moisture filled her eyes. She still had a chance.

"I'd like to cash in my rain check. Please kiss me."

Dalton couldn't allow that request to go unfilled, even though they still had things to sort out. He gathered Melanie into his arms and held her tightly as his lips found hers. Damn, he'd missed her with every fiber of his being. She wrapped her arms around his neck and held on as if she would never let go. Her mouth opened for him and she brought her legs up to encircle his hips. Her core called to his hardening manhood.

She pulled her mouth away from his and said, "I've missed you."

"I've missed you too." Dalton carried her to the couch and he sat down. She faced him as she remained in his lap. "We have to talk before this goes any further."

"What's there to talk about?"

"The fact that I love you and want you in my life forever."

She cupped his face and smiled at him. "I love you too."

Dalton's heart soared as he gathered her into his arms again. "Please say it again. I was afraid I'd never hear it."

She looked directly into his eyes. "I love you."

He kissed her. Long, wonderful minutes later, he released her mouth. "When did you decide to come down here?"

"Two days after you left."

He gave her a look of disbelief. "Why did you wait so long?"

"Because I had to wait until after the season was over. Had to work out my contract. Plus I needed to be around to make sure Rocket didn't sneak onto the field or was pushed."

"How did he take not getting to play?"

"Pretty hard at first, but he accepted it was in his best interest. He'll be ready for the next season and not lose his chance to ever play again. I agreed to let him suit up for the Championship game only because I was convinced it would mentally hurt the other team. For the Super Bowl I took no chances. Rocket wore his street clothes on the sideline."

"How about your father? Is he speaking to you?"

"He and Coach Rizzo didn't take it too well. I think winning the Super Bowl, Rocket or not, eased the pain. I quit my job and told my father I was going to work with children. That I wanted to be my own person."

"How did he take that?"

"He's coming around to the idea slowly. But I left on good terms. He gave me a glowing recommendation that helped me get a position at the children's hospital here in Miami. I start next week."

"You do? You were that sure of me?"

"No. Just hopeful."

"Well, I have some confessions of my own."

Her eyes had turned serious. "What are those?"

"You got me thinking about how I've dealt with what happened to me. I went to visit some of the places I lived and thought about how I felt when I lived there. I talked to one of my foster mothers, the one I felt closest to for a time. It was the home where I was the happiest...and the unhappiest. It turns out that the time I lived there in many ways made my life better. She knew what the other kids were doing to me. In her own way she protected me and gave me the groundwork to go on to school and become successful."

"You will have to take me to visit her sometime so I can thank her for the wonderful man I know today."

A knot lodged in his throat at how easy Melanie saw the picture that he'd painted with such broad strokes. "I would love for you to meet Mrs. Richie. I also have a surprise for you."

"What?" Melanie squirmed in his lap and he almost forgot what he was going to say.

"I had a colleague in my practice who specializes in young adults look at Josey Woods's chart. You remember Josey from the day we visited the hospital?"

Melanie nodded.

"Well, there's a new procedure and he thinks she's a perfect candidate. She'll be coming down in the summer to have her legs straightened. She'll be dancing at her prom the next spring."

"Have you talked to her family? Do they have a way to pay? Do I need to do something to help?"

How like Melanie to want to support people.

"That's taken care of. My foundation is covering all their expenses."

She leaned back and studied him. "You have a foundation?"

"I do. Most of the money goes to making foster children's lives better. But since it is mine, I can also use the money for other good causes. All those high fees I charge for my consults go into the foundation."

She kissed him and pulled away. "You really are wonderful."

"Thanks. Coming from you, I consider that the highest of compliments. Now, you mentioned something about a rain check a few minutes ago. If I remember correctly, that was for lovemaking. I'd like to cash that now, if you don't mind."

Melanie rubbed against him. "I don't mind at all. But I just need you to promise that I can come to the bank anytime."

"The doors are always open for you. Now and forever."

EPILOGUE

MELANIE INTERTWINED HER fingers with Dalton's as they sat on her father's couch. He leaned over and kissed her temple.

She looked at the Christmas tree and then around the room at all the people she loved. It was hard to believe that an entire year had passed.

"I hope we don't get snowed in," she said.

Dalton smiled. "If we do, I'm prepared this time. I won't have to borrow your brother's clothes."

"The only reason you are is because I did your packing."

Dalton squeezed her hand. "That's one of the perks of having a wife."

Her father came to sit beside her. "Hey, I saw a piece on the TV about the boy you helped have heart surgery. Smart kid and a big Currents fan."

Melanie squeezed Dalton's hand. His foundation had seen to it that Marcus was able to travel to Miami for the necessary surgery, which was at Melanie's hospital. He had even arranged for his grandmother to come and found them a place to stay for a couple of months afterward. "Marcus is doing great."

She and her father were closer than ever. He had seen to it that she'd had a beautiful wedding with all the trimmings. Her brothers and their families were in attendance. Even Mrs. Richie was there, proudly sitting in the mother of the groom's spot. Things weren't perfect between Melanie and her father, but they did speak every week on the phone and often talked about things other than football. She and Dalton had also made it up to one of the Currents' games during the year for a visit.

"Present time," one of her nephews called.

As usual it was loud and boisterous as the group unwrapped their presents.

Melanie was handed a box. She looked at the tag and then at Dalton. "We agreed no presents so all the foster kids would have a good Christmas."

"I didn't give you one last year so I owed you. Open it."

Melanie tore the paper away to find a snow globe with Niagara Falls inside.

"I couldn't pass it up."

She smiled at Dalton. "It's perfect. And so are you."

"Uncle Dalton, here's one for you."

He took the small box and looked at the tag. "We said no gifts."

"I couldn't help it either," Melanie said.

Dalton unwrapped the box and opened the top. He lifted the baby's rattle in Currents colors out. "What?"

The room quieted. Melanie watched as question, disbelief, wonder and then pure happiness settled on his face.

"We're having a baby?"

Melanie nodded.

"We're having a baby!" Dalton's arms encircled her as his lips met hers.

Her father said, "Great. Another for the team."

Melanie smiled softly. *No, a family for Dalton.*

* * * * *

MILLS & BOON®
Large Print Medical

June

Playboy Doc's Mistletoe Kiss	Tina Beckett
Her Doctor's Christmas Proposal	Louisa George
From Christmas to Forever?	Marion Lennox
A Mummy to Make Christmas	Susanne Hampton
Miracle Under the Mistletoe	Jennifer Taylor
His Christmas Bride-to-Be	Abigail Gordon

July

A Daddy for Baby Zoe?	Fiona Lowe
A Love Against All Odds	Emily Forbes
Her Playboy's Proposal	Kate Hardy
One Night...with Her Boss	Annie O'Neil
A Mother for His Adopted Son	Lynne Marshall
A Kiss to Change Her Life	Karin Baine

August

His Shock Valentine's Proposal	Amy Ruttan
Craving Her Ex-Army Doc	Amy Ruttan
The Man She Could Never Forget	Meredith Webber
The Nurse Who Stole His Heart	Alison Roberts
Her Holiday Miracle	Joanna Neil
Discovering Dr Riley	Annie Claydon

MILLS & BOON®
Large Print Medical

September

The Socialite's Secret	Carol Marinelli
London's Most Eligible Doctor	Annie O'Neil
Saving Maddie's Baby	Marion Lennox
A Sheikh to Capture Her Heart	Meredith Webber
Breaking All Their Rules	Sue MacKay
One Life-Changing Night	Louisa Heaton

October

Seduced by the Heart Surgeon	Carol Marinelli
Falling for the Single Dad	Emily Forbes
The Fling That Changed Everything	Alison Roberts
A Child to Open Their Hearts	Marion Lennox
The Greek Doctor's Secret Son	Jennifer Taylor
Caught in a Storm of Passion	Lucy Ryder

November

Tempted by Hollywood's Top Doc	Louisa George
Perfect Rivals...	Amy Ruttan
English Rose in the Outback	Lucy Clark
A Family for Chloe	Lucy Clark
The Doctor's Baby Secret	Scarlet Wilson
Married for the Boss's Baby	Susan Carlisle